The American Partnership

The American Partnership

Intergovernmental Co-operation
in the Nineteenth-Century
United States

Daniel J. Elazar

The University of Chicago Press

Library of Congress Catalog Card Number: 62-17132

The University of Chicago Press, Chicago & London. The University of Toronto Press, Toronto 5, Canada. © *1962 by The University of Chicago. All rights reserved Published 1962. Composed and printed by* The University of Chicago Press *Chicago, Illinois, U.S.A.*

To My Parents

Foreword

The nineteenth century is our next-door neighbor. Who can doubt that we know it well?

Daniel Elazar doubted. His concern was with an aspect of recent history that seemed completely understood and thoroughly documented: the relationship between the national and state governments. It is widely believed that during the nineteenth century the central government and the states acted as separate—and separated—sovereigns. They had distinct spheres of activity and touched each other, if at all, in unimportant ways.

This view of separation was based on apparently solid authority. Lord Bryce in *The American Commonwealth* (1888) described the federal and state governments as "distinct and separate in their action." The American system, as Bryce saw it, was "like a great factory wherein two sets of machinery are at work, their revolving wheels apparently intermixed, their bands crossing one another, yet each set doing its own work without touching or hampering the other." Bryce's view has been widely accepted. For example, W. W. Willoughby (*American Constitutional System,* 1904) stated the "general principle governing the exercise of governmental powers" in the United States in the following flat statement: "The powers of the Federal Government and those of the individual States shall be kept as distinct and independent as possible." Willoughby wrote in normative terms, but he clearly believed his prescription fitted the facts. To take only one more example, Leonard D. White also accepted the separatist view in his justly admired histories of public administration. For the earliest years of the century, "the federal government and state governments had little to do with each other in the conduct of public business except in the single field where the Constitution required them to work together, the militia." And for the years between 1829 and the Civil War, "the administrative systems [of federal and state governments] were autonomous."

These are statements that directly assert the fact of federal-state separation. They are views that, in my opinion, Elazar's work substantially destroys. He has informed his doubts with a careful sifting of the relevant state and national archives, and he has produced a radically revised picture of federal-state relations during the nineteenth century. He shows that the two planes of government worked together in every important public activity covered by his data.[1] There are no neat federal and state packages of functions. Each is involved with all. Nothing is done at arm's length. There is no exclusiveness of activity, no standoffish separation. Aside from the Civil War, there is a continuous involvement of both the federal and state governments in all the great domestic tasks of building and maintaining a continent-wide nation.

A new view of history, buttressed by voluminous data as this one is, has several kinds of significance. For one thing, it is important in and of itself as an intellectual achievement and, through that achievement, as a contribution to our deeper understanding of the nation's past. Second, research of this sort is important because it stimulates further scholarly efforts. For example, Elazar discusses a number of Supreme Court cases of the nineteenth century which had the effect of pulling the federal and state governments apart and confining them to separate spheres of action. Yet his own work on administration, as he recognizes, suggests that the total weight of Supreme Court decisions could hardly have been in the direction of separatism. From neither Marshall's theory of national supremacy nor Taney's view of national-state duality of power does it necessarily follow that central and peripheral governments need be separated in their administrative functions. Indeed, on the basis of Elazar's volume, one can hypothesize that court decisions of the last century generally allowed, if they did not encourage, an easy federal-state collaboration, notwithstanding some widely publicized cases to the contrary.

A final importance of Elazar's work lies in what it tells us about contemporary American government. A recent editorial in a Chicago news-

[1] Foreign affairs are not considered, but research by another participant in the University of Chicago's Workshop in American Federalism demonstrates that a significant sharing of responsibilities also existed in that field. See Dennis Palumbo, "The States in American Foreign Relations" (unpublished doctoral dissertation, Department of Political Science, University of Chicago, 1960).

paper opposed federal aid to education on the grounds that, historically, schools were an exclusive local concern and that, in any case, federal grants to states and localities were an evil invention of the New Deal and an aberration of traditional American standards. Even a casual reading of this book shows, on all scores, how absurd that argument is. One cannot hark back to the good old days of state and local independence because those days never existed. Government, to be sure, did far less in 1830 or 1890 than it does in 1962. (Federal expenditures in 1960 were three thousand times those in 1836.) Given the relative scale of public activities, it is probable that the extent of federal-state-local collaboration during the nineteenth century was equal to that which now exists.

Daniel Elazar's history not only adds to our knowledge of nineteenth-century government; it also provides a new base for understanding and evaluating the American federal system as it exists today.

MORTON GRODZINS

Preface

This study of intergovernmental relations in nineteenth-century United States was undertaken as one of a series of investigations into the American federal system pursued under the auspices of the Workshop in American Federalism, University of Chicago, and financed by the Ford Foundation. The primary purpose of this particular study is to examine the general hypothesis of the workshop, that government in the United States is shared government on all levels, and to test its validity in American history prior to the twentieth century.

The research for this study was undertaken in the states of Virginia, New Hampshire, Minnesota, and Colorado, and in Washington, D.C., as well as in Chicago. Supplementary research was undertaken in Arkansas, Illinois, California, Tennessee, and Oklahoma. The material in the following pages is based on the data gathered in the first group of states and the National Archives. The data gathered in the states investigated subsequently served to confirm the hypotheses presented below, though space limitations prevented their inclusion in the body of this study. In the course of further research on a related subject in Minnesota during November, 1959, the writer uncovered additional data which indicate that the conclusions advanced below are, in all likelihood, overcautious concerning the amount of intergovernmental co-operation in the nineteenth century and its impact.

The writer would like to gratefully acknowledge the assistance given him by the staffs of the following institutions: the Minnesota Historical Society and the Minnesota State Archives, St. Paul, Minnesota; the Virginia State Archives, Richmond, Virginia; the National Archives and the

Library of Congress, Washington, D.C.; the New Hampshire State Library, Concord, New Hampshire; and the Colorado State Archives, Denver, Colorado. The late Leonard D. White was instrumental in directing me to the problem of federal-state relations and encouraging my interest in this field. The members of the Workshop in American Federalism were of great and continuous help to me through almost daily discussions of the material and ideas that have been brought together in this study. Morton Grodzins, head of the workshop, has been of inestimable importance in the development and execution of this project. He furnished ideas, time, and funds, but, even more, he provided the climate and the encouragement needed for this project as well as others under the aegis of the workshop.

The Institute of Government and Public Affairs of the University of Illinois has been most generous in providing the time and facilities which have enabled me to prepare this manuscript for publication. Needless to say, the work itself and its conclusions are entirely my responsibility.

Contents

List of Tables

Introduction

This volume seeks to demonstrate that the pattern of American federalism —the American partnership—has been a constant one since the early days of the Republic. The principal hypothesis developed in the following chapters is that virtually all the activities of government in the nineteenth-century United States were co-operative endeavors, shared by federal and state agencies in much the same manner as government programs are shared in the twentieth century. Established in the first decades after the adoption of the Constitution, the character of the American partnership has changed relatively little over the years despite the great change in the amount of governmental activity at all levels of government in relation to the total activity of American society (the "velocity of government").

This study makes its case for the American partnership by emphasizing the actual sharing of responsibility for various endeavors by the federal and state governments. A series of overlapping cases provides a description of how that sharing was developed through the political and administrative processes of nineteenth-century America. The administrative agencies of the federal and state governments provide the setting. The political figures and public administrators of five generations serve as the cast of characters, and the action to be observed is the interaction between the two sets of agencies and their staffs. Behind the scenes, it will be possible to observe how the particular logic of political reality pushed the actors toward more formalized co-operation in practice, even when they spoke of the separation of functions in theory. From time to time certain characters will emerge who evinced greater understanding of the system in which they were working and who made signal contributions to its refinement.

1

These men, the architects of American federalism, and their contributions will be identified within the over-all scheme of American governmental development.

The method used in the following chapters is based on the principle of the "hard case." Rather than attempt an over-all history of American government in the nineteenth century, specific, well-screened programs in selected states were chosen for investigation with a view to demonstrating that co-operation occurred where it was least likely to be found. This method permits a thorough exploration of a smaller number of cases rather than a less detailed examination of many, on the principle that if co-operation is evident in places where it is least expected, and a superficial examination of other cases indicates that the same circumstances prevailed as in the ones studied carefully, the evidence from the hard cases can be generalized. In line with the concept of the hard case, the greater part of the research for this study was done at the state level. It would be easy to attribute a greater role to federal activity if one's investigations were confined to examining the record through what would be, in effect, federal eyes. The states, on the other hand, could be assumed to have a greater stake in asserting their independence or their domination of a given program if such existed. Thus, it was felt that if a pattern of intergovernmental co-operation similar to that with which we are familiar today should emerge from an examination of the states' records, it would lend additional support to the evidence in question. Furthermore, since the center of the political process generally lies in the party system, and since parties are state-based, a study of the operation of the federal system as a whole can justifiably be undertaken from the vantage point of the states, which lie at the center of the process.

Approaching the problem via the states has an additional advantage in that it places emphasis on the role of the states in the process so that the general hypothesis presented here will not be misinterpreted as an attempt to rewrite history from a centralist point of view. On the contrary, this study proceeds from the assumption that this is "an indestructible Union of indestructible states" in which the states and the federal government are in theory and in fact equally vital. It is not an attempt to shift the federal balance but to understand it.

The four states explored in depth in this study—Virginia, New Hampshire, Minnesota, and Colorado—were selected to implement the "hard case" idea in the various regions of the United States. Virginia, representing the South, was selected as the hardest case of all. It has traditionally represented the ultimate in states'-rights doctrine, and its articulate citizens have generally maintained a posture of independence, denying any and all co-operation or interdependence with the federal government that could possibly be denied.

Virginians have combined a long tradition of loyalty to their state with strong feelings for the concept of state sovereignty. This internally centered tradition stems from Virginia's own history, which extends over a period almost twice that of the history of the United States as a nation and longer than that of any other state. During the first fifty years of the American republic, the federal government was virtually dominated by sons of Virginia. At the time, the effect of this "Virginia Dynasty" was two-sided. On one hand the dynasty's role added to the high opinions of their state already held by citizens of the Old Dominion. At the same time the Virginians' positions of leadership in national affairs made their attachment to the Union greater than might have otherwise been the case. When Virginia's hegemony ceased as the tide of national expansion began to pass her by, the reaction of her citizens was to take further refuge in the past as exemplified by the complex of attitudes generally included under the term "states' rights."

As a consequence of this independent attitude, Virginians have always been wary about co-operating with the federal government. This wariness has sometimes prevented co-operation but, more often, has simply served to modify co-operative programs to meet local ideological needs while camouflaging their extent. Both local modification and ideological camouflage tended to be normal in a majority of nineteenth-century co-operative programs, as they still tend to be in the twentieth century.

The fact that co-operation between Virginia and the federal government was as prevalent as it will be shown to be does not alter the "hardness" of the extreme position of its citizens. Nor does it affect the value of the state's intransigence in viewing the federal system. While their conception of dual federalism may have prevented the development of better balanced co-operative programs, their feelings toward their state, along with feelings of the citizens of other states toward theirs, have been of no little importance in insuring that co-operative programs do not become centralized ones. Yet, it can be demonstrated that, where their conception of dual federalism became the ascendant one in the actual implementation of any program (including some that were formerly co-operative), the programs tended to drift toward federal control and were ultimately federalized under some form of "either/or" approach that prevented the development of co-operative patterns while not eliminating the need for national action.

While Virginia was moving from its position as dominant state in the nation to become the leading state in the South, New Hampshire was pursuing a much more stolid course as one of the smaller states in the Union, off the main track of westward expansion. New Hampshire was settled later than most of the original thirteen states, mainly in the second half of the eighteenth century. Some parts of the state did not emerge from the land-frontier stage until the 1840's. This rather late settlement was due to the relatively poor quality of the state's land, coupled with its northerly geographic position, which helped turn the immigrant tide elsewhere.

Despite this later over-all development, New Hampshire, like the other New England states, began experimenting with state economic activity a decade or more before the southern states did. Following the same trend, it also abandoned most of its state-controlled enterprises at an earlier date. Thus, the greater part of New Hampshire's development in the nineteenth century was in the hands of private entrepreneurs and corporate interests rather than under the full or partial control of the state government, as was the case in Virginia.

For the purposes of this study, New Hampshire is valuable for several reasons. Within its boundaries are areas that reflect virtually all the regional variations present in New England and the East. Its southern third was industrialized in the same period as Massachusetts, and even New York. Its central third and western border represent rural New England in its "classic" form, and its northern mountains presented challenges to developers as difficult as any east of the Mississippi River. At the same time, as a state with a less dynamic economy in the nineteenth century (and after), it represents the hard case in view of the plausible hypothesis that the amount of co-operative federalism is related to the extent of the dynamism present in the economy and society.[1]

This study's focus on New Hampshire will be primarily directed to the period after 1840, after the economic and social changes that came to a head during the administration of Andrew Jackson. The principle of economy of cases inherent in the "hard case" method dictates that the attention

[1] Where there is much activity, new problems tend to develop and the energies of many groups, public and private, must be mobilized. Where a relatively stable social and economic situation predominates, it should be more difficult to find evidence of intergovernmental co-operation (though, since no American state was a static society, co-operation should manifest itself in certain fields in every one).

directed toward the earlier period, which investigation has shown to follow much the same pattern as in Virginia, be mainly corroborative. In
order to add another dimension, the post-1840 period will be approached
from a legislative as well as an administrative viewpoint, commencing
with the statutory recognition of the co-operative programs by the state
legislature and covering their implementation through the normal course
of administrative operations.[2]

The New Hampshire political tradition is less one of state sovereignty
than one of Yankee conservatism. The state's major regional divisions tend
to reflect the struggle between industrialism and agrarianism, with a significant number of "old stock" urban residents pleased that the rural interests
dominate the legislature and thus maintain as many of the traditional
values as possible. This attitude seems to have been a persistent one, even
in the nineteenth century (though it was undoubtedly intensified with the
migration of the French Canadians to the state's industrial centers, in-
truding an alien religious element as well as representing social change).
As abolitionists or abolitionist sympathizers, citizens of New Hampshire
were impatient with states'-rights southerners. As conservatives, however,
they have also been opposed to the centralizers. Typically, in the middle
of the nineteenth century, New Hampshire had a strong Whig party,
which converted to Republicanism after 1855. The state's occasional ideological opposition to federal-state co-operation was based on a conservative view of dual sovereignties rather than on a fundamental opposition to
federal activity. At times this conservative view led to the support of exclusive federal action that would not involve the state, a position which
turned out to be as unusual in practice as the states'-rights position was.

Both Minnesota and Colorado are public-land states. Located in the
upper Midwest, geographically and politically Minnesota is a northern
state, a Great Lakes state, and a western state. Initially settled just prior
to the Civil War, much of Minnesota emerged from the land-frontier stage
only after the turn of the century. During the decade of the 1840's the land

[2] The administrative documents relating to the New Hampshire section of this study
are not readily available, since New Hampshire is one of the few states without an
official archives. Virtually all manuscript records of governmental operations are buried
in the basement of the state capitol, theoretically in the custody of the departments of
their origin. It was not possible, because of limitations of time, to explore any records except those available in the State Library, primarily the published reports and records
of the state. An examination of the actual correspondence, if it still exists, would undoubtedly add much depth to the following account, though much can be reconstructed
from the information that is accessible and from what is known from sources in other
states.

frontier was pushed back into the lower third of the future state, and the westward movement began to ascend the Minnesota river valleys. In 1849 Minnesota Territory was organized, and in 1858 Minnesota was admitted to the Union as the thirty-second state. The next several decades saw the frontier pushed back and new communities founded in the forests and on the prairies north and west of the area of initial settlement. However, it was not until 1907 that the land frontier in Minnesota was finally considered closed, with the completion of the railroad to Rainy River on the Canadian border.

Minnesota's problems were generally those of every nineteenth-century frontier area in the United States, and they have been relatively well recorded. Its citizens have a deserved reputation for progressive action, and its state government has always been numbered among the better ones in this country, one where federal "interference" has not been needed to counteract internal weaknesses. Furthermore, Minnesota's citizens have a long tradition of political independence, which has included an internal party system with a unique orientation since the period immediately following the Civil War. This high degree of political separation is partly the result of the state's relative isolation from the main stream of American development and partly because of its settlement by predominantly foreign-born pioneers who brought with them political traditions that remained relatively undiluted by American practice.

Minnesota, then, typifies another type of hard case. It used the mechanisms and benefits of co-operative federalism not out of weakness, to let the federal government undertake projects that the state and its localiites would not, but out of strength, to gain the most it could from federal benefits that supplemented the progressive action of its own governments.

Colorado, one of the oldest states in the mountain West, was admitted to the Union in the nation's centennial year, 1876, toward the close of the period of the great land grants. The majority of the land grants for transportation within the state had been made to private companies before capable government had existed in Colorado; and, by 1876, the great internal improvement boom was on the decline, not to re-emerge until the rise of the automobile. Furthermore, Colorado was developed primarily through mining and cattle raising, both fields of endeavor associated with private enterprise, particularly private corporate enterprise by the late nineteenth century. As a result, state economic intervention played a less obvious role than it did in the eastern or Mississippi Valley states, which were settled in the days when state economic activity was publicly more acceptable, or in other western states where conditions demanded more open state intervention in the economy at an earlier date. Colorado was settled during the period when the doctrines of laissez faire and dual federalism were most widely accepted, so its own political leadership was much more committed to such doctrines in theory than many of their counterparts of an earlier age, who had reached political maturity in a period of considerable state economic activity and comparatively open nationwide programs of intergovernmental co-operation.

In addition, of all the states in its part of the country, Colorado was able to benefit most from the attachment of its citizens. In other areas of the Rocky Mountain West, people came to make money and then left for more "civilized" parts of the country. For a number of reasons that cannot be discussed here, more of the people who came to Colorado decided to settle there permanently. This led to the development of strong and persistent attachments to the state. If such attachments are likely to breed more of a local orientation and less of an orientation toward Washington, as many people claim, this should make Colorado one of the hard cases. Perhaps more realistically, the state's isolation from the rest of the country and the absence of interstate problems that are so frequent east of the Mississippi River, where the states are smaller and more heavily populated, did influence the development of local attachments that can be examined by the accepted standards of judgment for possible evidence of less dependence on the federal government.

The aforementioned states provide the setting for the programs described in the following chapters. The programs, selected to represent some of the most important issues facing American government in the nineteenth century and some of the lesser areas of governmental activity as well, were studied in depth in each of the four states, further investigated in the records of the National Archives, and briefly examined for corroborative purposes in other states of New England (Massachusetts), the middle East (Pennsylvania), the border South (Maryland, Tennessee), the deep South (Alabama, Georgia), the western South (Arkansas), the near West (Illinois, Indiana, Michigan, Ohio, Wisconsin), the middle West (Montana, Nebraska, Wyoming), the Southwest (Arizona, Texas), and the Far West (California, Oregon, Washington). The evidence in all cases confirmed, without exception, the existence of extensive intergovernmental co-operation, involving federal, state, and local governments and pervading almost every governmental activity of the time. The evolution of co-operative programs, one by one, over three generations of American history, often in the face of an opposition based on the theoretical formulations of dual federalism as developed by the states'-rights school, will be chronicled in the following chapters. The sum of that evolution is the American partnership.

Part I

Programs and Policies in the Early Republic

1

Federalism in Theory and
Federalism in Practice

THE THEORY OF DUAL FEDERALISM

It is widely accepted that the American system of federalism was designed by the founding fathers as one embracing two separate levels of sovereignty. Almost every analysis of American federalism has started from this assumption that the dual sovereignties—federal and state—were to exist side by side, each virtually independent of the other in its own sphere. More important, it is widely accepted that what was desired in theory by the founding fathers was generally true in practice throughout the nineteenth century, the "classic" age of American federalism. These assumptions first developed as canons of American political thought in the pronouncements of public figures in the nineteenth century, and later in decisions of the United States Supreme Court. They were generally accepted by political scientists when the discipline emerged in the late nineteenth century, and were formally developed by the latter into the theory of "dual federalism" in the 1930's to describe a system which was considered to be passing away.

Edward S. Corwin was the first person to use the term "dual federalism" to describe the American system. He argued:

By the Hamiltonian theory, the national government, although a government of enumerated powers, is within the range of powers a truly sovereign government, and so is under no constitutional compulsion, either in the selection of means whereby to make its powers effective or in the selection of objects to be attained by their exercise, to take account of the coexistence of the states or to concern itself to preserve any particular relationship of power between itself and the states. And this also was the theory of the men who "put across" the

Constitution and who set the national government going. Also it is the theory which underlies Chief Justice Marshall's famous decisions.

For all that, the outlook embodied in the theory was not that of the great mass of the American people either in 1789 or even three quarters of a century later. Their experience was local, their immediate interest local, and through Jefferson and Madison this localistic outlook found expression in a far different version of the Constitution, one which treated it as resulting primarily from a compact among the states and which required that its interpretation be directed to the preservation in the states of their accustomed powers and to the maintenance of that greatest of constitutional contrivances, dual federalism. And in fact the constitutional jurisprudence of the Court conformed largely to these objectives for a full half century succeeding Marshall's death, save as it made accommodation for the more evident lessons of the Civil War.[1]

Corwin talks of the concept of dual federalism as one supported by popular action and referred to in the decisions of the Supreme Court. In his series of works on American administrative history, Leonard D. White extended this doctrine to show its applicability in the area of governmental administration.

In *The Jeffersonians* he says:

We may conclude that for twenty-eight years after the fall of the federalists the federal government and state governments had little to do with each other in the conduct of public business except in the single field where the Constitution required them to work together, the militia. The federal government came close to Jefferson's ideal: the common agent of the people for the conduct of foreign affairs and matters arising between the states. The scope of public business was narrow at best, and the domestic part of it was absorbed by the states, acting under their own constitutions and administrative systems. The limited activities of government reduced the points at which the two administrative systems might have been thrown in each other's way. Where they were required to join hands in the organization, training and maintenance of the militia, they made much trouble for each other.[2]

And in *The Jacksonians* he brings dual federalism down to the brink of the Civil War:

The general pattern of administrative relations between the federal government and the states was not altered during the years from 1829 to the Civil War . . . two administrative systems, as well as two judicial systems, [served]

[1] Edward S. Corwin, *The Twilight of the Supreme Court* (New Haven, Conn.: Yale University Press, 1934), pp. 47–48.

[2] Leonard D. White, *The Jeffersonians* (New York: Macmillan Co., 1951), p. 544.

the same citizens. The administrative systems were autonomous and each was complete in itself.[3]

Other political scientists have accepted the existence of "two separate federal and state streams flowing in distinct but closely parallel channels"[4] and not meeting except in rare cases, either implicitly or explicitly.[5] There were clear and obvious reasons for the acceptance of this theory. The pronouncements of most of the leading figures in nineteenth-century American political life seemed to indicate a deeply felt commitment to dual federalism both in theory and in practice. The dramatic issues that dominated the national stage seemed to reflect this separation. The doctrine of states' rights was matured on the slavery issue, in which, of necessity, the idea of separation was carried to its ultimate conclusion. Even westward expansion brought forth its share of separatist pronouncements, partly as a result of sectional differences and even more as another aspect of the ideology of frontier individualism, which did its best to conceal any form of outside aid given to the new worlds of the agricultural West and the industrializing East.

In addition, the most publicized decisions of the United States Supreme Court, particularly after the passing of John Marshall, who was popularly considered to be a nationalizing anachronism held over from Federalist days, seemed to reinforce this picture. When political history was less a history of political and administrative behavior and more a chronicle of legal and constitutional acts, the existence of these decisions carried great weight.

SEPARATION AND THE PRESIDENTS

The common method used to develop the theory of dual federalism by contemporary nineteenth-century statesmen and politicians was to talk of lines of demarcation between the federal government and the states. Thus,

[3] Leonard D. White, *The Jacksonians* (New York: Macmillan Co., 1954), p. 506.

[4] Jane Perry Clark, *The Rise of a New Federalism* (New York: Columbia University Press, 1938), p. 4. This pioneering work implies the end of dualism (or at least its drastic decline) with the rise of the new co-operative federalism.

[5] See, for example, George C. S. Benson, *The New Centralization* ("American Government in Action" [New York: Farrar and Rinehart, 1941]), Introduction; and Arthur N. Holcombe, *Our More Perfect Union* (Cambridge, Mass.: Harvard University Press, 1950), chap. xi.

James Madison wrote, shortly after the adjournment of the Constitutional Convention:

The double object of blending a proper stability and energy in the government with the essential characters of republican Form, and of tracing a proper line of demarkation between the national and state authorities was necessarily found to be as difficult as it was desirable, and to admit of an infinite diversity concerning the means among those who were unanimously agreed concerning the end.[6]

This concept of demarcation became the key to the entire concept of dual federalism. Dualism came to mean separation between the various levels of government in their dealings with governmental problems. Each level had, according to this theory, its own particular responsibilities, which were generally its exclusive province. While this theory was most often espoused by those advocating states' rights, nationalists also maintained its basic validity. Thus, Madison could demand that the federal government confine itself to its limited, enumerated powers, and leave the rest to the states; and Hamilton could demand that the states refrain from usurping those powers which his broad construction of the Constitution allotted to the federal government. In this way dualism and demarcation were inseparably linked in American federalist theory throughout the nineteenth century, though, in reality, a system of shared activities was developing that embodied its own type of dualism in which co-operation between governments, not demarcation of spheres of action, was the key.

Thomas Jefferson was among those who helped set this pattern of associating dualism with the demarcation of separate functions. Dual federalism was one of the theories he tended to advocate in the abstract, which, in practice, he had to circumvent in so many cases.[7] His description of the ideal federal system gave the states supremacy, generally exclusive, in domestic matters while confining the powers of the federal government to foreign affairs. Despite the fact that so many of the actions of his administration of necessity circumvented these principles, Jefferson never ceased to speak of dualism and demarcation in the same breath.[8] Many

[6] Gaillard Hunt (ed.), *The Writings of James Madison* (New York, 1900–1910), V, 1–2.

[7] Leonard D. White, in *The Jeffersonians*, describes this divergence of theory and practice in considerable detail, covering almost every aspect of government business in the Jefferson administrations.

[8] See Saul K. Padover (ed.), *Thomas Jefferson on Democracy* (New York: Penguin Books, 1939), and John Dewey (ed.), *The Living Thoughts of Thomas Jefferson* (New

of the accepted views of the nature of nineteenth-century American federalism have their source in his formulations.

In the *Federalist*, No. 46, James Madison provides a definition of dual federalism that has been generally accepted as accurate: "The federal and state governments are in fact but different agents and trustees for the people, constituted with different powers, and designed for different purposes."[9] On the basis of this position, he abandoned the mild dualism of his earlier years to become the first of a long line of presidents to veto legislation passed by Congress to involve directly the federal government in financing and constructing internal improvements. The first of these vetoes was the subject of a message to Congress delivered on March 3, 1817, containing the following summation of his theory of American federalism:

I am not unaware of the great importance of roads and canals and the improved navigation of water courses, and that a power in the National Legislature to provide for them might be exercised with signal advantage to the general prosperity. But seeing that such a power is not expressly given by the Constitution, and believing that it cannot be deduced from any part of it without an inadmissible latitude of construction and a reliance on insufficient precedents; believing also that the permanent success of the Constitution depends on a definite partition of powers between the Federal and State Governments, and that no adequate landmarks would be left by the constructive extension of the powers of Congress as proposed in the bill, I have no option but to withhold my signature from it, and to cherishing the hope that its beneficial objects may be attained by a resort for the necessary powers to the same wisdom and virtue in the nation which established the Constitution in its actual form and providently marked out in the instrument itself a safe and practicable mode of improving it as experience may suggest.[10]

Madison, like Jefferson, was not opposed to amending the Constitution to allow national participation in internal improvements, but he was not

---

York: David McKay Co., 1940), for scattered quotations illustrating Jefferson's approach, which is presented by the editors as a "theory of federalism."

[9] Alexander Hamilton, John Jay, and James Madison, *The Federalist* (Everyman's Library, No. 519 [New York: E. P. Dutton & Co.]), pp. 238–39.

[10] *The Complete Madison*, ed. Saul K. Padover (New York: Harper & Bros., 1953), p. 198. The issue of Madison's vetoes is not a simple one to analyze. On one hand, he was opposing not just federal-state co-operation, but direct and exclusive federal action in a field considered to be the preserve of the states under the Constitution. Thus his opposition to internal improvement legislation was based on his strict-constructionist leanings as much as his conceptions of dual federalism.

prepared to concede such power for potential intergovernmental co-operation or expansion of national activities without formal alteration of
the Constitution.

Thus, the accepted pattern of belief was established despite the simultaneous development of far different patterns of action. With the exception
of John Quincy Adams, who was notably unsuccessful in implementing
his program, and Abraham Lincoln, who spoke for national supremacy
during the Civil War when issues such as the nature of American federalism were closely associated with the survival of the Union itself, dual or
co-operative, the first president to veer publicly from the accepted posture of dualism as demarcation was Theodore Roosevelt, who already
stood at the threshold of the so-called new federalism.

On May 4, 1822, James Monroe vetoed a bill appropriating money for
the "preservation and repair of the Cumberland Road." In conjunction
with his veto, he sent to Congress a long paper, one of the fundamental
documents in American federal theory,[11] outlining his views on the subject
of internal improvements and setting forth his theory of dual federalism:

There were two separate and independent governments established over our
Union, one for local purposes over each state by the people of the state, the
other for national purposes over all the states by the people of the United
States. The whole power of the people, on the representative principle, is divided between them. The state governments are independent of each other,
and to the extent of their powers are complete sovereignties. The National
Government begins where the state governments terminate, except in some in-
stances where there is a concurrent jurisdiction between them. This Government is also, according to the extent of its powers, a complete sovereignty. I
speak here, as repeatedly mentioned before, altogether of representative sovereignties, for the real sovereignty is in the people alone. The history of the world
affords no such example of two separate and independent governments established over the same people, nor can it exist except in governments founded on
the sovereignty of the people.

Monroe continued the discussion with a chronicle of the probable consequences of any federal involvement in internal improvements unless the
Constitution were amended. What he feared primarily was a breakdown
of the line of demarcation between the federal government and the states
with a subsequent accretion of power by the former to protect its interests
in internal improvements that would destroy the balance of the federal

[11] James D. Richardson (ed.), *Messages and Papers of the Presidents* (rev. ed.;
Washington, D.C.: Bureau of National Literature and Art, 1908), II, 711-52.

system and, ultimately, the republican form of goverment. Like Jefferson and Madison before him, Monroe was not opposed to federal involvement in internal improvement. His message reveals his belief that national responsibility for internal improvements would not, of itself, bring evil consequences, but that violating the terms of the compact without resorting to the formal procedures for amending it would.

Andrew Jackson, protector of the national interest in the nullification controversy, also spoke out on behalf of this concept of dual federalism. In his second annual message, sent to Congress on December 6, 1830, he expressed his disapproval of federal investment in joint-stock companies:

The practice of thus mingling the concerns of the Government with those of the states or of individuals is inconsistent with the object of its institution and highly impolitic. The successful operation of the federal system can only be preserved by confining it to the few and simple, but yet important, objects for which it was designed. A different practice, if allowed to progress, would ultimately change the character of this Government by consolidating into one the Federal and State Governments, which were intended to be kept forever distinct.[12]

With the rise of the slavery controversy as a major national issue and the growth of the principle of states' rights as the South's doctrinal basis for preserving the "peculiar institution," dual federalism took on another connotation. Not only did it mean demarcation between the two levels of government, but demarcation to prevent encroachment by the "limited" federal government on the sovereign and inherent rights of the states— rights supposedly never surrendered under the terms of the constitutional compact between the several states.

A highly significant corollary manifestation attached itself to the concept of dualism in this period as dual federalism became a means to avoid governmental activity at any level. This concept was shifted from the slavery issue to that of laissez faire economics by the commercial and industrial interests of the northeast that were engaged in the destruction of the old commercial and agricultural mercantilist system and the creation of the free-enterprise capitalism of an industrial America. Without this added impetus, it is doubtful whether the southern doctrine would have received such a wide and favorable reception. Since a series of states'-rights Democrats occupied the White House during most of the

[12] *Ibid.*, III, 1072–73.

1840's and 1850's, this three-part interpretation of dual federalism became even more pronounced in the political literature of the period.[13]

After the Civil War, with its attendant nationalistic theorizing (which did not necessarily deviate from the general ideal of dual federalism), there was a general restatement of the principles of separation. This restatement came from several sources: southerners interested in re-establishing the status of the South as it had been before the war to as great an extent as possible, persons interested in preventing government regulation of the new corporate giants of the Gilded Age, and even some of the political leaders who were seeking a way to regulate the new big business.

In the last class stood Grover Cleveland. In his fourth annual message to Congress, on December 7, 1896, just before his retirement from office, he dwelt at some length on the problem of monopoly regulation:

Though Congress has attempted to deal with this matter by legislation, the laws passed for that purpose thus far have proved ineffective, not because of any lack of disposition or attempt to enforce them, but simply because the laws themselves as interpreted by the courts do not reach the difficulty. . . . The fact must be recognized, however, that all federal legislation on this subject may fall short of its purpose . . . because of the complex character of our governmental system, which, while making the federal authority supreme within its sphere, has carefully limited that sphere by metes and bounds that can not be transgressed.[14]

SEPARATION AND THE SUPREME COURT

In this manner down to the close of the century, American political figures tended to describe the federal system as duel and separate. Important sources for this view were to be found in the decisions of the U.S.

---

[13] The messages of these presidents provide good traditional statements of their position (*ibid.*, Vol. IV).

John C. Calhoun is generally considered to be the foremost exponent of this expanded doctrine of dual federalism, particularly in his later days. His theories did help form the foundation of the extreme states'-rights tradition, though that was not his aim. The arguments he presented for a balance of power within a co-operative confederacy were taken by others whose interest was to prevent co-operation and even disrupt the Union itself. A generally adequate statement of the states'-rights argument as he used it may be found in John M. Anderson (ed.), *Calhoun: Basic Documents* (State College, Pa.: Bald Eagle Press, 1952).

[14] Richardson, *op. cit.*, XIV, 6177.

Supreme Court. For a long time the Court did not directly comment on the issue in the terms that have gained currency in the twentieth century, probably because its members did not consider the question in the same fashion. They generally took the issue for granted, sometimes assuming co-operation between, and sometimes separation of, the governments. In general those decisions that were publicized, because of aspects that had little to do with the problem before us here, were those that assumed dual federalism. This was less true in the days of Chief Justice John Marshall. It became prevalent during the height of the slavery conflict in the 1850's, when southern opinion strongly influenced the Court, and was revived in strength after the Civil War in the interests of laissez faire. In the Court, as in the more openly political arena, the ideas put forth by a southern group found wide and ready acceptance by parties outside that section for the same good and sufficient reasons.

The first case publicized as invoking classic dual federalism was *Martin* v. *Hunter's Lessee* (1 Wheaton 304), decided in 1816. Justice Joseph Story stated in the opinion of the Court that "it is perfectly clear that the sovereign powers vested in the States' Governments, by their respective constitutions, remain unaltered and unimpaired, except so far as they were granted to the government of the United States." This is clearly not a statement of dual federalism, but it could just as clearly be interpreted as such, given the proper intellectual climate surrounding it. Actually the case was one that increased the powers of the federal judiciary in its interstitial relations with the state courts. Story's view was seemingly endorsed by John Marshall himself in *Cohens* v. *Virginia* (6 Wheaton 413-4) in 1821: "The states . . . are members of one great empire—for some purposes sovereign, for some purposes subordinate." Again, the doctrine of dual federalism was assumed from this statement, although not actually stated.

McCulloch v. *Maryland* (4 Wheaton 316), which will be analyzed in chapter v, was also generally interpreted as indicating the necessity for separation of federal and state governmental functions. Denial of the power of a state to tax federal instrumentalities was considered to be a direct ratification of dual federalism on the assumption that Marshall's view of the federal government as supreme within its sphere implied exclusive authority.

Cases dealing with interstate commerce provided a fertile field for dealing with the question of dual federalism. *Gibbons* v. *Ogden* (9 Wheaton 1) was interpreted as another example of Supreme Court ratification of that doctrine. This was partly because Daniel Webster, as counsel in the case, based his argument against the steamboat monopoly on exclusive federal jurisdiction over interstate commerce. Since Marshall ruled in Webster's favor, it was again assumed that he had also accepted his doctrines.

These examples from the Marshall era are only a few among many. They are examples from an era in which the Court was noted for its national orientation. After Marshall's death and the accession of the Jacksonians to power on the Court, this orientation seemed to change to one more favorable to the states. In this period the better-known decisions of the Court again seemed to be oriented toward dualism, particularly in those cases based on the slavery controversy, which tended to dominate the period in so many ways. The pattern was set in the first of these cases, *Prigg* v. *Pennsylvania* (16 Peters 539), decided in 1842. Justice Story, speaking for the Court, claimed exclusive jurisdiction over fugitive slaves for the federal government, denying the right of Pennsylvania or any other state to legislate in a field pre-empted by the United States.

Perhaps the best summary of the theory of dual federalism as set forth by the Court was made by Chief Justice Roger B. Taney in the opinion handed down in the name of the Court in *Ableman* v. *Booth* (21 Howard 506) during the height of this period, 1858:

The powers of the General Government, and of the State, although both exist and are exercised within the same territorial limits, are yet separate and distinct sovereignties, acting separately and independently of each other, within their respective spheres.

The circumstances of this case throw additional light on the acceptance of the doctrine included in the Court's opinion. It was a case involving a Wisconsin "usurpation" of federal powers in regard to the apprehension and return of a fugitive slave. Thus, it was related to the burning issue of the day and one of the crucial issues, in the popular mind at least, of the entire century. Furthermore, it was a decision not to reinforce the rights of a particular state, but to assert the authority of the federal government, which, in this case, was supporting southern interests.[15]

The period immediately following the Civil War witnessed the expansion of the heretofore assumed doctrine of dual federalism along the lines laid down by Taney. The dualism of the federal system was spelled out

[15] Edward S. Corwin, *Total War and the Constitution* (New York: Alfred A. Knopf, 1947), p. 173. Corwin attributes the development of a formal statement of this doctrine to Taney.

in a series of decisions. In 1871, *Collector* v. *Day* (11 Wallace 113) extended the separatist interpretation of *McCulloch* v. *Maryland* to the administration of the federal income tax. Justice Samuel Nelson used that case to restate the proposition that the states, within certain limits, "are as independent of the general government as that government within its sphere is independent of the states." In 1873, the great body of civil rights protection under the Fourteenth Amendment was given to the states in a separatist interpretation handed down in the Slaughterhouse cases (16 Wallace 36). In *Munn* v. *Illinois* (94 U.S. 113), Chief Justice Morrison R. Waite restated the position that Congress had exclusive control over interstate commerce, even while affirming the right of Illinois to regulate its intrastate commerce. In the decisions based on the "due process" clause that filled the Court's docket from then on through the days of the New Deal, dual federalism was assumed as a basic doctrine. In 1918, in *Hammer* v. *Dagenhart* (247 U.S. 251), Justice William R. Day repeated the dictum that the task of the Supreme Court was to act as umpire to prevent either sovereignty from encroaching on the province of the other and in this manner preserve the federal system. Chief Justice William Howard Taft restated the idea of dual sovereignty in *Ponzi* v. *Fessendan et al.* (258 U.S. 254) just four years later.

In the early days of the New Deal, this position was restated by the Court time after time as hallowed doctrine. Cases such as *United States* v. *Constantine* (296 U.S. 287), in 1935, and *United States* v. *Butler* (298 U.S. 238), *Carter* v. *Carter Coal Company* (297 U.S. 1), and *Ashton* v. *Cameron County Water Improvement District No. One* (298 U.S. 513), in 1936, highlighted this formal reiteration of the then accepted interpretation.

THEORIES OF FEDERALISM

As a result of the domination of the field of constitutional law by articulate southerners until relatively recent times,[16] the theory of dualism was further emphasized in its most extreme form by their view that the Union was really the product of a compact between the several states, rather than a sovereign entity in its own right with powers directly granted by

[16] See Edward S. Corwin, *The Commerce Power versus States' Rights* (Princeton, N.J.: Princeton University Press, 1936), for an astute analysis of this southern domination since the days of Madison.

the people of the nation as a whole. This view actually reached its ascendancy after the Civil War with the publication of Alexander H. Stephens' "Platonic dialogue," entitled *A Constitutional View of the War between the States*. Stephens, the former vice-president of the Confederacy, advanced the thesis that the outcome of the Civil War had in no way altered the basic nature of the constitutional compact. The Union was still a limited union of sovereign states. All that the South had forfeited by losing the war was the right to use military force to enforce the terms of this compact; it had not given up any part of the states' sovereign rights guaranteed by the Constitution.[17]

The doctrine of dual federalism, or some modification of it, became the generally accepted view of the nature of the Union, and was written into constitutional law by a willing Supreme Court. According to this theory, each of the two sovereignties has its own exclusive area of authority and jurisdiction, with few powers held concurrently. Every citizen is responsible to each of these sovereignties separately, within their respective spheres of authority, despite the fact that both occupy the same territory. Furthermore, the greater the separation of functions, the more truly federal the system is. It then becomes the role and duty of the Supreme Court to regulate the relationships between the federal and state governments in order to maintain this dual system. Dualism was equated with demarcation of areas of authority between the two levels of government and, later, with the prevention of certain forms of governmental activity at any level. It was considered to be the basis by which federalism would be able to survive as a vital and significant aspect of the American political system.

In the period since the New Deal, one basically different interpretation of the nineteenth-century attitude has been advanced. Some scholars, after examining the first thirty years of American government under the Constitution in more detail, have concluded that the Constitution was originally intended to establish a strong national government, that political events moved in that direction for a short while, and that the Constitution was then changed through interpretation into a compact favoring states' rights. Even this view does not do much to deny the basic separation of levels read into the system. It only allots a greater exclusive role to the

[17] Stephens, *A Constitutional View of the War between the States* (Philadelphia: National Publishing Co., 1868), II, 652.

federal government under the original Constitution.[18] On the other hand, polemicists for the extreme states'-rights position have maintained the older view of the prior existence of, and absolute necessity for, virtually complete separation.[19]

Both of these views are colored by differing conceptions of the nature and role of the federal system today. Both agree that dual federalism, for all intents and purposes, no longer exists. A "new federalism" has arisen, either since Wilson's administration or, at the latest, since the second Roosevelt's. This new federalism is viewed as having broken down the barriers between the federal government and the states, changing separation to co-operation. Co-operative federalism, as it is called, is viewed as a major departure from the traditional system by which the powers of the federal government have been broadened (or restored, according to some) into areas previously the sole responsibility of the states, leading to co-operation between the two levels of government in the implementation of new programs. Such programs involve an inevitable sharing of the same functions, with arrangements for joint financing and, generally, some type of federal supervision.

This revolution is evaluated in different ways. Radical states'-righters view what they call "coerced federalism" as the destruction of the true constitutional system and, consequently, the potential destruction of both the states and our traditional liberties. "Liberals" view it as a major step forward in providing the necessary governmental services, sufficiently within the spirit of the Constitution to be acceptable, yet in a manner different from the traditional pattern. Centralists, like the states'-righters feel that the states are being reduced to the level of administrative agents for the federal government, a change which the centralists view with approval.

If some of these theorists view this new development with favor and others view it with alarm, the common denominator that unites them all is their belief that co-operative federalism is a radically new approach that represents a real departure from traditional American values and practices. The remainder of this study will be devoted to demonstrating the unreality of the traditional picture of the nature of federalism in nine-

[18] Among those holding this view are Edward S. Corwin, Leonard D. White, and William C. Crosskey, who goes much further than this in his *Politics and the Constitution in the History of the United States* (Chicago: University of Chicago Press, 1952).

[19] See, for example, James Kilpatrick, *Our Sovereign States* (Chicago: Henry Regnery Co., 1956).

teenth-century America, the inability of the traditional theory of dual federalism to function when applied to concrete governmental problems, and the failure of students of American federalism to distinguish between fact and fancy in describing the system as it existed during the nineteenth century. It will demonstrate that the sources of this failure lay in the sharp dichotomy between theory and practice perhaps unwittingly set forth by the political leadership of the age, who continued to preach separation while practicing co-operation. Furthermore, this study will provide examples to indicate how the materials often used to infer separation, in practice inferred no such thing, as is evident when they are studied in context, and how other contemporary materials which infer or endorse federal-state co-operation have gone unrecognized in the studies of classic American federalism. At the conclusion of this study, it should be apparent that federalism in the United States, as practiced, has traditionally been co-operative, that dual federalism as demarcation of responsibilities has never worked in practice, and that governmental activities in the nineteenth century, as in the twentieth, were shared by the federal and state governments in collaboration despite formal pronouncements to the contrary.

2

Internal Improvements and Fiscal Relationships: The Setting

THE CREATION OF CO-OPERATION

The early period of American federalism overlaps the Federalist years, the Jeffersonian ascendancy, and the Jacksonian era, during which the foundations of most of the American political institutions were laid. Economic historians have referred to the first half of this period as the mercantilist era in American history, when the open and avowed purpose of government was to encourage and direct the economic development of the nation.[1] During this period the fundamental issue in public policy formation was not so much whether government had an active role to play or not, but what needed to be done by government and how it could be done best. The general consensus was that three problems in particular had to be met by governmental action: the development of a system of internal communication that would connect the various parts of the Republic, especially the East and the West; the establishment of a sound yet flexible national system of finance; and the development of an educational system that would serve the young Republic's citizenry.

The federal government, the states, and the localities moved to provide these services at virtually the same time. The joint action that resulted set a precedent for the future that is still being followed in the mid-twentieth century for the same reasons that it evolved originally. One common American myth is that, because primary responsibility for certain functions is constitutionally vested in the states, the states have been first to act to undertake those functions and the federal government has only

[1] See Curtis P. Nettels, "British Mercantilism and the Economic Development of the Thirteen Colonies," in *Journal of Economic History*, XII (Spring, 1952), 105–14.

moved in at a later date for reasons of national policy or nationwide pressure. This myth is generally at variance with the facts. The record of case after case confirms the general rule that when a problem has attracted the interest of government, it has done so throughout the United States, if not in every state, at least in some states in every section of the country. Thus, when the need for government action has been decided upon, it has generally been a decision for action by all levels of government at approximately the same time. Significantly, one or two states have often been pioneers in initiating specific programs and have provided some experience in governmental handling of a particular problem. The general rule has been, however, that the states have not made use of their powers before the federal government.

This was the case with internal improvements during the early period of American federalism. States were establishing boards of internal improvements in the period between the establishment by the federal government of the Corps of Engineers and the United States Board of Internal Improvement to co-ordinate activities under some form of national plan. Congress created the United States Army Corps of Engineers in 1802, with the understanding that the corps could be used for civil, as well as military, works. The first federal master plan for internal improvements was prepared by Albert Gallatin in 1808. The debate in Congress over the next two years indicated to the states that a substantial number of the projects contained within the master plan would be undertaken. Despite the delays engendered by the War of 1812, the Virginia General Assembly adopted a policy calling for a major internal improvement program to be developed in conjunction with that of the federal government; and the Virginia Board of Public Works was organized in 1816 at least partly as a result of federal activities in this field.[2] The creation of this and other state boards of internal improvement led to Congressional formalization of the existing internal improvement program of the Corps of Engineers by establishing a national Board of Internal Improvement in 1824.[3]

This situation prevailed because a problem of development for one section of the nation was almost without exception a problem for all sections in some measure. As the westward movement increased, this need for a national perspective in problem-solving grew, as did the national approach toward the solution of problems. The existence of nationwide problems

[2] Virginia Board of Public Works, *First Annual Report* (Richmond, 1816).

[3] The federal actions in this regard are described in Leonard D. White's *The Jeffersonians* (New York: Macmillan Co., 1951), pp. 260-62.

that displayed local variations but did not differ in their fundamental nature helped create a real need for a system of intergovernmental co-operation.

DEVELOPING AN INTERNAL IMPROVEMENT POLICY

When the vital role that communications plays in building and maintaining a nation is appreciated, the importance of developing a system of internal communications in the early United States becomes virtually self-evident. The major domestic problem facing the new national government after 1789 was the creation of the best possible means of communication between the various parts of the country. This problem was most evident in relation to the trans-Appalachian regions, which were at first so isolated from the settled parts of the Union that they were led to consider secession unless they could be united with the seaboard. No less important, though less dramatic, was the problem of facilitating communication and commercial intercourse between the North and South as a means of uniting those two diverse sections in a more firmly bound union.

The question of federal aid in developing an internal communications system was one that was hotly debated in Congress and in the country at large. The Federalists had been the first to think in such terms in the 1790's when they tried to have Congress authorize a system of post roads to meet the need.[4] Although certain routes were designated as post roads by Congressional action, no real plan for a nationwide system was submitted to the country until, at the request of the Senate, Albert Gallatin, Jefferson's secretary of the treasury, drew up a comprehensive program in 1808. While Gallatin's plan embraced the principle of intergovernmental co-operation, it provided for the allocation of specific programs to different levels of government rather than intergovernmental sharing within each program. His report determined the course of internal improvements prior to the coming of the railroads, though the War of 1812 prevented its formal adoption by Congress. Gallatin, like the rest of the Jeffersonians, was held back by the problem of constitutional interpretation. While he felt privately that the federal government had the power to engage in such enterprises, he deferred to the views of his leader, Jefferson, who felt that, desirable as the program was, a constitutional amendment would be needed to grant the necessary power to the federal authorities. Strict con-

[4] *Ibid.*, pp. 78–79.

struction being the dominant persuasion of the time, Jefferson's views prevailed.

After the war, however, the majority in Congress had changed its views and was ready to vote for internal improvements. It was at this point that the House of Representatives directed John C. Calhoun, then secretary of war, to prepare a second national plan for internal improvement. This plan was submitted to Congress in 1819. Calhoun had already emerged as the champion of internal improvements and as a supporter of federal action under the existing Constitution. During the postwar period, this complex and often misunderstood man became the leading architect of American federalism as we know it. He added a dimension to national action that had been omitted in earlier planning. Instead of dividing the field of internal improvements into separate programs, each to be assigned exclusively to a specific level of government, he developed the idea of two or more levels sharing in the implementation of each project. This idea brought both short- and long-range benefits. Despite the course of formal political action that led to the strict constructionists' triumph over the proponents of internal improvements in many Congressional actions, the idea of co-operative arrangements enabled Calhoun and his successors to provide federal assistance to the states within the limits of their discretion as department heads in many subsequent situations without antagonizing the majority of the strict constructionists.

Meanwhile, when Congress had established the United States Army Corps of Engineers in 1802, it had ordered the corps to constitute itself as a school of engineering, the first in the nation, with headquarters at West Point.[5] As virtually the sole source of trained civil engineers in the United States prior to the Civil War, the Army Corps of Engineers soon found itself deeply involved in the nationwide internal improvement effort. By virtue of the fact that their services were indispensable to the states embarked on internal improvement programs, co-operative relationships had to be developed. In 1824, after this fact became clearly apparent, Congress enacted the General Survey Act that formalized the co-operative patterns that had been suggested earlier and implemented in a piecemeal fashion under the aegis of various other federal enactments for well over a decade. This act authorized the President to use military and civil engineers "to cause the necessary surveys, plans, and estimates, to be made of the routes of such roads and canals as he may deem of national importance, in a

---

[5] Forest G. Hill, "Government Engineering Aid before the Civil War," *Journal of Economic History*, XI (Summer, 1951), 243.

commercial or military point of view, or necessary for the transportation of the public mail. . . ."[6]

The General Survey Act provided the basis for the major share of the internal improvements constructed over the next several decades. Before it was repealed in 1838, the Army Engineers had developed what amounted to a national master plan for roads, canals, and railroads (which the act was extended to include as they began to replace roads and canals as the dominant means of communication). Their availability as planners, engineers, and supervisors had also stimulated the states and private enterprise to undertake the construction of other such improvements themselves.

The Act of 1824 was repealed because the demands on the Corps of Engineers came to exceed the supply of engineers, and military projects began to suffer as a result. Although repeal ended one stage of planning for a national communications network, the task was carried on by the Engineers under less broad authorizations. Actually, by 1838 the pattern for intergovernmental co-operation was already set and the idea had proved its worth in a national system of communications that was capped by 1,899 miles of railroad, almost all of which had been constructed with the aid of the Army Engineers.[7]

THE FISCAL BEGINNINGS

Federal involvement in the fiscal system is almost as old as the institution of banking in this country. When the first Bank of the United States was established under Congressional charter in 1791 to inaugurate a central banking system for the nation, only four other banks existed in the entire United States and one of these four, the Bank of North America, had been chartered under the Articles of Confederation as a quasi-national bank.[8]

Prior to the Jacksonian era, the American banking system was operated as part of the mercantilist-oriented economy that had not yet been re-

[6] *Acts of the Eighteenth Congress,* in *Public Statutes at Large of the United States of America,* ed. Richard Peters (Boston: Little and Brown, 1846), p. 35.

[7] Hill, *op. cit.,* p. 242.

[8] Bray Hammond, *Banks and Politics in America from the Revolution to the Civil War* (Princeton, N.J.: Princeton University Press, 1957), p. 144.

placed by the laissez faire doctrines and practices that came to dominate American economic ideology for the next hundred years. The mercantilist approach centered around the idea that the state had a role to play in encouraging commerce—in the broadest sense of the term—and that the manipulation of fiscal affairs was a proper method for doing so.[9] It was in this spirit that the federal government and the states set about creating banking systems that they either controlled by charter and stockholdings or owned outright.

In addition to this general acceptance of government responsibility in the economic realm, there existed certain objective conditions that made it necessary for government to act and for different levels of government to act co-operatively. Chief among these was the advance of the frontier, coupled with the necessity for its large-scale development and the lack of funds readily available to do the job. Since funds were not easily available on the frontier, two courses were open to the country: to create paper money for the task on a local basis or to use the powers of the federal government to create a stable banking system that could also supply capital where it was needed. The first five decades of the Republic witnessed a struggle between the advocates of these two approaches, which was at first won by those favoring a national banking system and then, during the administration of Jackson, was reversed in favor of the localists. Significantly, each approach, however different one was from the other, provided for its own brand of co-operative federalism.

In the early period, the great majority of banks were either state-owned joint-stock companies in which the state was a major shareholder or were controlled by the state through special charter provisions. The Bank of the United States was controlled by the federal government rather than by the states, which meant that the bank served as the fiscal and banking arm of the federal government and as manager of the federal deposits. In this capacity it dominated the American financial scene prior to 1800. According to Shultz and Caine, "Through its branch organization it co-operated with and to some extent controlled the newly-created state banks throughout the country."[10]

Under the first and subsequent national banking programs, a significant

[9] See William W. Crosskey, *Politics and the Constitution in the United States* (Chicago: University of Chicago Press, 1953), Vol. I, Part I, for a thorough discussion of the meaning of the term "Commerce" in the mercantilist period.

[10] William J. Shultz and M. R. Caine, *Financial Development of the United States* (New York: Prentice-Hall, 1937), p. 125.

amount of intergovernmental co-operation developed. Some of this co-operation was formally written into law by both nation and state, while some of it evolved informally in response to obvious situations and needs. Political and ideological overtones that were attached to the immediate issue of banking itself introduced emotion-charged factors into the story of intergovernmental relations in the fiscal field that were quite unrelated to co-operative federalism as such. Over the years, the historian's interest in these factors has obscured the co-operative aspects of the nineteenth-century American fiscal system.

From the initial session of the First Congress, a climate of intergovernmental co-operation in fiscal matters began to develop, partly fostered by the almost immediate creation of the first Bank of the United States and partly by the implementation of the constitutional provision concerning direct taxation, which provides that, "Direct taxes shall be apportioned among the several states . . . and . . . no capitation or other direct tax shall be laid, unless in proportion to the census or enumeration hereinbefore directed to be taken."[11] This latter provision led directly to the necessity of apportioning any direct tax among the states, which, in turn, had to raise the money called for in their respective quotas and deliver it to the federal government.[12]

Because of Hamilton's maneuver to have the federal government assume the states' Revolutionary War debts, the direct tax was virtually the only tax levied by the states during the 1790's. One of the conditions in the Act of August 4, 1790, which provided for federal assumption of up to $21,500,000 in state debts, was that any part of the debts already paid by the states would be reimbursed by the federal government.[13]

---

[11] *U.S. Constitution,* Art. I, Secs. 2 and 9.

[12] For example, the Act of Congress of July 14, 1798, called for a levy of $1,315,000 to be raised on the basis of houses, $228,000 on the basis of slaves, and $457,000 on the basis of lands, to be distributed among the states on the basis of their respective populations. The states taxed lands to fulfill their quotas, all of them raising $734,224 in 1800 and $534,000 in 1801 (Shultz and Caine, *op. cit.,* pp. 110–11).

[13] I Stat. 142 (1790). Passage of this act was secured despite the initial hostility of the southern states through a compromise much in the tradition of American politics. When the assumption question was raised by Alexander Hamilton, there was much opposition to it, primarily because some of the states, particularly in the South, had paid substantial shares of their debts and others had paid little. New York in particular stood to benefit from federal assumption of its debts, since it had paid virtually none of them, had a large amount contracted, and was in a sound financial position otherwise. Situations like this generated considerable hostility among the southern states whose smaller populations would have placed on them a greater tax burden in

The federal bonds given to the states in repayment of the Revolutionary War debts they had voluntarily retired furnished sufficient income for most of the states to maintain themselves during the 1790's. With the addition of revenues from state-owned lands, more than enough money was available for state expenditures and very little taxation was needed.[14] The states began to develop a tradition of free spending with little responsibility for financing their activities, coupled with a reliance, albeit not officially recognized, on the federal government for funds to initiate and support major programs. While the money may have "rightfully" belonged to the states in the first place, in the last analysis it came from the federal treasury and, as such, could be used for projects that the state alone would not have been able to undertake because of local opposition to taxes—a situation familiar enough in mid-twentieth-century America. Virginia, among other states, used this technique to secure sufficient funds to establish a rudimentary public education system two decades later when the War of 1812 provided the occasion for another series of federal reimbursements. Thus, Hamilton successfully gauged the situation when he advocated assumption of debts as a means of strengthening the national government. However, in so far as he hoped to do so at the expense of the states, he failed, since Congress determined that, while the federal government might furnish the money, the states would spend it, another pattern that has persisted since that day.

THE ARCHITECTS AND THE PROCEDURES

Much of the co-operative pattern depended on the personalities and attitudes of the leaders who were responsible for creating it. These architects of American federalism fell into roughly two categories. The first group was composed of people whose main task was the formulation of policy. In general, they were second-rank leaders in the national government, cabinet members and some bureau chiefs. To some extent they had their counterparts on the state level. They were men such as Albert Gallatin and John C. Calhoun (Calhoun was perhaps the greatest single archi-

---

any national assumption. After initially defeating the measure in Congress, a compromise was arranged providing for the national capital to be located in the South and for reimbursement of the states by the federal government for any portions of their debts they had already repaid.

[14] Shultz and Caine, *op. cit.*, pp. 117–18.

tect of the system, with a well-formulated and reasoned approach that was entirely consistent with his general philosophy of government). They formulated the over-all policies for intergovernmental co-operation in a manner consistent with the goals of the nation and the rights of the states, and engaged in the political give and take necessary to achieve at least partial implementation of their programs. These men were not centralists like Hamilton; nor were they states'-rights anticentralists as Jefferson tried to be. They were true federalists who saw the need and desirability for national action within the framework of the federal system. They proceeded to experiment with ways to make this logically difficult concept a practical and political reality.

The second category consisted of professionals on both the federal and state levels who made the system work and who, in the manner of professionals, identified themselves with their programs so that they fought for them and sustained them during hours of trial. At first the influence of this professional group was most evident in the field of internal improvements where specialized training in engineering was necessary to qualify (this was before other governmental activities became professionalized). Numerous engineers served the federal government and the states when they could have earned more in private industry. These people dominated the field of internal improvements for many years, and in their concern with internal improvement without regard to the nuances of ideology, developed policy in the field favorable to intergovernmental co-operation.[15]

Particularly in the early period, most formal co-operative programs had to be developed around procedures other than those used to dispose of the public domain. This need for the development of co-operative procedures was common in the relationship between the federal government and all states without public lands.[16] Out of this need grew a number of experimental devices, most of which passed from the scene as they proved cumbersome or ineffective. Their abandonment has often been used as evidence in discussing the "failure" of early attempts at intergovernmental

[15] The parallel between the professional engineers and the professionals found in the various grant-in-aid programs of our own day is striking despite the greater numbers and strong professional associations that are products of our more complex society. For examples of the role of the latter, see the files of the Workshop in American Federalism, University of Chicago.

[16] These were the original thirteen states plus Vermont, Kentucky, Tennessee, Maine, and West Virginia. Texas was later admitted to the Union under special provisions that effectively placed it in this category also.

co-operation.[17] Actually, the entire period was one of experimentation in the development of co-operative forms in an attempt to satisfy both national and state interests. When one form failed, another was tried until a suitable method was found and the political situation developed sufficiently to permit its adoption.

The most formal method used in the early period was that of the joint-stock company, an arrangement particularly adapted for use in the creation of banks and specific works of internal improvement, such as canals and railroads. It involved the creation of a corporation to develop a specific project, the stock of which was purchased by the federal government (following Congressional authorization), one or more states (upon authorization from their appropriate legislative bodies), various municipalities, and, quite often, private individuals. Control was vested in a board of directors appointed by the several stockholders, with the voting powers of each party established in the charter of incorporation. Generally, control of any joint-stock company lay with the combined voting power of the federal government and the states involved, while the power to veto action rested informally with either government.

The joint-stock company provided a method for the federal government to supply funds, technical aid, and equipment to the states for internal improvements that were considered to be in the direct national interest, while retaining a sufficient measure of control over the plans, construction, and use of the improvement in question and without violating the letter of strict constitutional construction. Its use was not confined to federal-state projects. For projects in which federal participation in the joint-stock company could not be obtained, the states concerned, municipalities, and private individuals would provide the investment capital and management, with the federal government usually contributing technical assistance through the Corps of Engineers. In the case of intrastate projects, the state would form a corporation in conjunction with municipalities and private investors in a similar manner, obtaining technical assistance from the federal government if the project was judged to be in the national interest.

The joint-stock company was by no means the only structure used to implement federal-state co-operation in the early period, but like land grants a few decades later and monetary grants-in-aid since 1913, it was the major vehicle for introducing the pattern of collaboration in its time.

[17] See, for example, Leonard D. White, *The Jeffersonians* (New York: Macmillan Co., 1951).

Through numerous joint-stock companies in the banking and internal improvement fields and the federal technical assistance programs linked with them, the early architects of American federalism were given an opportunity to experiment with and develop routinized co-operative procedures that were highly influential in the evolution of American federalism. At the same time, federal monetary aid, often introduced through the reimbursement process, provided a fiscal climate for the growth of the American partnership.

3

The Dismal Swamp Canal

THE CANAL AND THE NATION

Prior to the coming of the railroads, canals were considered to be the most valuable form of internal improvement—a cheap, efficient means of transporting goods and people over varying distances in most kinds of weather. Since their only competitors at the time were poor highways and untamed rivers, they represented the height of man's progress in intracontinental communication.

One facet in the development of nationwide commercial intercourse was the construction of a waterway system along the east coast that would connect the northern and southern states and, at the same time, link the various water routes that were being developed to penetrate into the interior of the continent. The intracoastal waterway was designed to at once provide an all-weather north-south connection and also furnish the main stem of an integrated water transportation network that would embrace the entire United States east of the Mississippi River. The immediate targets for the first intracoastal waterway were a series of canals through Cape Cod in Massachusetts, the Maryland-Virginia eastern shore of Chesapeake Bay, and the region south of Norfolk along the Virginia–North Carolina capes. These canals were to eliminate the long hazardous sea trips around those jutting capes.

The idea for the continental system was first outlined for the nation as a whole by Albert Gallatin in his report to the Congress on internal improvements in 1808.[1] The idea for a canal through the Great Dismal Swamp was still older, having been considered seriously by George Washington and his associates in the immediate post-Revolutionary pe-

---

[1] *American State Papers: Miscellaneous* [hereinafter referred to as ASP:M], I, 725 (April 4, 1808).

riod.[2] The proposed canal was to penetrate the desolate water wilderness below Norfolk, Virginia, cutting some twenty miles southward into North Carolina where it would meet Albemarle Sound. It was originally designed simply to penetrate this area, a foreboding place rich in timber and other resources that had gone undeveloped since the earliest English settlement.

Virginia's interest in internal improvements was closely in line with that of the nation as a whole. Half of the state was relatively well settled and tied to the Atlantic seaboard, while the other half was just emerging from the rude frontier stage into that of a more complex civilization. Thus, the Old Dominion was faced with the problem of having to unify two diverse sections of her polity, much as was the nation as a whole. In addition, Virginians were as eager to tap the sources of trade in the trans-Appalachian region as were the citizens of the other coastal states.

In the last decade of the eighteenth century a company was organized and chartered by the states of Virginia and North Carolina to undertake the construction of a shallow canal that would enable barge traffic to haul lumber from the interior of the swamp to Norfolk. The company was capitalized at $100,000, of which Virginia subscribed $17,500.[3] By the time of the Gallatin report, this company had been successful in constructing a shallow draft canal, useful for local purposes only.

The preparation of Gallatin's report marked the first official Congressional interest in the canal. Gallatin himself followed up his report by having the possibilities for enlarging the canal investigated by the Army Engineers.[4]

No action was taken on Gallatin's proposals until 1816, when the Congress directed that a second national report on internal improvements be prepared under the auspices of the then secretary of war, John C. Calhoun. Calhoun sent Major James Kearney of the Army Engineers to conduct a survey of the proposed canal, and the project was again incorporated into a master plan submitted to Congress.[5]

Meanwhile, Virginia was also dissatisfied with the existing canal and

---

[2] Alexander C. Brown, "The Dismal Swamp Canal," *American Neptune*, V (1945), 203–22, 297–310; VI (1946), 51–70.

[3] *Ibid.*

[4] ASP:M, I, 725 (April 4, 1808).

[5] John C. Calhoun, "Report on Roads and Canals, Communicated to the House of Representatives, January 14, 1819," in *The Works of John C. Calhoun* (New York: D. Appleton and Company, 1888), Vol. V.

with the state of internal improvements within the Commonwealth generally. In an attempt to remedy the situation, the state general assembly ordered its committee on roads and internal navigation to prepare a report with suggested changes in the organization and financing of internal improvements. The report was submitted to the parent body in December, 1814, as the War of 1812 was drawing to a close and a new spirit of expansionism was sweeping the entire country. Its recommendations included the establishment of a state fund for internal improvements. All the state's holdings in existing internal improvements were to be transferred to this fund, and any profits accruing to the state by virtue of those holdings were to be used for additional improvements. A special board was to be established to manage the fund. A principal point in the committee's report was that the ordinary revenues of the state could not finance the extensive work necessary to develop the needed internal improvement system.[6]

The outcome of this report was the creation, in 1816, of a Fund for Internal Improvement and a Board of Public Works to manage the fund and the internal improvement activities of the state. From the beginning the board realized the national character of its task and desired to do its work in co-operation with the federal government. Its first annual report included the following statement of purpose:

There are several objects within the scope of the system devised by the General Assembly for the improvement of the interior of Virginia, which in the present state of her wealth and population, it is beyond the reach of her unassisted ability to accomplish; but which, being equally interesting to her sister states and to the government of the United States, it may not be impossible to further by their cooperation.[7]

Indeed, informal co-operation even preceded this statement. Since the supply of qualified civil engineers was generally monopolized by the United States Army at that time, Virginia officials had to turn to federal officials for help in securing a state engineer for the newly created board. Governor Wilson C. Nicholas, ex officio chairman of the board, was responsible for securing an engineer. In carrying out his responsibility he

[6] Virginia General Assembly, Committee of Roads and Navigation, "Report (December, 1814)," in *A Collection of All Laws and Resolutions of the General Assembly of Virginia Relating to the Board of Public Works, etc.*

[7] Virginia Board of Public Works [hereinafter referred to as BPW], *First Annual Report* (Richmond, 1816), p. 6.

turned to President Madison in Washington[8] and even to John Quincy Adams, then American minister in London.[9]

Another important federal official consulted was Benjamin H. Latrobe, then superintendent of public buildings in Washington, D.C. Latrobe, at that time the leading architect and civil engineer in the nation, had either trained or worked with every available man in his profession. Since he had come to the United States from England after becoming an engineer, he also had extensive contacts in Europe. Standing at the center of activity as he did, virtually every request for engineers passed through his hands.[10] Latrobe had been contacted by both the Governor of Virginia and the President of the United States. His correspondence with an agent of the Governor dwelt on the lack of trained canal engineers in the New World and the necessity for importing some from Europe for immediate use, which he endeavored to do. In addition to helping secure personnel, he offered advice on construction procedures.

On April 8, 1816, Latrobe wrote to Madison concerning the appointment of a principal engineer for the Virginia Board of Public Works, offering him "a few remarks on the subject," which were forwarded to Governor Nicholas by the President. In the letter he outlined what was required in the construction of roads and canals and recommended several possible candidates for the position.

8 *Ibid.*, p. 23. The President had inquiries made and submitted the names of several possible candidates, with evaluations of their work and abilities. In addition, he informed the Governor that the American ministers in Europe would be of every assistance if he desired to extend his search overseas.

General J. G. Swift of the United States Military Academy was also contacted by the President and submitted suggestions, not only for engineers but in regard to the securing of trained workmen. He suggested that men with experience be brought down from New England, and volunteered to make inquiry about them for Virginia if the Governor should want him to do so.

9 *Ibid.*, p. 15. Adams forwarded the application of at least one British candidate for the position.

10 Latrobe was one of the professional architects of American federalism. He is considered the founder of the architecture and engineering professions in the United States and was involved in either planning or constructing most of the internal improvement projects in the country prior to 1812, serving federal, state, and local governments both alternately and simultaneously. Out of the twenty-four-year span of his career in this country, twelve years were spent in the federal service and during three more he was engaged in federal projects (1800–1812, 1815–17). Since these were the years of his prominence, it was unavoidable that the states, even Virginia, should seek his aid and thereby enter into informal co-operative relationships with the federal government.

In this, as in other cases, President Madison considered Latrobe the federal consultant on roads and canals and, as such, endeavored to make his advice available to state officials who requested it. If the President, who vetoed more than one internal improvement appropriations bill as unconstitutional, was not ready to have the federal government appropriate money for internal improvements, he saw no reason why it could not offer its services in other ways. Nor did the states seem to dispute this.

A chief engineer secured, the board began to assume control of Virginia's internal improvement projects. The Dismal Swamp Canal, among the most important of these projects, was redesigned to be expanded as a part of the national waterway system at the same time that Major Kearney of the Army Engineers was undertaking his survey of the canal area for the Calhoun report. In the report of the Great Dismal Swamp Canal Company for 1817, this national purpose was officially recognized by the statement that the canal "will form the channel of internal communication between other great public works, both national and state."[11]

Despite these high intentions, progress was slow and financing inadequate. Every year the canal company filed its report of progress made and difficulties encountered with the Board of Public Works, as required by Virginia law from all joint-stock internal improvement companies.[12] Every year the company asked for additional state aid, and the state would repeat this request to the federal government. From time to time additional state aid was forthcoming, such as in 1819 when the board loaned the shares it held in the Bank of the United States to the company, in order that the dividends might be used to support construction.[13] At the same time the Congressional debate over the form of federal aid for internal improvements was resulting in one stalemate after another.[14]

Finally, in 1826, matters came to a head. The directors of the canal company had secured enactments from the Virginia and North Carolina legislatures authorizing the issuance and sale of six hundred more shares of stock, in addition to the six hundred forty then outstanding, which

---

[11] BPW, *Second Annual Report* (1818), p. 15.

[12] The procedures developed during these years by the various states engaged in internal improvements to control their subsidiary companies were later transferred almost intact to the supervision of railroad construction companies under the federal-state land-grant program.

[13] BPW, *Fourth Annual Report* (1819).

[14] Leonard D. White, *The Jeffersonians* (New York: Macmillan Co., 1951), pp. 480–82.

were valued at $150,000. However, no one purchased those shares during the time prescribed by the acts for their sale, leaving the company as low in funds as before and with little hope for the future. Just before the company's right to issue the new stock expired, an act of Congress was secured directing the secretary of the treasury to purchase the entire six hundred shares in the name of the United States. Under the terms of the act, the secretary was to purchase the stock at the price and terms set by the company. He was also to be responsible for voting for president and directors of the company in the name of the United States, "according to said number of shares," and for receipt of any dividends that might accrue. The act was not to go into effect until the United States Board of Engineers for Internal Improvement should "examine the canal and report in writing to the Secretary of War that, in their opinion the canal's plan will answer, as far as circumstances permit, as part of the chain of canals contemplated along the Atlantic coast and that the sum subscribed will be adequate to finish the canal by said plan."[15]

The $150,000 appropriated for purchasing the stock was expressly earmarked for completion of the canal only, not for settlement of any previous debts. To insure that this provision would be carried out, the secretary of the treasury was directed "to adopt such measures as shall insure the application of the same to the completion of the said canal, according to the plan proposed, and to no other purpose whatsoever, . . . before the payment of any part of the money subscribed on behalf of the United States."[16] Acceptance of the terms of this act was made possible by the grant of a substantial loan to the canal company by the Virginia General Assembly, enabling it to settle the outstanding debts and continue construction by relying largely on the new federal subscription. Thus, even when not specifically required by law, an arrangement to match funds emerged.[17]

---

[15] The United States Board of Engineers for Internal Improvement was established in 1824 after Congress had enacted legislation providing funds for the Army Engineers to undertake surveys of proposed internal improvements at the request of the states and companies involved. It was composed of senior Army Engineers, whose duties were to implement the Gallatin report and its successor reports in so far as possible and to oversee all internal improvement projects involving the federal government.

[16] U.S. *Statutes at Large*, LXV (May 18, 1826). The relevant sections of this statute are also reproduced in BPW, *Eleventh Annual Report* (1827).

[17] Brown, *op. cit.*, p. 21.

Under the terms of the new statute, the federal government would own 600 out of a total of 1,240 shares, thus becoming the largest single shareholder. The total investment in capital stock came to $310,000, of which $96,000 had been invested by individuals and $64,000 by the state of Virginia; $150,000 would be invested by the federal government.[18]

In compliance with the act of Congress, Lieutenant Colonel Gratiot of the Corps of Engineers was sent to survey the canal to ascertain what had already been done and to draw up a plan for its completion. He reported his findings to Major General Alexander Macomb, the chief of engineers, in August, 1826, while at the same time submitting a copy of his report and recommendations to the canal company. The report indicated that the canal would fit into the intracoastal waterway system and that the sum involved would be enough to complete it.

Since the company had no regular plan of construction, Gratiot prepared a plan that not only satisfied Macomb but was also accepted by the board of directors of the company, who submitted it to the Virginia Board of Public Works for approval. The Virginia board also accepted the plan and directed that it be followed by the company. With the assent of the three bodies concerned, it became the basis for completion of the canal.[19]

The co-operation that grew out of this report and its joint acceptance is indicative of the pattern of intergovernmental co-operation that was developing in the 1820's. In the first place, all three levels of government were involved in the project. (Among the so-called private shareholders in the company was the city of Norfolk.) The general goals of all three were the same, to construct a canal that would benefit both the national and the local interests; and the professional representatives of all three, namely, the several boards, also agreed on the technical details of construction. Gratiot even went so far as to provide for the depth of the canal to be eight feet in accordance with the decision of the United States Board of Engineers in the Chesapeake and Ohio Canal survey in order to standardize the new nationwide system.[20]

With the new money that became available, work toward completion of the canal could proceed. Nevertheless, certain leading Virginians

[18] BPW, *Eleventh Annual Report* (1827), p. 18.

[19] *Ibid.*, pp. 17–23.

[20] *Ibid.*, p. 20. Gratiot's report is incorporated in its entirety in the annual report of the Board of Public Works.

could not reconcile themselves to the gracious acceptance of this necessary federal aid. In his message to the General Assembly on internal improvements, delivered on December 4, 1826, Governor Tyler stated that Virginia had always favored the construction of the Dismal Swamp Canal and had even gone so far as to buy stock in the company and lend it money. Thus, it is "a subject of much regret that she should be deprived by the interposition of the Federal Government of the honor of having completed it, when it required but the mere finishing hand."[21] So words of separation masked facts of co-operation.

The "mere finishing hand" required two years of intensive work before the canal was opened, and even then it was not completed. Shortly after the federal subscription, Lieutenant Andrew Talcott of the Army Engineers assumed the position of superintendent of the canal. While it is unclear whether he received a formal order to take the position or whether he was simply loaned to the canal company to do the job, it is certain that the canal was opened for use under his direction. His formal position was that of an independent contractor, so that he, a federal officer, would not legally be an employee of the company, which paid all or part of his salary. The arrangement was a form of service-in-aid grant with matching provisions; that is, the federal government supplied the trained engineer, while the company paid all or part of his salary. This arrangement was a common one during the entire period in all parts of the country.[22]

Nevertheless, more capital was needed if the canal was to be completed according to national specifications. In 1829, the federal government purchased an additional two hundred shares of stock for $50,000.[23] No sooner was this transaction completed than the governor of the state felt compelled to denounce federal "interference" again, perhaps to salve his states'-rights conscience. In his message to the General Assembly of December 6, 1830, he stated that he was happy that Virginia had opposed federal action in the field of internal improvements as "unionist

[21] *Ibid.*, p. 110. In the same message he refers to the advocates of federal aid for the James River Canal to the effect that they just cannot get aid for that project, despite its national value.

[22] Dismal Swamp Canal Company, *Annual Report, 1827* (Norfolk: 1827) and *Annual Report, 1828.* The arrangement was evidently eminently satisfactory to the company, whose president said of Talcott in 1828, "To his science and unremitting attention, the Company particularly and the Country generally are eminently indebted."

[23] BPW, *Fourteenth Annual Report* (1830), p. 30.

and deleterious," and praised President Jackson's veto of several measures appropriating federal funds for internal improvements in other states.[24] But there is no record of his doing anything to prevent the federal government's additional investment.

Once the canal was open for traffic, attention could be focused on improving the details of its construction and maintaining it in proper condition. On July 4, 1836, Congress acted to meet the first task by appropriating $15,000 to improve the approach channels of the "grand internal line of water communication" and authorizing an additional $10,000 after the initial sum was expended.[25] Since the Corps of Engineers did not have an officer available to supervise the improvements, a civilian, Marshall Parks, was appointed to do the job as the agent of the federal government required by Congress. In addition to Parks, the Engineers Corps loaned the company a "mud machine" (dredge), which they ordered constructed especially for the improvement of Joyce's Creek, the southern approach to the canal.

Parks took charge of the work not only as agent for the federal government but as general agent and superintendent of the canal. As such, he reported to the company (and, through them, to the state) as well as to Washington. His reports speak of the interests of Virginia and the United States as virtually identical. At least in his eyes there were no conflicts, which was the reason the job could be done co-operatively. For a while he could not secure laborers for the project. In order to continue the work, he arranged to have laborers who were employed by the federal government in Norfolk, but who were temporarily unoccupied, loaned to him for work on the canal.[26]

In the course of the work, it was found that Deep Creek—the northern approach—could not be dredged because its banks were sandy and would only cave in again.[27] In order to remedy this situation, a larger canal with lock and dam was proposed to divert the channel into more stable banks. A measure to this effect was approved by the Virginia General Assembly for the Deep Creek approaches. On the basis of this legislative author-

[24] BPW, *Fifteenth Annual Report* (1831), p. 223. His comments on the proper relationship between government and private enterprise have a contemporary ring, as do his violations of those ostensible principles in practice.

[25] Dismal Swamp Canal Company, *Annual Report, 1837*.

[26] *Ibid.*

[27] Dismal Swamp Canal Company, *Annual Report, 1839*.

ization, an agreement was concluded between the company and the federal government whereby the former would pay for the necessary excavations and the latter would underwrite the cost of the new lock itself.[28] Responsibility for construction was vested in Parks, who had a wharf built and the lock practically excavated before the year was out. As a result of this progress, an unsuccessful attempt was made to secure an additional appropriation from Congress to aid in financing the work.[29]

Despite the lack of additional federal aid, the company pressed on with construction of the new channel under the direction of Parks, while continuing to petition Congress to live up to the terms of the agreement. The lock was completed by 1843 at a cost of $25,000. In 1845 the president and directors, by traveling to Washington to meet with Congressional leaders in person, were able to secure $5,000 as a partial reimbursement.[30]

The initial agreement had been made by the United States Topographical Engineers (a bureau of the Corps of Engineers) on the grounds that the new channel would greatly benefit the navy yard at Norfolk and the shipment of government supplies in general. This agreement was repudiated, at least in part, by Congress, which was much more reluctant to appropriate money for such projects than the professionals responsible to the national legislature were about pledging federal funds.[31] Yet despite the reluctance of Congress to appropriate money, the flow of materials from the federal government to aid in the improvement did not lessen. For example, timbers were provided from the naval stores for the lock and dam.[32]

The new Deep Creek channel was the last major improvement made in the canal prior to the modern era. Maintenance was continued by the co-operatively owned company until the outbreak of the Civil War, when the canal was seized by the Union army as part of the strategic hinterland of Norfolk. It was used by the Union army to transport supplies southward and in the process deteriorated from lack of proper maintenance. At the close of the war, of the 1,944 shares outstanding, the fed-

[28] Brown, *op. cit.*, p. 32.

[29] Dismal Swamp Canal Company, *Annual Report, 1839*.

[30] Brown, *op. cit.*, p. 32.

[31] Letter from C. W. Newton, Virginia proxy on the board of directors of the canal, to the Board of Public Works, November 28, 1839 (in the BPW files).

[32] Dismal Swamp Canal Company, *Annual Report, 1843*.

eral government still owned 800 and Virginia, 760. The state, impoverished and unable to shoulder any of the burdens of internal improvements, sold its shares to private parties in 1867. The United States continued to be a stockholder until 1871 when the canal was sold to pay debts resulting from a state-authorized bond issue. The last co-operative activity was the mapping of the canal by D. S. Walton in 1867. The canal underwent a continuing decline as a private enterprise. Congress was prevailed upon to grant its management $5,000 for repairs in 1894. Finally, in 1929, the United States purchased the canal outright and rejuvenated it as part of the intracoastal waterway system.

As a result of the destruction wrought by the Civil War, the rupture of relationships between state and federal government, Virginia's impoverishment, and the general trend toward complete laissez faire evident in the Gilded Age, this co-operative program was finally abandoned. Yet it had a record of some forty years of successful existence and left as its legacy a canal that is still in use today. Of the many internal improvements initiated in the early period of American history, few have such an enviable record, and those few, like the Dismal Swamp Canal, were generally co-operative endeavors.

CANAL ADMINISTRATION

In examining the course of these forty years of co-operation, a major question arises: How did the governments involved exercise control over the project? The shares owned by the Commonwealth of Virginia were in the hands of the state Board of Public Works, which appointed a representative to the company's board to serve at the state's pleasure. The federal government vested its proxy rights in the hands of the secretary of the treasury, who routinely delegated them to the collector of the port of Norfolk.

Both the company and the collector filed reports with the secretary of the treasury. The company filed copies of its annual report with the Board of Public Works in Virginia and the Treasury Department in Washington. The collector did not file his reports as regularly, though it seems that he was required by law to do so.[33]

Most of the letters on hand relating to the activities of the proxies are

[33] U.S. Treasury Department Records, *Canals, 1833–1849* (National Archives, Washington, D.C.).

those stemming from the occasional disagreements within the company as to the management of the canal. For example, in 1839 John N. Tazewell, representative of the state, wished to change the management of the company and wrote his superiors to that effect, asking them for their approval to initiate action to remove the current management. In his letter he indicates that the United States representative would be willing to support him:

These two interests—Virginia and the United States—combined give 328 votes out of 607. . . . Now such combination is not merely not improbable but the most certain event of which I am aware in this connection for as it would be difficult to conceive a case in which the interests of the two would be in opposition it is but fair to conclude that this identity of interest would produce concert in action between the proxies of these great stockholders and I am the more persuaded of the justice of this conclusion since in the many conversations which I have had with the proxy of the U.S. I have not known him to indicate any line of conduct by which the state would not be as much benefitted as his own immediate principal. In this view of the case then Mr. Whipple [the U.S. proxy] and myself are forced to regard our opinions as well nigh the regulations of the Co[mpany]. . . .[34]

Evidently the board did not approve of Tazewell's reforming spirit since he resigned his post on October 11 of the same year.[35]

Business had to continue and the dispute had to be settled, so the state immediately appointed another proxy, C. W. Newton. After the annual meeting of 1839, he reported to the board:

With the proxy of the United States I have recently had full and free communication. I find that his views in relation to the topics here submitted to your consideration [canal improvements, water flow, and the like] concur with those generally entertained by the stockholders and others—that convinced by personal observation of the existence of abuses, he is disposed to give his zealous cooperation to such measures as may be necessary to protect the company's interests from injury. . . . [36]

Though the incipient revolt seems to have dissipated itself, the co-operation between the two proxies continued as before. Newton continued as

[34] John N. Tazewell to the Board of Public Works, September 20, 1839, BPW files, box 1. It is also interesting to note the reference Tazewell makes to the continuing and prominent contacts that existed between him and the United States proxy for the purposes of determining their stand on company policy.

[35] Letter to BPW, October 11, 1839, BPW files, box 1.

[36] Letter to BPW, November 28, 1839, BPW files, box 1.

the state proxy for over ten years. In 1849 he was involved in a more serious fight over company policy. In that year, an opposition group arose within the company to challenge the existing board of directors. Up to that time whenever such opposition had arisen, both the state and the federal governments had joined with the major group of private stock-holders in support of the management. However, as a result of the change of administrations in Washington and the accession of the Whigs to the national presidency, the incumbent United States proxy holder had been removed from office as collector and the proxy had devolved upon his successor, of the opposite party, a Colonel Garnett. Garnett seemed disposed toward the opposition, which led that group to attempt to convince the Virginia Board of Public Works to change its position in favor of the opposition. Newton, still on the side of the management, endeavored to convince the board to stand pat.[37]

On November 2 Newton wrote to the board again, reporting that some citizens of Norfolk were trying to impute that the change of the holder of the United States proxy was a move by the secretary of the treasury to change federal policy in regard to the company. He said that this was not the case at all, but merely a change in collectors under the patronage system resulting from the change in political control of the national ad-ministration from Democratic to Whig. "The United States have always given its proxy to a federal officer, and for many years . . . to the Collec-tor"; thus he saw nothing more in the change than that. However, he did ask the board to investigate the situation.[38]

There were evidently grounds for Newton's fears, since a controversy had been raging since May, 1848, over the appointment of the collector of customs as United States proxy holder. Some of the businessmen of Norfolk, who represented the private capital in the canal company, wanted the federal government to emulate the state and appoint one of the local businessmen as its proxy, obviously in order to increase local control of the canal. Petitions to that effect were sent to Senator R. W. T. Hunter, of Virginia, by the merchants of the area.[39]

Conway Whittle, the collector who was replaced by Garnett, had at-tempted to defend himself and his position by enlisting the support of the secretary of the treasury, Robert Walker. He wrote to Walker saying

[37] C. W. Newton to BPW, October 19, 1849, BPW files, box 1.

[38] C. W. Newton to BPW, November 2, 1849, BPW files, box 1.

[39] Williams S. Mallory to Senator Hunter, May 21, 1848 (U.S. Treasury Department Records, *Canals: 1833–1849* [National Archives, Washington, D.C.], items 199 and 200).

that the attempt to oust him was part of a maneuver by certain local interests to gain control of the company by gaining control of the large bloc of votes held by the federal government. He suggested that no action be taken in Washington until the president and members of the board of the company wrote to Walker personally.[40] He also forwarded letters from other merchants in Norfolk who supported his position.[41]

The next day the president and directors of the company wrote to Walker on behalf of Whittle and to explain their own position. They informed the Secretary that certain Norfolk merchants were interested in gaining control of the company by placing the United States proxy in the hands of their representatives, since the "800 shares in a great measure controls the management of that company."[42]

By this time the Virginia delegation in Congress was fully involved in the controversy. Walker himself turned to the Virginians in Congress for advice in an already familiar pattern of executive-legislative co-operation, and both senators and representatives responded. Representative Atkinson wrote to the Secretary in support of Whittle and the company management, stating that he had already been approached by one of the directors on the matter.[43] Two weeks later he again wrote to Walker reaffirming his original position despite the memorial from the insurgents that Walker had sent to him.[44]

By the end of June, the rebels had retreated somewhat. In a letter to Senator Hunter, their spokesman, Mallory, conceded that his people did not disapprove of Whittle as collector but felt that a businessman would be better. Though he brought in the feelings of the local Democrats in a slightly veiled attempt to exert political pressure, the merchants' movement was revealed as obviously weak.[45] Hunter forwarded this last memorial to Walker, as requested, but the issue was resolved in favor of Whittle and the company management.[46]

[40] Whittle to Walker, June 2, 1848 (ibid., item 204).

[41] Josiah Wells to Whittle, June 3, 1848 (ibid., items 201 and 202).

[42] President and directors to Walker, June 3, 1848 (ibid., item 207).

[43] Atkinson to Walker, June 9, 1848 (ibid., item 205).

[44] Atkinson to Walker, June 22, 1848 (ibid., item 213). This memorial, incidentally, was the one originally transmitted to Senator Hunter by the insurgents and sent by the Senator to Secretary Walker (Hunter to Walker, June 19 and 22, 1848 [ibid., items 206 and 212]).

[45] Mallory to Hunter, June 26, 1848 (ibid., item 214).

[46] Hunter to Wallace, June 27, 1848 (ibid., item 215).

While the records are somewhat fragmentary, it seems clear that control of the canal was held by the governments involved, both federal and state; that either had a veto over policy by virtue of its own holdings; but that the two collaborated to control the company together since their interests coincided and were accepted as coincident by the principals involved—the way to gain control of the company was by gaining control of the government proxies.

Profits from the canal were allotted to investors, including governmental shareholders, according to the number of shares owned. Each year that dividends were paid out, the federal government and the state were credited with their just portions. These dividends were generally used to supply any funds needed for maintenance that could not be covered by the earnings of the company. Since most routine maintenance was covered by earnings before the distribution of any dividends, this meant that neither the federal government nor the state had to be petitioned for financial aid except in the case of major improvements.

To effect the latter, Congress ultimately provided for the use of any dividends accruing to the United States for canal improvements. The measure, enacted on February 26, 1845, as an outcome of company pressure for reimbursement of their outlay for the improvement of the northern approaches to the canal, clearly provided that

the said Company are hereby authorized to retain the Dividends hereafter to be declared, and now on hand, that is, held by the U.S. Treasury, on eight hundred shares held by the United States in the Stock of the said Canal Company, to be applied to refund the principal and interest on thirty-two thousand seven hundred and twelve dollars and thirty two cents; moneys advanced by the said Company to complete the work originally undertaken, and partly executed by the Agents of the United States; and that the same be paid to the Company, before any of the Dividends accruing in said Stock be paid into the Treasury of the United States.[47]

The process of crediting these dividends to the United States and then having them returned by the secretary of the treasury under the provisions of the act involved another series of administrative relationships between the company's treasurer and the United States Treasury Department concerning transmission of the funds, corrections of errors, and like matters of routine nature. Indeed, it is proper to infer that any program calling for co-operation between groups on one level will ultimately cre-

[47] As quoted in *ibid.*, item 179.

ate a problem of administrative co-operation. Even the most routine matters must be handled by men under some orderly arrangement.

STEPS OF CO-OPERATION

A summary of the Dismal Swamp Canal project reveals three major areas of federal-state co-operation: construction of the canal, maintenance and improvement of its facilities, and control over the administration of its operations. The first two areas involved both fiscal aid and the services of governmental personnel. The third involved co-operation between federal and state officials. While the federal government did not become a full partner in this enterprise until the canal was already under construction, once it entered the partnership its role became a crucial and even dominant one. Yet this did not come about through the lessening of the state's power but through a coincidence of interest between the state and the federal government. In addition to this coincidence of interest, the state as a whole and the locality involved both had the means of influencing federal policy and actions through their senators and representatives.

The institutional procedures involved in the co-operative process and the roles of the people involved in their operation can be summarized in the following manner:

1. Private individuals interested themselves in the project and campaigned for aid from the two states involved.

2. The states granted recognition and limited aid and a company was formed.

3. The canal idea was incorporated into a nationwide blueprint by the federal government through the actions of administrative agencies at the cabinet level and below, thus giving it federal recognition as a valuable project.

4. Informal co-operation between state and federal officials was necessary to advance construction. This included a survey by qualified federal engineers and federal assistance in securing a supervising engineer for the state. The highest administrative levels of both the federal government and the state were involved, including on the national level the President of the United States, cabinet officials (the secretaries of state, treasury, and war), the diplomatic corps, and government bureaus (such as the Army Engineers); and on the state level, the governor of Virginia,

his agents, and the Virginia Board of Public Works. Some of this co-operation came about through direct contacts through the normal administrative channels. Part of it came about through the use of the state's senators and representatives in Washington.

5. After a decade of informal co-operation, a formal co-operative relationship was established with federal purchase of shares in the joint-stock company in charge of constructing and maintaining the canal. Federal participation was secured through the activities of local interest groups working through their representatives in Congress, with the concurrence of the department in the executive branch of the federal government that had the responsibility for implementing the federal aspects of the project. A sharing arrangement was developed to insure joint participation by the federal and state governments, in this case through the joint-stock company. All this was achieved through the enactment of an appropriate statute by Congress.

6. The provisions of the act of Congress were accepted by the Virginia General Assembly by statutory enactment.

7. The federal executive then delegated the power of proxy to a federal official in the locality concerned (the collector of the port of Norfolk) and detailed other federal personnel to aid in the construction of the canal.

8. The state executive, pursuant to earlier acts of the legislature, provided for state administrative personnel to act as proxies and supervisors for the state, which, through its greater direct role in the company (a quasi-official state agent) became primarily responsible for actual construction. Co-operative procedures were then developed by the two sets of officials involved.

9. Construction proceeded under the direction of the company, supervised by the state Board of Public Works and utilizing federal engineers and equipment. The company reported to the state and to the federal government; and the state board also reported to the Treasury and War Departments.

10. Company policy was decided by the board of directors dominated by the United States and the state of of Virginia, whose representatives operated in concert within a community of interest. Attempts to change the policy were directed against both simultaneously by the non-governmental shareholders rather than by one government against the other.

11. The same processes of local pressure, action by the state's Congressional delegation, statutory enactments by Congress and the state legis-

lature, and administrative co-operation were used to maintain and improve the canal once the initial construction had been completed.

The fate of the Dismal Swamp Canal program illustrates the process by which programs of nationwide importance are nationalized when co-operative arrangements fail. After the combination of adverse circumstances begun by the Civil War had destroyed the co-operative program and the attempt to manage an essentially public project by private means failed, Congress was forced to intervene in the national interest. This time, however, the intervention was unilateral and the function became entirely a federal one in its formal aspects. In this case, then, co-operation was a means to forestall centralization rather than a centralizing device.

Thus, by the third decade of nineteenth century, the pattern of intergovernmental co-operation was already clear in projects such as this one. Changes were indeed made in subsequent years, but they were changes designed to improve the mechanism rather than to modify the basic relationships. While federal control over standards tended to grow, state control over processes grew as a counterbalance. All this was achieved through trial and error by men such as John Cowper, president of the Dismal Swamp Canal Company during this period, who could say in a request for federal aid, "Our friend . . . is strong in the Virginia Doctrine of state rights, not being clear in the right of the Federal Government to grant aids for such objects; I am of that school, but do not go so far."[48]

[48] Cowper to Levi Woodbury, U.S. Secretary of the Treasury, January, 1836 (*ibid.*, item 19). The "friend" is not identified.

4

Internal Improvements on the Eastern Seaboard

ORIGINS

The conclusion of the War of 1812 focused national attention on west-ward expansion, on the conquest of the land frontier, and on the necessity of internal communications—commerce in its broadest sense—to facilitate that conquest. In Virginia the magnitude of the task was first recognized by the Joint Committee of Roads and Internal Navigation of the Virginia General Assembly, which stated, in its 1814 report on the state's internal improvements, that even prior to the war the ordinary revenues of the state were unable to furnish sufficient funds for internal improvements. That body suggested that the money to be paid to Virginia by the federal government in reimbursement for military expenditures be devoted to the task; but the General Assembly allotted those funds to the Literary Fund for the support of public education in the state (see chap. vii), and the internal improvement interests were forced to look elsewhere for support.[1]

The state Board of Public Works, created as a result of the committee's report to manage the Fund for Internal Improvement[2] and serve as the

[1] Virginia General Assembly, *A Collection of All Laws and Resolutions of the General Assembly of Virginia Relative to the Board of Public Works, etc.* (Richmond: 1819), p. 52.

[2] One of the major investments made by the board was the purchase of 710 shares in the second Bank of the United States, which was created at approximately the same time. These shares were loaned to various internal improvement companies in Virginia that the board controlled, wholly or in part, giving those companies the income from the shares for their work. This tended to tie the interests of the board, and consequently

directing agency for the various internal improvement projects of the day, well understood its problems—both the scope of the improvements needed and the lack of the necessary money. In its first annual report, the board outlined its prospective program, which included

the contemplated connection . . . between the eastern and western waters, by extending the navigation of James River to Dunlap's Creek, and constructing an ordinary Turnpike from thence to the falls of the Kanawha, or an iron rail way across the Allegheny . . . to the same point . . . [and] the extension of the United States Road from Wheeling to Winchester; by which, with the aid of the companies already incorporated in Virginia, a permanent highway would be completed from the seat of the Federal Government to the River Ohio.

In line with this program,

"The Board of Public Works" beg leave, therefore, to recommend it to the General Assembly, to invite the cooperation of the Governments of the United States, and of the States of Kentucky and Ohio, in the accomplishment of those objects.[3]

This very first public statement of the board set the stage and the tone for the work of the next thirty years. It is evident that the men involved in the work were thinking in national terms as well as in terms of Virginia, and considered the needs of both to be complementary and their joint consideration to be natural. Virginia's system of internal communications would be part of a national network, tied in with the Cumberland Road (which they called by its formal name, the United States Road), which was already considered to be the backbone of a national road network that was to connect all settled parts of the nation. In this light, their interest in receiving federal aid and in otherwise co-operating with the federal government is understandable in terms other than the mere search for a handout.

It has been seen how this desire for co-operation was immediately put into effect in the board's search for a chief engineer. However, formal collaboration remained at a minimum for about eight years after the board's creation. This was at least partly the result of the failure of the states and localities to convince President Monroe, as they had Congress, of the constitutionality of direct federal aid for internal improvements. In

---

of the state, more closely to those of the nation by providing another set of overlapping interests that tended to break down the walls of separation.

[3] Virginia Board of Public Works [hereinafter referred to as BPW], *First Annual Report* (Richmond, 1816), pp. 6 ff.

large part (and perhaps most important) it was also due to the almost total occupation of the United States Topographical Engineers with the improvement of the nation's coastal defenses in the years between 1816 and 1824 to prevent a repetition of the disastrous experiences of the War of 1812. This project, which cost $8,500,000 between 1816 and 1829, brought the Topographical Engineers, who had been given responsibility for the civil engineering functions of the United States Army Corps of Engineers, to the attention of the public, particularly since the greater part of their work was done in the most populated areas of the nation to prepare defenses for the great port cities of the east and gulf coasts.[4] It also caused the creation of the Board of Engineers for Coast Defense, which, in turn, provided the model for the Board of Engineers for Internal Improvements established by act of Congress in 1824.

The public, interested as it was in national internal improvement, was not slow to grasp the possibilities inherent in this new corps that had been brought to their attention through the work on coast defenses. Calhoun's plan, submitted in 1819, called for nationwide internal improvements as a military necessity. In his report, he laid down a series of criteria for judging when and how federal aid and co-operation would be desirable and necessary. These criteria can be abstracted in the following manner:

1. Federal aid should be extended in programs "immediately beneficial to more than half of the states of the Union, and, which without the aid of the Federal Government, would require their cooperation."

2. Federal action is desirable when it is in the interest of national defense and the movement of a civilian army reserve to needed points. He elaborated on this point by stating that:

Many of the roads and canals which have been suggested, are no doubt of the first importance to the commerce, the manufactures, the agriculture, and political prosperity of the country, but are not, for that reason, less useful or necessary for military purposes. It is, in fact, one of the great advantages of our country, that, whether we regard its internal improvements in relation to military, civil, or political purposes, very nearly the same system, in all its parts, is required.

3. In regard to the form of federal aid to be given: "For the construction of the roads and canals which Congress may choose to direct, the

[4] Leonard D. White, *The Jeffersonians* (New York: Macmillan Co., 1951), pp. 260–61.

army, to a certain extent, may be brought in aid of the moneyed resources of the country."

4. For programs initiated by Congress (i.e., the federal government): "The disbursement of the sums appropriated for the purpose might be made by the Department of War, under the direction of the President."

5. "Where incorporated companies are already formed, or the road or canal already commenced under the superintendence of a state, it perhaps would be advisable to direct a subscription on the part of the United States, on such terms and conditions as might be thought proper."

6. "Where the army cannot . . . execute it, the work ought to be done by contract, under the superintendence and inspection of officers of the engineer corps, to be detailed for that purpose."[5]

7. In projecting the surveys for internal improvements:

The whole Union must be considered as one, and the attention directed, not to those roads and canals which may facilitate intercourse between parts of the same state, but to those which may bind all of the parts together, and the whole with centre; thereby facilitating commerce and intercourse among the states, and enabling the government to disseminate promptly, through the mail, information to every part, and to extend protection to the whole.

Here Calhoun adds the following analysis:

By extending these principles, the line of communication by roads and canals, through the states, the Federal Government, instead of interfering with the State Governments within their proper spheres of action, will afford the only means of perfecting improvements of a similar description which properly belong to them.[6]

Although the strict constructionists prevented direct cash appropriations from being made by Congress for most projects, various other steps could be taken. In 1824 the General Survey Act was passed authorizing comprehensive surveys to be undertaken of routes for roads and canals deemed by the President to be in the national interest. In essence, this

[5] John C. Calhoun, "Report on Roads and Canals, Communicated to the House of Representatives, January 14, 1819," *The Works of John C. Calhoun* (New York: D. Appleton and Co., 1888), V, 45, 51, 53.

[6] "Report on the Condition of the Military Establishment and Fortifications, Communicated to Congress by the President, December 7, 1824," *ibid.*, p. 141. To this writer, the entire set of criteria, with slight modifications to take into consideration the growth of the federal service to a point where all the talents needed for co-operative projects are no longer located in the U.S. Army, is as applicable today as it was then, and provides a basis for implementing a co-operative approach in the field of internal improvement.

provided a basis for the establishment of a national system of internal communications, even though it was to come about through federal assistance and suggestion rather than direct federal action.

The survey act provided a basis for one other development of great importance. Most proposals for federal action in the field of internal improvements were based on the separatist premise operating in reverse; that is, they provided that the federal government would not only contribute initial funds and personnel, but would actually construct, maintain, and administer roads and canals. These were the measures that failed of passage. The survey act, on the other hand, of necessity was directed toward co-operative activity. Federal engineers would survey roads or canals which would be the responsibility of the states to construct. This created the first major comprehensive co-operative program to be enacted by Congress in the internal improvement field. Although it was supported for only a relatively short duration, it served to accomplish its original end. When it was abandoned by Congress, it was as much because a national system had already been surveyed and projects were becoming increasingly local in nature as it was because of opposition from the strict constructionists.[7]

CANALS

Virginia responded to the survey act with great interest. Claudius Crozet, principal engineer of the state Board of Public Works, commented on federal policy toward internal improvements in his report for 1826, explaining the activities of the United States Board of Engineers in the two years since 1824 by quoting extensively from Calhoun's report, which has been summarized above. Indeed, he quoted several of the same passages, indicating that, among the professionals at least, Calhoun's approach had become a statement of policy. Crozet then commented on the effect of the national board on Virginia's internal improvement projects. He indicated that according to the report of the national board, the first and most important work would be the extension of a canal from Washington, D.C., to the Ohio River and thence to Lake Erie. This canal would have to cross Virginia at some point and would follow the state's borders for a considerable distance. After that route was surveyed, there

[7] Thomas Hart Benton, *Thirty Years' View* (New York: D. Appleton and Co., 1854–56), I, 26.

were three proposed canals of secondary priority that would receive the attention of the Corps of Engineers. One of these would be the James and Kanawha Canal, designed to connect Richmond and Norfolk with the Ohio River. In discussing the latter project, Crozet echoed the previously stated views of the Virginia Board of Public Works that the spirit behind the construction of that canal was a national one, a desire to connect East and West.[8]

The same year, the Army Engineers were engaged in the survey of the embryonic James and Kanawha Canal. Upon completion of their survey, they filed a report with the secretary of war, who, in turn, forwarded a copy to Virginia's principal engineer. The state official, in his report to the Board of Public Works for 1827, reported with satisfaction that the federal engineers had confirmed his choice of alternate routes as the better one. To document the federal report, he included a copy of a letter containing the topographical information that had been written by Captain William McNeill of the United States Topographical Engineers, who had directed the survey, to Major General Alexander Macomb, chief of the United States Board of Engineers for Internal Improvements.[9]

The James and Kanawha Canal, unlike the Dismal Swamp and Chesapeake and Ohio canals, could obtain the services of federal engineers but no federal monetary aid since the project was entirely within the boundaries of the state of Virginia. Without much formal promulgation, other than Calhoun's remarks, a distinction between interstate and intrastate projects had been established, with the latter category divided into two classifications, whereby intrastate projects that were tied in with the national interest or some major national improvement could receive federal services-in-aid but no federal funds. This principle generally held true whenever direct contributions of federal funds or services were involved. In cases involving land grants, this distinction tended to disappear, so that in the public-land states federal financing became available even for intrastate projects with tenuous national connections. The important thing to note is that attempts were being made to establish criteria by which to justify projects. While these were often simply attempts at justification of projects that had been approved for political or other reasons, they did indicate the development of a concern for the maintenance of the *institutions* of dualism, which was a necessary condi-

[8] BPW, *Tenth Annual Report* (1826), pp. 444 ff.

[9] BPW, *Eleventh Annual Report* (1827), p. 106.

tion for successful co-operation between the different levels of government. Consultations between the state engineers working on the James and Kanawha Canal and their colleagues from the Army Engineers continued on an informal basis for a number of years, based on McNeill's initial report, which was referred to and quoted quite often during the course of construction.

The state hoped to make the canal a vehicle for national traffic. With such a goal in mind, it had to conform to the standards established by the federal engineers, particularly to those set for the Ohio River, which was to be its western terminus. The Army Engineers were given the task of improving the Ohio River for navigation as part of the federal constitutional responsibility for navigable rivers. In this capacity, they prepared a report for the War Department based on their survey of the river in 1836–37, in which they set standards of maximum tonnage and average water depth for the Ohio, based on those set in earlier federal canal and river improvement surveys. The principal engineer of Virginia was pleased to point out in his annual report for 1839 that the maximum tonnage prescribed by the charter of the state canal and the water depth he proposed were in accordance with federal standards. He also gave a résumé of Army Engineers' reports to indicate how the two systems could be linked.[10]

The Chesapeake and Ohio Canal was another matter entirely. Rated first on the list of vital national improvements, it was also an interstate canal, involving Virginia, Maryland, Pennsylvania, and the District of Columbia. As a result of this powerful combination of interests, the project became one of the foremost co-operative endeavors of the nineteenth century. Since the history of this canal is relatively well documented, this study will deal briefly with its co-operative nature only.[11]

The canal was constructed by a joint-stock company whose shares were originally owned, and actively voted, by Virginia, Maryland, and Pennsylvania, a number of cities and towns along the right-of-way, private individuals, and the federal government.[12] The company was established

[10] BPW, *Twenty-third Annual Report* (1839), p. 251.

[11] The most thorough work on the Chesapeake and Ohio Canal, from the historical viewpoint, is Walter S. Sanderlin's *The Great National Project* (Baltimore: Johns Hopkins Press, 1946). While this study does not examine the co-operative nature of the project from a political-administrative point of view, it does describe the construction of the canal and places it in proper perspective among the internal improvements of the day.

[12] As late as 1889, when the canal was sold to private parties, the federal government held $2,490,000 in capital stock out of a total of $3,857,600 outstanding. The remainder

through the acts of the United States Congress and the legislatures of Virginia, Maryland, and Pennsylvania, which defined the organization of the company, its method of government, and the respective roles of the federal and state governments in the making and implementing of company policy.[13]

United States Topographical Engineers surveyed the route of the canal and drew up the plans and specifications for its construction, which were rigorously followed in the work as it progressed. Some of these same engineers were detailed by the secretary of war to supervise the actual construction for several years. Officers of the company were bound, by a vote of the shareholders (which was dominated by the several government blocs), to refrain from "active political interference," a precursor of the Hatch Acts of a much later date. The company was required to report annually to each state and the federal government, the latter having the right to inspect the work in progress. Whenever a section of the canal was completed, the company treasurer would report that fact to the secretary of the treasury to allow for federal inspection. The treasury secretary was responsible for handling federal interests in the Chesapeake and Ohio Canal project, as he was in the Dismal Swamp Canal.

In addition to the states mentioned and the federal government, the cities of Alexandria, Georgetown, and Washington purchased stock in the company—2,500, 2,500, and 10,000 shares, respectively, out of a total of 60,000 shares for sale at $100 each. This is an early example of local participation in such projects. Of course, these cities were represented at the stockholders' meetings, and at one time the mayor of Washington was even appointed by the federal government to serve as its proxy on the board.[14]

---

was owned by Maryland, Virginia, the city of Shepherdstown (Virginia), the Baltimore and Ohio Railroad, and private individuals, though only Maryland remained an active participant in the governing of the company. See *ibid.*

[13] *Acts of the States of Virginia, Maryland, and Pennsylvania, and of the Congress of the United States in Relation to the Chesapeake and Ohio Canal Company, etc.* (Washington, D.C.: 1828).

[14] Documentary records, from which the above items were selected, include: U.S. Treasury Department Records, *Canals: 1833–1849;* the annual reports of the Virginia Board of Public Works; the journal of the Virginia House of Delegates; and U.S. Army Corps of Engineers, *Bulky File,* case 1, drawer 3, boxes 1–13.

ROADS

Construction and maintenance of roads also became a matter of federal and state interest in Virginia in this period. The federal government had entered the field of highway construction in 1802 through what Leonard D. White termed "the inventive genius of Albert Gallatin," who discovered a way to permit Congress to appropriate money for the construction of the Cumberland Road, a national road designed to connect the east coast with the Ohio River.[15] Gallatin's device is an interesting illustration of the growing impact of the new states, or the frontier, on American federalism. Whereas the means, and often the spirit, for developing co-operative programs in the original states were generally harder to come by, the new states had both the means, the public lands, and a strong desire for co-operative programs. They, in turn, greatly influenced their senior sisters. What Gallatin did was to have Congress include in the compact providing for Ohio's admission to the Union a clause setting aside 5 per cent of the net proceeds of the sale of public lands in the new state for "the laying out and making [of] public roads, leading from the navigable waters emptying into the Atlantic, to the Ohio, to the said state, and through the same."[16] Construction of the road through other states could be undertaken with the approval of their respective state legislatures. After a reduction of the amount to 2 per cent, the first appropriation was made in 1806. Subsequently, appropriations were made in advance of the revenues received and credited to the fund. This legal fiction enabled the federal government to extend the road well into Illinois and survey the route across the Mississippi River into Missouri.

The Cumberland, or National, Road was not designed to be a co-operative endeavor, except in so far as approval for its construction had to be obtained from each of the states it was to cross. It soon became clear, however, that this was not the way to run a road. The project is often pointed to as a symbol of the non-existence of intergovernmental co-operation in the nineteenth century owing to the strength of the states'-rights position. It would be better to view it as a step toward the evolution of later formal co-operative programs, such as the land-grant roads to be discussed in later chapters, and as the catalyst for semiformal and

[15] White, *op. cit.*, p. 484.

[16] 2 Stat. 173, § 7 (3), April 30, 1802.

informal co-operation in the creation of a national road network based, in great part, on local needs.[17]

The first impact of the Cumberland Road on the government of Virginia came through the possibilities it offered as a backbone for a co-ordinated national road network. The state Board of Public Works decided that by using it as a focal point, the prospective state road network could be connected to the embryonic national system. Actually this was one of Gallatin's intentions in having the road constructed, and the state rose to implement it in the same manner that it had accepted his views on the three great Virginia canals.

Even the Virginia General Assembly, jealous guardian of state sovereignty that it was, agreed with this plan. Exemplifying this agreement was its resolution of January 11, 1823, instructing the board to direct the principal engineer to mark and lay out a road from the Ohio River via Morgantown (in what is now West Virginia) to intersect with the National Road at, or near, the Yohoghany bridge.[18] The annual reports of the board indicate that such resolutions were the rule during the heyday of Virginia's internal improvement movement. In fact, those roads not designed to link up with the National Road were frequently designed to connect the interior of the state with the Chesapeake and Ohio Canal.

Meanwhile, the road itself had been slowly pushed westward through the state.[19] By 1818 the road had reached the Ohio River at Wheeling, Virginia (now West Virginia), at a cost of close to $1,500,000 for its construction. As the only significant road to the region beyond the Appalachians, the National Road was so heavily used that the need for maintenance developed almost immediately. This led to the question of who was to maintain it, the federal government or the states. Reluctantly Congress assumed the burden in a haphazard manner after the states'

[17] As in the case of the Chesapeake and Ohio Canal, this study will not include a detailed history of the National Road but will be confined to indicating its meaning in the scheme of intergovernmental relations from the vantage point of Virginia's relations to the project. For a brief account of the political-administrative history of the road from the national viewpoint, see Leonard D. White, *The Jeffersonians*, pp. 484–87. For a more detailed account, see Jeremiah S. Young, *Political and Constitutional Study of the Cumberland Road* (Chicago: University of Chicago Press, 1902).

[18] BPW, *Eighth Annual Report* (1824).

[19] White, *op. cit.*, p. 485. An early precedent had been set for state influence over even those projects ostensibly entirely federal when the state of Pennsylvania attempted to dictate the route of that section of the road which passed through its borders. While Jefferson was displeased with this attempt, he yielded to Gallatin's political astuteness and compromised rather than risk losing the state at the next election.

inactivity had indicated that they would not assume the responsibility by default. Here, then, was an early example of a "federal" program that remained federal, not because of any desire of the federal government to usurp the powers of the states, but by decision of the state governments themselves.

The problem was finally adjusted in the 1830's, when Congress ceded the road to the states through which it passed. This means of eliminating the problem of maintenance is often interpreted as a rejection of the principle of federal participation in internal improvement, a product of the states'-rights temper of the time. It is more accurate to view the cession as a victory for the principle of sharing. The co-operative approach was established as the precedent to be followed. Rather than allocate internal improvements to one level of government exclusively, it was decided that, even when the federal government would construct a road, it would be transferred to the states it crossed for maintenance. The National Road was the first and only all-federal road to be constructed through already existing states. Following this precedent, later roads constructed by the federal government in the territories and newly admitted states were turned over to the states for maintenance upon completion. The role of the federal government in the construction of roads, canals, and railroads did not end when this road was turned over to the states. On the contrary, it was just beginning to expand, only in the form of a partnership in a co-operative venture rather than as an exclusive agent.

The Virginia Board of Public Works accepted responsibility for the state's section of the Cumberland Road in 1835 after some protracted negotiations between it and its federal counterpart over the terms of the transfer.[20] In April of that year, once an informal agreement had been reached and it was known that the state would accept responsibility for the road, the federal government formally ceded it.[21] The road retained

[20] The Virginia General Assembly had authorized the state government as early as 1832 to take control of the section of the road in Virginia whenever the federal government would relinquish it. The act of Congress in 1833, however, which assented to the act of the General Assembly, stipulated that it should retain the power to resume control of the road at its discretion. The Board of Public Works felt that this stipulation was not covered in the Virginia enabling legislation and refused to accept the responsibility until the matter had been clarified in the General Assembly and in Congress. This is what delayed the transfer. See BPW, *Annual Reports*, for 1832, 1834, 1835, and 1836.

[21] BPW, *Twentieth Annual Report* (1836).

its designation as the National Road and was so considered by all concerned with it, but after 1835 it was locally maintained. When the highway construction boom of the early twentieth century brought a revival
of the federal-state highway program, the old National Road was extended to the Pacific coast and given the designation U.S. 40.[22]

The influence of the surveys undertaken by the Topographical Engineers extended beyond the reaches of specific projects. For example, in
1834 the principal engineer of Virginia, James Herron, reported to the
General Assembly as directed on a proposed railroad and turnpike to
connect the James and Kanawha Canal and the Virginia-Tennessee
border. In his report, he made use of the Topographical Engineers' report
on the canal itself, as a technical document and as a model for his
endeavor.[23]

Again, on a survey for a proposed Shenandoah Canal, Herron referred
to the work of the United States Board of Engineers for Internal Improvement and discussed the method used by the board to estimate the
necessary dimensions of the Chesapeake and Ohio Canal. He then applied the same method to his estimates for the Shenandoah Canal.[24] It
is evident that the federal service not only provided the great majority
of trained engineers in the country, but it also developed and set the
standards for construction of roads, canals, and, somewhat later, railroads,
which were accepted and utilized by professionals no matter which government, or private corporation, they served.

One of the customs of the period that promoted intergovernmental
co-operation was the federal government's practice of "lending" its engineers to individual states for their internal improvement projects. This
practice grew in the 1830's as it became evident that the Jacksonians

[22] It seems that after the road was ceded to the state, the federal government became
involved in its maintenance by loaning its personnel to the state from time to time to
serve in some capacity in connection with the road as well as to provide advice. For
example, there is a letter on file from Joseph Brown, second auditor of Virginia, to
Colonel Gratiot, chief engineer of the U.S. Army Corps of Engineers, notifying him that
his letter to the Board of Public Works relative to the compensation of Mr. McClure,
as superintendent of part of the Cumberland Road, had been placed before the board.
He reported that the board had adopted a resolution that he hoped would supply the
voucher requested by Mr. Hagner (third auditor of the U.S. Treasury Department, in
charge of federal-state fiscal matters in this and other cases), which he enclosed with
an account for $1,463.86 rendered by McClure. BPW, *Letter Book "B"* (April 5, 1837,
to May 15, 1840), p. 25.

[23] BPW, *Eighteenth Annual Report* (1834), pp. 236 ff.

[24] BPW, *Nineteenth Annual Report* (1835), p. 345.

were abandoning the established forms of co-operation and a need arose to develop new ones. This lending arrangement was furthered by the common spirit that embraced those professionally engaged in internal improvement at every level of government. Their interest was in getting the work done as efficiently as possible on any level of government, an outlook which has traditionally provided the atmosphere most conducive to the growth of co-operation.

Thus, in 1836, Charles B. Shaw, Virginia's principal engineer, went to Washington to arrange for officers of the Topographical Engineers (which had been separated from the Corps of Engineers in 1831) to be detailed to Virginia for survey work. As in all such arrangements, the state would pay the engineers' salaries during the time of their detached service. (This was the "matching" provision of this services-in-aid program.) Shaw's first trip proved to be unsuccessful since no engineers were then available, but, on his second trip, in mid-June, 1836, he was able to obtain the services of federal personnel to augment his own staff sufficiently to form five field parties—two for railroad surveys, two to locate the routes of turnpikes, and one to examine rivers. Since his own staff included only two qualified men, he was obviously quite dependent on this federal assistance.[25]

The lending program ran into difficulties two years later when the states' demand for the services of the United States engineers became so great that federal programs, primarily river and harbor improvements, were threatened. Then, as now, river and harbor improvements held a high place in the affections of Congress, which promptly passed a bill recalling all engineers who had been placed on detached service and who wished to remain in the employ of the federal government. In 1851, after the policy embodied in that measure had been modified and United States engineers were again being detailed to help with non-federal improvements, Colonel J. J. Abert, commanding the Topographical Engineers, gave the following explanation of the law and the policy it embodied:

The object of the law was to prohibit details of officers for such duties, which would give the companies a right to object when the officers were withdrawn; and to appease an ill founded apprehension on the part of the Civil Engineers of the Country, that their employment injured their expectations. These objects can be accomplished by the clear understanding that the Officer can be ordered on such duties only temporarily, and at the pleasure of the War De-

[25] BPW, *Twenty-first Annual Report* (1837), p. 387.

partment, so as to obstruct or embarrass no public duty, and secondly, their orders could be limited to cases of application from the executive of a state.[26]

The original enactment and its subsequent modification indicate the magnitude of the number of state and local requests for federal aid in the mid-nineteenth century. Even when such requests had little chance of being satisfied, people looked to the federal government and petitioned Washington for aid.

NEW HAMPSHIRE AND THE INTERNAL IMPROVEMENT BOOM

Though not on the main routes westward, New Hampshire was not totally bypassed by the internal improvement boom of the period after 1812. This very fact testifies to the pervasiveness of the boom as well as to the power of local interests in Congress, a power that required the distribution of the national bounty to all parts of the nation. Upon the passage of the federal General Survey Act of 1824, the War Department created a special survey district to embrace Maine, New Hampshire, and Vermont, and assigned a group of United States Topographical Engineers to undertake the surveys prescribed for that district. In all, routes for ten proposed canals were surveyed. Most of them progressed no further than the original surveys because of their impracticality, on one hand, and the rise of the much more practical railroads, on the other. In 1829, J. J. Abert, of the Topographical Bureau, who was later to become the federal representative on the board of the Chesapeake and Ohio Canal,

[26] U.S. Topographical Engineer Corps, *Letterbook Number 5*, p. 57, Abert to Secretary of War, April 11, 1851. This letter was written in response to a request from Governor Brown, of Florida, for some topographical engineers to be detailed to work on the railroads of his state. Abert had to reply that none were available since all were engaged in work on federal projects and undoubtedly would be for some time to come. In his report to the Secretary, however, he suggests that "under these views [see quotation in text], Lieut. Col. Long could be directed to correspond with Governor Brown, and to give his attention to any general directions or instructions in reference to the location of this road, with the understanding that the Department cannot furnish Officers or instruments for the purposes of locating the road." The reorganization of the War Department in 1831 abolished the Board of Engineers for Internal Improvement and in its place substituted an independent Topographical Engineers Corps, the commander of which reported directly to the secretary of war. This new corps became in effect a bureau of internal improvement. For an excellent study of its role in internal improvements before the Civil War, see Forest G. Hill, *Roads, Rails, and Waterways* (Norman, Okla.: University of Oklahoma Press, 1957).

was directed to proceed to northern New England to undertake surveys in that area. Of his work in New Hampshire, he reported:

In the surveys and examinations made in New Hampshire, I was aided and accompanied by Colonel P. Carrigan, as commissioner on the part of that state. This gentleman is well known as the compiler of a very excellent map of that state, and as active promoter of all the subjects connected with its prosperity and improvement. His intelligence and urbanity of manner made the association highly valuable and agreeable, and his zeal induced him after my duties called me elsewhere to remain with the surveying parties in the field in order to assist them by his knowledge of the country, and to facilitate their accommodation by his universal acquaintance with the inhabitants.[27]

In so far as the division of labor between the state and the federal government was concerned, Abert reported that

he [Carrigan] was authorized on the part of the state, to go into the actual location of the routes, and to aid in making the estimates. But as your orders to me were silent on these subjects, and as I knew from the arrangements of your Department [Abert reported to the secretary of war] to divide the labour of these duties, that the business of making the estimates was reserved for another branch, and as also what was particularly ordered required all my time to accomplish, I was obliged to decline his proposition in relation to these objects.[28]

It is clear that with respect to the survey for internal improvements, the state was prepared to enter into more extensive co-operative arrangements than was the federal government, but the latter made the final decision. Abert remarked that other state representatives in the area had submitted requests along the same lines, but he had refused them also, since his instructions precluded locating the routes and estimating canal costs.

These surveys, conducted by a team of topographical engineers under Abert's direction, were designed to establish a canal system that would connect the Lake Champlain area with the Atlantic Ocean above Cape Cod for commercial purposes. This formally justified the work in terms of the national interest and the Constitution and made each proposed local canal part of a regional, interstate system.[29]

[27] Report of J. J. Abert to Secretary of War, 1829, National Archives, Record Group 77.

[28] *Ibid.*

[29] J. J. Abert, Supplementary Report on the LeMoille Canal, to the Secretary of War, January 27, 1829, National Archives, Record Group 77.

In some cases, the state even contributed to meeting the costs of the surveys. In 1835 (the work of the survey team for northern New England continued for at least six years), Major Graham, of the Topographical Engineers, reported on the survey of the Oliverian Canal, which was designed to connect Connecticut with New Hampshire:

I take occasion here also, to acknowledge the valuable services which were rendered throughout the survey by John McDuffee Esquire, of Bradford, Vermont. To an accurate knowledge of the topography of the whole country explored by us, he united a zeal and intelligence in demonstrating its facilities, which tended very much to the success of our investigations. His survey of Great Squaw Lake, executed under my instructions, upon the ice, in February and March 1831, is very accurate and satisfactory, and reflects credit upon him. His services were rendered chiefly at the expense of the State of New Hampshire, as the funds allotted by the Department for this service did not admit of my commanding them at an adequate compensation from that source.[30]

After the collapse of the canal boom, railroads came to occupy first place as a means of transportation in New Hampshire as elsewhere. The new railroads were constructed by private enterprise, and the government of New Hampshire left the field of major internal improvements.

[30] Report of Major Graham on the Oliverian Survey to the Secretary of War, 1835, National Archives, Record Group 77.

5

The Treasury and the Banks

THE FIRST BANK OF THE UNITED STATES

The first Bank of the United States was chartered in the year following federal assumption of the state Revolutionary War debts. In its twenty-year charter, Congress provided for federal purchase of 5,000 of its 25,000 shares of stock. States could also buy stock in the bank, but were limited to a maximum borrowing power of $50,000. The charter was enacted by Congress on January 20, 1791, after a great struggle. A national bank was opposed as an unconstitutional infringement of states' rights and an unwarranted centralization of power, on one hand, and as a corrupting influence in a pure agrarian society on the other.[1]

In the House of Representatives' affirmative vote of 39 to 20, 33 of the favorable votes came from New England, New York, New Jersey, and Pennsylvania, and 15 of the negative votes came from the South. The entire Virginia delegation opposed the measure.

The bank was established with an authorized capital of $10,000,000, of which $2,000,000 was contributed by the federal government. Located in Philadelphia, its directors did not originally intend to establish branches in other parts of the country, but pressures from stockholders in other cities soon forced them into widespread branch banking. Four branches were opened in the spring of 1792 after some attempts were

[1] Bray Hammond, *Banks and Politics in America* (Princeton, N.J.: Princeton University Press, 1957), pp. 114–43. While the opposition to the bank was couched for the most part in constitutional terms, it was basically an opposition to banking in general as an evil, no matter who controlled it. The use of the constitutional issue to camouflage basic opposition to a program per se has become a standard feature of American politics. This is not to say that there was no constitutional issue, or that it was not a legitimate approach to the problem: it is merely that the issue has more often than not been raised for reasons other than constitutionalism for its own sake.

70

made to absorb the four existing state banks. This latter move was resisted by many of the same people who had supported creation of the
national bank. Just as they recognized the need for some centralized
banking institution, they also feared too much centralization and resisted
any attempts to create a monolithic structure.[2]

Virginia did not get a branch until 1800 when one was established in
Norfolk, despite Jeffersonian attempts to prevent its establishment. Actually the citizens of Richmond had endeavored in vain to secure a
branch for their community. Defections to central banking were developing even among Jeffersonians in high places. Albert Gallatin, Jefferson's secretary of the treasury, had become a strong supporter of the
bank and encouraged its use as an important fiscal instrument of the
nation.

The Norfolk branch was the second bank to be established in the entire
Commonwealth of Virginia, the first being the very minor Bank of
Alexandria, founded in 1793. Not only was the United States Bank (and,
by implication, the federal government) safe from charges of usurping
state powers, but it had to transact almost all of the banking business in
Virginia until 1804 when the state legislature incorporated the Bank of
Virginia as a central bank for the state, modeled along the lines of the
Bank of the United States, much as the latter was modeled along the
lines of the Bank of England. The new Bank of Virginia was so much a
replica of the national bank that its charter was practically copied from
that of the latter. The state subscribed one-fifth of the capital, and the
legislature elected a proportionate share of the bank directors.[3]

THE FISCAL BACKGROUND

During the first decade of the nineteenth century, state government
expenditures remained low. The few expenditures continued to be met
for the most part by income from federal bonds obtained through the
Revolutionary War debt assumption, as well as by earnings from stock
in the United States Bank and from stock in the respective state banks.
Until the War of 1812, taxation remained a supplementary source of

[2] *Ibid.*, pp. 126–27. This also became typical of the pragmatic attitude toward federalism that was already emerging and has persisted.

[3] Davis R. Dewey, "Banking in the South," *The South in the Building of the Nation*
(Richmond, Va.: Southern Historical Publication Society, 1909), V, 462–64.

state revenue. This was particularly true in southern states such as Virginia, which had yet to embark on large-scale internal improvements.

Virginia received federal aid during this period for the greater part of its governmental activities, virtually all of which involved state collaboration with the federal government. The Marine Hospital at Norfolk was a federally financed co-operative project. A large part of Virginia's responsibility for compensating its Revolutionary War veterans was met through a co-operative program involving grants of federal lands in the Northwest Territory (subsequently Ohio) that had been set aside by act of Congress for use in compensating the Virginia line.[4] Additional revenue was raised by sale of the Gosport (now Norfolk) lands to the federal government for a navy yard—the famous Norfolk base that has since become one of the great naval bases of the world. As in the case of the Marine Hospital, this involved selecting the lands through negotiation, determining their value, and transferring title to the United States, all of which was done through commissioners appointed by both governments.[5]

The few internal improvement companies that were active in this period obtained much of their operating revenue from "stock of the United States," which they had acquired for the most part as repayment of the state debt under the assumption act. For example, the Potomac River Company (a quasi-governmental organization similar to the Dismal Swamp Canal Company), which was designed to improve navigation on the Potomac River, reported to the governor of Virginia in 1802 that it had sold at least some of the "six per cent stock of the U.S." it held and had used the proceeds to build locks around the great falls of the Potomac and otherwise improve navigation.[6]

Militia affairs, a major governmental activity in this period, were also primarily supported by federal aid. State support of the peacetime militia was almost non-existent, but whenever the militia was called upon for active service, such as guarding federal stores during a slave insurrection[7] or turning out to join with the United States Army garrison in Norfolk to protect the naval base after the "Chesapeake" affair,[8] the state was reimbursed for its expenses by the federal government. These

[4] *Calendar of Virginia State Papers,* Vol. IX. The complex administrative relationships between the federal government and the state that grew out of this program will be dealt with at greater length in chapter viii.

[5] *Ibid.*   [6] *Ibid.,* pp. 311–14.

[7] *Ibid.,* Secretary of War Dearborn to Governor, June 13, 1803.

[8] *Ibid.,* pp. 513–615.

reimbursements furnished almost the entire public support for the militia before 1808. In the Chesapeake affair, the records show that securing reimbursement was a full-scale administrative project in itself, since the state had to produce records of all expenditures, have them approved by the secretary of war, and then have them acted upon by Congress. After 1808, the militia was at least partly equipped by the federal government, by Congressional enactment, thus further reducing the financial obligations of the state.

THE IMPACT OF THE BANK'S OPERATIONS

In the field of banking itself, the United States Bank operated as a clearing house and source of capital for the various state banks, as well as serving as fiscal arm of the federal government. As such, it was accepted as an asset by the more conservative banks and as an undesired threat by the more reckless and speculative ones. Hammond describes its operation in these words:

Being the main government depository and having offices in the principal commercial cities, the Bank was the general creditor of the other banks. It had the account of the largest single transactor in the economy—the federal government —and the receipts of the government being mostly in the notes of state banks and these notes being deposited in the Bank, it could not help being their creditor. By pressing them for payment of the notes and checks received against them, the Bank automatically exercised a general restraint on the banking system. . . . This restraint upon bank lending came later to be designated central bank control of credit.[9]

Though the Jeffersonians had opposed the bank at the time of its establishment, the operations of the bank were in fact expanded during its Jeffersonian decade. This reversal was due, in great measure, to the support that Albert Gallatin—that loyal Jeffersonian and sensible statesman—gave to it. Gallatin realized the importance of a national banking system and understood the good work being done in that direction by the bank. As a result, he was able to persuade first Jefferson and then Madison to accept it. Although he never converted Jefferson to the belief that banks were sometimes useful and not by nature pernicious, he did

[9] Hammond, op. cit., pp. 198–99. For a brief but thorough description of the creation and development of this national banking system and the support and opposition it engendered, see chapter viii, pp. 197–226, in Hammond.

influence Madison along the lines of his thought in this matter. As in the case of internal improvements, Gallatin emerges as one of the prime architects of American fiscal federalism.

The character of the political opposition to the bank provides another indicator of its role in the political economy of its day. Some businessmen opposed it out of a desire to engage in greater speculative activity, whereas political conservatives did so on the grounds that such an institution was a threat to the sovereignty of the states and to the American constitutional system. Virginia was in the forefront of this opposition, which culminated in the defeat of the attempt to renew the bank's charter when it expired in 1811.

The defeat of the charter, despite administration support for its renewal, came through a coalition of extreme states'-rights conservatives and spokesmen for eastern businessmen interested in speculation on the frontier, where less control over fiscal matters would aid their highly speculative ventures. Among the former were the most influential members of the Virginia Congressional delegation, including Senator W. B. Giles, who had opposed the original charter grant, and Representatives J. W. Eppes and W. A. Bunnell. The arguments this coalition used against the bank were those of unconstitutionality but the motivations were those of business.

The new agrarians, primarily westerners, wanted to maintain the national bank because the state banks had already proved their inability to meet what were, in essence, national needs.[10] They accused the "great states," among them Virginia, whose legislature had "instructed" the state Congressional delegation to vote against renewal, of an avaricious desire to obtain the federal deposits for their own state banks in order to gain revenue from the use of the national funds via the dividends received by the states from the bank stock they owned.

Without a national bank to balance their relative poverty against the much greater commercial and fiscal power of their older sisters, the frontier states knew they would be at a great disadvantage in their future development and in obtaining what they considered to be their just share of federal deposits, which meant so much to a money-short region. Their opponents were not their neighbors, but the eastern interests who were

[10] Westward expansion was such a need: for example, it was possible for the federal government to direct the national bank to establish a branch in New Orleans at the outset of American settlement of Louisiana, thus providing a broader, more stable financial system that could draw on the credit of the whole nation, rather than requiring the area to wait for a state bank that could come only after sufficient settlement had already taken place.

in the process of making their fortunes in the West. Representative Samuel McKee of Kentucky stated the issue quite clearly: refusal to renew the bank's charter would increase the power of certain states through the deposit of federal revenue in their "entirely foreign banks . . . not for the public service or public good but for the express purpose of putting it into the pockets of the wealthy capitalists of Pennsylvania; the state bank stockholders of Massachusetts, Maryland, and Virginia; . . . providing all the evils of the United States Bank without any of the advantages."[11]

From the perspective of this study in federal-state co-operation, the most interesting aspect of the bank controversy is the fact that the opponents of the bank did indeed want to have the federal revenues deposited in the state banks. In terms of federalism, all they were doing was proposing to substitute one form of co-operation for another; and this is exactly what came about. As long as the federal government refrained from creating its own system of depositories and the state banks were at least quasi-governmental, it was impossible to avoid co-operation, no matter which program was in vogue.

As early as 1802 Jefferson had requested Gallatin to deposit a larger proportion of federal funds in the various state banks, much to Gallatin's displeasure. The Secretary, on the other hand, was interested in strengthening the co-operative nature of the national bank's program and suggested, when the charter was brought up for renewal in 1808, that the federal and state governments participate in its management. After the expiration of the charter, however, Gallatin was forced to implement the other program of co-operation by arranging for deposit of federal funds in the state banks.

On February 25, 1811, Gallatin wrote to the collector at Norfolk instructing him to withdraw the federal funds from the erstwhile United States Bank branch in Norfolk and to deposit them in the Bank of Virginia, commencing March 3, 1811. In his letter he stated that

the only condition that is previously required of that Bank of Virginia is the following: that in making their discounts, other things being equal, they shall consider it as a rule, that paper offered by persons having Custom House bonds to pay, and intended to be applied to such payment, shall have the preference over all other paper offered for discount.[12]

---

[11] M. St. Clair Clarke and D. A. Hall, *Legislative and Documentary History of the Bank of the United States* (Washington, 1832), pp. 209, 297–98.

[12] U.S. Treasury Department, *Letters to Collector, Norfolk, Va., 1803–1833*, February 25, 1811 (in the National Archives).

The elimination of the national bank and the consequent availability of federal deposits to provide capital for local banks to begin operations led to the establishment of one hundred twenty new state banks between 1811 and 1815. In Virginia one other bank was created, the Farmers' Bank of Virginia, chartered by the General Assembly in 1812 under provisions almost identical with those in the charter of the Bank of Virginia, including the same degree of state ownership and control. As was to be expected, the new bank wanted its share of the federal deposits also and, after some delay, succeeded in obtaining one-third of the deposits in the state, the Bank of Virginia retaining the other two-thirds.[13]

THE SECOND BANK OF THE UNITED STATES

In 1812 the country went to war, and the difficulties of national fiscal operation without a national bank that were already becoming apparent were intensified. The federal Treasury found itself unable to negotiate the loans it needed to pay for the war. It had difficulty in transferring the funds in its possession from the point at which they entered the Treasury to the point at which they might be needed. In addition, without central control, many of the state banks engaged in unsound note-issuing practices, which led to "runs" on the banks for specie and, ultimately, to suspension of payments.

In some cases the state legislatures attempted to regulate the situation, but this regulation could help only in the case of local suspension. As suspension became general, only federal action could be of any help, and there was no way for the federal government to act. Once again, this time by suffering the consequences of avoiding action, it became apparent that the United States had a nationwide interlocking economy that had to be dealt with as such, despite the political desires of states'-rights advocates and other elements to view it as fragmentary in nature and capable of complete local control.

The leading opponents of federal action generally opposed control of the banks by any level of government. The distinction between those interested in states' rights and responsibilities as a political principle and those interested in states' rights to prevent governmental intervention on any level had become apparent even earlier. The former group believed

[13] *Ibid.*, Secretary of the Treasury Dallas to Charles K. Mallory, Collector, August 31, 1815.

that governmental action should take place primarily at the state level, but did not necessarily oppose such action by the states. The latter did not want governmental action in any form on any level, but often found it convenient to resist action at the federal level in the name of states' rights rather than in the name of laissez faire. When states did attempt to take action, this latter group even supported the federal government against the "offending" states in order to serve the same ends of non-intervention.

The two groups were allied only part of the time. On other occasions, when men like Gallatin and Calhoun, who believed in the rights of the states, recognized the need for governmental action but wanted a fair sharing of that action by the federal and state governments, the proponents of state action resorted to the use of intergovernmental co-operation. In such cases, they were opposed by the non-interventionists. The resort to co-operative federalism led to the gradual development of a system in which the duty and ability of the states to take action were both stimulated and guaranteed by the federal government. Under this system, co-operative federalism preserved the greater part of the states' powers while developing a climate in which they could be used.

The major example of this realignment within the ranks of states'-rights supporters in the fiscal field was the creation of the second Bank of the United States. The movement began in 1814 and, after some conflict between President Madison and Congress over the role the federal government was to play in the revived institution (in which Madison supported a larger governmental role), a suitable bill was passed and signed by the President on April 10, 1816. The fact that the issue of constitutionality was not raised at all during the protracted discussions on the nature of the institution to be formed was an indication that the states'-rights argument had been used as a subterfuge in the debates of 1811. Madison himself indicated why this was so when he dismissed the question "as being precluded . . . by repeated recognitions, under varied circumstances, of the validity of such an institution, in the acts of the legislative, excutive, and judicial branches of government, accompanied by indications in different modes of a concurrence of the general will of the nation. . . ."[14] In the course of debate on the measure, Rep-

---

[14] Hammond, op. cit., pp. 233–34. This is an excellent statement of the pragmatic approach that has been used in the United States for every "informal" modification of constitutional doctrine. However, Madison himself refused to apply it to the question of internal improvements only a year later, creating a new set of problems that were not substantially resolved for almost a century.

resentative Robert Wright of Maryland, an opponent of the first bank, in 1811, concluded that the court had given tacit approval of its constitutionality "by often recognizing it" in court decisions.[15] This exposition of the role of the court's tacit approval was one that could subsequently be applied to the bulk of the co-operative activities in the nineteenth century.

The most able argument for federal responsibility in monetary matters from the constitutional point of view came from John C. Calhoun, who had assumed Gallatin's role as leading architect of co-operative federalism in his generation. Calhoun's view, which could have been used a century later to justify expanding the powers of government, was that any private enterprise (in this case, the banks) which has grown strong enough to exercise a power granted to the federal government under the Constitution must be subject to control in the public interest. This control is best achieved by reassumption of power by the federal government in the interests of the public and of the states and by its entry into the appropriate sphere of activity to do so.[16]

Characteristically, Virginia still held to its views on state sovereignty despite its record of co-operation with the first bank in specific situations. While the South and the West voted overwhelmingly for the new bank, the Virginia delegation in Congress went against it, albeit by a margin of only one vote (11 to 10), the only state of those two sections to oppose it.

Unlike the first United States Bank, the second one was chartered after numerous state banks had come into existence. This led to a formal discussion of the relations between them that had been absent in 1791 simply because there were so few state banks at that time. The state banks represented a powerful pressure group before Congress and could undoubtedly have had their will done if they had been all of the same mind on the issue. As it was, some of the state bankers heartily opposed any national bank as a threat to their positions, but others, among them some of the most powerful men in America (including Stephen Girard and John Jacob Astor), supported such a bank with equal or greater vigor. As a result, the large group of Congressmen who felt that a national bank was a necessity but that state banks had an important place in the fiscal system carried the day and a framework for co-operation between the

[15] *Ibid.*, p. 234.

[16] *Works of John C. Calhoun* (New York: D. Appleton and Co., 1855), Vol. II. Calhoun's views are expressed in a series of reports and papers written by him in this period.

two banking systems was consciously established. In this way, the some-what halting and experimental co-operation that existed during the second decade of the first United States Bank was replaced by a more consciously recognized need and desire for co-operation on the part of the Congress itself. The plan that was finally adopted was based on the recommendations submitted by Secretary of the Treasury Dallas, an ardent supporter of co-operation. It is a matter of record that the administration would have been willing to formalize the co-operative nature of the proposed banking system even further by introducing the states into the management of the national bank.[17]

NEW FORMS OF CO-OPERATION

The charter that was finally enacted made it quite clear that the second bank was a continuation of the first with only minor differences. In effect, it may be said that the same national banking system served the country for forty of the forty-five years between 1791 and 1836. The differences were primarily in the way of strengthening federal control over the bank. Aside from increasing the capitalization and lowering the price per share, the new charter gave the federal government the power to require the bank to establish at least one branch in each state under certain conditions. In addition, the bank was specifically designated as the principal depository of the United States Treasury (though the state banks were allowed to keep some deposits because they were so dependent on them to stay solvent). The bank was required to report to the Treasury and was subjected to Treasury inspection. Five of the twenty-five directors were to be appointed by the President of the United States with the consent of the Senate.

The first positive act of co-operation after the establishment of the new bank was the securing of an agreement with the state banks of Pennsylvania, New York, Maryland, and Virginia to resume redemption of their notes in specie, which they had suspended in 1814. To effect this agreement, representatives of these banks met with representatives of the United States Bank and decided to resume redemption on February 20, 1817.[18] This made it safe for the national bank to redeem its notes with-

---

[17] Clarke and Hall, *op. cit.*, pp. 613–19, 636–38.

[18] Specie redemption meant that people could exchange their bank notes for their face value in gold and silver. When the War of 1812 was in progress, the currency, often

out fear of losing its specie to the state banks. At the same time it made it possible for the United States Treasury to accept the notes and checks of the state banks who were party to the agreement for payments due the federal government. In addition, the United States Bank agreed to the establishment of a nationwide system consisting of the banks who were parties to the agreement, whereby they could draw upon the credit of the United States Bank for checks on other participating banks where they had funds, practically eliminating the necessity of transporting specie from one to another to make payments. By assuming the state banks' deposit liabilities while allowing them half a year to transfer the federal funds, the national bank essentially lent them what they owed to the Treasury for immediate repayment to that institution. The bank also agreed not to demand payment of other balances due it from the state banks before lending those banks sufficient funds to maintain the local money markets during the transition. The Virginia banks could borrow up to $500,000 under this arrangement.

Aside from the immediate problems of transition from a fragmentized to a national system again, provisions were made for long-range co-operation. It was agreed that the United States and state banks would settle their note balances with each other daily. Furthermore, the banks pledged "good faith and friendly offices" to each other and agreed to "contribute their resources to any reasonable extent" to support each other should any emergency arise that might menace the credit of any of the participants. In order for this agreement to take effect, it had to be approved by the secretary of the treasury, who was prompt in doing so.[19] Specie payments were to some extent resumed, and a bad situation remedied. The agreement and its resultant success can be considered the personal triumph of the secretary of the treasury, William H. Crawford of Georgia. Bray Hammond sums up his achievement in the following words:

Though imperfect and incomplete, resumption was an achievement and the Secretary's own. The Bank supplied the machinery, and the Secretary supplied the brains. He tutored, corrected, and prodded the Bank's president. Central

weakly supported in any case, was threatened by the use of specie (gold and silver) for war expenditures and the issuance of too much currency with too little specie behind it. With the absence of a national bank with powers to regulate the amount of currency issued by refusing to accept bills with insufficient backing, the state banks just stopped redeeming their bills. This led to a general cheapening of the currency, one of the evils which a national banking system was designed to remedy.

[19] *American State Papers, Finance* (Washington, 1832), IV, 769.

banking policy was more intelligently developed in the Treasury than in the central bank itself. Mr. Crawford also had to mediate between the state banks and the federal bank, for each feared the other.[20]

Crawford's assurances to the state banks of Pennsylvania, Delaware, and Maryland in his general letter of January 28, 1817, are indicative of his concern that the two systems would and should co-operate with each other: "The deep interest which the U.S. Bank must feel for the credit of the paper system and its intimate connection with the government are considered sufficient guarantees for the intelligent and disinterested manner in which this operation will be effected, independent of the power of the Treasury Department to control its proceeding at any moment by changing the deposits to the state banks."[21] This is one of the earliest statements on record indicating federal willingness to use its powers to enforce co-operative arrangements by virtue of its authority as the federal government. In support of this commitment to the state banks, Crawford wrote to William Jones, president of the United States Bank, on February 7, 1817, that, "If the state banks can be brought, by a concession of this nature, to move harmoniously with each other and with the Bank of the United States, the beneficial consequences resulting from it will be cheaply attained by such a concession."[22]

Co-operation in fiscal matters generally involved the United States Treasury Department primarily through its secretary, chief clerks, and collectors of customs in the field; the Treasury of the United States through the treasurer or his chief clerk, who handled actual payments and transfers of funds; and the Bank of the United States through its branches and their respective officers (primarily presidents and cashiers of the branch offices of discount and deposit) on behalf of the federal government.

During the period of the second United States Bank, a majority of the state banks were still at least partly owned by their respective states and served as central banking agents for them. Even those which were privately owned were closely regulated by the states because of the quasi-monopolistic role they played in the state's financial system. Though eastern banks were already moving toward fully private ownership, those

[20] Hammond, *op. cit.*, p. 249.

[21] "Correspondence Relative to the Public Deposits," *American State Papers, Finance* (Washington, 1832), IV, 495–99.

[22] *Ibid.*, pp. 974–1077.

in the South and West were only beginning to reach the full expansion of their existence under state control. Where private banks existed alongside the state banks, the latter were the ones generally chosen by the United States Treasury Department and the national bank as partners. In general, state banks served as federal depositories wherever there were no national bank branches to handle the federal revenues or wherever it was otherwise considered expedient to maintain them as such. They, through their officers and cashiers, served in the co-operative program at the state level. Occasionally, a governor would also take a hand in the proceedings when political rather than technical administrative questions were at issue. As in every other case to be examined in this study, the ubiquitous senators and representatives of the several states were always on hand to serve as means of access to the federal executive.

On January 7, 1817, the main office of the new United States Bank opened in Philadelphia. Following the aforementioned agreement with the state banks, sixteen branches were designated in March of 1817 and the number was raised to nineteen in October of the same year. Two of the branches were in Virginia, in Richmond and Norfolk. As soon as the branches were opened, newly received federal funds were deposited with them, while the federal government continued to make payments from the $23,000,000 already on deposit in ninety-four state banks around the nation. Since the state banks had committed the federal deposits in long-term investments and their immediate transfer would have caused many banks to collapse, the federal funds were removed over a period of time sufficient to prevent such catastrophes. Even these transfers were made only in areas where there were branches of the national bank to receive them. All the transfers were made at the state bank's convenience, usually in installments. Occasionally, the state bank would keep the funds by paying the interest earned to the federal Treasury. In addition, the United States Bank replaced withdrawn deposits with large loans to enable the state banks to resume specie payments. This policy brought mutual benefits where it was operative, since it kept the United States Bank from being flooded with state bank notes to redeem, and also gave the federal government a good measure of control over the national banking system through the debtor banks. It was particularly attractive in the northeastern states, whose banks were most interested in resuming specie payments and co-operated actively with the federal government.[23]

[23] William J. Shultz and M. R. Caine, *The Financial Development of the United States* (New York: Prentice-Hall, 1937), pp. 172–74.

MC CULLOCH V. MARYLAND

Shortly after the inauguration of the second Bank of the United States, the state of Maryland created a situation designed to test the entire fabric of the national banking system. This situation led to the famous decision of the United States Supreme Court delivered in *McCulloch* v. *Maryland* (4 Wheaton 316 [1819]). As it is commonly interpreted by constitutional lawyers today, this decision is considered a landmark in the delineation of nineteenth-century dual (meaning separate) federalism. When Chief Justice John Marshall issued his famous dictum that "the power to tax is the power to destroy" and ordered the state of Maryland (and the other five states engaged in the same practice) to desist from taxing the United States Bank, it was considered to be a ratification of the doctrine that federalism means separation of governments through division of powers, and it has been so used since then in constitutional interpretation. Even when historians have examined the decision, they have interpreted it as an expression of Marshall's nationalist approach, which was designed to transfer powers to the federal government at the expense of the states.

When the decision is examined in light of the actual operations of the American banking system of the time, an entirely different interpretation comes to light, one more consistent with the temper of the times. There can be little doubt that *McCulloch* v. *Maryland* reinforces a dualism in governmental organization, but it is a dualism that leads to co-operation, not one designed to promote separation. It is in fact an answer to and a refutation of the position that demanded separation in favor of the existing co-operative arrangement. Maryland and her sister states objected to the co-operative fiscal program that had evolved by 1819, which had been reintroduced in 1817 by the establishment of the second United States Bank. By taxing local branches of the bank, they hoped to force it out of business in their states, thus leaving the local field entirely in state hands. By rejecting this approach, the Supreme Court ratified the co-operative program in existence and prevented its destruction through interference by individual states.

Examination of the details of the case reveals much to support this interpretation. The counsel for Maryland tried to have the Constitution construed as a compact between the states (which possessed the only true sovereignty), with only limited powers, thus precluding the establishment of a national bank. This would have rendered the existing bank illegal by virtue of being unconstitutional. In the opinion of the court,

Marshall invoked the principle of implied powers, leaving to Congress the discretion, within broad limits, to decide what could be implied. In setting forth this doctrine, he used the terminology of dualism that has already been shown to have been present alongside clearly co-operative activities. While this has obscured the actual consequences of the decision, it does not change them. Marshall talked in terms of a division of sovereignty and powers as was customary at the time. He also talked of the limited powers of the federal government. In both cases, he accepted the stated doctrine of his age, but he accepted it as a superstructure for intergovernmental co-operation, not as a demand for isolation of individual activities. Just as federal powers are not really limited if Congress can add any others that are necessary to effect them, so division of powers is not really separation if the consequences of a Supreme Court decision reinforce a federally initiated system of co-operation.

The Virginia General Assembly waxed indignant over Marshall's decision, as did many people in other sections of the nation, considering it a direct encroachment on the rights of the states. While the General Assembly passed a resolution to that effect, the state bank it had created and continued to control maintained the already routine patterns of co-operation with the United States Bank and the federal Treasury.

THE LATER DAYS OF THE BANK

After 1828 the operations of the United States Bank centered around forcing the state banks to adopt more conservative banking practices. This attempt came just as the more radical business elements were attaining political power under the Jacksonian Democracy. As a result, their cries that the bank was strangling business expansion in the interests of a few wealthy eastern capitalists fell on willing ears and doomed the second bank in much the same manner as the first. Even so, the actual political struggle that led to Jackson's veto of the recharter bill in 1832 sealed the fate of the bank more because of conflicts between persons in the political arena than for reasons of principle.

Beginning in 1833, the $6,500,000 in federal deposits were gradually withdrawn as the funds were spent (in order to prevent a sudden collapse of the nation's finances, a tribute to the role played by the bank as the central force in the national monetary system). Newly received funds were deposited in the state banks once again. In an attempt to gain re-

newal of the charter, bank president Nicholas Biddle created a national deflation by curtailing credit extensions, ostensibly in anticipation of losing the federal deposits. While this provided an excellent test
for the future historian to use in measuring the extent of the United
States Bank's influence on the national financial scene, it alienated almost
all the remaining supporters of the recharter movement and ended any
chance to maintain the central banking system that was needed by the
nation to continue sound growth patterns.

Meanwhile, the originally high standards of federal supervision of
funds deposited in the state banks began to decline, in great measure because of political pressures on the federal government by local business
and political leaders. For example, many western banks were created
solely for the purpose of serving as federal depositories and earning the
interest that might accrue from investment of the federal funds they obtained. In these cases, the federal funds in effect formed their original
capital.[24]

This perversion of the idea of co-operative fiscal organization came
about because of a general change in the nation's banking system. Originally, the depository system had been based on the ideas of central banking imported from England, whereby only a few banks were created by
special governmental charter, each being owned (in full or in part) or
controlled by the federal or state government which had created it.
While this condition existed, there was co-operation between the central
bank of the nation and the central banks of the several states as the
agents of their respective governments. Under these conditions, the constituent elements of the system could co-operate successfully and fill a
great need.

By the 1830's, the rise of the new laissez faire economy and the decline
of the earlier mercantilist system had wrought changes in the banking
system, replacing the idea of central quasi-public banking with that of
private banking, or banking as a private enterprise. This meant that
banks were no longer specially chartered but could be established by almost anyone under the provisions of a general banking law, just as any
other type of corporation could be founded under a general incorporation statute. Banks became private, competitive, and often speculative
businesses rather than agents of government. This quite naturally resulted in changing the co-operative system from one which operated to
equalize fiscal benefits throughout the nation to one which, through the

[24] Shultz and Caine, *op. cit.*, p. 219.

very same acts of co-operation, discriminated in favor of the few banks that had sufficient political influence to secure federal deposits as safe working capital. While this development did not take place in all the states—many of which maintained their government-controlled central banking systems until the Civil War—by 1835 a sufficient number had adopted the new system to cripple a program designed with the old system in mind. This banking revolution, not the issue of states' rights, brought about the political reaction which led to the abandonment of the national co-operative fiscal system. In fact, the states oriented toward states'-rights—those in the South—were generally the ones which maintained their central banking systems longer than their sisters. It was not until new forms of co-operation were evolved many years later that a new central banking system was attempted, one much different from the relatively streamlined model of the early years of the Republic.

Before abandoning the system, several attempts were made to save it. In 1836 Congress passed an act setting statutory qualifications for depository banks to replace the large amount of administrative discretion previously left in the hands of the secretary of the treasury. Under the terms of this statute, federal deposits could not exceed 95 per cent of a bank's capital, bank notes had to be redeemable in specie, and no bills of under five dollars could be issued by depository banks. Federal deposits were to be credited as specie and the secretary could not shift deposits between banks to support individual institutions.[25]

Then the Panic of 1837 struck the nation at a time when its fiscal affairs were already in a weakened condition because of the loss of the staying power of a national bank. The crisis forced many of the overextended state banks first to suspend specie payment (May, 1837) and, in many cases, to close their doors. This served to freeze millions of dollars of federal funds in state banks and led the secretary of the treasury to order (May 12, 1837) federal collecting officials to retain all federal receipts for use in immediate disbursements rather than deposit them in state banks where they might also be frozen.

The Panic of 1837 led to the re-emergence of the idea of a national bank. Martin Van Buren, Jackson's successor, was as opposed to the revival of such an institution as was his illustrious mentor. In its place, he proposed a system of independent federal subtreasuries to be located in different parts of the country to hold the federal funds. After protracted debate, he secured the necessary legislation from the Congress at the end

[25] *Ibid.*, p. 220.

of his administration, and in 1840 a series of "independent treasuries" was established. This system was extremely short-lived, however, because political power passed into the hands of the Whigs, who desired the reestablishment of a national bank. After letting the treasury-system act expire, they passed a bill that would have permitted such a great amount of power over the states to be placed in the hands of Congress that it was vetoed by President John Tyler, of Virginia, without hesitation. A second measure was passed, supposedly in conformity with Tyler's views; but the President, who was so much a supporter of states' rights that he was later to serve in the Confederate Congress, vetoed it also, much to everyone's dismay. His whole cabinet, with the exception of Daniel Webster, of Massachusetts, resigned in protest. Nevertheless, Tyler's action ended any hope of reviving the bank. From then on, although some federal funds were placed in eastern banks, they were generally held by the collecting officers, who disbursed them on treasury draft. The first phase of intergovernmental banking co-operation was virtually at an end.

THE RECORD OF FISCAL CO-OPERATION

In view of the historical record, it can safely be said that government banking in the United States was a co-operative effort during the first fifty years of the Republic. The United States Treasury Department, the two national banks, and the several state-controlled banks operated within a single banking system in which the federal government acted as a stabilizing agent. Banking set the pattern for most subsequent government functions by emerging at the federal and state levels at the same time. The first national bank preceded all but four other banks in the entire country and was directly responsible for the creation of other banks in the states to co-operate with it. The co-operation that began on a rather *ad hoc* basis in the days of the first national bank was demonstrated to be so essential to the nation's welfare that it was formally included in the legislation that established the second Bank of the United States. It was then upheld by the Supreme Court, albeit in a roundabout way, in *McCulloch* v. *Maryland*, after some of the states that were opposed to the fiscal control exercised by the bank had attempted to levy a confiscatory tax on it to drive it out of business. The bank finally did die as a consequence of personality politics and changing times, not as a result of any rejection of co-operation as such.

Even without the national bank, co-operative relationships developed between the United States Treasury and the state banks. The latter served as federal depositories and disbursing agents during periods when the national bank did not exist and as parallel institutions when it did. As long as the mercantilist view of the role of government in the economy prevailed over a majority of the nation, this co-operation continued. It was only when this view was abandoned that the forms of co-operation created under it became inadequate.

Aside from co-operation in banking and fiscal administration, the states were dependent on federal financial resources to a great extent, at least until the 1820's. Starting with Hamilton's victory and the compromise that led to the assumption by the federal government of state Revolutionary War debts, federal payments virtually eliminated the need for the states to levy their own taxes until the post-1812 internal improvement boom. In this way, the first several decades under the Constitution set the pattern of federal-state relations for the future. Financial aids to the states through assumption of debts, day-to-day co-operative administrative arrangements of the national banking and monetary system, and the Supreme Court decisions of John Marshall endorsing all these as being within the powers of the federal government, laid the foundation for a co-operative federalism in the United States.

6

Co-operative Routine in the Banking System

VIRGINIA AND THE FEDERAL TREASURY

Since the state banks continued to hold federal funds after 1817, provisions had to be made for their utilization. At the same time new provisions were needed to govern the relationships between the branches of the Bank of the United States and the United States Treasury. The extent of the co-operative arrangements between the Treasury and the state banks was revealed in Secretary Crawford's reply to an inquiry from J. B. Dandridge, cashier of the Office of Discount and Deposit, of the Richmond branch of the United States Bank, regarding the manner and time of making returns to the Treasury Department on the federal funds held by his branch. Crawford instructed him to adopt the report form used by the Bank of Virginia and, like that institution, report returns weekly.[1]

On June 30, 1817, the old arrangement expired by which federal deposits in designated state banks were subject to withdrawal. In a general letter sent to the banks concerned, including the Bank of Virginia, Crawford announced a new set of regulations under the new conditions that obtained. Each bank had to signify its continued acceptance of the federal deposits on these terms.[2]

These rules were made permanent on July 11, 1818, with a few modifications. On September 30 of that year, the state banks were to transfer all the money left in their hands that had been deposited to the credit of the United States Bank since June 30 to the credit of the treasurer of the

[1] *American State Papers: Miscellaneous,* Class III, Vol. IV, 537 (June 25, 1817).

[2] *Ibid.,* p. 588 (July 1, 1818).

United States. After that date, the banks would make their returns directly to the treasurer. Withdrawals would otherwise continue in the same manner. Returns were made in duplicate, one copy sent directly to the treasurer and the other sent to the secretary of the treasury. The former was for disbursement purposes and the latter for general supervision of the funds.[3] Returns of the Treasury account had to be rendered monthly only, rather than weekly, "promptly at the close of the month."[4]

While some banks resisted removal of the federal funds with all the means at their disposal, relationships between the branches of the Bank of Virginia and the Treasury Department were good enough to earn the commendation of Crawford himself, who praised them for the readiness with which they met his views on the transfer.[5] In every case, Crawford tried to have the funds transferred to the accounts of those branches of the United States Bank located where federal expenditures were the greatest to necessitate only one transfer and expedite the use of the money involved. Under this arrangement, funds in the Virginia banks were generally transferred to the United States Bank offices in Richmond, Washington, D.C., or Norfolk.[6] In any case the transfers continued over a period of many years, so that a continual stream of correspondence relating to the use of the funds was maintained between Washington and the Virginia institutions. This correspondence became quite routinized, consisting of discussions of specific transfers, changes in routing and personnel, and, of course, the regular reports of the depository banks.

During the lifetime of the second United States Bank, the co-operative system introduced in 1817 continued to function. In Virginia, as in a majority of the other states where state-chartered banks existed, the co-operating banks were state-controlled. In large parts of the West, the state banks had not recovered from the hard times of the previous decade, so that during the 1820's the branches of the United States Bank were the only banks serving those areas.[7]

Veterans' pensions were disbursed by the local branches of the United

---

[3] *Ibid.*, p. 590 (July 11, 1818).

[4] *Ibid.*, p. 596 (Crawford to cashiers of the Bank of Virginia, Petersburg and Fredericksburg branches, November 12, 1818).

[5] *Ibid.*, pp. 636, 656, 660, 681.

[6] *Ibid.*, pp. 644–45 (Crawford to R. K. Jones, cashier of the Bank of Virginia, Petersburg branch, October 8 and 14, 1819).

[7] William J. Shultz and M. R. Caine, *The Financial Development of the United States* (New York: Prentice-Hall, 1937), p. 182.

States Bank on drafts issued by the United States Treasury after the pensioners had been certified as legitimate by the governor of Virginia and the War Department.[8] Federal deposits remained in the state bank throughout the entire period, despite a Congressional resolution of 1824 calling for their complete withdrawal.[9] Thus, the Bank of Virginia continued to transmit returns to the treasurer of the United States. When such returns were not forthcoming on schedule, prompt reminders were sent out by the treasurer to the erring bank cashiers.[10]

THE END OF THE NATIONAL BANKING SYSTEM

The return to the system of using the state banks as federal depositories after 1836 created the need for some new co-operative procedures. Despite the fact that the eastern states had begun to liquidate their holdings in state-chartered banks, the newer southern and western states were increasing their role in banking operations, often to the point of owning banks outright. Thus, in these states the amount of intergovernmental co-operation in banking operations actually increased during the 1830's.

In addition, the Treasury Department attempted to impose even more stringent conditions on those state banks desiring to become depositories for federal funds. The contract between the secretary of the treasury and the Bank of Virginia is a typical example of this new policy. The Bank of Virginia agreed to receive and deposit to the credit of the United States Treasury all money presented on account of the United States. It agreed to provide collateral security, submit weekly returns of the funds on deposit, transfer funds to other banks at the request of the secretary of the treasury on receipt of reasonable notice, and submit all its records (not only those concerning the federal deposits) for examination by federal inspectors, excepting only personal accounts. Furthermore, it agreed to serve the federal government in all the ways the United States Bank had, to pay the expenses of the federal bank examiner, and to furnish bills

8 U.S. Treasurer, *Letters Sent*, Book I (July 3, 1828–July 19, 1831), p. 25 (treasurer to pensioner, July 30, 1829).

9 *Ibid.*, pp. 86–87 (Report to the U.S. Senate via the secretary of the treasury, January 23, 1830).

10 *Ibid.*, p. 79 (John Campbell, treasurer of the United States, to F. Sydnor, cashier of the branch Bank of Virginia at Lynchburg, December 28, 1829).

of exchange on London at cost. The secretary of the treasury reserved the right to terminate the entire arrangement at will if it was in the public interest to do so.[11]

Secretary of the Treasury Roger B. Taney notified the bank of its selection as a federal depository on October 9, 1833, in a letter that included the contract to be signed as well as forms notifying the proper public officials, which were to be sent out by the bank after signing the contract. On October 17, John Brockenbrough, president of the bank, returned the signed contract with a promise of faithful compliance with its terms. He requested a modification in the reporting procedure to allow monthly rather than weekly reports from each branch and also asked for clarification of the bank's role in paying federal pensioners. Taney replied on October 22 acknowledging receipt of the contract and putting it into effect. While he was willing to accept a single report from the main office to cover the entire bank and all its branches, he insisted on its submission on a weekly basis as a uniform rule for all federal depositories. He also informed Brockenbrough that the Treasury Department did not intend to have the depository banks pay the pensioners as yet.[12]

The expected reaction of orthodox states'-rights Virginians to such a

[11] Virginia House of Delegates, *Journal for the 1833–1834 Session,* p. 172.

[12] *Ibid.,* Document 20, Part 3. The Congress withdrew the pension disbursement duties from the expiring Bank of the United States in 1836 (Act of April 20, 1836). The secretary of war was given the task of assigning the duties to "individuals and corporations under rules he would devise." The secretary wanted to appoint the officers of the banks with federal deposits as federal pension agents in their respective states. He hoped that this would facilitate the payment of the pensioners, since the funds for their payment would be in the hands of the disbursing officers. In Virginia, the officers of the two depository banks could not become pension agents. Any appointment to federal office was impossible for them to accept because they were state employees by virtue of Virginia's control over their banks. The U.S. Congress made it possible, through legislation, to circumvent this barrier to effective co-operative action. In place of the officers themselves, the Bank of Virginia as a corporation was appointed federal pension agent. This seems to have satisfied the constitutional provisions in question, the local states'-rights doctrines, and the administrative needs of both parties. [This information came to the writer's attention through a similar case in New Hampshire, where the legislature of that state was called upon to determine whether a governor-elect could assume office while remaining a United States pension agent. They turned to the Virginia decision as a precedent. See New Hampshire, *House Journal, 1833.*]

This is a typical example of the type of correspondence that continued to pass between the Treasury Department and the state bank during the life of the arrangement. It was correspondence that dealt with routine matters and small problems between men of good will and with general agreement on both sides as to the goals and operations of the program.

strong and comprehensive agreement was not long in coming. Governor John B. Floyd, one of the original strict constructionists, dwelt upon it at length in his message to the Virginia General Assembly of 1833, attacking the contract as a threat to the states and an enhancement of federal power by placing all fiscal matters under federal control. Floyd pointed out that the new system gave the secretary of the treasury the authority to put a value on state bank notes as he saw fit, raising or lowering their value or even rejecting them entirely. (The question of federal control over state bank notes had been an important area of disagreement for several decades, with constant attempts by the federal government to gain some measure of control over their issue through the United States Bank.)

The contract was also denounced for the powers it gave to the secretary to dissolve the agreement at his discretion and to select the depository banks. The Virginia governor, with justice, argued that in effect the secretary of the treasury determined which banks would be in good financial positions with their notes in demand and which would be relegated to second place or worse because they lacked the insurance of stability furnished by federal deposits. Floyd felt that this favoritism would ruin the South and West in favor of New York, a not unfamiliar cry in the history of fiscal affairs in the United States and one that contributed much to the inhibition of ongoing co-operative programs in the banking field.[13]

The Governor was also incensed at the federal right to inspect at will banks that were creatures of the state and at the willingness of the banks to pay the costs entailed in such inspections. He quoted the Bank of Virginia as acknowledging itself to be "in the service of the government." Concerning the weekly returns of its accounts that were to be submitted to the Treasury Department, the Governor felt that this was claiming "a privilege not heretofore deemed necessary by this commonwealth, which has so deep an interest in this bank itself." He concluded that the entire arrangement was made even more dangerous by the fact that the Bank of Virginia was a state depository also, thus giving the federal government an indirect supervisory role over state funds and even a measure of

[13] The tendency of the money power to gravitate eastward meant that the South and West would continue to oppose a national banking system until such time as one could be created that would at least face this problem. Some eighty years after the end of the second United States Bank, the Federal Reserve System was created in a rather decentralized fashion to meet the objections and, hopefully, the needs of these sections.

control over them through the collateral-security provisions of the contract.

The entire problem was aggravated by the fact that it came in the midst of the tariff controversy and at the same time that the famous "Force Bill" was passed by Congress to counter South Carolina's nullification attempt. Floyd used the same occasion to denounce that piece of legislation as representing the destruction of the states, the usurpation of all power by the federal government, the end of the compact, and its replacement by a unitary state. This attitude did not make the rather stringent terms of the depository contract more palatable to the group Floyd represented.[14]

Shortly after the contract was signed, the treasurer of the Commonwealth, who also served as Virginia's proxy on the board of the state-controlled bank, forwarded a copy of the agreement with a report to the speaker of the House of Delegates.[15] On the basis of this report and the Governor's message, a Select Committee on the Subject of the U.S. Deposits was established to investigate the matter, headed by John Barbour. The net result of these investigations was to continue the co-operative program despite the inflammatory statements against it.

Barbour immediately entered into correspondence with the officers of the Bank of Virginia and the Office of Discount and Deposit of the United States Bank at Norfolk (which had also been a party to the contract since it had previously held the deposits).[16] On December 18, Brockenbrough, president of the Bank of Virginia, replied to Barbour's queries, reporting that federal deposits under the new agreement had been made at the Richmond and Norfolk branches of his bank: $15,759.94 at the former and $9,000 at the latter. He did not anticipate that the total amount deposited would ever exceed $200,000 at any one time. As long as the capital stock of the bank stood at $2,740,000, the bank did not expect to be required to give collateral security, since federal deposits would have to exceed half the bank's capitalization, or $1,370,000, for it to be required to do so. In demonstrating this, he indicated the extent to which the bank would serve as the agent of the federal government by stating that "the greater part of the receipts must be from the transfers

[14] Virginia House of Delegates, *op. cit.*, pp. 6–7.

[15] *Ibid.*, Document 5, L (Burfoot, treasurer of the Commonwealth, to the speaker of the House of Delegates, December 2, 1833).

[16] *Ibid.*, Document 17 (Report of the Select Committee on the Subject of the U.S. Deposits).

of money. This is immediately paid over to the proper officers, and by them speedily disbursed, and the chief benefit the bank has in this operation, is that of paying out of its own notes for the money it thus receives."

Thus, in actuality, the arrangement provided the federal government with a local disbursing office at the same time that federal funds were utilized to bolster the value of state bank notes. Customs receipts were expected to equal about $200,000 per year and were subject to withdrawals on the warrants of the treasurer of the United States to meet operating expenses of the Treasury Department. Brockenbrough felt that if the secretary thought it necessary to demand collateral for such a small proportion of funds in relation to the capital stock of the bank, he would so mistrust the institution as to withdraw the deposits altogether.[17] It seems clear that the question of furnishing collateral security was the one that really perturbed the legislators, primarily because the state and its agencies held 10,486 shares of the bank's stock worth $1,184,360 (or slightly less than half of the institution's total capitalization), and, at the same time, half of the state's revenue was deposited in it.[18] Brockenbrough concluded his reply in the following manner:

The bank is at a loss to conceive any objections to the agreement as a *pecuniary* [his emphasis] matter. It pays nothing for the use of the deposits. If the operation be one of any profit, the commonwealth gains its due proportion of it, and that the deposits may be of some value is fairly inferred from the claim for compensation made by the bank of the United States on Congress for the withdrawal of them. If there be no profit to the bank of Virginia, then the officers and clerks will have had additional labour to no purpose. On the *political* [his emphasis] bearing of this measure, it probably does not become the bank to express an opinion.[19]

At this point, the stockholders of the bank, Virginians to the core, passed a resolution disapproving all sections of the contract that imposed federal controls on the institution and directing them to be abrogated.

---

[17] *Ibid.*, Document 20 (Correspondence between Chairman John Barbour of the Select Committee and the Bank of Virginia and the Office of Discount and Deposit of the Bank of the United States at Norfolk, and Bank of Virginia to Chairman, December 18, 1833).

[18] This seems to have been less a question of economics than of politics. If the bank should furnish collateral security, it would indicate the submission of an agency of the state to federal regulation in a manner inconsistent with states'-rights theory.

[19] Virginia House of Delegates, *loc. cit.*

This resolution was forwarded to the House of Delegates early in 1834.[20] The resolution did not seem to affect the status of the bank as a federal depository, since its reports to the General Assembly continued to refer to the federal funds on deposit.

The Select Committee on Banks then turned its attention to the broader problem of the state's banking and capital needs in the light of the extinction of the United States Bank, which had evidently been a prime source of capital for the large-scale internal improvements then under way in the Commonwealth. In a letter which was circulated to interested parties and institutions throughout the state, the committee asked,

What effect will the winding up of the Bank of the United States have upon the present state of the banks and upon the commerce of the state? Especially, does it suggest the propriety of increasing the banking capital of the state; and does it indicate the present, or some future time, as the period proper for such increase?[21]

In the same letter the committee asked the two Richmond banks about their business relations with the federal government.

Responses to this inquiry generally reflected the need for state action to fill the gap left by the impending demise of the United States Bank and its attendant national banking system. Thomas Rutherford commented that the United States Bank had had a good effect in controlling the state banks and strongly implied that the investments made by individuals and cities in internal improvements were made possible by the existence of the United States Bank with its available capital.[22] That is to say, local lack of investment capital in the "underdeveloped" sections of the country was alleviated, at least to some extent, through the mediation of the national bank, which could supply such capital because of its nationwide operation. This, in turn, made it possible for local governments to participate in internal improvements (which were generally undertaken through joint-stock companies) along with the states and the federal government, developing the three-level co-operation that has become characteristic of the American federal system.

S. I. Harrison, Maurice Langhorne, Jr., and John G. Meem wrote that the state's money needs had been provided jointly by the state banks and the United States Bank and that there was greater danger of joint con-

[20] *Ibid.*, Document 23 (January 6 and 7, 1834).

[21] Virginia House of Delegates, *Journal for the 1834–1835 Session*, Document 23.

[22] *Ibid.*, letter of February 2, 1835.

traction of their issue as a result of the demise of the latter.[23] By way of summary, Brockenbrough wrote that the accounts of the United States Bank and the Bank of Virginia were about equal though they had fluctuated earlier, usually in favor of the former, and that, "a liberal intercourse has always existed between the two institutions."[24]

As a result of this inquiry, the General Assembly passed an act to increase the amount of banking capital in Virginia. Almost on the heels of that action came the distribution of the federal surplus in 1837. Virginia took advantage of that largess to expand the state's investments in the banks, under the terms of the Acts of March 22 and March 25, 1837 (general regulations for incorporating banks and increasing banking capital in Virginia) and June 24, 1837 (authorization for the state to use part of the surplus revenue for investment in banks). There is good ground to believe that the acts themselves were at least partly in response to the impending surplus distribution, which would be governed by requirements set by Congress.[25]

In 1838, the total amount on deposit for the federal government in the state banks well exceeded the $200,000 estimate made five years earlier. In addition, the second state-controlled bank, the Farmers' Bank of Virginia, had also been made a federal depository. There was $478,388.54 on deposit in the Bank of Virginia and $122,301.41 in the Farmers' Bank.[26]

NEW HAMPSHIRE IN THE MID-NINETEENTH CENTURY

During the mercantilist period, federal-state relations in the field of fiscal affairs in New Hampshire followed the general pattern of those in Virginia with two exceptions. In the first place, New Hampshire, as a small state out of the main stream of financial activity, did not have as much banking activity as did Virginia. Its banks were primarily designed to serve local needs. Just as Richmond was the financial center of Virginia and perhaps even of areas beyond its borders, Boston was the financial center of New England, including New Hampshire. In the second place, the state of New Hampshire did not retain control or stock owner-

[23] *Ibid.*, letter of January 29, 1835.

[24] *Ibid.*, letter of February 3, 1835.

[25] Virginia House of Delegates, *Journal for the 1838 Session*, Document 1, p. 50.

[26] *Ibid.*, pp. 10–11.

ship in its banks as long as Virginia did. In the northeast, state control came earlier and was given up earlier than in the South and West.

At the same time, the federal government and the state did collaborate in some important ways during the period in which the banks served as federal depositories, indicating that it was not just an accident of ownership that brought about co-operative relationships. The New Hampshire secretary of state had to file copies of the returns of the New Hampshire depository banks with the secretary of the treasury in Washington during those years.[27] In this way, the states were involved in supervising the federal-depository banks even when they did not own an interest that gave them participant supervision, as in Virginia.

After the abandonment of the deposit system and the failure to recharter a national bank, the confused deposit situation was brought into some order in 1846 with the re-establishment of an independent treasury system under which federal funds were deposited either in the Treasury Building in Washington or in vaults located in United States mints and customhouses around the country. This served to divorce the federal finance system from the now generally privately owned banks and their vagaries.[28]

This system was encouraged by many state governments, among them New Hampshire. In 1845, Governor John Steele and the General Court went on record as encouraging the idea of independent federal depositories, not on the grounds of separation of governmental functions, but on the grounds that public and private finance should not be mixed.[29] After the independent treasury system had been functioning for close to two years, Governor Jared Williams endorsed its existence as exercising a healthy control over commerce in the country. He was particularly impressed by the ability of the federal depositories to withhold specie from circulation simply by holding on to their deposits. It was also beneficial, he thought, that banks were restrained in their issuance of notes since they could no longer depend upon the federal deposits to keep them solvent. Since these were the two major criticisms of using privately owned banks as federal depositories, he could well feel satisfied with the situation as it then stood.[30] The revived independent treasury system, with its

[27] U.S. Treasury Department, *Letters from Banks: 1835–1837, New Hampshire.*

[28] Shultz and Caine, *op. cit.*, p. 263.

[29] New Hampshire, *Message of the Governor,* June, 1845.

[30] *Ibid.*, June, 1848. It would no doubt be revealing to investigate whether the deposit of federal funds in local United States customhouses, whose collectors were

scattered subtreasuries, remained in operation until its functions were assumed by the Federal Reserve System in 1920.

The New Hampshire experience can be summed up so briefly because it was so much like that of Virginia. Its own variations have been outlined to indicate two important aspects of American federalism. Even in the original thirteen states, with their different patterns of development prior to the formation of the United States and their radical differences in size, position, wealth, and geography, co-operative programs were more alike than different. Yet, at the same time, these universal co-operative programs could be, and were, adjusted in their particulars to meet the different needs of each state. These two fundamental elements of the co-operative approach are as old as the co-operative system.

---

political appointees and were generally from the same localities that they served, had any effect on the management of the funds, since political contacts and relationships no doubt did exist between state and federal officials.

7

Federal Reimbursements and Public Education

FEDERAL FUNDS AND THE VIRGINIA SCHOOL SYSTEM

One of the major points of contention in the debate on the course of American federalism revolves around the financial self-sufficiency of the states vis-à-vis the federal government. Today there is almost general agreement that state reliance on federal funds and initiative to undertake governmental programs is a relatively new phenomenon that has lessened the role of the states in the federal system. Earlier parts of this study have already indicated that this view is open to serious re-examination. This chapter will focus more attention on the financial relationships of Virginia and New Hampshire with the federal government in the early period as exemplified in the field of public education.

Just as the importance of the Revolutionary War reimbursement funds declined, the War of 1812 provided new stimuli for federal participation in financing state governmental activities. During the war, the federal government had to borrow money from the states in order to maintain the army. The states were called upon to raise, equip, and pay their own troops, with reimbursement promised for all expenses incurred while the state troops were in the federal service. Virginia accepted this arrangement with the full expectation of reimbursement. Washington's chronic lack of funds forced the state to wait until the war had ended before pressing its claim, at which time the governor and senators of the Commonwealth actively attempted to secure the funds due it.

Complications arose almost immediately. The burning of Washington by the British in 1814 had destroyed expense vouchers that the state had already submitted, and no payments could be made without proper documentary evidence of the outlay. This meant that decisions had to be made in the national capital as to which claims could be settled by the War Department through the use of available records and which ones would have to be settled by Congress because of lack of statutory authorization for reimbursement on the basis of incomplete records. Virginia had to secure additional vouchers for expenses not yet claimed and submit them. The process of reimbursement created a series of administrative contacts that continued for the following two decades.

There would be little point in discussing this problem in a study devoted to describing so-called normal situations rather than unique products of wartime co-operation, except that in Virginia, as in other states, the funds finally repaid by the federal government were used to found the common-school system of the state. In this case, the unique became the normal, since the funds were invested in a trust fund the revenues of which provided virtually the sole state support for the common schools until 1870. Since federal reimbursements for the state's war expenditures were nearly universal, many of the thirteen original states, which did not receive federal land grants for common schools (as did the public-land states), made use of this form of federal financing for the same purpose. While it is quite true that the funds were technically only reimbursements, not new grants, the historical record indicates that the large sums of money secured by the states for defense in time of war could never have been raised for educational institutions in peacetime. Virginia's record is an excellent example of this, since it was not until 1870 that the state was prepared to spend any tax money on public education. The recorded public attitude toward state support of education strongly indicates that if it had not been for the "fortunate" circumstances of the War of 1812, there would not have been any public schools in Virginia prior to 1870.[1] Furthermore, the federal officials, under pressure from Congress and knowing that the funds were to be used to aid education, were considerably more liberal in allowing the state's claims, many of which were highly dubious. The federal government did not exercise any control over the use of the funds, it is true, but neither did the state. Virginia

[1] For the history of education in nineteenth-century Virginia, the reader is referred to two works on the subject, which, though ignoring the role of federal money in the Literary Fund, do describe the fund's importance. They are J. L. Blair Buck, *The Development of Public Schools in Virginia* (Richmond: State Board of Education, 1952), and A. J. Morrison, *The Beginnings of Public Education in Virginia, 1776–1860* (Richmond: State Board of Education, 1917).

merely took the money received from the federal government, invested it in a permanent Literary Fund, and made it available annually to those of its counties and cities that were interested in providing educational facilities to use as they saw fit. The significant point is that, even in this case, it was not a question of the states functioning where the federal government did not, but of both functioning minimally together.

The history of public education in Virginia is one of public refusal to devote resources to its development. After much talk about the need for an enlightened citizenry to maintain the Commonwealth, a bill was finally put through the General Assembly in 1810 establishing the Literary Fund, to be used to aid in the establishment and support of free schools. The fund was to be made up of all escheats, penalties, and forfeitures due the state, and to be managed by a group called the President and Directors of the Literary Fund, consisting of the governor of Virginia, the lieutenant-governor, the treasurer, the president of the court of appeals, and the attorney-general. The fund was to be used for indigent children only; but since it represented the only source of public revenue for schools in the Commonwealth, the schools it helped were virtually the only common schools established prior to 1870.[2]

In actuality, no public education system developed, even in rudimentary form, until 1818. The amount entering the fund from local sources was too little to encourage an unwilling public to add to it for schools. However, in 1816 the first of the war reimbursement money, totaling $1,210,550, was returned to the state. This sizable sum, added to the fund by act of the General Assembly, gave the state the resources with which to establish a rudimentary system of common schools at no additional cost to its citizenry.

[2] Buck, *op. cit.*, pp. 25–29. The ex officio composition of this board was by no means unique. In this connection it is interesting to note the deep involvement of most of the state officials in co-operative programs. The Virginia state auditor's report of 1833 lists the following distribution of duties:

Governor: ex officio president of the Literary Fund, the Board of Public Works, the James River Canal, and the Northwestern Turnpike Company.
State treasurer: director of the Board of Public Works, the James River Canal, the Literary Fund, and Northwestern Turnpike Company, and the Bank of Virginia.
First auditor: director of the James River Company, the Board of Public Works, the Literary Fund, and the Northwestern Turnpike Company.
Second auditor: same directorships as first auditor and auditor of their accounts, superintendent of the Literary Fund and clerk to its Board of Directors, secretary to the Board of Public Works [he was the official particularly involved in the day-to-day contacts with the federal government].

THE ADMINISTRATION OF REIMBURSEMENT

The means by which the money due Virginia was acquired are illustrative of the way in which a state works to secure almost any benefits from the federal government. Realizing the administrative difficulties involved in securing the funds and the necessity for concerted action on the political and administrative levels to overcome them, Virginia's Governor Wilson C. Nicholas appointed John Chew as the state's agent in Washington to be responsible for untangling the complicated skein.

Chew's first step was to present the War Department accountant with as complete a collection of vouchers showing state expenditures as he was able to assemble. The War Department took the position that the state had to abide by the same rules for submitting claims that applied to individuals and that the department's province was to decide only to what extent the law authorized payment, not what was equitable. Under these terms, Chew had to report that no settlement satisfactory to Virginia could be obtained at that time. The state would not even be reimbursed for established claims pending an additional Congressional appropriation.

War Department regulations were strict. Claims for pay, subsistence, and forage for the militia had to be separated, and the accounts and vouchers presented to the paymaster of the army. Purchases had to be listed in an abstract following a particular form; expenditures had to be listed in another. The authority under which the state troops were called into federal service or were subsequently recognized by the federal government also had to be produced in all cases. Any parts of the claims that were not so sanctioned were to be submitted separately since they would not be allowed without the formal approval of Congress.

After a trip to Richmond to obtain additional vouchers, Chew returned to Washington to resume negotiations. This time he enlisted the aid of William Wirt, prominent Virginia politician and United States attorney in Richmond. Together they met directly with the secretary of war. According to Chew, the secretary "sent forthwith for the accountant and requested that he would devote his attention as exclusively as possible to our business."[3] Accordingly, a special clerk was assigned to the accountant's office to examine the Virginia accounts with Chew and Wirt. How-

[3] *Calendar of Virginia State Papers* (Richmond, 1875–93), X, 423–24 (Chew to Governor, August 30, 1815).

ever, even the secretary suggested that some items would need Congressional sanction, such as those expenses incurred when the militia was called out without prior presidential order; but he felt that a great amount of discretion in interpretation would be allowed. In the conversation, the secretary conceded that every claim resulting from repelling invasions was justified. The secretary even agreed to the Governor's request for an advance payment on the claims, up to $600,000, if the immediate checking of the accounts would show that much indisputably due.[4]

On January 5, 1816, Wirt had a second interview with the secretary of war to confirm the availability of the $600,000 advance payment, which was being held pending the receipt of the remaining vouchers covering the period from May 15, 1815. In order to facilitate the examination and approval of the vouchers, Wirt wrote to Governor Nicholas requesting that they be forwarded as soon as possible. He also informed Nicholas that he hoped to proceed to determine how much could be settled without going to Congress. He indicated that he had been in close contact with the Virginia Congressional delegation, which did not recommend approaching the national legislature on this issue. He also requested the figures on the number of troops called out by the Governor to repel invasion, since only the general orders were in Washington and the War Department wanted to make sure that a number disproportionate to the emergency had not been mobilized.[5]

On January 16, Wirt was able to forward the first $200,000 installment of the advance.[6] On January 30 the rest of the initial payment was obtained. The agent's efforts were then directed toward the more difficult claims, where progress was much slower. This task continued during the 1820's, with others conducting the negotiations.

In 1824, Chapman Johnson, then the state's agent in Washington, wrote to the Governor reviewing the entire case in preparation for a possible appeal to Congress should the War Department's authority be too limited to settle those claims still outstanding. Of the almost $2,000,000 that had been advanced by the state, some $1,781,330 had been repaid, $100,000 at the end of 1814 and the remainder between February 26, 1816, and January 22, 1823. The disagreement over repayment stemmed

[4] *Ibid.*, p. 427 (Chew and Wirt to Governor, December 27, 1815).

[5] *Ibid.*, pp. 428–29 (Wirt to Governor, January 6, 1816).

[6] *Ibid.*, p. 429 (Wirt to Governor, January 16, 1816).

from its mode of collection. Unable to raise sufficient funds for defense by taxation, the state had resorted to borrowing the money from the two state banks and from the small state Literary Fund. Though only $319,000 of the advances had not been repaid by the federal government, the state had spent an additional $486,853.54 to pay the interest due on these loans. Virginia wanted at least part of the interest costs to be paid by the federal government, excepting only the interest on the money borrowed to pay Virginia's share of the United States direct tax (collected under a co-operative arrangement) and that borrowed after the federal government had begun the repayments.

In preparing his case for presentation to Congress, Johnson made a point of comparing it to the federal assumption of state Revolutionary War debts in the 1790's on the theory that if the federal government thought it necessary to pay debts incurred by the states before there was a United States, how much more were they obligated to do so after the adoption of the Constitution. He then informed the Governor that if any additional arguments for repayment were needed, it would be well to indicate that Virginia had dedicated the money received from the claims to the encouragement of learning by investing its proceeds in the Literary Fund and by appropriating $50,000 from the sum to equip the University of Virginia.[7]

The latter was a particularly telling argument at the time, since there had been much talk around the country of the need to support education and of the fact that the public-land states were receiving support from the federal government through the land grants for common schools, while the states without public-land grants were not receiving any such aid. Proposals had even been placed before Congress that would have allotted the revenues accruing to the federal government from the sale of public lands to the several states in proportion to population for the support of education.[8]

In Virginia the Literary Fund had been an important source of funds for the University of Virginia from the time of its founding in 1818, in great measure because of the increase in the Literary Fund resulting from the federal payments of 1816. Once it became evident that some type of public education system could be established without resorting

[7] *Ibid.*, pp. 506–17 (Johnson to Governor, March 23, 1824).

[8] For a collection of documents that provide a sample of the discussion of such an idea, see Virginia House of Delegates, *Journal for the 1833–1834 Session*, pp. 88–97, Document 1: Public Land Matters.

to public taxation for its support, the General Assembly became sufficiently interested in the matter to request the President and Directors of
the Literary Fund to present a report outlining such a system. While the
report was too radical for the legislators as it stood, since it asked for a
comprehensive school system from the primary grades through college, it
did lead to the passage of a bill in 1818 establishing a system of primary
schools and a university. As a result of Thomas Jefferson's indefatigable
campaigning for a state university, the General Assembly included a provision in the Act of February 21, 1818, that gave the new university
$15,000 annually from the income of the Literary Fund, an appropriation
that was continued until after the Civil War.[9] This was the beginning
both of the university and of the use of the Literary Fund to support the
greater part of the higher educational facilities that existed in Virginia in
the nineteenth century. The next great infusion of support for the state
college system came from the federal government through the Morrill
Act (establishing the land-grant colleges) and the Freedman's Bureau
after the Civil War. In Virginia, the state's system of higher education is
almost entirely the result of co-operative action involving federal financial aid in the founding and maintenance of the state's colleges.

The case of reimbursement was then taken before Congress by the
Virginia senators, who submitted a bill to authorize payment of the interest as well as the principal. They were supported by President Monroe, who had been kept informed on the issue by Secretary of War Calhoun as well as through a series of meetings with the senators from Virginia. The President sent a special message to Congress endorsing the
validity of the Virginia claims and supplying relevant documents from
the files of the state and federal governments.

Virginia's decision to dedicate the reimbursement to the advancement
of education was brought into the Congressional deliberations by the
President himself, no doubt with considerable effect. Among the documents he submitted was a copy of the letter from Chapman Johnson to
Governor Pleasants advancing that argument. He also submitted a letter
that he had received from Joseph C. Cabell, member of the board of vis-
itors of the soon-to-be-opened University of Virginia, who had been in

---

[9] Buck, *op. cit.*, pp. 28–33. The act created a twenty-four-member board of commissioners to establish the university and administer the annual Literary Fund grant.
Jefferson, a member of this board, was responsible for the board's report, which became the plan used to organize the university and its curriculum. In it his famous ideas
on religious freedom in an academic institution were set forth.

Washington at least in part for the purpose of lobbying the state's cause with Monroe and Calhoun. Cabell set down on paper his reasons for requesting full reimbursement, no doubt to bring the essence of his conversations with Monroe and Calhoun to the attention of Congress. He commented on the vital necessity of securing the funds from the federal government so that the state university would be able to open its doors with the necessary library and scientific apparatus, which were to be purchased with the federal payments.[10] On March 2, 1825, Senator James Barbour notified the Governor that after much difficulty the measure had been passed; he enclosed a copy of the bill and advised immediate submission of the state's claims for adjustment.[11]

By this time the position of state agent had reached the level of virtual professionalization, since other states had also found it necessary to have expert representation in Washington to oversee their interests in claims against the federal government.[12] Thus, one week after passage of the bill, one Cary Seldon wrote to the governor of Virginia, sending him a copy of the measure and offering his services as agent for the state to adjust the claims.[13] He was duly appointed and commenced work almost immediately. To the great good fortune of Virginia, James Barbour was appointed secretary of war before the month was out. One of the architects of co-operative federalism in the field of internal improvements, he soon indicated his desire to co-operate as fully as possible with the state within the limits of departmental regulations.[14]

In order to substantiate its claims, the War Department required the state to submit an accounting similar to that required for the first set of reimbursements, accompanied by vouchers for the sums paid in interest to the banks and the Literary Fund as well as proof that the loans were used for troops in the service of the United States. The records were as-

[10] U.S. Senate, *Message of President Monroe Relative to the Virginia Claims*, 18th Cong., 1st Sess. (1824), Doc. 64.

[11] *Calendar of Virginia State Papers*, X, 519 (Barbour to Governor, March 2, 1825).

[12] The role of the state agent in Washington is one that has gained additional importance today. While this study can only suggest some of the areas of his activity in various periods of American history, it is a topic that would bear further investigation in order to throw more light on the course of federal-state relations in the United States. Some records of the role of state agents in the twentieth century are in the files of the Workshop in American Federalism of the University of Chicago.

[13] *Calendar of Virginia State Papers*, X, 519–20 (Seldon to Governor, March 9, 1825).

[14] *Ibid.*, p. 521 (Barbour to Governor, March 18, 1825).

sembled in Richmond and forwarded to Seldon in Washington. They were then given to Peter Hagner, third auditor in charge of claims, in the War Department. Hagner had formulated the requirements for filing claims and was responsible for their administration. The third auditor felt that the full claim could not be allowed because the records submitted by the state were incomplete under the terms of the act of Congress. He persisted in this opinion after further examination of the vouchers, insisting that the claim be reduced by one-third. Seldon was not satisfied with this, and the matter was submitted to the secretary of war. Ultimately, the decision was made by the attorney-general of the United States, called in by the secretary of war for a ruling, who decided in favor of Virginia.[15] On the basis of this decision, Hagner proceeded to process the claims. Four months later, Virginia received $178,480.11, the entire amount claimed less $140.85.[16]

In his account to the Governor, Seldon praises the secretary of war and the attorney-general for their help in settling the claims so speedily but does not mention the third auditor, with whom the major part of his dealings were conducted.[17] It seems clear that in the process of negotiation, the third auditor was somewhat more zealous in guarding what he conceived to be the national interest than were his superiors. As an official whose primary responsibilities were administrative, it would be expected that his orientation would be toward the War Department and, indeed, toward the federal government. The secretary of war and the attorney-general, on the other hand, were political officials first and

[15] Meanwhile, Jefferson, a member of the board of commissioners of the new University of Virginia, was anxious to obtain the $50,000 appropriated by the General Assembly from the funds to be secured from the federal government, since the money was needed for construction at the campus. Accordingly, he wrote to the governor that he had heard "authentically" that Congress had passed the reimbursement measure, that the claims would certainly cover the sum appropriated for the university, and that the state act appropriating the money had provided for payment to the university directly from the federal funds. Therefore, he urged action to be taken as soon as possible to secure the money (Jefferson to Governor, March 10, 1825). Governor Tyler then wrote to Secretary Barbour requesting that the money be advanced to the state by the War Department to expedite Jefferson's request. Barbour, however, was forced to refuse even the ex-President, since regulations forbade any such mode of payment. It is evident that the states were, on the one hand, able to obtain redress from the federal government within the limits of national policy, but were not able to exceed those limits no matter how minimal they might be.

[16] An error in the state's calculations. *Calendar of Virginia State Papers*, X, 528 (State Treasurer Jarman Baker to Governor, undated).

[17] *Ibid.*, pp. 526–28 (Seldon to Governor, July 12, 1825).

foremost. Their previous experiences, which led to their respective appointments to the cabinet, were experiences in national and state politics. These experiences in the locally oriented party system, if not political expediency, would certainly have influenced their decision in this and similar cases. In many respects a greater gap existed between the orientations of the political officials in the federal government and their administrative subordinates than between the same federal political officials and the Virginia political leaders.

It was the existence of this state of affairs as part of the fundamental American political tradition that gave the states relatively easy and continuing access to the federal bureaucracy. This access, in turn, made it possible for co-operative federalism to develop without weakening the states by centralizing power in Washington. The system as it evolved was not planned that way. It grew in the course of myriad small administrative relationships like this one.

This did not end the question. Seldon himself stated that after the successful completion of this part of his mission, he was turning his attention to the list of unsettled and suspended balances, which were expected to prove more difficult to adjust.[18] In 1831, Thomas W. Gilmer was appointed agent pursuant to new legislation passed by the Virginia General Assembly and the United States Congress. Gilmer, who had been active in the preliminary legislative struggle, departed for Washington to continue the task so successfully prosecuted by his several predecessors.[19] As the claims issue completed its second decade, it had become a program of longer duration than many others of more formal origins.

THE CONSEQUENCES OF FEDERAL AID

What were the consequences of this monetary windfall for the Literary Fund and education in Virginia? (It must be borne in mind that despite the apparently small sum, this was a monetary windfall. Not much money was being spent by any government of that time, and sums such as these could and did represent a large proportion of the total.) Under the General Assembly's Act of 1818, a system of primary schools was established to serve the indigent children of the state. The measure re-

18 *Ibid.*

19 *Ibid.*, pp. 574–76 (Gilmer to Governor Floyd, June 26 and 28, 1831).

quired each county court (the governing body of the county) to appoint school commissioners who were to determine how many indigent children were to be educated and to report directly to the President and Directors of the Literary Fund. The annual income from the fund, $45,000, was to be used for education of the poor. Most Virginians failed to be sufficiently moved by the idea of public education to take advantage of even the limited resources offered them through inadvertent federal benefits. Without local initiative, little could be accomplished even when funds were made available by the federal and state governments. This is a phenomenon to be noted in virtually every case of governmental action on record. In some way, each successful project has been locally initiated and, if it involves a service of some sort, is ultimately locally administered, with the locality in both cases heavily influencing the nature and performance of the service in question.

Still, such public education as did develop was the result of the Literary Fund distribution. Governor James Pleasants, Jr., reported to the General Assembly in 1823 that

returns from 74 counties give us the number of 6,105 indigent children within these counties who have been sent to school in the year 1822 by the aid of the fund at the average expense of $7.33 for tuition, books, and other things.[20]

In 1829, the legislature empowered the county school commissioners to establish district free schools for all classes of children; the district's residents were to pay for three-fifths of the expense for the school plant and at least one-half of the teachers' salaries, while the Literary Fund was to pay the balance. It seems that this arrangement still involved more local taxation than the Virginians desired. Prior to 1846, only six counties out of a possible one hundred took advantage of the act.[21]

In 1832 three counties reported district schools established under the Act of 1829. In one of them, Washington County, 1,067 students were enrolled and the total compensation for teachers was $4,081, of which $914 was paid from the Literary Fund.[22] The second auditor of the state

[20] Buck, *op. cit.*, p. 38. The Governor seems to have arrived at his per capita figure of $7.33 by simply dividing the annual income of $45,000 assigned to the schools from the fund by the total number of students involved. Buck estimates the actual per capita allotments were nearer $2.00. The Act of 1829 established a per diem payment of 4 cents per student, which was in effect until 1861, but the number of school days per year was small.

[21] A. J. Morrison, *op. cit.*, p. 11.

[22] Virginia House of Delegates, *Journal for the 1845–1846 Session*, Document 4: The Literary Fund Report.

had the actual responsibility of handling the administration of the fund, thus acting, in effect, as state superintendent of those schools supported in whole or part from its revenues. At least some of the holders of that position were men sincerely concerned with the cause of public education, but the schools they helped were still stigmatized by the charity concept.

Lack of interest in public education at the primary level helped provide funds for use at the secondary (academy, in the terminology of the day) and college levels. A majority of Virginia's colleges, aside from the state university, received grants or loans from the fund, including some grants made on a continuing annual basis. In March, 1833, the General Assembly appropriated the excess of the fund, not to exceed $10,000, for the support of an institution for the deaf, dumb, and blind, thus placing the Literary Fund in the role of founding father for the state's welfare program also.

In return for these grants and loans, services to the state were sometimes extracted from the colleges. In 1842, the General Assembly passed a measure requiring all state-supported cadets (there were up to forty of these) at the Virginia Military Institute to teach for two years in some school in Virginia in return for two or more years of education at V.M.I. This regulation supplied the state with a high proportion of its teachers. In 1850, an arrangement was made with Emory and Henry College to pay the annual interest on a loan of $18,000 they had received from the Literary Fund in 1843 by admitting sixteen young men as state students, who would also be pledged to teach for two years upon completion of their college education.

Both the University of Virginia and the Virginia Military Institute continued to receive annual appropriations from the fund. Other colleges and academies could receive the unexpended remainder of the primary-school allocations under the terms of the acts of 1821, 1841, 1846, and 1849. V.M.I., a recipient of federal aid in the form of military equipment under the militia acts as well, furnished the state with approximately 150 teachers prior to the Civil War.[23]

During the 1840's, agitation for public education increased among certain elements of the population. As a result, in 1841 the General Assembly instructed the president and directors of the Literary Fund to present another plan for an educational system for the Commonwealth. The minor reform that resulted from this and other reports improved the sit-

23 Morrison, *op. cit.*, p. 78.

uation slightly but still could not touch the root of the problem—local apathy. As more counties began to develop school systems, the role of the Literary Fund as an agency for the collection and exchange of information increased. The second auditor for the period between 1823 and 1853, Joseph Brown, Jr., was a particularly good friend of education and was diligent in his efforts to utilize the power given him by the fund, little as it was, to best advantage. At the same time, the fund was growing also, though the bulk of its funds was still of federal origin. In 1845, the fund had permanent capital of $1,782,208.41, of which $1,210,550.41 had come from the federal reimbursement.[24]

In 1849, the fund received a new infusion of federal funds from the adjustment of claims remaining from the Revolutionary War. Virginia had paid certain claims of individual citizens and veterans for losses incurred and services rendered during that conflict which had not yet been reimbursed by the federal government. Once again the state sent an agent to Washington; and a procedure similar to that described earlier in this chapter was followed, culminating in a Congressional appropriation of $93,586.80 to be paid to the state. Of this money, the agent, Thomas Green, received $2,722.82 for his services, and $77,216.28 was appropriated by the General Assembly to be added to the Literary Fund.[25]

Aside from the addition of the fees prescribed in the original Act of 1810 and unexpended income from investments, federal funds were the only additions to the Literary Fund prior to 1851, when half of the state's capitation tax was appropriated under a provision of the new constitution. In 1853, the General Assembly added the other half, providing the only new state appropriations for education prior to 1869.

Although up to thirty counties experimented with district schools prior to 1860, the Literary Fund report of that year lists only nine counties and four incorporated communities as receiving aid; the number had been higher in previous years. Perhaps as many as five municipal school systems were also in operation in the state.

With the development of the capitation tax fund, the Literary Fund had to share its role as the source of school funds. However, its administering board still retained its function as the central agency for educational activities in the states. By 1860 every county had a school superin-

[24] Virginia House of Delegates, *Journal for the 1845–1846 Session,* Document 4: The Literary Fund Report.

[25] Virginia House of Delegates, *Journal for the 1849–1850 Session.* Documents 2 and 4: Reports of the First Auditor and the Literary Fund.

tendent who at least reported to the second auditor on local expenditures of the fund within his county, though such expenditures were still primarily for the education of the poor. The United States Census Bureau reported in 1860 that "of all the states in the Union, Virginia was perhaps the least disposed up to this date (1860), to adopt the common school system of the northern states of the Union."[26] Little exception can be taken to that statement.

The Civil War changed the course of the Literary Fund, as it did most of Virginia's institutions. The Virginia Convention of 1861 which passed the Ordinance of Secession also appropriated the revenue of the fund for use in the military defense of the state, excepting only the annual allotments to the University of Virginia and V.M.I. This led to the suspension of those primary schools that had been established. The federal funds involved had come full circle. Acquired originally in repayment of a military debt from the War of 1812 in defense of the Union, the earnings from their investment served to arm the Commonwealth of Virginia in its attempt to disrupt the Union.

The subsequent fate of the Literary Fund is of some interest. After 1870 it ceased to be the mainstay of state public school financing, though its revenues were still used as part of the larger financial pattern. As other, more direct state and federal aids were entering the educational picture, the fund declined in importance. In 1906 it was revived in an important new capacity. Under the terms of the Williams Building Act of that year, it was converted into a revolving loan fund from which local school boards could borrow money to construct school buildings. This new function has played a highly significant role in stimulating better schools in the state. By 1931–32 the fund's principal had increased to $6,288,821.93. During the Depression of the 1930's, it provided a means for continuing school construction in conjunction with new federal grants for that purpose. Of the $8,275,925 principal in 1939–40, $7,921,703 was reported on loan to local school boards, thus making a sizable revolving fund. This was increased by the addition of $11,000,000 from the sinking fund by an act of the General Assembly in 1950. Though the original funds are all but submerged, the Literary Fund continues as an important adjunct to education in Virginia.[27]

[26] Buck, *op. cit.*, p. 46.

[27] Buck, *op. cit.*, pp. 144, 349–50, 417.

REIMBURSEMENT AND THE COMMON SCHOOLS
OF NEW HAMPSHIRE

New Hampshire also increased its common-school funds by securing federal reimbursement of expenses incurred "in the defense of the state." As in the Virginia cases, extensive use was made of state agents to adjust the state's claims with the Treasury Department. The major New Hampshire reimbursement between 1812 and 1861 was more in the nature of a politically engineered federal grant than a normal reimbursement for expenses incurred. The Indian Stream region of northern New Hampshire, now the town of Pittsburg, was once embroiled in a boundary dispute between the United States and Canada. Claimed by both countries after the American Revolution, it was left as a no man's land for fifty years. Its settlement in the late 1820's raised the usual problems of government, which the settlers solved in approved frontier tradition by creating their own. On July 8, 1832, the settlers organized the "Republic of Indian Stream," with a written constitution embodying an executive council, an assembly of all adult males, and a court system. After three years of "independent" existence, violent disagreements between settlers of Canadian and American origin caused Lower Canada (Quebec) to lay formal claim to the area, which in turn led to direct action on the part of New Hampshire. The state militia occupied the "Republic" in 1835 and for a year fought the "Indian Stream War" in a desultory manner. The state incorporated the town of Pittsburg (embracing the disputed territory) in 1840, and in 1842 the issue was formally settled in the Webster-Ashburton Treaty between the United States and Great Britain.[28]

With the cessation of "hostilities," the state turned to Washington, to wage a campaign to obtain reimbursement of funds expended in dispatching and maintaining the militia in the disputed territory on the grounds that the state had acted to protect United States interests against a foreign nation. Not surprisingly, Congress was quite reluctant to honor the state's claims. The militia had been dispatched on state orders alone and had served what was fundamentally a local purpose under the state's police powers—the protection of law and order. There had been no conflict with the government of Lower Canada, as such, but only with some individual Canadians.

[28] Federal Writers' Project, *New Hampshire: A Guide to the Granite State* (Boston: Houghton Mifflin Co., 1938), pp. 45, 335.

In 1837, the governor submitted an account of the amount ($6,028.63) spent by the state to President Van Buren. After twelve years of negotiation, conducted in the main by a state agent in Washington, Congress was finally prevailed upon to enact a measure providing for reimbursement. Actual adjustment of the claim was achieved through negotiations between the state's agent and the second auditor of the United States Treasury Department. In 1850, $5,362.56 (the amount allowed on the claims themselves) was paid, and in 1852 an additional $4,390.86 was obtained "for interest on advances made in repelling invasion and suppressing insurrection at Indian Stream."[29] The money was quickly assigned to the support of the schools by the General Court.

The Indian Stream case was by no means an isolated incident. The practice of federal reimbursement of at best dubious claims on the national treasury became so widespread during the first century of the Republic that there is reason to believe that other policy considerations were involved in the Congressional appropriations. If this was indeed the case (and some evidence to this effect has been uncovered), it is possible to infer that reimbursement of state militia expenses for quasi-national activities (war-scare mobilizations, border troubles, and Indian alerts) was one of the methods used to provide the states with additional federal aid in the form of cash payments, which the conservatives in Congress otherwise opposed, and to provide the states without public lands with aid of the type that public-land states received through land grants. Causes upon which these claims could be based arose frequently during the first century of the Republic. With the passing of the land frontier (and co-incident with the introduction of monetary grants-in-aid), their incidence declined rapidly. Also, it seems to have become increasingly difficult to obtain Congressional appropriations for reimbursement for those that did arise. Considering the difficulty entailed in securing support for direct federal aid, the popular desire for assistance, and the uses to which the reimbursement funds were generally put, the reimbursement method would not have been an unlikely means of avoiding the highly combustible issue of federal cash grants for many years.

[29] The records of this case may be found in New Hampshire, *Laws* (1849); New Hampshire, *Governor's Messages to the Legislature* (Samuel Dinsmoor), June, 1849; and New Hampshire State Treasurer, *Annual Report*, 1846, 1850, 1852.

8

Early Co-operative Social Services

SOCIAL WELFARE IN NEW ENGLAND

Though social service matters were primarily of local concern in the period before the Civil War, joint federal-state programs began to emerge for services which exceeded the scope of local authority and the limits of local fiscal resources. The major example of such joint programs in New England was the Hartford (Connecticut) Deaf and Dumb Asylum, a formal co-operative program involving the federal government and the six New England states, with other states participating informally from time to time.

The Hartford Asylum is the oldest permanent school for the deaf and dumb in the nation. It was founded in 1817 by Thomas Hopkins Gallaudet, the father of education for the deaf in the Western Hemisphere, with private and church support. In 1819, Gallaudet succeeded in securing a land grant of one township in Ohio from Congress for the support of the institution, which, as a result, was then named the American Asylum for the Deaf and Dumb.

The institution was designed to be a co-operative one from its inception. Its support was to come from the Congressional land grant, annual appropriations from the New England states, private contributions, and fees paid by the other states in the Union for the privilege of sending their citizens to the school—a privilege conferred on them by the terms of the land-grant act.

The school was designed to be an experimental institution, a pilot plant in the education of the deaf and dumb, a service which had not been previously attempted. It was to serve as a model for the other states, to encourage the establishment of such institutions by the larger ones or by several banding together as had the New England states. It was also

116

designed to stimulate federal participation in the education of the handicapped.

Gallaudet remained at the head of the school until 1830. He developed the institution along the lines he had set forth when he founded it and trained the first group of professional educators of the deaf and dumb in the country. They, in turn, went out and established similar institutions in all parts of the land.

The question may well be asked as to why the federal government and the states were willing to undertake a program for the improvement of the lot of the deaf and dumb at a time when they were rejecting other programs of an educational, scientific, and commercial nature of equal validity and importance. It is in asking, and trying to answer, this question that a significant clue is revealed as to the manner in which American federalism developed. It seems clear that in this case a man appeared who combined the necessary conviction and the ability to move indifferent or opposing forces sufficiently to mobilize the support he needed to give his ideas a practical test. Gallaudet was able to persuade private groups to support him until he could obtain government aid. He was able to persuade Congress to grant him the aid necessary to stimulate the states. And he was able to persuade the states to take up their share of the work on that basis. It is quite true that conditions were ripe for his movement and that the American people, or sufficient numbers of them, were prepared to be aroused on behalf of the handicapped group he was trying to help; but they were equally prepared to be aroused for other endeavors for which no man emerged capable of leading them.

Gallaudet's influence was such that the second major school for the deaf and dumb, founded by the state of Kentucky in 1823, was able to obtain a federal grant in 1825. Both of his sons followed in his footsteps, one of them, Edward, becoming principal of the new District of Columbia Institution for the deaf and dumb when it was founded in 1857. Edward Gallaudet was able to fulfil a lifelong dream that had been given him by his father to establish the first institution of higher education for the deaf and dumb, an outgrowth of the advanced division of the Columbia Institution. He was also able to obtain an appropriation from Congress, even in the midst of the Civil War, for faculty and buildings for the new institution. Fittingly enough, it was named after his father in 1894 and has been known as Gallaudet College since then. The American Asylum is now the American School for the Deaf.

It would be somewhat inaccurate to include Gallaudet among the architects of American federalism. Like most Americans, it is highly questionable whether he was concerned with the functioning of the federal system when he undertook his campaign. His interest was in founding the school. It was exactly because of his uncomplicated outlook that he contacted all levels of government and sufficiently influenced each of them to support his undertaking. It remained the province of the politicians and administrators in the federal and state governments to work his plan into the system.

If it was a result of his general approach that both levels of government were informed of the project, it was the impact of the national political mores that assured that both levels would be involved in it. The values of federalism coupled with the local interests of congressmen meant that the federal government would confine itself to the role of stimulator and partner rather than exclusive manager of this program or any other. The majority of the state legislators, on the other hand, saw this as a legitimate partnership because of its very structure and not as an insidious attempt to usurp their rights. With this outlook prevalent on both sides, combined with the basic influence behind the program, it would have been hard for it to develop in any other manner. It was when one of these two ingredients (federal stimulation and state partnership) was lacking, or weak, that co-operative programs did not develop. Generally, in such cases the programs themselves did not develop to any great extent.

By the terms of the Congressional grant, the township located in Ohio was either to be sold or leased; the funds obtained were to be placed in a permanent fund, and the interest used to defer the expenses of the asylum. Since the fund was not sufficient to cover the entire cost of the institution, it was matched by appropriations from the legislatures of the several states maintaining students at the asylum. In return, the asylum made an annual report to each state and to the federal government, sending copies to officials in the executive and legislative branches of the respective governments. The federal funds were actually used to supplement the state appropriations as well as to stimulate them, so that they served to reduce the cost per pupil per state equally and thus provided every participant state with an equal share of the benefits. Students were accepted from all parts of the Union, with particular emphasis on New England. They were supported by their states of residence, except for one student who was supported by the federal government directly. Students were recruited at the age of twelve for a five-year course. By

1833, the school had been sufficiently successful as a pilot to influence the founding of three others, and by 1842, a fourth had been founded.

The asylum actively cultivated the support of its constituency through a series of visits by the instructors and pupils of the institution to the various state legislatures to demonstrate the work of the school. One such visit was made to the New Hampshire General Court in Concord in November, 1842, which was personally led by the principal of the asylum, Lewis Weld. Weld described one of the purposes of the asylum as an attempt to pool the efforts of all interested states to maintain a good school, rather than have several poor schools maintained by individual states. To this end, even two southern states had been brought into the program on a continuing basis by 1842, though primary responsibility for the school remained in the hands of Congress and New England.

Weld pointed out the amount each state saved by virtue of the interest from the Congressional grant by demonstrating how much New Hampshire saved on the fourteen pupils from that state then in the school. Without the federal aid, the expenses for each pupil would have been $160 to $170 per annum. By applying the fund equally to students from all the states, the actual cost to New Hampshire was reduced to "*one hundred dollars* [his emphasis] per annum."

Hence the state and the Asylum are co-workers—the state bearing the larger share in the expenses of the pupils' education, the Asylum however doing what it can—never perhaps bearing less than one third of the whole expense, and generally more. In this way the benefits of the fund granted by the Federal Government are enjoyed equally by all who send children to the Asylum.[1]

New Hampshire continued annual appropriations to the asylum through the end of the nineteenth century.

THE NEW HAMPSHIRE INSANE ASYLUM

Less formal programs developed around the movement to establish insane asylums around the nation.[2] The New Hampshire State Insane

[1] New Hampshire House, *Journal*, November, 1842, pp. 414 ff. In Virginia a report was prepared for the legislature that discussed Virginia's contemplated participation in the organization of a regional asylum in the South. According to its figures, the American Asylum had 446 pupils in 1833: 123 privately supported, 322 supported by the New England states, and one by the federal government (Virginia House of Delegates, *Journal for the 1833-1834 Session*, Document 7).

[2] This is another example of a movement stimulated by a guiding spirit—in this case, Dorothea Dix. There would likely have been no nationwide movement to improve

Asylum was a product of Dorothea Dix's earliest campaign outside of her home state of Massachusetts. It was founded in 1842 with funds provided by the federal government's surplus distribution of 1837. At the time of the distribution, Concord was attempting to secure a state institution for itself; and the only one planned, but as yet unlocated, was the asylum. The town fathers managed to maneuver a measure through the General Court giving the city the right to divert its share of the surplus distribution to the asylum in return for its location in Concord, rather than invest it in a permanent fund as was required by the initial act distributing the money among the towns.[3] This measure was passed in 1839, and the next year Concord granted the asylum $9,500, its share of the surplus, and the institution was located there, where it has remained.[4] The state, matching the federal funds that came by way of the town, provided the land for the site just outside of the city limits. This was the only public institution for the care of the insane in New Hampshire.

The subsequent development of the asylum also marks the entrance of a national professional association into New Hampshire administrative history. One of the moves made by Miss Dix and her followers to co-ordinate their activities on behalf of the insane throughout the nation and promote better practices in the field of care for those unfortunates was the organization of the Association of Medical Superintendents of the American Asylums for the Insane, which met biennially to discuss mutual problems and exchange information.

In 1846, the superintendent of the New Hampshire Asylum, Dr. Andrew Erhard, attended the second biennial meeting of the association, which was held in Washington, D.C. He was much impressed with the association and its purposes, as reflected in the meeting, and reported: "A large amount of good will result from the interchange of views

---

the condition of the insane if a person like Miss Dix had not appeared on the scene. She stimulated those few states that already had rudimentary insane asylums to improve their institutions and many of the others to establish their own. Her efforts before Congress and the state legislatures gained governmental support for these institutions, though her attempt to obtain formal federal aid failed because of opposition generated by political disagreements in entirely different fields at the time her aid program was brought before Congress.

[3] New Hampshire, *Laws*, 1839, chap. 438, July 4, 1839. This act provided that the money could only be diverted from the standard procedures if the asylum were located in the town as a consequence of the diversion. It also reaffirmed the provisions for the return of the money should the state be asked for it.

[4] New Hampshire House, *Journal*, 1841 (Report on the Insane Asylum).

by such an association; and by the publication of its proceedings, its suggestions will become of influence in exalting the conditions of the insane."[5]

In that same year, the Superintendent first acknowledged the receipt of federal government publications from the Patent Office and the state Congressional delegation.[6] Although federally appropriated funds were often impossible to secure, the distribution of public documents was always available through interested congressmen. This distribution to the state institutions continued through the years in such volume that it came to constitute a quasi-formal program in its own right. The reports of the various state institutions constantly refer to the "great fund of interesting reading" contained in the "reports, speeches, and other congressional matter," sent them either by their congressmen directly or by the Patent Office and its successors in the field of federal publications at the behest of their congressmen. (Considering the variety of government publications and the general formality of the printed page at that time, it is possible that this was indeed interesting reading matter to the inmates of the institutions.) These publications formed the basis for many an institutional library, which would later be expanded through donated books and, ultimately, developed along scientific principles of library organization. The initial appreciation of the role of a library and reading material in such institutions seems to have stemmed from this steady stream of free reading matter received from the federal government.[7]

AID TO VIRGINIA'S VETERANS

Until after the Civil War, veterans of American wars were primarily rewarded by grants of land rather than cash pensions. Just as it was more expedient for the federal government to grant land to the states for various purposes to be sold by them for cash rather than grant cash directly, so it was more convenient for the federal government and the states to grant land rather than cash rewards to veterans for their service. In great part this was true simply because land was plentiful and already belonged to the granting government, whereas cash was scarce and could

[5] New Hampshire, Trustees and Superintendent of the New Hampshire Asylum for the Insane, *Report*, 1846.

[6] *Ibid.*

[7] *Ibid.* See also the other annual reports at least to the end of the century.

only be raised by the unpolitic method of raising taxes. So long as farming or other primarily land-based pursuits provided a major means for individual advancement, this was an equitable solution to the problem of rewarding veterans. Although bureaucratic delays frequently decreased the usefulness of the grant, in theory and often enough in practice, a bounty grant provided even more than a cash pension would have, since it provided a source of livelihood for the recipient that could be made to last a lifetime.

At first those states of the original thirteen that had established claims to the western lands made grants to their soldiers directly. However, those states that did not have western land claims began to agitate for limitations on their more fortunate sisters even prior to the signing of the Declaration of Independence.[8] Four years later, in 1780, New York became the first state to surrender its claims. By 1790 (in the case of Georgia not legally until 1802) all the western lands were actually in the hands of the federal government.[9]

Virginia ceded its western lands to the Confederation Congress in 1784 after five years of negotiation, with the proviso that Congress would reserve a tract between the Scioto and Little Miami rivers in what later became Ohio and a small tract near Louisville in what is now

[8] The history of the demands for cession of the western lands is an interesting piece of evidence in the somewhat tangential but related question of the sovereignty of the states and the national government. It is one of several refutations of the argument advanced by the southern theory of American federalism that sovereignty passed from Great Britain to the individual states, which later ceded a limited part of it to a general government. The demands of a large minority of the states that the Continental Congress assume control over the western lands are good evidence in support of the opposing view that Great Britain and the American colonies had been in a rudimentary federal system prior to the break (or so they were viewed by a majority of the American revolutionists) and that those powers which had belonged to the king of England under the old system passed directly to the Continental Congress, thus creating the dual sovereignty legally inherent in the American federal system from the outset. Under this view, the federal government did not exist on sufferance of the states, but had its grant of sovereignty directly from the people, as did the states themselves. While the conception of the English colonial system may have been that of the Americans and not of the British, it was the one upon which the Americans legally based their revolutionary actions and subsequent constitutional movements, which is the important factor in judging the theory. For a further exposition of the entire question in a manner that covers most of the evidence and its ramifications most thoroughly, see Carl Becker, *The Declaration of Independence* (New York: Alfred A. Knopf, 1941), chap. iii.

[9] For a brief but comprehensive view of the western land cessions, see Richard B. Morris (ed.), *Encyclopedia of American History* (New York: Harper and Bros., 1953), pp. 417–19.

Kentucky as bounty lands for Virginia soldiers who had served in the Continental Army. In 1788, the Confederation Congress passed a law to that effect, which was confirmed and revised in 1790 by the first Congress under the Constitution.[10] That act provided for the reservation of federal lands north and west of the Ohio River to supplement state lands south and east of it to be granted as bounties to qualified veterans (under state law) of the Virginia Line. The actual procedures for granting bounties involved a series of interlocking co-operative activities on the part of the War Department, the State Department, the president, the Virginia executive council, and their respective agents.

The secretary of war was to determine how much land in the aggregate was due Virginia's veterans by listing all eligible persons and the lands due each in conformity with the state laws. This information was to be forwarded to the Virginia executive. State agents were then to locate the lands until the total had been reached. After the locations, surveys, and allotments had been made, the agents were to file records of the entire process, including the names of the grantees, with the secretary of state. The president would then cause patents to be issued to each grantee, or his heirs, with the endorsements of the secretaries of war and state to the effect that all legal conditions had been complied with. The secretary of state would then send the patents to the Virginia executive for distribution among the grantees.

The program established by the Act of 1790 lasted for over eighty years, finally ending in 1871 after years of legislation, litigation, and administrative co-operation. In Ohio, lands could be chosen from a reservation of 4,204,800 acres (6,570 square miles). In Indiana, 150,000 acres near the falls of the Ohio (now Louisville) had been set aside for veterans of George Rogers Clark's expedition to Illinois, all considered to be Virginians by virtue of their service in that Virginia-authorized campaign.

The secretary of war had to obtain a list of the Virginia veterans entitled to the grants in order to compile the official federal list. Every such veteran had received a certificate from the state as his official record of eligibility, which indicated how much land he was entitled to receive. In response to the secretary's request, the Virginia Land Office (a state agency) forwarded a copy of the register of certificates that had been issued to the War Department.

As it turned out, the register had not been maintained during some

[10] 1st Cong., 2nd Sess., chap. 40, August 10, 1790.

periods. A sizable number of men who held certificates were refused lands by the federal government because their names were not in the register, although they were listed in other records of the state land office. Each time a case like this arose, it necessitated a complete investigation by federal and state authorities to properly certify the individual applicant.

In 1800, Edward Carrington, United States marshal for the state of Virginia, former lieutenant colonel in the Continental artillery, and active participant in Virginia politics for many years, had occasion to contact the governor about such an applicant for a grant—one who was not on the state's list in Washington but was discovered on the lists in the state land office. In the process of adjusting this claim, he indicated that such omissions of names had impeded deserving applicants in obtaining their rightful grants while extended investigations were undertaken. To rectify this situation, he suggested that the governor should have a complete return made and sent to the War Department.[11] This suggestion was taken up, and Samuel Coleman, of the state land office, prepared and forwarded such a list to the War Department, to the great pleasure of the latter.[12]

After fifteen years of claim adjustment, Congress enacted a measure setting a time limit after which no bounty land claims in the reserved lands would be accepted (March 23, 1804) and sent a surveying party to mark off the boundary between the general public domain and the Virginia military lands. Virginia's agent at Chillicothe, Ohio, E. Landham, wrote to Governor William H. Cabell on behalf of the claimants, presenting the case against the new Congressional enactment. They felt that the time limit was too short. Once the warrant was issued, the claimant took it to the surveyor's office to have his parcel surveyed for entry. Many of the warrants were still in the surveyor's office waiting to be filled, and others had yet to be issued. The Virginians also believed that the new line being run to divide the bounty lands from the general public domain was encroaching on Virginia's allotment. They thought that it should be run by a joint federal-Virginia commission and paid for out of federal funds; Langham personally volunteered to serve on such a body. The state legislature, which had to accept the terms of the act of Congress before it went into effect, as in a grant-in-aid procedure, was

[11] *Calendar of Virginia State Papers,* IX, 103 (April 1, 1800).

[12] *Ibid.,* p. 117 (June 16, 1800).

urged to refrain from doing so until this modification had been obtained.[13]

In essence, this is what was done. The first of many Congressional attempts at setting a time limit was modified; and in 1811 acts of the General Assembly of Virginia and the United States Congress established a joint commission of three federal and two state members to re-examine the original line drawn by the federal surveyor in 1805. The joint commission met at Xenia, Ohio, on October 26, 1812, and proceeded to draw a line that provided for sufficient land to meet the then recognized claims.[14]

The establishment of this official boundary line created new problems. Some grantees had located their lands outside of the district set aside for that purpose. Secretary of War William Eustis wrote to Governor John Tyler in 1810 in an attempt to find a remedy for the situation that would be applicable in most cases. He suggested that the Governor instruct Colonel Anderson, the Virginia surveyor-general in charge of surveying the bounty lands (this was a Virginia-controlled operation on and for federal lands on behalf of the federal government), to add a clause to his survey authentications of such locations specifically stating that the lands were not to be considered as being outside the boundaries or as having been previously surveyed as United States lands. This would prevent inconvenience to the settlers and future litigation.[15]

After the running of the boundary line, the program settled down into routine administrative action, punctuated by periodic Congressional attempts to set a time limit on claims. Correspondence between the federal government and the state was channeled through the War Department and the governor's office. In 1833, the federal government published a list of Virginia veterans entitled to land who had not yet claimed it. At the request of interested parties in the state, the governor procured copies of the list. This led to a rash of claims from those who were mentioned and from those who were omitted. These claims were directed to the governor, who passed them on to Washington if they were justified by the state's records.[16]

As available land disappeared in the allotted areas, legitimate claimants had to be satisfied by other means. At first, the state tried to secure an additional Congressional grant of a bloc of land, as had been done

13 *Ibid.*, pp. 454–55 (October 30, 1805).

14 *Ibid.*, X, 180–82 (Abram Trigg, Virginia commissioner, to Governor James Barbour, January 12, 1813).

15 *Ibid.*, p. 95 (December 19, 1810). 16 *Ibid.*, pp. 593–618.

originally. This proved impractical, however, so an arrangement was made whereby legitimate Virginia land warrants could be exchanged for land scrip to be used in acquiring land elsewhere in the public domain. This device was utilized particularly in the settlement of claims to the Kentucky tract, which had been small at the outset and was soon exhausted.[17]

By 1852, Virginia had ceded its remaining claims in Ohio on the condition that all of its citizens who still held warrants would be granted land directly by the Secretary of the Interior. In carrying out this task, the secretary demanded detailed proof of the validity of the claim in each case, rejecting many of them. In 1855, Governor Joseph H. Johnson asked the General Assembly to join him in protesting to Congress and in applying the pressure of the state toward rectification of this situation.[18] This led to a new exchange of correspondence between the Governor and the secretary of the interior in an attempt to sort out the evidence and adjust conflicting claims, a process which was ended only by the Civil War.[19]

On February 18, 1871, Congress granted the as yet unsurveyed and unappropriated lands in the Virginia Military District to Ohio, giving each settler on those lands pre-emption rights to 160 acres. Ohio accepted this grant the next year and conveyed the lands to its land-grant college to supplement the Morrill Act lands. This ended the Virginia bounty land program—four years after the death of the last veteran of the Revolutionary War.

Meanwhile, one good claim had led to another. With the success of the bounty program in securing lands for Virginia veterans of the Continental Army, the idea was put forth that similar grants should be secured for Virginia state troops who had served during the war without ever entering the Continental service. Of course, this required Congressional action, so consultations were begun between the governor and Congressional delegation of the state to find a way to support such a request in Congress. After some discussion, the governor submitted a formal request to James Monroe, then secretary of state, in 1813. Monroe, in co-operation with the Virginia delegation, submitted the proposal to Congress, which was too busy with the War of 1812 to give it much

[17] Virginia, *Executive Papers,* January, 1835.

[18] Virginia House of Delegates, *Journal for the 1855–1856 Session,* Document 45.

[19] Virginia House of Delegates, *Journal for the 1855–1860 Session,* Document 1.

attention. The claim was renewed after the war on the grounds that the state owed its veterans land but had been unable to grant any to them after ceding its western territories. It was not until 1830 that Virginia succeeded in obtaining a Congressional enactment providing bounty lands for state troops.[20]

The administration of this new program increased the co-operative activity between the two governments. Virginia veterans with land warrants issued by the state had to exchange their state warrants for federal land scrip, which was issued and signed by the secretary of the treasury and countersigned by the commissioner of the General Land Office. If the original state warrant had been lost or destroyed, it had to be replaced by a certified copy from the state and then presented to the secretary of the treasury with an affidavit from the claimant to the effect that the original was truly lost. The state warrants had to be endorsed by the proper state officer to confirm that they had been granted under the terms of state laws in effect prior to the cession of 1784. Along with the warrant and state certification, the claimant had to furnish certificates from the register of the land office in Kentucky (a federal officer) and the surveyor of the military lands of the Virginia Line (a state officer), indicating that he had not located his claims in Kentucky. (This provision was probably added to the original act at the request of the Kentucky Congressional delegation.)

In addition to the procedures involving individual claimants, the commissioner of the General Land Office was required at the outset to obtain a complete list of all outstanding warrants covered by the act from the governor of Virginia. This list had to include the name of the recipient, the number of the warrant, the date of issue, and the number of acres granted. After providing the initial list, the governor was required to furnish a monthly statement covering any additional warrants issued. Since a significant number of warrants had not been issued during the time that there was no land available for their redemption, this promised to be a program of some magnitude.

Congress had provided that lands claimed under the warrant program were to be located in the open public domain in Ohio, Indiana, and Illinois. Though the act specified that claims had to be made by January 1, 1835, this part of the bounty land program benefited from the same extensions granted by the national legislature for its older counterpart.

---

[20] 21st Cong., 1st Sess., chap. 215, May 30, 1830.

All told, fourteen extensions of the time limit were made by Congress between 1807 and 1855.

Three important points stand out in any discussion of the Virginia military lands program. First, the lands in question were part of the federal public domain, not Virginia territory. Even the original military district was not set aside exclusively for Virginia bounty claims but only as much of it as would prove necessary. The earmarking of the area was to give Virginia claimants a prior right to file with the federal government, not a proprietary one. When the program reached the stage at which the federal government began to grant land scrip rather than land in the military district, there was no question about the federal ownership of the land claimed, since it was situated in various parts of the open public domain.

Second, the amount of land to which each claimant was entitled was determined entirely by the state under the terms of its laws, which had been formally approved and accepted by Congress when the program was initiated. Congressional legislation provided for federal enforcement of the grants after they were determined by the state.

Third, the acts of Congress contained specific provisions for the administration of the program, provisions that described—and bound—the actions of state officials from the governor on down. Included were provisions on surveying, filing, record-keeping, location of the land, and so forth. They were put into effect by the Treasury, War, and State Departments and the General Land Office; and they were followed.

Virginia was not the only state that participated in a bounty land program. At least half of the others also participated under provisions similar to the ones outlined above. Even New Hampshire, a state without western lands to claim and cede, took part. To satisfy Connecticut claims, the famous "Western Reserve" in Ohio was set aside by the federal government, just as was the Virginia Military District. The city of Cleveland is a scion of the federal-state program implemented there.

Part II

Co-operation and Expansion in the Maturing Republic

9

The Great Grant Programs and the Public Domain

OHIO SETS THE TONE

While intergovernmental co-operation in the states without public lands developed by fits and starts, dependent on specific negotiations between the parties involved in each case, co-operative federalism in the public-land states rested on the firm basis of the public domain. Federal land-grant policy actually preceded any other form of intergovernmental co-operation, having its origins prior to the adoption of the Constitution in the famous Northwest Ordinances of 1785 and 1787. That legislation pledged the federal government to grant one section of land in each township of the Northwest Territory for the support of common schools. When Ohio, the first of the states carved out of the Old Northwest, was admitted to the Union in 1802, a grant for this purpose was made. This initial grant not only set a precedent for Congressional authority to grant lands in subsequent cases, but also established the precedent that the grants were to involve co-operative action on the part of the federal and state governments.

The original grant was made by Congress directly to the townships concerned. Ohio, then a territory, could not quibble over this procedure, since it had secured the grant on the basis of a political compromise in the first place. In order to make the western lands attractive and induce buyers to purchase them, Albert Gallatin wanted to have public lands exempted from taxation temporarily after purchase. The school lands were granted to Ohio's townships to keep the state from suffering a major loss of revenue because of this exemption. Their sale and the funds that

131

would accrue to the several townships were to compensate for any tax losses. This compromise is particularly significant in that it shows that the land grants were not a gift from the federal government to Ohio, but "the result of a bargain in which the United States purchased from a state exemption of its lands from taxation for a term of years after they had been sold."[1]

The federal government had reserved four large tracts, similar to the Virginia military lands, within the boundaries of Ohio for national purposes prior to the settlement of the new state. After its admission to the Union, Ohio's consent was necessary in order to maintain these reservations. The new state grasped this opportunity to remedy what it conceived to be a grave defect in the original school land grant. In parts of the four reservations, the land grant was not operative. Accordingly, the state refused to ratify the necessary compact unless compensation for the excluded school lands was included. Congress responded by granting the state legislature the right to select lands in other parts of the state, where necessary, to equal one thirty-sixth of the reserved tracts.

Two major precedents were set by this action. The principle of indemnification was established, which lifted the land grant out of the category of a gift to a specific locality and made it a grant to the state as a whole. This refinement was written into the statute books along with the principle that federal grants would be made to the states, not to the localities. Partly because the lands were to be selected outside the townships whose schools they would help support and, more important, because the state legislature of Ohio wanted to control the distribution of the grant, a precedent was established that led to the channeling of all federal land grants for local purposes through the states.

This first land grant contained within it the seeds of the principles and procedures that evolved in later federal grants of land or cash. The legislation authorizing the grant applied a general law to a specific state. It was not a special grant for Ohio. The amount of the grant was set down in the general law and was uniform for all the states admitted to the Union while it was in effect. (When the amount was subsequently

---

[1] Mathias N. Orfield, *Federal Land Grants to the States with Special Reference to Minnesota* (Minneapolis: University of Minnesota Press, 1915). This monograph is among the most thorough published descriptions of the federal land-grant programs. While not particularly analytical, it does relate the grants to their political backgrounds. Orfield describes each program, its origins, and the changes in its structure over the years. For a more detailed description of the various programs that will be mentioned below, his work should be consulted.

increased, it was increased uniformly.)[2] Specific conditions as to the use of the grant were attached—in the case of Ohio, provisions for the creation of township or state-administered trust funds to be used exclusively to promote the common schools. These rudimentary first provisions were expanded in later grants as the need for their improvement was demonstrated.

The Ohio experience illustrates another facet of American federalism. The desire for statehood in newly settled territories was two-edged. It embodied a desire for local self-government and also a desire to secure better (i.e., more powerful formal) access to the national councils. Statehood has meant not only the right to elect local officials but the right to send representatives to Washington who could speak with the authority and power necessary to back up local desires and actions. In particular, statehood has been a means to obtain better access to the resources of the federal government, including grants-in-aid, which generally have not been fully available until statehood had been achieved.

THE PERVASIVENESS OF THE GRANTS

It would not be amiss to say that virtually every major governmental function in the public-land states benefited directly or indirectly from federal land grants. The grants directly stimulated, financed, or helped to finance all vital governmental operations. Indirectly, the pervasiveness of the public domain and the need for its proper disposition to enable a state to grow served to involve the state government, either formally or informally through the political process, in all federal land activities that took place within its boundaries. In this manner the public domain came to serve as the integrating factor in the development of co-operative action between the federal government and the states. This was also true in some measure in relation to the states without public lands, as indicated in the examples of the veterans' bounty lands and land-grant college programs that involved Virginia and New Hampshire.

Land-grant programs fell into three basic categories. First was the system of land grants made by the federal government to the various

[2] Five states and part of a sixth received one section per township. After 1849, the grant was increased to two sections, and after 1894, to four sections. In 1958, Alaska received the standard four sections per township for its common schools. Oklahoma, the only exception, received a Congressional grant of five million dollars in lieu of land, since its lands had already been settled or allotted to the Indian tribes by 1906.

states to aid them in developing education, internal improvements, and welfare programs. Over the years grants were made to the states for elementary education, higher education, general internal improvements, land reclamation, river and harbor improvements, public buildings, public institutions, and veterans' benefits. These were grants designed to make basic contributions to the growth of vital public services in the various states in a manner closely resembling the monetary grants-in-aid of the twentieth century.

There was also a system of federal land grants for education and internal improvements made through the states to private companies, primarily for roads, canals, and railroads, but also for academies and colleges. Under such arrangements, the states became the implementing agencies administering the distribution and proper use of the grants.

Finally, there were the federal programs designed to dispose of the public domain without formally including the states in their administration. These programs, in the main, consisted of the various homestead, mineral, and tree-culture acts; grants to certain western railroads situated primarily outside of state boundaries at the time of the grants; and some town-site and local improvement grants that generally were made to embryonic towns prior to statehood. Even those programs did not function outside of the sphere of federal-state co-operation.

THE INTERNAL IMPROVEMENT GRANTS

Typical of the evolution of the great land-grant programs were those that developed in the field of internal improvement. It has already been indicated how important internal improvements were to the successful development of the United States as a modern continental nation. As the line of settlement advanced across the continent, the problem was magnified. At the same time, new and better solutions appeared, ranging from roads to canals to what became the foremost among these in the nineteenth century, the railroads.

The financing and construction of the National Road through Ohio, Indiana, Illinois, and Missouri were the first major uses of revenues received from the sale of public lands for improvements in the field of transportation. The federal government arranged to do this by the device of advancing money to those four states from the Three Per Cent Fund.[3] Ini-

[3] This fund was a federal distribution to the public-land states from the annual proceeds of the sale of public lands within their boundaries to be used for internal

tially, only 2 per cent of the proceeds from land sales were granted. When it became apparent that this amount was not sufficient to maintain the needed rate of construction, Congress speeded the process by increasing the grant to 3 per cent and then "loaning" the money to the states until the loan could be repaid from future land-sale revenues. This system was maintained until the road was turned over to the states.[4]

Even earlier, some federal grants had been made to private individuals for the construction of specific roads. Such grants proved to be wasteful and unmanageable. Once state governments were established in the newly settled areas and were able to furnish the necessary governmental controls, the federal government ceased making large-scale grants directly to private individuals or corporations and turned to co-operation with the states.

The first of these co-operative arrangements involving land grants passed the Congress in 1823.[5] A grant of land was made to the state of Ohio to aid in the construction of a road to the border of the Michigan Territory. This grant was justified on the grounds of national security, under the war powers of Congress, much as John C. Calhoun had recommended in his report of 1819. Actually, its greatest value was as a means of connecting the then isolated settlements of the Michigan Territory with the settled parts of the country. In the debate in the House of Representatives, it was openly opposed by only one person, Cooke of Tennessee, who argued that if the Michigan settlers thought such a road was necessary, they should build it themselves. When the vote was taken, all those voting nay were from the states without public lands, who opposed the measure as discriminatory rather than unconstitutional.[6]

This grant set the pattern for many subsequent ones. It consisted of a right of way 120 feet wide plus a mile-wide strip of land on each side that was to be sold to raise money for actual construction of the road. Although the grant contained no provisions for revocation, the federal government included a provision that the land could not be sold for less than

---

improvements, particularly roads. The procedure was specified in the Congressional act making the grant and in the constitutions or legislative enactments of the recipient states (Orfield, *op. cit.*, p. 98). Today similar distributions are made from the proceeds of timber sales in the national forests.

[4] Subsequently, the Three Per Cent Fund was maintained to aid the states' internal improvement projects and was increased to 5 per cent in 1831. *Ibid.*, p. 78.

[5] *Ibid.*

[6] *Ibid.*, p. 92.

the minimum price of other lands in the public domain ($1.25 per acre) and that the road had to be completed in four years.[7]

Other land grants to the states for roads were made until the close of the Civil War. In many cases, construction of major roads was begun by the Army Engineers prior to statehood. These so-called military roads generally opened up new territories and contributed significantly to the creation of new states and their development after achieving statehood. When a territory achieved statehood, uncompleted roads would either be finished by the Army Engineers and then turned over to the state for maintenance or the entire project would be given to the state to complete under conditions similar to those current in other land-grant programs.[8]

In 1827, a grant of land was made to the state of Ohio for the construction of a road by the Columbus and Sandusky Turnpike Company. The land was granted to the state to be held in trust for the company until it completed the road. This was the first grant along the lines later used for railroad construction grants. It set the precedent for the use of co-operative procedures to supervise and regulate projects constructed by private companies and financed by federal land grants. It marked the introduction of the provision for lands to be granted in alternate sections along the right of way to enable the federal government to profit directly from the construction of the proposed road by having the value of the retained lands increase.[9] In addition to the military roads begun by the Army Engineers, thirteen land grants were made to the states for road construction. By 1911, a total of 3,047,428 acres had been patented to the states under the terms of these grants.[10]

[7] 4 Stat. 234 (1823).

[8] For a complete account of the role of the federal government in road construction west of the Mississippi River which summarizes the programs referred to above, see W. Turrentine Jackson, *Wagon Roads West* (Berkeley: University of California Press, 1956). Though military roads were as extensive and probably even more significant east of the Mississippi, no comparable study has come to the writer's attention. (Forest G. Hill's *Roads, Rails and Waterways* [Norman, Okla.: University of Oklahoma Press, 1957] does contain a discussion of road building within the context of a larger study of the role of the U.S. Army Corps of Engineers in internal improvement before the Civil War.) U.S. 18 in Wisconsin, U.S. 41 in Illinois, Wisconsin, and Michigan, U.S. 112 in Michigan, and U.S. 68 in Kentucky are only a few examples of present highways that were first constructed as military roads under this nineteenth-century program.

[9] 4 Stat. 242 (1827).

[10] U.S. Department of the Interior, *Annual Report of the Commissioner, General Land Office*, 1911.

Canal construction programs were the next beneficiaries of this type of land grant. Between 1827 and 1866, ten land grants were made for canal construction, all to Mississippi Valley states. A typical example of a canal grant was that made to Illinois in 1822 for a canal to connect the Illinois River with Lake Michigan, thus linking the Mississippi River system with the Great Lakes. Ninety feet on each side of the proposed canal was reserved for the right of way.[11] In 1827 this grant was increased to include alternate sections along the right of way that were to be sold to obtain funds for construction of the canal.[12] In addition, the state was authorized to use materials on the adjacent public lands for construction purposes. In return for these benefits, Illinois was required to survey the route and transmit a map of the survey to the secretary of the treasury within three years, complete the canal within twelve years, and agree never to use the land for other than canal purposes. The penalty that could be invoked for not fulfilling these requirements was forfeiture of the grant. Another precedent-establishing provision was the requirement that, after its completion, the canal be open for free passage of federal troops and property.[13]

Debate on these measures in Congress dwelt primarily on the ques-

[11] 3 Stat. 659 (1827).

[12] 4 Stat. 234 (1827). This grant was quite possibly one of the most significant acts of government in nineteenth-century America. It resulted in the linkage of the two major inland water systems of the North American continent. This linkage has not only been maintained through the years but has been extensively enlarged. It set precedents and indicated pitfalls to be avoided in later grants for construction of the major part of the American railroad system. One of the provisions of the Act of 1827 was that town sites were to be set aside from among the lands granted and platted as termini at either end of the canal. The eastern terminus was so reserved and platted by the canal surveyors and, shortly thereafter, incorporated as a town. The new town, named Chicago, included the designated canal lands, a section from a school land grant, and part of the Fort Dearborn military reservation donated for the purpose. With its location at the point where the Great Lakes and the Mississippi River were linked, and with the addition of the Illinois Central Railroad by virtue of a subsequent land grant, it was soon on its way to becoming the second largest city in the United States. The school lands are now the heart of the city's financial district. Unfortunately, local pressures secured their immediate sale at a fraction of their potential value. The military lands were donated by the federal government on condition that they be used only as a public park or commons. They are now part of Grant Park and Michigan Boulevard, kept free from buildings as a result of the conditions imposed by the federal grant and confirmed by the Illinois Supreme Court.

[13] There are several histories of the Illinois and Michigan Canal, among them James W. Putnam's *The Illinois and Michigan Canal* (Chicago: University of Chicago Press, 1918). A total of 4,597,805.37 acres was granted to the states for canal construction.

tion of whether such grants gave unfair advantage to the public-land states, all in the West, to the disadvantage of the rest of the Union. For example, Senator Smith of South Carolina argued long and forcefully that such grants were prejudicial to the interests of the eastern states since they favored one section of the country over the others. It was only as a footnote to his argument that he publicly expressed concern that continued grants would "constitutionalize" actions which he considered to be basically unconstitutional.[14]

A similar form of Congressional land grant to the states was inaugurated in 1828 for improvement of navigation on various rivers. Supervision and control of commerce on navigable rivers were specifically placed under federal jurisdiction in the Constitution; and in most cases, river improvements were undertaken by the Army Engineers. Nevertheless, large-scale improvements were frequently made by the states under co-operative arrangements. This land-grant program is illustrative of the by no means rare example of movement in the other direction, in which programs allotted in the Constitution to the federal government are transformed into co-operative ones that are shared by the other levels of government. One important new feature emerged from this program. In a grant to Wisconsin for the improvement of the Fox and Wisconsin rivers in 1846, restrictions on the scheduling of the land sales were imposed. Only enough land could be sold at the outset to raise $20,000 for initial costs of construction. After the governor of the state certified that $10,000 of the initial amount had been properly expended under the conditions of the grant, enough additional land to raise another $10,000 would be released by the General Land Office to the state for sale. This series of steps would be repeated until completion of the project. This condition was imposed to prevent the waste of lands and funds that had sometimes occurred in previous projects. With variations, it became standard in later land grants and led to very close and complex administrative relationships between the federal government and the state involved.[15]

In 1841, Congress passed a general measure authorizing the future appropriation of five hundred thousand acres of land to each public-land state for internal improvements not necessarily of a national character. The act granted the acreage to already admitted states, and subsequent enabling acts continued to grant a similar bounty to each new state. The state legislatures were assigned the duty of selecting the lands within the

[14] Orfield, op. cit., p. 94.   [15] Ibid., pp. 97–98.

boundaries of their respective states. Subsequently five states asked for, and received, permission from Congress to use their grants for education rather than for internal improvements. Since the initial grant included a strict forfeiture provision limiting its use to the specified purpose, it was necessary to secure an act of Congress to divert it to other uses.[16] This program is particularly significant because it was the first major internal improvement grant for projects not ostensibly of an interstate character. (Virtually all previous and subsequent grants were to further projects either interstate in themselves or linked to similar works in other states.) This grant could be used for county and township roads and bridges if the state so desired. In many cases it was so used.

While the land-grant system was developing, new forms of transportation were emerging. Chief among them was the railroad, which, in conjunction with the growing land-grant system, soon came to dominate the American transportation scene, provided the strongest links between the various sections of the United States, and contributed greatly to the conquest of the land frontier.

Congress was not slow to perceive the potential significance of railroad operations in the nation's development. As early as 1825, the House of Representatives had its Committee on Roads and Canals investigate the utility of railroads and compare the costs of railroad and canal construction.[17] The first practical results of these investigations came in 1830, when Ohio was authorized to divert an 1828 canal grant for use in the construction of a railroad between Dayton and Lake Erie. In 1833 Illinois was given the option to do the same with its canal grant of 1827, thus providing for either a canal or a railroad to connect the Illinois River and Lake Michigan.[18]

Beginning in 1834, land was granted to railroads for rights of way on federal property at Harpers Ferry, Virginia, in Florida, and in Alabama. These grants were based on conditions virtually identical with those set down in grants for rights of way for canals. Such right-of-way land grants soon became widespread and were made to both railroad and turnpike companies. As with earlier grants, federal-state co-operation was required. Since the lands were often parts of federal reservations, not public lands for sale, they were often granted directly to the companies involved. Even such lands could be granted only after the legislatures of

<hr>

[16] *Ibid.*, p. 102. [17] *Ibid.*, p. 102.

[18] *Ibid.*, p. 103.

the states concerned had authorized construction of the roads and chartered the companies.[19]

In 1852 a general law was enacted by Congress that granted a right of way one hundred feet wide (two hundred feet where necessary because of construction problems) to all railroad and macadamized and plank road companies then chartered, or that would be chartered by the states within ten years from the passage of the act, subject to the provisions cited above. The companies were further authorized to make use of any materials necessary for the construction of the roads that were found on public lands adjacent to the rights of way. Additional plots of land, not less than ten miles apart, were granted for stations and water towers along the routes of the railroads. Aside from the need for authorization from the states, the companies had to submit maps of the roads to the commissioner of the General Land Office. The roads had to be started within ten years and completed within fifteen years of the passage of the act. If a project were discontinued, the land reverted to the federal government.[20]

This form of land grant has had a long history. The 1852 act was extended for five years in 1862 and modified by an act of 1875 that increased the amount of land in each grant. The last revision remained valid well into the twentieth century with provisions and conditions basically the same as those of the original act.[21]

Between 1830 and 1850, no true railroad land grants were enacted. While several passed the Senate, the House of Representatives rejected them all. This seems to have been due to the fact that the House, with its representation based on population, was controlled by eastern interests that still opposed such grants, while the Senate, where the new states had come to form a majority, was more liberal in dispensing the public domain in line with the sectional interests of the West.

In 1850 a grant was made to the states of Illinois, Alabama, and Mississippi, of every even-numbered section of land, six sections in width, on both sides of the right of way for a railroad that was to extend from Chicago to the Gulf of Mexico.[22] Other provisions in the act were modeled after those of previous grants. A one-hundred-foot-wide right of way was included, as in canal grants. Construction was to commence at both ends of the proposed line simultaneously, as in a river improvement

19 *Ibid.*, p. 104.   20 *Ibid.*   21 *Ibid.*

22 Kentucky and Tennessee did not receive grants because they had no public lands within their borders.

grant made to Alabama in 1827. The lands could be sold only as construction progressed, as in the grant to Wisconsin for improvement of the Fox and Wisconsin rivers in 1846. The alternate sections remaining in the possession of the federal government could not be sold for less than double the minimum price, a standard feature of all grants after 1828. The usual provision for free transportation of federal troops and property was included. The railroad had to be completed within ten years or the unsold lands would revert to the federal government, as in the canal grants, and the state would also have to pay the federal government for any lands that had been sold. Two new provisions were added. The first provided for the selection of indemnity lands within fifteen miles on either side of the route in case any of the original sections had already been sold. The second provided for mail to be carried at a price set by Congress. All of these conditions were definite obligations that were assumed by the individual state legislatures and the railroads as part of their acceptance of the grant itself.[23]

In Congress the vote was by state and sectional, rather than party or ideological, lines. The congressmen from the public-land states, north and south, supported the grant, while those from states with no public lands generally were in the opposition. In the Senate, a total of forty votes was cast, twenty-six for the measure and fourteen opposed. Twenty senators were from the western states, and eighteen of the twenty voted for the measure. Of the twenty from states without public lands, twelve were opposed to the grant and eight approved.[24]

Fairly strong opposition to railroad grants continued to exist until 1856, though several grants were made during the interim. After 1856, grants for railroads were made recklessly for over a decade. Public opinion supported the grant programs so overwhelmingly that Congress did not care to resist the trend. Land grants for railroads were conceived to be so much in the national interest that even the states'-rights Democrats found a rationalization in order to support them; they explained that the grants were made by the federal government in its role as landowner rather than as sovereign.[25]

Opponents of the land grants turned once more to the two arguments

[23] Orfield, *op. cit.*, pp. 104–5.

[24] *Ibid.*, p. 105. For other voting statistics on similar grants, see John B. Sanborn, *Congressional Grants of Land in Aid of Railways* (Madison: University of Wisconsin, 1899), pp. 19–61.

[25] *Ibid.*, p. 14.

of discrimination and unconstitutionality. Senator Niles of Connecticut summed up the position of his side in the following words: "To say that we can get around the Constitution by granting the public lands, instead of taking the money directly out of the treasury, is certainly trifling with the judgment of this body."[26] As a statement of fact, as well as from his point of view, he was quite right in stating that there was no real difference between land and money grants. An overwhelming majority of the American people, however, seemed to feel that it was constitutional enough. Proponents of the grants defended their program against the charges of sectional favoritism by pointing out that the supposed advantages of the West were offset by the appropriations for forts and custom-houses built in the eastern states. John C. Calhoun argued that by increasing the value of the surrounding lands, such grants would increase the revenue flowing into the federal Treasury. Calhoun was a consistent supporter of such grants even as late as 1848.[27]

There were many constitutional rationalizations created to enable the strict constructionists who wanted land grants to justify their position. As Sanborn says in his study of the political origins of the railroad land-grant program (published in the days of supposed dual federalism, 1899), "The true basis of the land grants was national benefit, but to take this ground required an extension of the 'general welfare' clause which few at that time were willing to make."[28]

By the late 1860's, public sentiment began to question the policy of granting lands for railroad construction. For one thing, so many railroads had already been provided for; for another, the abuses of many of the companies had become apparent and were raised as questions of political concern. In 1867 California received the last railroad grant made to a state, and in 1871 the last corporation grant was made to the Texas Pacific Railroad.[29] However, under the terms of those grants already made, the railroads were able to claim lands as late as 1943, when a final settlement was made whereby the companies relinquished all their remaining claims in return for an adjustment in the rates of payment for transporting federal troops and property.

[26] *Congressional Globe*, 30th Cong., 1st Sess. (1817), App. 535 (quoted in Sanborn, p. 27).

[27] Sanborn, *op. cit.*, pp. 27–28.

[28] *Ibid.*, pp. 28–29.

[29] *Ibid.*, p. 106.

LAND GRANTS AS GRANTS-IN-AID

Were the land grants true predecessors of the monetary grants-in-aid of the twentieth century? The inescapable conclusion is that they were. Why was land granted in place of money? Land was plentiful and money was not. Also, the federal government was trying to dispose of its great landholdings in a manner best calculated to advance settlement and internal development. When many of the grant programs were first discussed in Congress, both money grants and land grants were advocated. At the same time, strict constructionists objected to federal grants in any form. In the process of political give and take, the congressmen favoring federal grants discovered that a number of their strict-constructionist colleagues, who recognized the utility of federal aid, would not object to land grants. Everyone wanted to see the then vast public domain put to use, and land grants could be rationalized as gifts by the federal government in its capacity as property owner rather than grants made in its governmental capacity. Since the land could be sold and funds thereby obtained, this legal fiction did not bother the nationalists, who readily accepted it in return for the votes necessary to enact the grant-in-aid programs. This was a reasonable compromise that avoided serious political conflict, yet provided federal aid. As such, it was in the great American political tradition of compromising to avoid a head-on clash of beliefs whenever possible, an eminently good reason to accept the land grants in place of cash.

No serious effort was made to change this policy until the supply of readily salable land was exhausted toward the close of the nineteenth century. At that time, the issue was reopened, and in a surprisingly short time cash grants became common. In 1890, the United States Census Bureau declared the land frontier to be closed. Four years earlier, the first modern cash-grant program had been initiated. The transition had been made as the need arose. Despite this, the myth that the earlier land grants were gifts persisted and served to cloud the true nature of the land-grant programs.

About midway through the nineteenth century, the states of the West, as the new majority in the Union, began to set the governmental pattern nationally. The land-grant programs then became the dominant form of intergovernmental co-operation, though many had come into being years before. Just as joint investment programs had set the tone of federalism in the early Republic, after 1850 federal-state co-operation, even in the states without public lands, was shaped by the great grant programs.

10

Developing Partnership in Railroad Construction

THE IMPORTANCE OF THE RAILROADS

A dramatic illustration of the role of the railroads in the development of most of the states west of the Great Lakes was the closing of Minnesota's land frontier by the construction of a railroad in 1907. The extension of the railroads in Minnesota opened up the prairie for settlement and the forests for exploitation. The building of the railroad enabled Minnesota's settler-farmers to transport their produce to markets and the pioneers of the iron ranges to transport their ore to refineries. Before the advent of the internal combustion engine, the railroad served as the lifeline of the new society, usable in virtually all types of weather and feasible in terms of cost. It was not a luxury to be acquired after the land was settled and the settlers established, but a vital necessity that in many cases preceded settlement and made it possible. No one knew this better than the settlers and prospective settlers themselves.[1]

In his first message to the territorial legislature on January 11, 1854, Governor Gorman reflected his constituents' community-wide concern for the construction of railroads:

To get out from here, during the winter . . . is far above and beyond any other consideration to the people of Minnesota. To accomplish this, in my judgment, you must concentrate all the energies of the people to one or two rail roads.[2]

[1] For an excellent history of nineteenth-century Minnesota, see William Watts Folwell, A History of Minnesota (St. Paul: Minnesota Historical Society, 1921–30), in four volumes. He discusses the politics of railroad land grants in some detail.

[2] Folwell, op. cit., I, 329.

144

Action to obtain railroads meant essentially one thing to the people on the Minnesota frontier, just as it did to the people in every new western state—federal aid in the form of land grants. Their goal was to obtain grants of land from the national government in sufficient quantity to finance construction and to attract potential investors by encouraging their desire to profit by selling the lands. To achieve that end, memorials were passed by the legislature, representatives were sent to Washington to press for aid, and, in co-operation with prospective investors, considerable lobbying was carried on. After some years, this activity was successful, and lands were made available to Minnesota for the construction of railroads within its borders. The railroad land-grant program that resulted spanned almost the entire period of federal grants for railroad construction. From an initial grant in 1854, while Minnesota was still a territory, through 1866, when the final grants to the state were made, and up to 1935, Minnesota received 8,315,327.92 acres from the federal government for railroad construction.[3] For many years supervising railroad construction was a major activity of the state government.

AN ABORTIVE GRANT AND THE SUPREME COURT

Minnesota's first attempt to secure a federal land grant served only to give the United States Supreme Court an opportunity to reaffirm the principle that Congressional land grants were not gifts but conditional grants of the federal government. When the citizens of Minnesota saw the enactment of the Illinois Central grant in 1850, their hopes were raised for similar aid to be granted to their own territory. Their major doubt was whether Congress could be persuaded to grant lands for that purpose to a territory, since all previous grants had been to states. With usual frontier directness, they determined to make the test and in 1853 chartered five railroad companies through the territorial legislature, while at the same time requesting Congress to make the necessary grants for construction. While this was being done, the leading citizens of the territory were negotiating for backing from eastern capitalists. They were successful in interesting several, since the potential for development in Minnesota was becoming apparent in the East.

The year 1854 opened with such promise that the legislature chartered two more railroads. Everything seemed to be running smoothly in St.

[3] Minnesota State Auditor, *Biennial Report, 1935–36* (St. Paul, 1937), p. 48.

Paul; no one openly opposed federal aid, and the citizens of the territory certainly gave no public indication of feeling that they were about to sell their rights. However, in Washington the idea of railroad land grants was still new enough to require more than frontier exuberance to bring about the enactment of the necessary statutes.

Henry Rice, delegate to Congress from the Minnesota Territory, petitioned that body on February 6, 1854, calling for a grant to build a railroad from Lake Superior through St. Paul that would connect with the Illinois Central, thereby spanning the width of the continent while simultaneously connecting Minnesota with the outside world. His petition coincided with action already being taken, and a land-grant bill submitted by Senator Shields of Illinois passed the Senate "without debate or division" on February 7, 1854.[4]

The Senate bill was sent to the House and on March 7 was taken up by the committee of the whole. Greater representation from the eastern seaboard in the House made the bill's passage more difficult. The opposition centered primarily around the question of the potential corporate gain such a grant would bring to a few favored individuals who controlled the recently chartered railroad companies—an unfair contribution to the gain of a few by the representatives of the many. To save the day, the congressmen from the public-land states submitted a compromise measure. In order to avoid favoring any existing corporations, whose backers were suspected of having an untoward interest in the pending legislation, the substitute bill granted the land to any *future* territorial legislature to grant only to corporations not then chartered. This new bill passed the House on June 20, received quick Senate approval, and was signed into law by President Pierce on June 29, 1854. One million acres of land, to be selected along a right of way extending from the northern border of Iowa to Lake Superior, were included in this grant, subject to the usual conditions.[5]

At this point, when victory seemed won, it was discovered that the bill had been engrossed with two basic alterations in the text that changed its entire meaning. The alterations enabled the bill to be construed as allowing the territorial legislature to grant the land to a company that had been chartered but not yet formally organized. It soon became clear that this was not an accident. While the bill had been debated in Congress, a

[4] Folwell, *op. cit.*, I, 332.

[5] Theodore Christianson, *History of Minnesota* (New York: American Historical Society, 1935), p. 261.

new corporation, named the Minnesota and Northwestern Railroad Company, had been chartered by the territorial legislature to build a road along the general route specified by Congress in the act granting land. When the corporation pushed its claim to the newly granted lands, cries of protest were raised in the national legislature. A select committee of investigation was established to determine the origins and purposes of the textual change.

The select committee soon determined that Congressman Stevens of Michigan, who had delivered the bill for engrossment, had been persuaded by "gentlemen interested" to change the wording and had done so with the approval of the chief clerk of the House, evidently quite innocently believing that it was only a matter of clarification. A short investigation of this incident served to point up the presence of skulduggery, but the "gentlemen interested" were never located and forced to explain their actions. The altered bill was repealed, but no replacement was enacted. Not until the territory reached the verge of statehood could Minnesotans again muster enough support to receive the help they needed to construct railroads.

Minnesota was bitterly disappointed. The territorial legislature convened on January 3, 1855, and in his message, Governor Gorman expressed the hope that Congress would reconsider and not punish the entire territory for the attempted peculations of a small group. The Minnesota and Northwestern Railroad Company brought suit in the courts, claiming that, once granted, the land was out of Congressional hands and that any attempt at repeal was unconstitutional. After several years of litigation, the case was carried to the United States Supreme Court on a writ of error. In January, 1862, the Court ruled in a four to two decision that

the Act of Congress of June 29, 1854 did not vest the territory with ownership but devolved upon it "a mere naked trust or power to dispose of the lands" for a purpose and under conditions. Congress had the right to rescind the trust and withdraw the power. The repealing act of August 4 was therefore "a valid law."[6]

In this decision the Court affirmed that land grants were not gifts and that conditions and controls imposed by the Congress were valid and enforceable. This decision was not the first one that indicated Supreme

[6] *Rice* v. *Railroad Company*, 1 Black 381 (1862), as quoted in Folwell, *op. cit.*, I, 350.

Court recognition of intergovernmental co-operation via land-grant programs, but it is a landmark as one of the most explicit.[7]

THE GRANTS AND THEIR CONDITIONS

When Minnesota applied for admission to the Union in 1857, her citizens felt that the time was ripe to renew their request for railroad land
grants for their state-to-be. By that year, an optimistic legislature had
chartered fifteen railroads, presenting a multiple confusion of companies
for Congress to choose from. In order to present a more coherent plan to
Congress (and, incidentally, to assure themselves dominant positions in
the coming railroad boom), four of these companies united under Edmund D. Rice (brother of the Minnesota delegate to Congress) to pro-
pose a railroad system that would cover the whole state, dividing the
territory among themselves.[8]

With sympathy built up because of the sad circumstances that surrounded the loss of the 1854 grant, Congress quickly moved to remedy
Minnesota's situation.[9] On March 3, 1857, a generous grant of land was
made by that body to Minnesota in conjunction with a grant to Alabama
for the same purpose. The "big four" had presented their plan to Congress and had lobbied for it so successfully that it was incorporated in its
entirety into the act granting the land. This was somewhat of a departure from precedent. Normally Congress granted the lands to the state
legislature, to dispose of as it saw fit. Here the routes were assigned by
Congress first, leaving little discretion to the legislature. This was possible in good measure because the territorial and state officials were sup-

[7] For further evidence of Supreme Court support, see Daniel J. Elazar, "Federal-
State Cooperation as Reflected through Supreme Court Decisions, 1851–1858" (research
paper prepared for the Department of Political Science, University of Chicago, February, 1957).

[8] The four railroads, with the sections assigned them, were (1) Minnesota and
Pacific Railroad, the central and northwestern parts of the state; (2) Minneapolis and
Cedar Valley Railroad, a line due south from Minneapolis; (3) Transit Railroad, a
line west from Winona; and (4) Root River and Southern Minnesota Railroad, southwest from St. Paul.

[9] Folwell states that although there was little or no opposition to the bill on its
merits, $200,000 worth of bonds of the St. Paul and Pacific Railroad (Minnesota and
Pacific) had to be promised to thirty members of the House of Representatives to
guarantee their support. After the measure was passed, the custodian of the bonds
disappeared, and none were ever delivered (Folwell, op cit., II, 38 n.).

porters of the plan. The compromise had been made prior to the passage of the legislation, and the state had no reason to feel constricted by this step. All parties seem to have been satisfied. This successful maneuver virtually assured the participating railroads of a share in the division of a land grant of four million acres—provided they could construct the lines under the conditions laid down under the acts of Congress and the Minnesota legislature.

By the Act of March 3, 1857, Congress made the territory and future state of Minnesota[10] the agent of the federal government for the purposes of implementing the provisions of the land grant in the same way that the states were constituted as agents of the federal government for almost all of the land-grant programs. The provisions of the act set forth definite terms and conditions that had to be fulfilled for the grant to be legally obtained.

First, the act specified the routes of the railroad lines in the state. The governor was named responsible for the selection of the lands and was instructed to send agents to select them. Any agents appointed and lands chosen by them were subject to the approval of the secretary of the interior before the lands could be patented to the state. The act further directed the order in which the lands were to be selected (in groups of sections) and the areas of their selection (every alternate section for six miles on each side of the right of way), with the provision that indemnity lands could be chosen within fifteen miles on either side in place of original choices already pre-empted or otherwise unavailable.

Congress also prohibited the disposal of the land other than as directed, that is, in groups of sections as the work progressed. All lands that had previously been granted to the state for education or internal improvement were reserved and exempted from this grant, except in so far as they conflicted with the right of way of any of the railroads. In that case, their relinquishment and replacement (for regranting to the railroad concerned) could be effected with the approval of the President of the United States.

The price of the lands in the alternate sections retained by the federal government had to be at least double the minimum price currently asked for public lands in order to protect the railroads receiving the grant and to enable them to secure a decent price for the lands they received. Actual disposal of the lands was vested in the legislature, with the condition that the lands be disposed of for the purpose of the act and for no

[10] Admitted to the Union on May 11, 1858.

other. It was also specified that the railroads constructed under this act would be public highways for the free use of the federal government to transport its troops and property and carry the United States mails at rates set by Congress.

The act set forth the methods and conditions required for disposal of the lands by the legislature. For every twenty continuous miles of railroad track constructed, upon certification of the work by the governor to the secretary of the interior, a company would receive 120 sections of land. An initial 120 sections were to be granted upon location of the first twenty miles of road, subject to the same process of certification, to facilitate construction in its early stages. If the roads were not completed in ten years, all land sales were to be stopped and unsold lands were to revert to the federal government.[11]

In order to take advantage of the grant, the state legislature had to enact appropriate enabling legislation that would accept the conditions imposed by Congress and make provisions for implementing them. In a special session called to pass enabling legislation for Minnesota's impending statehood, the legislature enacted measures[12]

to execute the trust created by an Act of Congress entitled "An Act making a grant of land to the territory of Minnesota . . . to aid in the construction of certain railroads in said territory . . ." and granting certain lands to railroad companies therein named.

The act contained three chapters, each granting lands to specific railroad companies along specified routes with specified junction points. In addition, each chapter granted the power of eminent domain to the railroad, subject to state review, for use in acquiring a right of way. The act specified the capitalization, method of selling stock, amount of interest to be paid, and the nature of the dividends to be earned. It provided for the mode of election and the responsibilities of the board of directors of each railroad company and actually specified the members of the first boards. The powers of the board to manage the company and to set rates were qualified by certain obligations to the general public. The act specified the width and type of track to be used, the rules governing railroad crossings, and regulations for bridges and signals. The board had discretion in the choice of equipment and rolling stock. In general, the method of

[11] Stat. 195–97 (1857).

[12] Minnesota, *Session Laws of the Territory of Minnesota*, Extra Session, 1857, pp. 3–26.

organization and financing of each company was set forth in considerable detail. A timetable for construction had to be met based on initial goals for each company for the first two-year period and then thirty miles per year for ten years, or until the road was completed; the timetable restated the conditions in the act of Congress almost verbatim and then elaborated on them. Construction engineers of the railroads were required to report to the governor on the location of routes as the right of way was located. Agents of the state, under the supervision of the governor, were to inspect construction as it progressed. The responsibilities of the railroads to the federal government were also made binding in state law. The granted lands were exempted from taxation until they were sold, and the companies were required to pay 3 per cent of their gross earnings in lieu of taxes, with specified procedures for reporting their earnings.

The act also included a number of safety provisions to safeguard the public interest. Each railroad was confirmed in its right to construct a telegraph line along its right of way, as provided by Congress. Any future consolidation with a non-Minnesota railroad company required the approval of the state legislature.

Like the act of Congress that stimulated this statute, the state legislation specifically provided for intergovernmental co-operation on the administrative level in supervising the construction of the railroads. Indeed, this was the case in all such grants. These administrative interrelations were specified in some detail, though much of their realization was left to the discretion of the Department of the Interior and the governor. The railroad companies were required to accept these conditions within ten days after passage of the act, just as the state legislature was required to formally accept the Congressional act, and they did so in most cases with the same alacrity.[13]

INITIAL PROBLEMS OF CONSTRUCTION

All this legislation could not solve the basic problem of raising sufficient capital to begin actual construction of the planned railroads. Minnesota suffered, as did the rest of the nation, from the effects of the Panic of 1857. The resulting depression put a temporary end to virtually all land sales. There was just no available cash on the frontier. The construc-

[13] For a list of the railroads' acceptances and dates, see Minnesota, *Executive Documents,* 1879, p. 17.

tion of railroads into as yet unsettled territory would have been a speculation under the best conditions. In the midst of a depression, it became
too great a risk. The railroad companies could not even raise the capital
necessary to survey and locate the twenty miles of right of way that
would have entitled them to claim 120 sections in advance of construction.

In order to break the impasse, it was suggested that Minnesota should
follow the example of the federal government and other states and provide some immediate aid for railroad construction.[14] Proponents of this
scheme found the major barriers to its implementation to be in the state
constitution, which prohibited the legislature from contracting a debt in
excess of $250,000 and forbade the giving or loaning of the credit of the
state "in aid of any individual, association or corporation."[15]

The ingenious minds of the railroad promoters soon developed what
seemed to be a sound method of bypassing the restrictive clauses. With
the aid of a good deal of connivance on the part of the railroad interests,
a measure speedily passed the legislature in March, 1858, submitting a
constitutional amendment to the voters. The amendment retained the
original clause but provided that up to $5,000,000 in special bonds, bear-
ing 7 per cent interest to be paid semi-annually, could be issued as a loan
of public credit to the four railroads to enable them to begin construction.[16] Despite more vocal opposition than had been met in the legislature, the amendment passed by an overwhelming majority on May 6,
1858.[17]

In emulation of the federal government, the governor was to issue
bonds in lots of $100,000 only in return for work completed—after the
preparation of ten miles of roadbed and, subsequently, upon the comple-

[14] The idea that state aid would be in emulation of the federal government was
expressed by the people involved in the project at the time; see "Report of the Select
Committee on the Five Million Loan Bill," in Minnesota, Senate Journal, 1858, pp.
172–79. Folwell also cites such suggestions in the series of pamphlets written in behalf
of the loan (Folwell, op. cit., II, 44 n.).

[15] Minnesota, Constitution (1857), Art. 9, secs. 5 and 10.

[16] Corruption has been charged but never proved. Folwell maintains that the legislators were so eager to have railroads that they would have been seduced by any
halfway plausible scheme and that bribery was unnecessary (Folwell, op. cit., II, 46).
I would tend to agree with this. A later generation was only too ready to treat any
misfeasance in railroad construction as a product of corruption, not realizing the in-
tense desire and need for railroads at the time.

[17] For a full description of the loan, see Folwell, op. cit., II, 44–50. The vote was:
yeas, 25,023; nays, 6,733.

tion of each ten miles of track. Presumably the state was lending its name only, since the companies had to agree to pay for the bonds as the interest and principle came due. The railroads were required to set aside their net profits for payment of the interest and to return the first 240 sections of granted land to the state. The governor was to sell these lands and use the proceeds to establish a special fund to meet payments of either principal or interest if necessary. As an additional guarantee for the state, the companies had to exchange an equivalent amount of their own first mortgage bonds for any bonds obtained from the governor. The railroads quickly accepted these conditions, and by midsummer, contracts had been awarded and some actual work begun.

ADMINISTRATIVE PROCEDURES

Meanwhile, activity had been initiated on the administrative level to supervise the land grant and its transfer to the railroad companies. From the very first, the railroad companies tried to exert pressure on the governor to obtain lands prior to meeting the statutory conditions. Early in 1858, the first governor of the state, Henry Hasting Sibley, had to answer the presidents of two of the railroad companies on this issue. He refused their request by quoting copiously from the act of Congress setting down the rules for land transfers, thus showing the gentlemen that his instructions were clear and that such a transfer would be impossible. Nor was this the only request of this nature.[18]

At the same time, lands were being selected from the areas specified in the land grant. This selection was made by the governor through his agents for the companies. Lands were opened for selection after first being surveyed by the staff of the United States surveyor-general for the state of Minnesota, a federal official assigned to each of the public-land states and territories.[19] Once the survey was completed, an agent of the state would examine the lands and choose the sections most desirable for his purposes.[20] Then he would send a list of recommended sections to the

[18] Minnesota State Archives, Governors' Archives, file 57.

[19] The surveyor-general was a federal official who had very close political and administrative connections with the state government, usually being a politically influential citizen of the state in which he served who had been appointed through the patronage of the party in power.

[20] By the act of Congress, alternate sections along the right of way were automatically reserved for the roads within the area set by law. However, these sections had

governor, who would transmit duplicate copies of the list to the register of the local United States land office in the district from which the lands were selected.[21] The register would keep one of the copies and would reserve the lands listed therein if they had not been previously claimed, selected, or otherwise reserved.[22] He would send the second copy to the General Land Office in the Department of the Interior. In Washington, the lands would be approved for selection and the local United States land office would be notified that they were to be held for the state. The General Land Office would also notify the governor, who, in compliance with the terms of the act of Congress, would file claim to the lands with the same local land office, paying the proper filing fees. As soon as the General Land Office was apprised of this by the local land office and as soon as the governor's certification was in their hands, the land would be patented to the state for the railroad concerned. The state could then turn the lands over to the railroad.[23]

At times, a state agent would neglect some of the procedures involved. In those cases, the federal officials were quick to point out errors to the governor and to require him to rectify them before any further steps were taken to secure the lands requested. The governor, always careful to

---

to be determined according to the right of way, and many of them had already been pre-empted by settlers, who were allowed to legalize their claims. In such cases, the roads would be compensated with lands selected by the state agents from the replacement zones set up by the same law.

[21] In each public-land state and territory, there were several public-land districts (federal), each with a United States land office and a register and receiver to handle the land business of the district. These offices maintained records of all land transactions involving federal lands and were directly responsible for the lands in their districts. As the public domain within a state shrank, these offices were progressively consolidated, as were their records. When the last one in a state was closed, its land records, which by that time included all those pertaining to public and formerly public lands in the state, were turned over to the state government for its future reference and use. The Minnesota records, obtained in the 1930's, are in the State Archives in St. Paul. The federal government has also kept copies of all these records in Washington.

[22] To reserve lands meant to withdraw them from the market temporarily, subject to their subsequent formal disposal or return to the market.

[23] Records of such transactions can be found in the Minnesota Governors' Archives and in the National Archives in Washington. These procedures were basically the same for all the land grants to the states. Of course, those granted to the states for their direct disposal and not for transfer to another group did not involve the consultations and communications that developed between the state government officials and the railroads. The United States land office records in Minnesota are basically registrations of tracts of land plus some copies of communications between the different officials referred to above.

see that his agents followed the regulations, made the necessary adjustments when errors did occur.

When the governor erred in some way, the same reaction was forthcoming. A case in point is found in the early stages of the program. In 1859, Governor Sibley forwarded a map of the Transit Railroad to the General Land Office as part of a request for adjustment of parts of its land grant. In doing so, he omitted his official seal on the map. The commissioner of the General Land Office returned the map with a letter describing the omission and stating that the matter could not be considered until the documents were in order. The Governor hastened to remedy his error and returned the map, with his seal, forthwith.[24]

After passage of the constitutional amendment, the railroads began to make the necessary arrangements with the state in order to be eligible for the land grants. Among these arrangements was the requirement (federal) that all contracts and related documents dealing with any phase of construction be filed with the governor for his examination. In May and July of 1858, the first two contracts between the Minnesota and Pacific Railroad and their construction manager, specifying certain details of construction, were submitted to Governor Sibley who reviewed and approved them.[25]

THE STATES'-RIGHTS ARGUMENT IN MINNESOTA

The doctrinal paradox of dual federalism was not confined to the South and East. On one hand, the state officials of Minnesota showed no hesitation in accepting federal aid and spoke freely of emulating federal programs on the state and local levels. They did not hesitate to accept the conditions that accompanied federal grants and were willing to use them in support of their dealings with railroad officials, undoubtedly with sincere respect for the federal requirements. In their capacity as administrators, elected officials of the state had entered into co-operative relationships with the federal administration and accepted such relationships seemingly without complaint. Yet in their public political roles, and probably with the conviction of their political persuasions, they could denounce every "encroachment" on the rights of the states by the federal

[24] Minnesota State Archives, Governors' Archives, file 74 (1859).

[25] Ibid., file 57 (May 26, 1858) and file 60 (July 15, 1858).

government. Witness Governor Sibley's message on June 3, 1858, to the first meeting of the legislature of the new state. One of the most important items in his speech was the problem of railroad construction, which he dealt with at some length. At first he stressed the state financing program as a good plan that emulated the approach of the federal government toward internal improvements. Then he abruptly changed to a discussion of states' rights, stating that the federal government should confine its activities to specific powers and areas. No doubt this public attitude of political officials and community leaders was a large factor in the development of the image of nineteenth-century dualism.

At the same time, the federal grant was actually strengthening and expanding the operations of the state government. Twelve days after his denunciation of federal encroachment, Sibley presented a plan to the state senate which called for the appointment of a state engineer to examine the railroads before they were certified to insure full compliance with the conditions set down by the state and the federal government. This plan was adopted and the state engineer served as a valuable aid during the next several decades.[26] This was one of the first technical positions to be created in the state government of Minnesota, one which opened up a new field of state governmental involvement.

Meanwhile, on August 26, 1858, the Minnesota and Pacific Railroad returned its first 240 sections of land to the state in order to qualify for the bonds. However, the arrangement was obviously not satisfactory to that company. On August 29, the secretary of the railroad wrote a letter to Governor Sibley, ostensibly to press the cause of states' rights. In this letter he expressed hearty disapproval and great fear of the co-operative program that had been established to administer the railroad land grants. He suggested a more forthright approach to obtain the lands quickly and "preserve the rights of the states." His scheme was to have the railroads take possession of the lands reserved for them and to have the governor simply notify Washington to that effect. He disputed the right of the executive branch (as represented by the Department of the Interior) to interfere with the legislative process (in this case, the act of Congress) on the grounds of a violation of the separation of powers; he reasoned that all the state had to do was obey the act of Congress and only the judiciary could determine whether it was doing so or not.[27]

On the face of his reply, the Governor agreed that states' rights should be protected, but he obviously felt that this maneuver was less concerned

[26] *Ibid.*, file 57 (June 15, 1858).   [27] *Ibid.*, file 60.

with states' rights than with corporate claims. Nothing was done to test this theory of constitutional interpretation, and the co-operative program continued unimpeded. This type of activity provides much information as to who was particularly interested in developing a theory of dual federalism. As could be expected, it was developed in response to the practical needs of certain important interests, rather than as an a priori philosophy of government.

By mid-November, 1858, the state engineer could report to the Governor that thirty miles of the Transit Railroad had been graded and found to be satisfactory after his inspection.[28] The president of the Southern Minnesota Railroad reported substantial progress in grading along his road in strict compliance with the law;[29] and by April, 1859, a record of the route of that railroad was on file in the United States land office.[30] All during that year, similar records were deposited with the governor.

For a year, the railroads were able to maintain a construction program of sorts probably by paying the contractors with bonds valued much below par; but by July, 1859, the bonds had become almost valueless. They could no longer be used even as collateral to raise funds. On the advice of the railroad companies themselves, the contractors halted their work. This only added to the depressed conditions within the state, since many of those Minnesotans involved in the construction were either unpaid or owners of virtually unnegotiable bonds.

On December 2, 1859, the legislature convened and Governor Sibley officially advised them of the unfortunate facts. He ascribed the failure of the state bonds to acquire a market value to "the determined and mischievous efforts of a portion of our own citizens" (speculators?) and reported that at the time of the suspension of the construction, 239.5 miles, fairly equally distributed, had been graded. Bonds worth $2,275,-000 had been delivered to the companies.[31]

The legislature attempted to breathe some life into the dying bond issue and, after a series of proposals, emerged with a refinancing plan that was approved by the voters at the next election.[32] For a short time it looked as if they had saved the day, but the program could not be translated into effective action. By the end of 1860 the scheme was aban-

[28] *Ibid.*, file 61 (November 15, 1858).   [30] *Ibid.*, file 67 (April 29, 1859).

[29] *Ibid.*, file 61 (December 6, 1858).   [31] Folwell, *op. cit.*, II, 53.

[32] This plan is described in *ibid.*, pp. 53–57. Since it had no real effect on construction, it will not be treated here. It was essentially a paper scheme that produced no action other than a trading of securities.

doned, leaving conditions in Minnesota more depressed than before and
saddling the state with a debt of $2,275,000 that could not be redeemed.[33]

[33] In the election of 1860, the voters of the state repudiated the debt in its entirety,
and it was not until 1881 that the bonds were redeemed at almost double the original
cost to the state. A good deal of maneuvering had to take place to obtain the passage
of the redemption measure. The people were not inclined toward it, since the bonds
had meanwhile passed into the hands of a few speculators. They were the ones who
were instrumental in seeing the measure through to their own advantage. The funds
used to redeem the bonds came from a federal grant of 500,000 acres for internal
improvements that the state had not previously claimed.

11

Tightening Procedures and Building Railroads

MINNESOTA

After two years of patient exploration of ways and means to provide adequate financing, the state government and the railroad companies were able to work out a plan which met conditions in Minnesota and the terms of the federal grant. The administrative operations of the land-grant program were begun again with the resumption of railroad construction in 1862. On March 17, 1862, Edmund Rice, who had automatically passed into the presidency of the St. Paul and Pacific, wrote to Governor Ramsey to request that Elias Drake be appointed agent of the state, to select lands for his railroad.

This was not an unusual request by any means, but another illustration of the interrelatedness of the whole governmental program on all levels. The state, which was officially charged with appointing and supervising agents to select the lands, and the railroads worked out a compromise policy whereby they would consult together on appointments, with the railroad usually suggesting a person they felt would do the job well. The governor would normally appoint the man suggested, communicating the fact to the General Land Office, which had to approve the appointment. Normally the federal agency raised no questions and accepted the governor's choice.[1]

[1] See Minnesota State Archives, Governors' Archives, files 114 and 133b, for examples of such appointments. Correspondence between Washington, St. Paul, and the railroad companies fell into the following categories: (1) requests for lands, (2) certification of construction, (3) transfers of title, (4) conflicting and overlapping grants, (5) settlers on lands claimed by the railroads, (6) requests for relinquishments, (7) requests for information, (8) legal opinions, and (9) clarifications of authority and responsibility.

For the first time in the history of the program, Rice was also able to request that the Governor inform the secretary of the interior that grading, locating, and surveying had been completed on varying lengths of both the main and branch lines in compliance with the conditions of the land-grant acts, so that the appropriate lands could be transferred to the railroad. Evidence of this work had been submitted earlier, as Rice reminded Ramsey. The Governor immediately transmitted the necessary information to Washington, informing the General Land Office of the work completed and of the appointment of Drake as a state land agent. That fall, the first ten miles of track in Minnesota were opened, connecting St. Paul with St. Anthony (now Minneapolis) and bringing the state into the railroad age.

On January 7, 1863, Commissioner Edmunds, of the General Land Office, transmitted to Governor Ramsey certified transcripts of the lists of lands inuring to Minnesota under the 1857 grant for the St. Paul and Pacific and the Winona, St. Peter, and Missouri [sic] railroads. The lands listed were then released to the companies, and the actual railroad construction program was under way. From that date, the Governors' Archives are full of communications between railroad officials, land selection agents, governors, state attorneys-general, commissioners of the General Land Office, officials of the local United States land offices, and secretaries of the interior, submitting records, maps, and transcripts with progress reports and certificates of inspection in return for receipts, patents, certified land lists, titles, and certificates of registration as the grant lands passed from the federal government to the state of Minnesota to the railroads.[2]

In July of 1863, Henry Swift assumed the governorship. In his message to the legislature, he summarized the progress of railroad construction in the state and made two signal recommendations. First, he recommended that a railroad be constructed to link Minnesota with the newly chartered Union Pacific Railroad, a connection provided for by the act of Congress that chartered the transcontinental line.[3] Second, he recommended that the legislature supplement the basic Congressional railroad grant of 1857 with a grant of swamp lands to the railroads to aid construction. These swamp lands were themselves part of a grant from the federal government. In 1849, Congress had passed an act granting

[2] Another source of records pertaining to these activities is the Executive Department Records in the Minnesota State Archives.

[3] Minnesota, *Executive Documents*, 1863, p. 9.

all swamp and overflowed lands within the public-land states to the respective states. This grant required the states to use the proceeds from
the sale of said lands for the draining of the swamps and the construction
of levees to make the land fit for cultivation. As each new state entered
the Union, it was entitled to claim the swamp lands within its own
boundaries under the Act of 1849.[4] The lands could be selected by the
federal surveyor-general in each state, but the state would be required
to pay the expenses involved in surveying and selecting them. As Minnesota was just beginning to claim its share, Rice's plan was accepted and
subsequently the legislature granted close to three million acres of swamp
lands to various railroads in addition to the grants obtained from the
Congress specifically for railroad construction.[5]

In the course of administering the program, it was found that some of
the lands chosen for transfer to the railroads were already occupied by
settlers. Some of these settlers were bona fide claimants and others were
pre-emptors who had never filed claims but who had traditionally received recognition and the right to secure their lands legally. All of them
were potential voters and could command a good deal of attention from
local and national politicians. These pioneers bitterly protested the
possibility of losing the lands they had worked so hard to improve. For
many reasons, some humanitarian and some political, the federal, state,
and local governments usually supported them, just as Congress regularly
supported the pre-emptors by special legislation legalizing their status.
As early as 1860, Governor Ramsey engaged in correspondence with the
General Land Office over the proper interpretation of the federal pre-
emption laws in regard to the rights of these squatters. Federal law
specifically reserved all lands subject to entry under the terms of Congressional grants from settlement once the general grant had been made.
Thus, all squatters who had settled on the lands in question after the
acts of Congress were subject to eviction. Because of the general concern
over evicting squatters who could vote, and who, in addition, had invested so much time and effort in creating farms out of wild country,
Ramsey was able to secure a gentleman's agreement with the General

[4] Mathias Orfield, *Federal Land Grants to the States with Special Reference to
Minnesota* (Minneapolis: University of Minnesota Press, 1915), pp. 112 ff. This was
basically a reclamation grant with matching provisions (see chap. xv).

[5] Minnesota Railroad and Warehouse Commission, Engineering Division, Railroad
History Files, compiled by H. S. Hayes. See Table 1 (pp. 166–67) for a summary of the
railroad land-grant program in Minnesota.

Land Office to apply "a liberal interpretation" of the pre-emption laws that would allow the squatters to claim the land that they had worked.

The Governor was particularly interested in adjusting this question in a way that would benefit both the squatters and the state. If the squatters were to get their land, it would have to be on condition that the state would have the right to select other lands to compensate for their losses. As part of this procedure, the state attorney-general became involved in the proceedings. For example, whenever a squatter applied at a local United States land office to obtain title to lands set aside for schools, the state wanted to be notified and represented. Accordingly, in 1860 the Minnesota attorney-general contacted the United States Department of the Interior and secured a change in the regulations of the General Land Office by which the local land offices were ordered to require all such applicants to notify the governor when they filed their claim. This gave the state the opportunity to appear and present its claims either in support of, or in opposition to, private claimants. In his report of that year, the attorney-general describes one such case. Application was made to pre-empt a portion of section 36 (one of the sections reserved for schools in every township) in one of the townships in Meeker County. Notice was served on the Governor, who referred it to the attorney-general's office. The latter official filed a protest with the United States land office at Forest City, which had jurisdiction over the matter; and the Meeker County attorney was requested to appear on behalf of the state to contest the claim.[6]

Whenever it was discovered that settled lands had been included in a land transfer, the General Land Office would request the governor to relinquish the state's title to the lands in question to the federal government. The first relinquishment requests came in 1864. The Governor did not know whether he could legally relinquish lands already patented to the state. In a ruling issued on November 15, 1864, the state attorney-general stated that under the terms of the federal and state acts of 1857, the governor could relinquish the lands to the federal government as long as he had the right to make alternate selections.[7] This settled the constitutional issue in a manner that strongly supported the co-operative nature of the land-grant program. The Governor did not hesitate to accept this solution, which was not only administratively sound but politically advisable. From then on, almost all federal requests for relinquishment

[6] Minnesota, State Attorney-General, *Report* (1860), pp. 3 ff.

[7] Minnesota State Archives, Executive Department Records, C, p. 9.

were honored by the governors of Minnesota, as long as title to the lands concerned was still vested in the state.

A more difficult problem was posed when title had already passed to the railroads. In such cases, the governor could only request the railroad company involved to relinquish the lands to the state, which could then relinquish them to the federal government to be granted to the people who had settled on them. While the railroads could often be induced to comply with such requests, since they could choose alternate lands often of higher quality, there were numerous occasions when they found it more to their advantage to refuse to do so. This led to complications and considerable discussion between the four parties concerned before any agreement could be reached. In such cases, the governor was usually the middleman in the negotiations.

Occasionally, the relinquishment problem would result in strained relations. For example, on March 19, 1872, the commissioner of the General Land Office requested the governor to inform that office of the relinquishment by the state of certain railroad lands to which a homesteader had prior claim. The commissioner politely scolded the governor for delaying the relinquishment for a year, since it had been promised in 1871.

As the state population increased, this problem was met with greater frequency. In such cases, the homesteader would petition the federal officials for a hearing, normally at the district United States land office. After holding the hearing, the records would be forwarded to Washington where a final decision would be made. The governor would be notified as to the decision and was expected to see that the local interests concerned complied with it. If either side still considered the decision to be wrong, the aggrieved party had the right to appeal for a rehearing.[8]

The state government was continually disposed to support the individual settlers. In response to pressure by the homesteaders, who made up a sizable bloc, if not a majority, of the voters in Minnesota, the state legislature passed a measure in 1875 that required the railroads to relinquish to the state any lands that had been properly pre-empted or homesteaded, so that the state could then relinquish them to the federal government to be transferred to the individual settlers who claimed them. Enforcement of this law seems to have been rather erratic.[9]

[8] *Ibid.*, file 258.

[9] The governor is not on record as having used it in his subsequent requests to the railroads, though some recently discovered files that could not be examined for this study might indicate that he did in some cases.

Relinquishments were also called for when two grants conflicted, either because grants to different railroads overlapped at some point or because of conflicts between different types of grants (such as a railroad grant and a swamp land grant). In the former case, hearings would be held and the Department of the Interior would make a decision, usually in favor of the company whose Congressional grant was earliest. For example, some of the lands granted in 1864 to the Minnesota Central Railroad conflicted with a grant made at the same time to the St. Paul and Sioux City line. On December 20, 1872, the commissioner of the General Land Office instructed Governor Austin to divide the lands in conflict equally between the companies whenever they both should apply for them.[10] After the administrative decisions were made, the losing party could appeal to both state and federal courts, and on occasion did so. Where different types of grants were involved, the lands in question would be awarded under the grant that had first been used to select them. Thus, if the lands had been selected by an agent of the governor under the school land grant and later selected by another agent of the governor under a railroad land grant, the lands would be considered as accruing to the state as school lands. However, even if the lands were school lands but had been selected under a railroad land grant first, they went to the state for the railroad in question. The time of selection took precedence over the year of the act of Congress in such cases.[11]

In 1865 Congress extended the ten-year time limit, so that the grant of 1857 would not be automatically forfeited and the heirs of the original recipients of the grants would be able to continue their work.[12] Under the Congressional extension, the St. Paul and Pacific Railroad completed its main line from St. Anthony to Breckenridge by 1871, which was within the time limit set by the legislature. In the same year, the railroad (renamed the First Division of the St. Paul and Pacific) requested permission to change the route of its branch line for a more direct one to the Canadian border. Since any such change involved changing the terms of the land grant, it had to be approved by both Congress and the state legislature. Approval was obtained from both bodies before the year was out. A section of the act of Congress revising the earlier act provided:

[10] Minnesota State Archives, Governors' Archives, file 283.

[11] *Ibid.*

[12] 17 Stat. 631 (1865).

That the St. Paul and Pacific Railroad Company may so alter its branch lines . . . to intersect with the Northern Pacific Railroad . . . so as to form a more direct route to St. Vincent, with the same proportional grant of land, to be taken in the same manner along the said altered line as is provided for the present lines by existing law: *Provided However,* that this change shall in no manner enlarge said grant, and that this act shall only take effect upon the condition of its being in accord with the legislation of the State of Minnesota, and upon the further condition that proper releases shall be made to the United States by said company of all lands along said abandoned lines.[13]

Similar conditions were applied in other railroad land-grant changes.

The branch line was being completed on schedule when the company went into bankruptcy in 1876. A receiver was appointed to operate the road for its bondholders and did so until 1879 when the system passed into the hands of the St. Paul, Minneapolis, and Manitoba Railroad, headed by James J. Hill. The St. Paul, Minneapolis, and Manitoba became the foundation stone of the Great Northern Railway System in 1890. Under Hill's direction, construction was pushed, gaps were eliminated, and the St. Vincent branch, which connected the road with the Canadian Pacific Railroad, was completed in 1881. The line was then turned westward, reaching Minot, North Dakota, in the 1880's and, finally, Seattle, Washington, in 1893, thus completing the transformation of the St. Paul and Pacific into one of the major American railroad systems.

The second part of the original Root River and Southern Minnesota Railroad grant went to a third corporation called the Southern Minnesota Railroad in 1864. Congress made an additional grant to Minnesota in 1866 for a railroad to run between Houston, Minnesota, and the Dakota line.[14] This grant was conferred upon the Southern Minnesota by the legislature in 1878, with the condition that the line be completed by the end of 1880.[15] In building the railroad, the company deviated slightly from the line of the original grant. This raised the question as to whether it had forfeited the lands by doing so. After some discussion, the Department of the Interior ruled that the deviation was not sufficient to warrant forfeiture of the lands.[16] In time, this road also became part of one of America's major railroads as a link in the Chicago-to-the-Black-Hills route of the Milwaukee Road.

[13] 13 Stat. 195 (1871).   [14] 14 Stat. 84 (1866).

[15] Minnesota, *Special Laws* (1878), p. 537.

[16] John Bell Sanborn, *Congressional Grants of Land in Aid of Railways* (Madison: University of Wisconsin, 1899), p. 105.

TABLE 1

ORIGINAL LAND GRANTS CONVEYED TO RAILROADS IN MINNESOTA BY THE FEDERAL GOVERNMENT AND THE STATE OF MINNESOTA*

Present Ownership	Recipients of Original Grants	Acres of Railroad-Grant Lands Conveyed by Congress	Acres of Swamp Lands Conveyed
Chicago, Milwaukee, St. Paul, & Pacific Railroad	Hastings & Dakota Ry. (Hastings to Glencoe)	375,856.01	......
	Minnesota Central Ry. (Minneapolis & Cedar Valley)	173,756.28	......
	St. Paul & Chicago Ry.	......	462,336.00
	Southern Minnesota R.R. (Ext.)	511,614.05	36,777.84
	Total	1,061,226.34	499,113.84
Northern Pacific Railway	Lake Superior & Mississippi R.R. (St. Paul & Duluth)	855,423.09	694,399.35
	Taylors Falls & Lake Superior R.R.	......	91,829.96
	Stillwater & St. Paul R.R.	65,113.64	......
	Western R.R. of Minnesota (St. Paul & Northern Pacific) to Northern Pacific	195,296.40	......
	Little Falls & Dakota R.R.	......	265,856.00
	Northern Pacific R.R. (chartered July 2, 1864)†	1,614,156.62	......
	Northern Pacific Ry. (to Feb. 23, 1943)	291,740.34	......
	Total	3,021,730.09	1,052,085.31
Great Northern Railway	First Division St. Paul & Pacific—Main Line	3,247,413.20 (St. Paul & Manitoba)	......
	First Division St. Paul & Pacific—Branch Line		......
	St. Paul & Pacific R.R. (St. Vincent Ext.)		425,664.00
	Minneapolis & St. Cloud		......
	Total	3,247,413.20	425,664.00

* Taken from Minnesota Railroad and Warehouse Commission, Engineering Division, Railroad History Files, compiled by H. S. Hayes.   † Not shown on state auditor's report, as it was conveyed by the General Land Office of the federal government.

TABLE 1—*Continued*

Present Ownership	Recipients of Original Grants	Acres of Railroad-Grant Lands Conveyed by Congress	Acres of Swamp Lands Conveyed
Chicago, St. Paul, Minneapolis, & Omaha Railway	St. Paul & Sioux City R.R. (Minnesota Valley R.R., 1865–85) .... St. Paul, Stillwater & Taylors Falls R.R. .... Sioux City & St. Paul R.R.	855,199.86 44,246.27 234,556.88	....
	Total................	1,134,003.01	....
Chicago Great Western Railway	Minnesota Central R.R. (Cannon River Improvement Co. [Wisconsin, Minnesota & Pacific]; Cannon River Manufacturing Assoc. retained 24,190.45 acres	....	275,000.00
	Total................	....	275,000.00
Chicago & North Western Railway	Winona & St. Peter R.R.	1,756,862.24	....
	Total................	1,756,862.24	....
Duluth & Iron Range Railroad	Duluth & Iron Range R.R. (sold 125,064.47 acres by agreement to C.R.I. & Pac.)................	....	606,720.00
	Total................	....	606,720.00
Total		10,221,224.88	2,858,583.15

Total acreage of Congressional and swamp land grants ....13,079,808.03‡

‡ This equals 20,473.2 square miles, or about 25 per cent of the total land area of the state. The present amount of carrier land owned by the railroads and used for transportation purposes is 151,495 acres, or about .3 per cent of the total land area of the state.

The Minneapolis, Faribault, and Cedar Valley Railroad, which failed in 1862, was revived as the Minnesota Central Railway. In 1866 the right of way and immediate approaches of this line were sold to the Iowa-chartered McGregor Western Railroad. This sale provided the first railroad link between Minnesota and the rest of the Union, bringing St. Paul to within thirty hours of Chicago. By the terms of the sale, the Minnesota Central retained the lands granted it, since the route of the McGregor Western passed to the east of the lands included in the Act of 1857 and the new ownership could not claim the grant. In 1870, the Minnesota Central resumed construction and fulfilled the Congressional provisions by building the road to the state line via Austin to the west of range sixteen. This railway also became part of the Milwaukee Road.[17]

Once the railroads began operations, the reports of their construction progress became more detailed. On May 16, 1871, Walter W. Smith, the acting secretary of the interior, sent the governor a number of circulars clarifying the authority of the federal government in the administration of the railroad land-grant program. According to these circulars, the primary responsibility for inspection of railroad construction under the grants lay with the state officials, but as a check "the United States has reserved the right, or shall reserve it, to appoint directors, engineers, commissioners or other agents to examine said roads."[18]

This approach is very similar to the one used to provide a federal check on the twentieth-century grant-in-aid programs. No record was found in this study of any cases of actual federal inspection, but a thorough investigation of the railroad grant program in the United States might very well turn up such cases. The officials of Minnesota had administered their part of the program very well, much better than seems to have been the case in most of the other states. Thus, there would have been little need for direct federal inspection.

When a section of a railroad line was completed, the governor had to be supplied with evidence to that effect (letters and maps) from the chief engineer of the company involved before certifying that the company had complied with the terms of the land grant. When he was satis-

[17] Minnesota Railroad and Warehouse Commission, Engineering Division, Railroad History Files. See Table 1 for a summary of the railroad land-grant program in Minnesota: the amount of lands granted by both the federal and state governments, the railroad companies that received the grants, and the present ownership of those companies.

[18] Minnesota State Archives, Governors' Archives, file 258.

fied that they had, he would forward to the General Land Office the documentary evidence with his certification and a request for patents to the lands concerned. The Interior Department did not demand a firsthand inspection of the certified track, but allowed the governor to use his discretion in ascertaining its fitness. However, he was responsible for correct and proper certification.

At times there were attempts made by the railroads to circumvent the procedures involved in obtaining the granted lands. All such attempts were rejected by the federal officials. When a railroad tried to obtain federal approval for work completed or projected without first clearing things with the state authorities, its request was always returned with instructions to the effect that any communications had to be channeled through the state, and the state was informed of the attempt. For example, when the Minnesota Valley Railroad sent a map showing construction completed directly to the General Land Office, that agency immediately returned it as incomplete as it had not passed through the proper state channels (and had none of the proper seals).[19]

THE TRANSCONTINENTAL RAILROADS

Until 1862, all Congressional land grants for railroad construction had been channeled through the states. In that year a new policy was initiated with the precedent-setting Union Pacific land grant, in which, for the first time, lands were granted directly to railroad companies, bypassing the states.[20] There were several reasons for this, which, when analyzed, show that it was not so much a change in the policy of co-operative federalism, as an adaptation of the national internal improvement policy to new and different conditions.

Up to the time of the Union Pacific grant, all the railroads that had received federal assistance for construction were within the boundaries of states or organized territories on the verge of statehood. Moreover, for the most part, the grants were for railroads that would operate entirely within the state that administered the grant. The early interstate railroad systems that had begun to develop in the East were united after the completion of the various sections in each state; in some cases they were subsidized by land grants, and in others they were put together through

---

[19] *Ibid.*, file 44 (1866).   [20] Sanborn, *op. cit.*, pp. 65 ff.

private means, various forms of state aid, and federal mail contracts. Since the land-grant railroads were generally confined to single states, or at the most to two or three, the grants could be made through those states.

As the idea for a transcontinental railroad gathered momentum, and pressure for federal aid for such a project increased, it became evident that the usual form of such aid would not do. A transcontinental road would begin on the fringes of organized settlement and mainly cross lands that were still unorganized territories, or at best organized ones with small and scattered populations. No governmental mechanisms existed that could be interposed between the federal government and the private parties concerned to administer the land grants. It seemed obvious that any land grants would have to be made directly to the companies that would undertake construction. Whatever supervision there would be would have to come from the federal government itself.

The new policy, therefore, was not a repudiation of federal-state partnership. Indeed, grants of the earlier type continued to be made until the entire program was ended. The new approach was simply designed to meet a new situation that could not be dealt with as the old one had been. In order to handle the contacts with states that would be necessary under direct grants, a provision was included in the acts of Congress specifying that the railroads chartered therein had to obtain the consent of the legislature before they could build within a state's boundaries.[21]

On July 2, 1864, Congress chartered a transcontinental railroad to be built along the northern route—from Lake Superior to Puget Sound in Washington Territory—to be named the Northern Pacific Railway.[22] It was to receive ten sections of land per mile in the states it would cross and twenty in the territories, and was to be completed by July 4, 1876.[23] On March 2, 1865, the Minnesota legislature gave its consent to the construction of the railroad within the state (as required by the act of Congress) on the condition that the company build a branch from the main line to Duluth. The company agreed to do this.[24]

Construction was soon begun, accompanied by the usual conflicts between the railroad, the settlers, and the state. On January 14, 1873, the

[21] Minnesota Railroad Commissioner, *Annual Report, 1883* (St. Paul, 1884), p. 40.

[22] Sanborn, *op. cit.*, p. 123.

[23] This time limit was later extended several times, ultimately to July 4, 1879, and figured in later attempts to revoke parts of the grant on charges of fraud.

[24] Minnesota Railroad Commissioner, *op. cit.*, p. 56.

state railroad commissioner asked the governor to request the General Land Office to forward copies of the lists of all lands granted to the Northern Pacific within the boundaries of Minnesota. Since the land grant was a direct one, the state had no records of the actual transfers of land to the company. The governor agreed that this was an undesirable situation and wrote to the General Land Office requesting copies of those records.[25] Information concerning direct land grants was subsequently sent to the state from time to time.

TABLE 2

ESTIMATED VALUE OF FEDERAL, STATE, AND LOCAL GRANTS
MADE TO RAILROADS IN MINNESOTA*

Character of Grant	Value at Time Conveyed	Total
Congressional lands granted to Northern Pacific R.R. by federal government directly: 2,354,000 acres....................................	$ 5.00 per acre	$11,770,000
Lands granted to railroads by the federal government through Minnesota in the co-operative program: 8,315,000 acres......................	5.00 per acre	41,575,00
Swamp lands from federal grant to Minnesota, granted to railroads by the state: 2,895,000 acres	2.50 per acre	7,237,000
State of Minnesota bonds........................	....	2,275,000
State of Minnesota—240 miles of graded roadbed..	2,500.00 per mile	610,000
Bonds issued by villages, cities, and counties under Chap. 17, Minnesota Laws of 1871	....	3,000,000
Total		$66,467,000

* Taken from Minnesota Railroad and Warehouse Commission, Engineering Division, Railroad History Files, October 10, 1916. Figures are given in round numbers.

The separation of the Northern Pacific Railway from the general pattern of federal-state railroad land grants was short-lived. As soon as that railroad began expanding and acquiring smaller roads, it came under joint federal-state jurisdiction, since with the absorption of each intrastate line, the railroad also acquired its status under the appropriate land-grant acts of Congress and the state legislature. Thus, in order to qualify for the lands granted and to complete construction on an acquired line, it had to subject itself to the same terms and conditions as the road it had absorbed. This was the case with all the interstate railroad systems that came into Minnesota and her sister states. As they acquired smaller lines within the state, they also assumed the benefits and obligations that were included, and were brought into the co-operative programs.

[25] Minnesota State Archives, Governors' Archives, file 308.

TABLE 3

Tax Benefits from Land-Grant Railroads in Minnesota

	1866	1875	1880	1885	1890	1895	1900
Total state revenue	$450,861	$980,604	$1,417,174	$2,077,664	$3,296,287	$5,426,936	$6,903,296
Total railroad tax	$ 4,078	$106,873	$ 209,464	$ 673,303	$ 685,433	$ 851,394	$1,443,992
Number of operating railroads*	4	10	14	17	29	39	38
Tax from land-grant railroads*	$ 4,078	$106,873	$ 209,464	$ 673,303	$ 620,761	$ 729,210	$1,105,955
Number of land-grant railroads*	4	10	14	17	10	10	8
Total tax from top five railroads	......	......	......	......	$ 517,519	$ 639,991	$ 959,100
Number of land-grant railroads in top five	......	......	......	......	5	5	5

* Declining numbers indicate mergers and consolidations.

TIGHTENING PROCEDURES AND BUILDING RAILROADS

By 1872 the railroad had come to Minnesota to stay; 1,906 miles of railroad track were in operation. In addition to the grants described in the preceding pages, eleven other Minnesota railroads participated in the co-operative land-grant program. (See Table 2 for an estimate of the value of the grants made to railroads in Minnesota.) The state was connected with the rest of the country through Chicago in the south and Duluth in the north. As the railroads advanced, so did the frontier; the settlers followed the tracks, moving northward and westward, and taking up lands near the new sources of readily available transportation. After the rails reached Duluth, Minnesota became a gateway to the world and a port for shipping grain not only from its own farms but also from an empire embracing the American and Canadian northwest as far west as the Rocky Mountains. In fact, the railroads had reached a position of such strength that the movement to regulate them through administrative action had already led to legislation in the legislative session of 1871.

Some idea of the immediate impact of the railroad land grants can be ascertained by examining Table 3. From 1880 to 1900, railroad taxes supplied between one-seventh and one-third of the state's annual revenue. During this entire period, the land-grant railroads supplied the major share of the total. Until 1890, the land-grant railroads were the only ones producing taxable revenues. After that time, they remained the foremost revenue producers and ultimately absorbed most of the non-land-grant companies.

The railroads continued to extend their lines in Minnesota for another quarter of a century and continued to claim lands as late as 1943, although on a greatly diminished scale after 1890.[26] Since construction did not cease, the co-operative administrative program also continued, even increasing in scope as more lands were claimed, located, and transferred. Rival claims had to be adjudicated, and conflicts between the settlers and the railroads had to be resolved. All these and other problems provided for an ongoing program of co-operative federalism that was crucial to the continued growth of Minnesota.

COLORADO

Co-operative programs in internal improvement took on a somewhat new dimension in Colorado, less because of its location in space than because of its position in time. Statehood came to Colorado almost at

[26] Minnesota State Auditor, *Biennial Report, 1935–36* (St. Paul, 1937), pp. 46–48.

the end of the great transportation boom of the nineteenth century. Canals had obviously long passed from the scene. The state's major roads had been built by the federal government during territorial days or by the United States Army to facilitate the defense of the frontier. Many of the roads into the mountains were built by private enterprise prior to statehood to provide access to the mining areas and a means of bringing the minerals out. Nevertheless, the railroads, which were of vital importance in opening up the area, connecting it with the outside world, and making Denver a regional center, were the products of intergovernmental and public-private co-operation, which, though differing from the midwestern states' experiences, was just as real.

Early Colorado was faced with the same problem as Minnesota in its need to secure relatively inexpensive and dependable connections with the outside world in order to grow. But while Minnesota was favorably situated geographically along the logical northern route to the west coast, Colorado's location was extremely poor. Since the state was blocked from the western third of the continent by the highest mountain ranges in the United States, and flanked by territories with considerably lower and more accessible passes through the mountains, no real national advantages were to be gained by constructing a transcontinental railroad through it. However, the future state's leading citizens knew that without a railroad they would be bypassed by the westward movement. Denver, in particular, was concerned over the implications of this, since it possessed no natural advantages to aid its growth; it needed a railroad to survive. Only by becoming a commercial center for the Rocky Mountain region could it exist, and the natural barriers against achieving that goal were formidable.

In the early days of the territory, the territorial representatives in Washington lobbied without success to make the Pacific Railroad grant run through Denver. United States Army Engineers surveyed a route via Denver, along with the other suggested routes, and decided against it in favor of the overland route that passed through Cheyenne one hundred miles to the north, even though citizens of Colorado were prepared to give the capital that had been raised in a vain attempt to build their own railroad to the Pacific in return for location on the transcontinental route. The project was too large for them to undertake alone, and their offer was nowhere near attractive enough to be an inducement for the Union Pacific. That railroad company did report an interest in building a branch line to Denver from Cheyenne to tap the mineral wealth of Colorado, provided a federal land grant could be secured. Congress, however, limited its grant to a main-line railroad; and the Union Pacific was not willing, or financially able at the time, to construct the branch line without assistance.

The stalwarts among the citizens of Denver would not give up. While many of the city's four thousand inhabitants were preparing to leave for Cheyenne, others were hard at work in the halls of Congress. In 1866, Congress granted lands to the state of Kansas for the Kansas Pacific Railroad Company to construct a railroad across the state to Pond Creek at its western edge and instructed the company to build as far as Denver, which was designated as its western terminus. But the Kansas Pacific was in poor financial straits and could not build past the end of its land grant, which terminated at the Colorado line, so the Congressional authorization did nothing to alleviate Denver's position.

In 1867, Thomas J. Carter, one of the federally appointed directors of the Union Pacific, came to Denver to negotiate for aid from the local governments in the Colorado Territory to construct the branch line from Cheyenne. He proposed that counties along the right of way share the costs of construction with the Union Pacific by issuing bonds. While the four counties concerned and the city of Denver accepted this arrangement, rivalry between Golden and Denver over the site of the terminus prevented any bonds from being issued, and the plan died quietly.

The struggle between Denver and Golden then spread to embrace the rival Union Pacific and Kansas Pacific railroad companies. Denver entered into negotiations with the Kansas Pacific to extend its tracks westward from Pond Creek and, at the same time, created its own railroad, the Denver Pacific, to build directly to Cheyenne, bypassing Golden. The latter road was jointly financed by local businessmen and Arapahoe County[27] under an arrangement with the Union Pacific similar to that proposed by Carter for the other railroad, which had never been fulfilled.

Meanwhile, the territorial governor, John Evans, was busy seeking funds in the East to finance the Kansas Pacific line westward. Meeting with little success in his dealings with the eastern capitalists, he turned once more to Congress to obtain a land grant for the company to be used west of Pond Creek. At first he was opposed by the company itself. In

---

[27] The local businessmen subscribed $280,000, and the county issued bonds for $500,000 more. So enthusiastic were Denverites over this turn of events that the bond issue passed by the astounding vote of 1259 to 47. See Wilbur Fisk Stone (ed.), *A History of Colorado* (Chicago: S. J. Clarke, 1918), I, 336–37.

this anomalous situation, the Kansas Pacific Railroad Company was fighting the territorial governor of Colorado to prevent him from securing a land grant from Congress for their own railroad. They succeeded in delaying passage of the grant for one session, but in 1869 an agreement was reached between the three parties and Congress made the standard grant of alternate sections of land (totaling eight hundred thousand acres) in March of that year. The grant was for the Kansas Pacific to Denver and for the Denver Pacific from Denver to Cheyenne, with the former company operating the railroad over both routes. Governor Evans himself became president of the latter company.[28]

Two railroads were thus to be constructed to connect Denver with the outside world. One of them, the Kansas Pacific, was a United States chartered company that was subsidized by the federal government, partly at the instigation of the citizens and territorial officials of Colorado. The other one, the Denver Pacific, though ostensibly supported by direct federal aid, was actually a substitute for what would have been a federal-state program if Colorado had been a state. Arapahoe County was serving in lieu of the state by providing the major share of the local capital in the initial stages. The county bonds paid for the grading of the roadbed and the company's prior indebtedness.

In 1870, both railroads reached Denver, and the initial connection was complete. Railroad construction then entered the next phase, penetration of the mountains and the opening of the interior of Colorado for settlement. In most cases, the railroads were created and empowered to build by state law; and construction was financed by eastern capital, federal grants of land for rights of way and materials, and local bond issues. Whenever one of these sources was cut off, the entire process stopped. For example, the Colorado Central Railroad, under a territorial charter, built into the mountains between 1870 and 1873 over public lands granted by the federal government with eastern capital contributed through the Union Pacific and $550,000 in bonds provided by Gilpin County. Similar financial arrangements were made to build in Boulder and Weld counties. The purpose of this railroad was to connect the mountains with the railroads from the plains at Golden, bypassing Denver. United States public lands for rights of way were available once the railroad was chartered by the territorial legislature. Nevertheless, the entrance into the mountains proved to be too expensive until a second Gilpin County bond issue that added $300,000 to the original bond issue of $250,000 provided the

[28] *Ibid.*, pp. 335–38.

necessary stimulus and resources. Then the Panic of 1873 cut off the flow
of eastern capital, smashing the grand plan to bypass Denver.

By 1880 Denver had triumphed, and the struggle was ended with the
consolidation of the Union Pacific, Kansas Pacific, and Denver Pacific
railroads as the Union Pacific Railway Company and its leasing of the
Colorado Central Railroad under terms quite favorable to the Denver
interests. The city's future was thus secured by its success in attracting
railroads.[29] In subsequent years, the Burlington Railroad and others were
to enter Denver with the aid of land grants, but these were simply wel-
come additions after the great success of 1880.[30]

Colorado's greatest railroad remained to be constructed. If the progress
of the Union Pacific and its antecedents is illustrative of intergovernmental co-operation of a somewhat makeshift sort in the days before statehood, the construction of the Denver and Rio Grande Western Railroad
is the best example of the development of federal-state-local-private co-
operation after 1876—co-operation that did for Colorado what James J.
Hill's Great Northern and Northern Pacific did for Minnesota and its
hinterland. As in Minnesota, the commanding figure of one man, General
William J. Palmer, stands out in bold relief. Like Hill's railroads, the
railroad he created almost singlehandedly was not built into a region
with wealth ready for harvesting but into one that had to be opened up
by the railroad itself.

Palmer's venture was pioneering in its classic sense. It has also been
considered a classic example of the achievements of laissez faire private
enterprise in the American West. The claim that this is a classic example
of American enterprise will not be disputed here. Indeed, it was that; but
like the other truly classic American enterprises, it was not a product of
laissez faire. It was, rather, a classic example of private initiative mo-
bilizing and utilizing the American system of intergovernmental and
public-private co-operative procedures.[31]

Palmer first conceived his idea for a railroad from Denver southward
in the early 1860's, when he crossed the area with a federal surveying
party seeking possible transcontinental railroad routes. He combined the
knowledge gained from that firsthand experience with information

---

[29] *Ibid.*, pp. 342–45.

[30] For an account of the other railroads and their land grants, see *ibid.*, pp. 365–82.

[31] For a brief history of the Denver and Rio Grande Western Railroad, see *ibid.*,
pp. 346–64. Documents pertaining to the history of the railroad are located in the
Denver and Rio Grande Western Archives, Denver, Colorado.

gleaned from other federal and local surveys for the Kansas Pacific and Denver Pacific railroads. On the basis of this information, he mapped out the route his railroad was to follow and then proceeded to create the railroad.[32]

The Denver and Rio Grande Company was incorporated under the laws of the Colorado Territory on October 27, 1870. Its first seventy-four miles were constructed in 1871 without any governmental aid. In June, 1872, on the basis of the territorial charter, the railroad received a Congressional grant for a right of way over the public domain, which extended one hundred feet on each side of the tracks,

together with such public lands adjacent thereto that may be needed for depots, stops and other buildings for railroad purposes, and for yard room and sidetracks, not exceeding twenty acres at any one station and not more than one station in every ten miles, and the right to take from adjacent public lands stone, timber, earth, water and other materials required for the construction and repair of its railway and telegraph lines.[33]

It also received the same condemnation rights, powers, and privileges as had been conferred on the Union Pacific, provided that it reached Santa Fe within five (later increased to ten) years from the passage of the act. It was also required to complete fifty miles of track below Santa Fe each subsequent year.

In the federal right-of-way grant programs, the recipient companies could select lands for a right of way along any route that had been specified in their articles of incorporation, as passed by the legislature of the state in which they were building. This was a standard provision in all right-of-way grants, which actually made those grants subject to state approval. While the company would deal directly with the General Land Office in claiming the lands in question, the lands were granted by the federal government only in accord with the state's specifications. In a sense, the federal government was here acting as an agent of the states in promoting railroad construction within their boundaries, though it set the conditions whereby the grants would be made.[34]

The United States grant stimulated others. The town of Pueblo voted

[32] The magnitude of his vision can only be realized when one learns that in 1870 no more than five hundred people lived in the area that his railroad was to traverse and that the Pueblo-Denver stagecoach line carried no more than three passengers each way on its daily trips. Neither Leadville nor Cripple Creek had begun to boom when he began the D.&R.G.W., nor were their potentialities known.

[33] Act of Congress, June 8, 1872.

[34] Two exemplary acts of Congress providing for right-of-way grants are those of March 2, 1861, and March 3, 1875.

$200,000 in bonds for the railroad, which reached it on June 29, 1872. Pueblo's population in 1870 had been only five hundred. The coming of the railroad increased it to thirty-five hundred by 1872.[35] Canon City subscribed to $50,000 of D.&R.G.W. stock to have the railroad extended in its direction. Out of this Canon City extension came the famous Royal Gorge War.

The conflict in the Royal Gorge War was between the D.&R.G.W. and the Santa Fe Railroad to determine which would get the only possible right of way into the mountains to tap the riches of the Leadville silver boom, then at its peak. The gorge was too narrow for more than one railroad, so that the one able to prove its prior claim would win a total victory. The D.&R.G.W. based its claim on the grounds that even though it had not been able to actually occupy the gorge before April, 1878, it had placed its prospective route through that defile when Palmer had first mapped his envisioned railroad, and it was so registered in the legislature's act of incorporation. Thus, according to the terms of the act of Congress (the Royal Gorge was public domain), it was entitled to the right of way through the gorge on the basis of state recognition of prior claim.

After a prolonged "shooting" conflict, the issue was finally resolved by the United States Supreme Court, which ruled in favor of the D.&R.G.W. on just those grounds. The Santa Fe Railroad's contention was that the D.&R.G.W.'s right to the public domain was contingent on completion of the line to Santa Fe within the five-year limit. The Congressional extension of the limit to ten years coincided with the occupancy of the gorge by the D.&R.G.W., allowing Justice Harlan to write the opinion in its favor.[36]

The Rio Grande continued to expand during this protracted war. The conflict was settled and reopened, then settled again by litigation in state and federal courts. The final settlement determined the future of the Rio Grande Railroad as a westward-oriented road and ended its dream of expansion farther southward. United States lands continued to be used to furnish rights of way and the other benefits, while local bond issues, along with eastern capital, helped finance its construction.

[35] James H. Risley, *How It Grew: A History of the Pueblo Public Schools* (Denver: University of Denver Press, 1953), pp. 14–17.

[36] The history of the Royal Gorge War is actually considerably more complex than this brief view of its implications for co-operative federalism indicates. There is a whole literature on the subject available to the interested reader. Wilbur Fisk Stone's *A History of Colorado* provides a good starting point; the Denver and Rio Grande Western Archives, in Denver, contain the documentary records of the conflict.

MODES OF INTERGOVERNMENTAL CO-OPERATION:
A SUMMARY

Intergovernmental co-operation in building railroads in the public-land states took three forms. The classic co-operative mode followed the pattern of federal grants-in-land to the states, which then administered the transfer of the granted lands to specified railroads by supervising construction of railroad lines. This method was evolved from previous grant-in-land programs and reached its highest development in the states of the Mississippi Valley from 1830 to 1870.

The best-known mode of sharing the responsibility for the promotion of railroad construction was the use of direct federal grants-in-land for the great transcontinental railroads, which were constructed westward from the Mississippi Valley to the Pacific Coast through what was then sparsely settled or vacant land. The federal government made these grants directly to the railroad companies for about a decade (1862–71) because no effective state or territorial governments existed to provide the necessary supervision of the grants in most of the area. However, the railroads that benefited from the transcontinental grants soon either absorbed, or were absorbed by, railroads created under federal-state co-operative programs and thus became involved in the procedures established for those programs as well.

The third mode involved state-chartered railroads that received federal grants from the public lands for rights of way and natural materials for construction. In this case, the federal government, by its own laws, became virtually an agent of the states, supplying aid to railroads created by the states under terms laid down by the state legislatures. By far the longest lasting of the three modes, the right-of-way grants were made for almost three-quarters of a century.

These three modes of co-operation were often used concurrently within the same state. It would be difficult to find a railroad located west of the Appalachians that was not constructed through co-operative action in at least one of these three modes. Certainly, the railroads that survived the "time of troubles" of their construction period were those linked to the American system of federal-state-local-private partnership.

12

Public Purpose Grants and Their Administration

Intergovernmental co-operation was so pronounced in virtually every aspect of government in the public-land states that its forms and objectives were rapidly institutionalized. The procedures of co-operation were just as rapidly made standard and routine. Colorado, as one of the public-land states created after the Civil War, displayed the full range of federal grant-in-land programs at their institutionalized best, from the incorporation of standard provisions in the state's constitution to the routinization of day-to-day intercourse between public officials. Although this chapter is devoted to a description of the institutionalization of collaboration and its consequences in Colorado, it could, with minor modifications, be used to describe the situation in Minnesota or any other state west of the Mississippi River and, with slightly greater modification, the public-land states to the east of the river as well.

COLLABORATION AND THE COLORADO CONSTITUTION

Congress passed the Colorado Enabling Act on March 3, 1875, with provisions for the standard land grants. Sections sixteen and thirty-six in each township were granted to the state for common schools. Fifty sections of unappropriated public land within the state were granted for the erection of public buildings at the state capital for legislative and judicial purposes. Another fifty sections were granted for the erection of a penitentiary, and seventy-two were set aside for the state university. Five per cent of the proceeds of the sales of agricultural public lands (which were to be sold within the state after its admission to the Union) was to be granted annually for internal improvements to be used within the state as the legislature might direct. The Act of 1841 was extended to Colorado, giving the state five hundred thousand additional acres for internal improvements, and the Morrill Act of 1862 gave it ninety thousand acres for an agricultural college. All salt-spring lands were also granted to the state, as had been customary since the days of George Washington.

Certain conditions were included in the act, some more far-reaching than in earlier grants to other states. Just as extensions of governmental services have tended to develop simultaneously on all levels, so have methods for their administration. Congress was learning that more than minimal control was necessary to promote profitable use of the granted lands for the intended purposes. The state governments were learning the same lesson. As in the case of Minnesota (see chapter xvii), state officials of Colorado and other new states had noted the wasteful misuse of the lands granted to older states of the Union and were as anxious to remedy the situation as were the national officials. Congress could thus find substantial agreement on the subject and make provisions for better utilization of the grants in the new enabling legislation. The inclusion of these new conditions was thus made possible through consensus rather than by federal coercion. As in the cases examined earlier, the change in policy was based on a foundation of rather widespread national agreement. So far as is known, there were no great outcries that these more stringent conditions were robbing the states of their rights or powers.

The common-school lands were of particular concern to the Congress and to the states. The act required that they be sold only at public sale and at a price of not less than $2.50 per acre; the proceeds were to become a permanent school fund, with only the interest to be expended for support of the schools. All mineral lands were excluded from claim under the act for any of the grant programs. When lands that should have been allocated for the common schools were found to contain minerals, provision was made for alternate selections. Similar provisions for alternate selections were included for lands due the state but previously sold or otherwise disposed of by the United States. The act gave the state the right to choose equivalent lands "in legal subdivisions of not more than one quarter-section, and as contiguous as may be." This became an important provision in the administration of the grant program in Colorado, where judicious selection of indemnity sections laid the foundation for a substantial income for the permanent funds.[1]

[1] 18 Stat. 476. Mathias Orfield (*Federal Land Grants to the States with Special Reference to Minnesota* [Minneapolis: University of Minnesota Press, 1915]) places

The terms of the common-school grant were incorporated into the state constitution, making the school fund permanent and inviolable. The other land grants were also protected by the state constitution under provisions establishing the ex officio State Board of Land Commissioners (SBLC), composed of the governor, secretary of state, attorney-general, superintendent of public instruction, and a register elected by the board members to manage the lands.[2] It was the duty of the SBLC to "provide for the location, protection, sale or other disposition of all the lands heretofore, or which may hereafter be granted to the state by the federal government, under such regulations as may be prescribed by law, and in such manner as will secure the maximum possible amount therefor."

It was through the use of state constitutional provisions that federal control over the grants was originally developed and maintained. Before the rise of the modern administrative state, the judicial apparatus was the means most often used to insure government control or supervision of any kind. In chapter x, this was shown to be the case in public supervision of the railroads. The same held true for federal supervision of land grants to the states. Since no state was admitted to the Union until the Congress accepted its draft constitution, the latter could require the inclusion of proper guarantees (not that the state was unwilling to include them). Enforcement of grant provisions could then be maintained through the state courts, or if poorly maintained there, through the federal courts on appeal. An examination of an annotated copy of the Colorado constitution will indicate how this system worked out in practice so long as the number of decisions were few. It was only with the rise in the number and complexity of decisions that had to be made, which coincided with the rise of the cash grant-in-aid, that an administrative apparatus had to be created to handle such enforcement procedures.[3]

The constitution also included a semiformal matching provision that, although not required by the terms of the Congressional grant, was com-

the Colorado grants in national perspective as including the first of the strictly conditional school land grants and the last of the general internal improvement grants, pp. 48–51, 101–2.

[2] In 1910 this was amended to create a board composed of three persons appointed by the governor, with the consent of the state senate, for six-year staggered terms.

[3] An examination of the reports of the U.S. Supreme Court in the nineteenth century will indicate that this procedure was carried to the very pinnacle of the federal judicial system when necessary. See Daniel J. Elazar, "Federal-State Cooperation as Reflected in Supreme Court Decisions, 1851–58" (research paper prepared for the Department of Political Science, University of Chicago, February, 1957), for some exemplary cases.

monly included by custom in most of the states (including states without public lands, such as Virginia and New Hampshire). All "estates that may escheat to the state; also all other grants, gifts or devices that may be made to this state for educational purpose" were to be added to the permanent school fund.

When the constitutional convention submitted its product to the people, its members included a statement on the virtues and value of statehood, a goal by no means unanimously supported in the territory at the time:

. . . Believing that you [the citizens of Colorado] fully appreciate the inestimable prize secured by entering the sisterhood of states, whereby you gain those privileges that flow only from that form of government, which is the offspring of your choice . . . we may reasonably assume that the chief objection made . . . will . . . be founded upon . . . the alleged and supposed increase of expenses and consequent taxation. We meet this objection directly, by conceding that a state government will, of course, involve an increased expense over that of our present form, but we assert that this expense will be more than balanced by the pecuniary gain alone which we will receive by becoming a state. . . . The increase in our expenses under a state government will be about $50,000 per annum, which, in five years, will amount to $250,000. This would be saved to us, or more properly, be delayed in payment, by remaining out of the Union five years longer.

Now, let us see what we would lose in that time: The Act of Congress granting Sections Sixteen and Thirty-six for school purposes allows the state to select an amount of public land equal to that which has been sold out of said Sections to settlers prior to survey. Under this arrangement we will be entitled to select about fifty sections of land.

The Enabling Act grants fifty other sections for public buildings, fifty sections for the penitentiary, and seventy-two sections for general purposes [This is an error; the seventy-two section grant was earmarked by law for the university.]—making a total of two hundred and twenty-two sections, or one hundred and forty-two thousand and eighty acres of land, which, at $2.50 per acre, amounts in value, to $385,200.

It will also be remembered that, upon becoming a state, Colorado will be entitled to five hundred thousand acres of public lands within her borders, by virtue of a grant heretofore made by Congress. This amount, if selected now, would be worth to us at least $50,000.

The Enabling Act also grants the state five per cent of the proceeds from the sale of the public agricultural lands after the adoption of this Constitution. The amount to be derived from this source for the next five years would exceed one hundred thousand dollars, which, added to the value of the land above mentioned, would make a total of about $1,000,000 which is four times the estimated amount of the increased expenses of the state for this period, so that we would really gain over three-quarters of a million dollars in five years by becoming a state.[4]

The convention enlarged on this estimate by including a saving of ten to twenty-five thousand dollars per year in school taxes from income of the common-school grant and dwelt on the dangers of delay that would allow the sale of additional public lands in Colorado without local pecuniary benefit. On this basis, the convention estimated that delay would cost them an additional million-dollar loss. On July 1, 1876, the voters indicated their agreement with this assessment of the value of statehood by voting 15,443 to 4,062 for ratification.

THE IMPACT OF THE EDUCATION GRANTS

Colorado's educational system is almost completely a product of the original co-operative relationship between the federal government and the state. Aside from providing the direct financial support that enabled the system to get under way, the grant program exercised a strong influence on the administrative organization of the school system.

The federal grant, of course, provided that the state government administer the permanent school fund. The state, in turn, used this as a lever to establish a state-wide educational system that included state controls over the local school districts. The state constitution itself included a provision to that effect.[5] Any school district failing to maintain a school within its boundaries for at least three months each year was denied any portion of the school fund for that year.

The administration of the grant soon came to involve even local officials. The state treasurer was to manage the fund, invest it, and distribute the interest annually among the counties and school districts as prescribed by law; and the state guaranteed to make up any investment losses. The county treasurers were made the collecting and disbursing officers for the funds on the local level. The county superintendent of schools was to be the ex officio commissioner of school lands within his

[4] As quoted in Wilbur Fisk Stone (ed.), *A History of Colorado* (Chicago: S. J. Clarke, 1918), I, 188–89.

[5] Colorado Constitution, Art. 9.

county and was to manage them under the supervision of the State Board of Land Commissioners.

Once statehood had been achieved, the lands accruing to the state under the terms of the appropriate federal grant programs had to be selected and properly disposed of so as to create permanent funds; and the funds had then to be employed to create a comprehensive school system. Among the responsibilities of the SBLC was the examination of sections sixteen and thirty-six in each township to ascertain whether they were mineral lands or previously settled (and thus unavailable), or whether steps could be taken to have them patented to the state. In the former case, equivalent selections had to be made by state agents from open lands; and in both cases, the SBLC had to secure the transfer of the lands from the General Land Office.

The state superintendent of public instruction directed the county superintendents to investigate the prospective school lands in their respective counties. The county superintendents then reported on the location of the lands, their mineral or non-mineral character, and whether they had been surveyed by the United States surveyor-general for Colorado. The state superintendent collected this information and reported to the SBLC, which then proceeded to handle the actual selection of the lands.

SELECTING THE LANDS

Filing, claiming, and patenting procedures followed the standard forms taken in the other states. As might be expected in Colorado, the major item of controversy between the federal government and the state in the administration of the program was the determination of whether lands contained minerals. The meaning of the term was vague, as was the rule to be used in applying it. Often the General Land Office would rule that certain lands highly desired by the state fell into that category, and a whole series of actions would be initiated before a final decision was reached. The federal claim was always based on an assessment of the lands as more valuable for mineral purposes than for any other. In any selection made by the state, the agent of the SBLC had to submit an affidavit attesting that this was not the case. If challenged by the General Land Office, the burden of proof lay with the state authorities.

Two methods of land selection were used. Generally, engineers and agents were appointed by the SBLC and went out on periodic expeditions to locate the lands to be selected immediately after the federal surveyors had completed an area survey and had opened it for filing. They would cover a specified area, making such selections as were allowable and, in their judgment, advantageous to the state. As a basis for their selections, they used the United States Geological Survey maps. They could only select lands already surveyed.

The state agents tried to select lands in blocs in areas with the best drainage and the most water, which would be good for leasing to cattlemen for grazing purposes, preferably in river basins and along river banks whenever possible. The state had decided rather early that, in most cases, leasing the lands and insuring a permanent income that could be added to the permanent fund were preferable to selling them outright; and during most of the subsequent years, the state's land selection policy was shaped to that end. When lands rightfully due the state under the common-school grant were subject to conflicting claims, the state agents were sent to the United States land office to procure their relinquishment, so that they could then be turned over to the state. This was a rather delicate matter, since it generally meant providing alternate lands for the settler and convincing him to take them.

Often private citizens were desirous of leasing or, where allowed, purchasing certain specific tracts from the state that were then in the hands of the federal government. For example, a cattleman might want exclusive control over a waterhole and not be able to claim it from the federal government under the Homestead Act. He would then approach the SBLC and request them to investigate the tract with a view to acquiring the land for lease to him. The board would send an agent to examine the land and appraise it. If it was good land and met the state's conditions, application for it would be made. If it was patented to the state after the normal procedures had been followed, it could then be leased to the interested party. In this way, many cattlemen seem to have supported their herds, particularly after the close of the open range. By using the wide expanses of the federal public domain for grazing purposes and the land leased from the state for water, they could have benefits of a silent three-way partnership to promote the cattle industry.

The state board filed the lists of lands selected with the local United States land office in the district where the lands were located. The land office then posted a copy of the list for public examination as part of the process of clearing title before transfer to the state. Notice was placed alongside the lists instructing any claimants to submit their claims to the land office; and copies of the list and notices were sent to the SBLC. If no claimants came forward within the set time limits, the land could be patented to the state.

From time to time the General Land Office issued instructions as to how the states were to make their selections. These were uniform national rules sent to every state and United States land office; and all selections were governed by them. As in Minnesota, the federal officials did not hesitate to demand full compliance with their conditions.

In some cases, land claimed by private citizens under United States law was relinquished to the federal government after arrangements had been made for the state to claim it and lease it back to the original claimants. This was a particularly common occurrence in the case of lands claimed under the timber culture acts. When a private claimant discovered that he would have to forfeit the land for not growing trees, he would arrange to have the state select it for re-leasing. The SBLC would be willing to do this, if the lands were suitable, since it insured them an income. There are a number of cases in which the filing fees (which even the state had to pay to the federal government to obtain lands) were paid by the prospective private lessees.[6]

All expenses for selecting, locating, appraising, leasing, and selling the lands were provided by state legislative appropriations, since none of the money earned from the lands themselves could be used for any purpose other than the appropriate permanent fund. The SBLC was authorized to sell school lands or lease them at its discretion, subject to applicable state and federal laws. Sale could not be made for less than the state-appraised price. The annual rent for leased lands was also determined by a proration of their appraised value. No lease could be given for more than five years without a reappraisal,[7] except when minerals were found on the land (if the minerals were found after transfer to the state, the mineral lands remained state property) and suitable royalties were paid the state for their extraction.

[6] Abundant records of cases illustrating all aspects of land selection, location, and leasing are on file in the Colorado State Archives, State Board of Land Commissioners' Records.

[7] In 1881, this provision was changed to allow leasing for twenty years, with the board retaining the right of reappraisal every five, if "they shall deem it best for the interest of the State" (Colorado, *Statutes,* Act of February 18, 1881).

ADMINISTRATION OF THE GRANTS-IN-LAND

Intergovernmental collaboration was a major feature in the administration of the land grants as well. As in the later cash grants, local officials were involved in the administration of the grants through the state and only infrequently came into direct contact with federal officials. The local share in the partnership was no smaller because of this indirect relationship. Rather, it is testimony to a continued ability of the states to absorb federal grants and utilize them without branding the grants with federal markings. This is no less true in the twentieth century than in the nineteenth.

The county superintendent of schools in each county was responsible for enforcing the leasing arrangements for all state lands located in his county. If people continued to occupy state lands in his county, he administered the procedures for removing squatters or legitimizing their residence in co-operation with the county attorney, who could institute any legal proceedings against them under the state law. Expenses incurred in this process were paid by the state board from its appropriation.

The county commissioners were also involved in this program as a rudimentary appeals board. When a resident of their county had occupied and improved lands prior to their selection by the state, he could present his case to the county commissioners, who could then petition the state board to appraise and sell the lands in question, up to 160 acres per person, to the settler "for the good of the citizens of the county." Upon receipt of such a request, the board would appoint "three disinterested householders residing in said county" to appraise the lands and improvements and report to the board. If the board thought it advisable, it could then have the lands sold in the regular manner. As in the Minnesota railroad land-grant cases, the settlers were citizens and voters and as such commanded the attention of holders of public office on all levels of government. Consequently, elaborate provisions were developed for safeguarding the rights even of squatters, which provided for compensation for improvements and options to lease the land on which they had settled. School lands were as a rule exempted from this procedure as permanently inalienable;[8] however, even they could be sold in some very specific cases. When situated within, or adjacent to, an organized city or town, the SBLC could have them platted and sold as subdivisions. They

[8] Colorado, *Statutes,* Act of February 10, 1879.

could be sold to cities for schools, parks, or public buildings, provided that the local authorities submitted the highest bids at a public sale. Local authorities had the right to request the board to put lands they desired up for sale.[9]

Leasing arrangements also involved state-local collaboration. The state was obliged by law to allow one renewal if the leaseholder had complied with the conditions, posted a suitable bond, and would pay a year's rental based on a new appraisal. The secretary of the SBLC would order the county school superintendent to appoint an appraiser, the leaseholder would appoint a second one, and the two appraisers would appoint a third. Their appraisal, as communicated to the secretary, could not be lower than the previous one. After the first renewal, however, the board could refuse to renew in the best interests of the state. If the leaseholder should not want to renew his lease, he had the right to remove or otherwise dispose of any improvements he had made on the land prior to the lease's expiration.

In 1887, the SBLC was given wider discretion as to the sale of school lands when they considered it to be in the best interests of the school fund. Any school lands that were to be sold had to be auctioned publicly with a minimum price of $3.50 per acre. Mineral lands could be leased on a royalty basis; but no leases of any kind could be made for more than five years. It had been too easy for leaseholders to avoid reappraisal under the previously granted twenty-year leases. As usual, the provisions for state land sales virtually duplicated those of the federal government. Generally, the only variations were in the size of the tracts that could be sold and the mode of payment. Even when lands could not be sold, the board was authorized to grant rights of way for irrigation ditches, reservoirs, railroads, roads, or telegraph lines. They could also grant land to localities for school building sites. These provisions also conformed with federal land laws, or as in the last case, with the terms of the common-school grant.[10]

Although these administrative activities were ostensibly state-local in character, they brought the SBLC, its agents, and, occasionally, the county officials working with the state agency into almost daily contact with officials of the federal government either directly through the local United States land offices and surveyors or by mail with the General

9 *Ibid.*, Act of February 12, 1881.

10 *Ibid.*, Act of April 2, 1887.

Land Office or the secretary of the interior in Washington. As in Minnesota and the other public-land states, the line between public and private, direct federal and federal-state grants, was obscured. The problems revolved around one central feature, the public domain, and could not be divided by level of government, particularly since private citizens did not find it in their interests so to divide it.

POLICY, POLITICS, AND ADMINISTRATION: THE PERMANENT SCHOOL FUND

While the foregoing procedures for implementing the various land-grant programs were being refined, the permanent school fund was growing, as shown in Table 4. In one decade the fund had become an estab-

TABLE 4

GROWTH OF THE COLORADO PERMANENT SCHOOL FUND, 1881–88*

Biennium	Amount in Fund	Annual Earned Rental	Amount Distributed to Counties	Acres under Lease
1881–82........	†	†	$31,000	†
1883–84........	$ 75,000	$ 22,484	†	†
1885–86........	114,220	109,545	†	449,850
1887–88........	488,685	69,821	86,836‡	1,280,559

* Total grant: 3,500,000 acres. Statistics in the table are from Colorado, *Governors' Messages.*
† Not available.
‡ Distribution based on earnings in previous biennium.

lished means of state support for the common schools. At the time, it was the only source of state aid to the localities for education.

The growing trend toward state supervision of the local school districts continued to be abetted by the fund. The state was attempting to standardize administrative procedures and did so by distributing such materials as standard forms and registers to the local school districts, which were paid for through deductions from the permanent fund distribution.[11] In 1887, actual distribution of the funds was made contingent on the receipt of annual reports from the county superintendents. Following the months of June and September, the state auditor would notify the state superintendent of public instruction as to the amount of money credited to the Permanent School Fund for distribution. The state superintendent then

[11] *Ibid.*, Act of February 4, 1879.

apportioned the money among the state's counties that had filed reports with his office on the basis of the county's share of the state school population. He would certify this apportionment to the state auditor, who would then issue a state warrant to each county treasurer for the amount due his county.

State land policy became an important question in Colorado politics in 1876 and has remained one since. Generally, these policy questions have revolved around two differing views of the most profitable way to employ the state lands. Traditionally, some have advocated sale of the lands and investment of the proceeds while others have supported leasing the lands and the investment of the income.

During the eighties, the fund's rate of growth continued to be great, partly because, under the Democratic administration of Governor Adams, the state's policy of not selling school lands was altered. For nearly a decade, lands were sold, but only to actual settlers in tracts not exceeding one half-section, or to encourage the construction of irrigation canals.[12] In the latter case, the state followed the federal lead and sold only alternate sections, with a view to enhancing the value of the ones it retained.

In 1893, however, Republican Governor John L. Routt reinstated the original policy of the state in regard to the land grants, particularly the school lands:

These lands, bequeathed by the wise policy of our National Government, as a heritage to assist in the education of our children, and in the construction of needed internal improvements, should be always strictly guarded from spoliation at the hands of unscrupulous speculators and from the cupidity of designing officials. I am happy to report . . . that the present Board has, upon all occasions, unanimously held to a very conservative policy in dealing with this question. The report of its transactions show that during the entire incumbency in office, less than 4,000 acres have been disposed of, and a large proportion of this was sold for use as reservoirs and for other special purposes. We have held that unless some special occasion demanded it, that the proper policy, under present conditions, was to save the land, and secure for the school fund the benefits of the increased value which is accruing upon these lands.[13]

Since the Routt administration inaugurated the reform movement that reinstated the original policy of leasing the school lands, it secured

[12] Colorado, *Governors' Messages* (Alva Adams), 1888.
[13] *Ibid.* (John L. Routt), 1893.

amendment of the state's land laws incorporating this policy revision. However, it was not as a result of the statutory requirements that the reform was maintained, since they did not appreciably alter the previous legislation on the subject. The amount of discretion that had, of necessity, to be left with the state board could be interpreted either conservatively or liberally. The success of the reform movement lay in its acceptance by the people and by Routt's successors. His immediate successor, the Populist Governor Waite, reaffirmed this policy,[14] but Governor Adams, who was returned to office after eight years, changed the board's policy back to what it had been during his previous term as governor:

The present board has deemed it wise to sell lands to actual settlers, chiefly, for two reasons. One, because of the necessity of securing water upon the lands before all of the water shall have been taken by owners of other land, in which event, the state lands would have value only for pasturage purposes. Second, because such sales would result in the settling up of the agricultural regions resulting in a development of those sections, and the payment to the state of taxes.[15]

The differences in land policy between Routt and Adams were closely tied to the party politics of the era. Both men were leaders in the state and in their respective parties from the advent of statehood. Routt, the Republican, had been territorial governor and first governor of the state. After a decade "in retirement," he had been recalled as a compromise candidate in the midst of an intraparty struggle to run for the governorship again. Adams, a member of one of Colorado's leading Democratic families, served non-consecutive terms as governor and ran for office many times in the days when the Democrats were by no means the majority party in the state. The differences between the two men in land policy were based on two honestly held but diametrically opposed premises that were not new to Colorado. The question of whether the public domain is to be held in trust for the people as a whole or sold to individuals to promote the general prosperity is an old one in American history; and Colorado in the late nineteenth century provided the setting for a practical expression of the conflict. If the political tide sometimes flowed one way and sometimes the other, it is indicative of how important the issue was among the issues facing the state at the time.

The school lands due the state were virtually all selected by the turn

[14] *Ibid.* (David H. Waite), 1899.

[15] *Ibid.* (Alva Adams), 1897.

of the century, yet their role in promoting education in Colorado, though already great, was to persist and grow. The following tables are illustrative of their status in recent years.

In the first place, the Permanent Fund is still growing. Table 5 gives the sources of cash receipts for Colorado's Public School Permanent Fund, which is based on the United States common-school land grant. These cash receipts, which came to over $1,700,000 annually in the mid-1950's, stem primarily from sales of the granted lands and royalties earned through sales or lease of mineral rights on the lands. Under the

TABLE 5

CASH RECEIPTS OF THE COLORADO PUBLIC-SCHOOL
PERMANENT FUND, 1954–56*

Source	July 1, 1954, to June 30, 1955	July 1, 1955, to June 30, 1956
Sales (lands, improvements, rights of way)....	$ 261,336	$ 287,735
Royalties (minerals, etc.).................	684,695	605,364
Repayment of loans......................	106,335	153,638
Transfers..............................	2,705	14,483
Investments liquidated...................	955,345	661,632
Total receipts.........................	$1,722,711	$1,722,852
Cash balance on July 1.................	243,769	166,900
Total...............................	$1,966,480	$1,889,752
Investments purchased...................	$1,798,500	$1,834,448

* Source: SBLC Report, 1954–57.

terms of the federal grant, the fund is invested in various ways and the proceeds of the investment comprise the public school income fund.

The total income earned by the investments of the permanent fund comprises the Public School Income Fund, which is distributed to the state's schools. In 1954–55, income from land, timber, and mineral rentals and interest on investments totaled $3,035,250. In 1955–56, this total increased to $3,341,612.

The Public School Permanent Fund is invested in a number of ways, primarily in United States and local government bonds and United States insured loans. As of June, 1956, the permanent fund had assets of $20,517,-786. Its major investment—$8,375,281 in school district bonds—is indicative of the fund's continuing secondary role as a revolving fund for meeting the capital needs of local school districts.

Of the 3,757,447 acres in the original common-school land grant, 938,-226 acres have been sold and 2,774,221 acres remain in the possession of the State Board of Land Commissioners. In 1956, 2,666,044 acres were being leased by the SBLC, 120,826 were used for agricultural purposes and 2,511,835 for grazing. Every county in the state, except fully urban Denver, has state-leased agricultural or grazing lands within its boundaries. The fifty acres leased by the state in Denver form the major part of the Denver municipal golf course attached to City Park.

In 1955–56, the legislature of the state of Colorado appropriated $14,-000,000 (in round figures) as the state subsidy to the local school districts. With the addition of the two federal-state funds (the permanent school fund and the revenues from federal mineral leases), which are automatically distributed to the local districts, the state provided a total of $19,472,000 (in round figures) to aid the localities. Of this amount, $3,146,000 (in round figures), or over 16 per cent of the total, was from the fund established as a result of the federal land-grant program, a figure fully comparable to the percentage of federal contributions in more recently enacted grant-in-aid programs.

IMPACT AND SCOPE OF THE GRANTS-IN-LAND

Despite Colorado's relatively late achievement of statehood in relation to the land-grant programs, the state still benefited (and continues to benefit) immeasurably from the grants it received. The land grants played a significant role in the creation of the state's public school system. They were in great part responsible for the creation of the state system of higher education. Money from the internal improvement fund provided virtually all the state aid for road and bridge construction prior to the passage of the Federal Highway Act well into the twentieth century. The foundations of Colorado's irrigation system were laid as a result of the land-grant programs. Even the railroads that came into the state benefited from federal-state partnerships based on grants of the public domain.

Tables 6 and 7 illustrate the progressive disposal of the acres received by the state and the funds that accrued as a result. These charts cover the formal federal-state land-grant programs, all the lands that passed from the hands of the federal government to the state, which handled their disposition in accordance with the specific land-grant acts. The charts do not include the right-of-way grants, the percentage-of-proceeds grants, or the cash grants.

Many questions have been raised as to the actual value of the lands when they were sold by the state. In theory, the lands were valued at $1.25 to $2.50 per acre throughout the land-grant period. Congress was quite specific in this assessment of their value, as indicated by the price it attached to the alternate sections in the railroad and canal land grants, which were retained by the federal government. The Congressional valuation is an unmistakable sign that the Congress had every intention of grant-

TABLE 6

SUMMARY TABLE OF STATE LAND SALES, ACREAGE SOLD,
AND AVERAGE PRICES PER ACRE IN COLORADO*

Biennial Term	Acres Sold	Average Price
1885–1886..........................	12,836.00	....
1887–1888..........................	67,738.00	$ 7.80
1889–1890..........................	78,464.00	7.85
1891–1892..........................	28,320.00	....
1893–1894..........................	9,621.00	....
1895–1896..........................	41,980.00	4.57
1897–1898..........................	12,980.00	14.71
1899–1900..........................	3,130.00	4.35
1901–1902..........................	10,329.00	6.25
1903–1904..........................	11,120.00	6.25
1905–1906..........................	29,926.00	6.90
1907–1908..........................	60,356.25	8.31
1909–1910..........................	287,340.63	11.59
1911–1912..........................	79,639.33	10.38
1913–1914..........................	91,215.57	7.35
1915–1916..........................	134,218.87	10.27
1917–1918..........................	224,005.57	14.37
1919–1920..........................	156,502.25	21.38
1921–1922..........................	33,753.99	17.74
1923–1924..........................	10,346.52	12.62
1925–1926..........................	21,384.28	13.28
1927–1928..........................	25,513.04	15.33
1929–1930..........................	99,135.85	10.96
December 1, 1930, to June 30, 1932...	25,030.32	9.55
July 1, 1932, to June 30, 1934........	4,374.89	12.03
July 1, 1934, to June 30, 1936........	9,218.07	11.76
July 1, 1936, to June 30, 1938........	19,769.71	11.76
July 1, 1938, to June 30, 1940........	30,757.50	8.18
July 1, 1940, to June 30, 1942........	15,304.62	9.73
July 1, 1942, to June 30, 1944........	62,079.97	8.22
July 1, 1944, to June 30, 1946........	57,392.53	16.40
July 1, 1946, to June 30, 1948........	49,159.01	18.66
July 1, 1948, to June 30, 1950........	36,584.02	27.57
July 1, 1950, to June 30, 1952........	39,599.71	38.73
July 1, 1952, to June 30, 1954........	24,683.27	45.22
July 1, 1954, to June 30, 1956........	23,857.95	43.16

* SBLC Report, 1954–56, p. 37.

ing lands with a specified value in lieu of cash and that the two types of grant were not regarded as essentially different. Later, as in the case of the Colorado school land grant, a minimum price of $2.50 was set by federal law for all of the acreage involved. A two-section school land grant was supposed to provide $1,600 for schools in each township if the lands were sold. The actual price per acre of granted land in Colorado after

TABLE 7

SUMMARY TABLE OF RECEIPTS OF THE COLORADO STATE BOARD
OF LAND COMMISSIONERS*

Biennial Term	Receipts
1877–1878	$ 44,000.00
1879–1880	112,000.00
1881–1882	112,184.09
1883–1884	239,508.89
1885–1886	291,251.99
1887–1888	642,044.87
1889–1890	758,377.76
1891–1892	479,705.74
1893–1894	255,757.28
1895–1896	231,561.96
1897–1898	238,008.60
1899–1900	355,305.97
1901–1902	372,372.79
1903–1904	574,176.04
1905–1906	684,683.62
1907–1908	825,901.67
1909–1910	1,294,064.08
1911–1912	1,596,428.96
1913–1914	1,364,763.66
1915–1916	1,788,430.54
1917–1918	2,509,238.52
1919–1920	3,160,643.02
1921–1922	2,053,990.53
1923–1924	1,908,170.37
1925–1926	2,275,575.33
1927–1928	1,912,416.68
1929–1930	1,895,065.05
December 1, 1930, to June 30, 1932 (19 months only)	1,040,210.14
July 1, 1932, to June 30, 1934	826,385.51
July 1, 1934, to June 30, 1936	1,157,404.50
July 1, 1936, to June 30, 1938	1,371,369.74
July 1, 1938, to June 30, 1940	1,146,778.58
July 1, 1940, to June 30, 1942	1,275,934.85
July 1, 1942, to June 30, 1944	1,924,808.59
July 1, 1944, to June 30, 1946	2,218,557.15
July 1, 1946, to June 30, 1948	2,498,499.15
July 1, 1948, to June 30, 1950	2,733,258.63
July 1, 1950, to June 30, 1952	4,513,679.63
July 1, 1952, to June 30, 1954	5,714,053.29
July 1, 1954, to June 30, 1956	7,982,905.42

* SBLC Report, 1954–1956, p. 38.

1885 exceeded the theoretical value established by Congress. The lowest average price per acre was $4.35, and in the 1897–98 biennium, the average price per acre rose to $14.71. It is true that in the earlier days of the land grants many of the states did not sell their lands at a proper price. As experience was gained and lands became less plentiful, the newer states were able to earn much more from sale of the lands. The Colorado case illustrates this clearly.

Apart from the money received from land sales, which had to be invested in the appropriate permanent funds to insure a steady flow of income, there were the proceeds of these funds coupled with the rentals of leased lands. The most direct benefits emerging from the land-grant programs were those that came from the use of this annual income from investments and rentals (and, later, mineral royalties). In the case of Colorado, this income has been substantial. Only in the first biennium after statehood was the revenue from the grants below $100,000. Between 1879 and 1900, the biennial revenues from the land grants varied between $112,000 and $758,000, no mean sum in a nineteeth-century state budget.

Federal-state co-operation in the implementation of the land-grant programs has not fully ended (as of 1962). By the middle of the twentieth century, the co-operative activities had been reduced to mere shadows of their former magnitude but continued in the transfer of small parcels of land under the authority of one program or another. For example, Minnesota received some acreage under the Swamp Land Grant in 1958, after a survey of lands still in the public domain revealed some swamp lands previously not surveyed that belonged to the state under the terms of the grant.

In the same year, the grants-in-land aspect of the federal grants-in-aid program took a new turn. With the admission of Alaska to the Union, a temporary revival of the entire range of land grants was initiated. Under the terms of the Alaska Statehood Act, Congress extended all the relevant land-grant programs to the new state, subject to the same co-operative administrative procedures described above. When all the selections are completed, Alaska will have received 102 million acres of public lands, the largest over-all land-grant transfer in American history.

It is possible that the Alaska grants presaged a modest revival of land grants to other states as well. In the summer of 1961, the Kennedy Administration's secretary of the interior, Stewart Udall, announced the establishment of a new program to enable the eighteen remaining public-land states to acquire federal lands within their boundaries for school purposes for the nominal price of $2.50 per acre. This program turned out to be the first step in a larger federal effort to aid American cities by enabling them to acquire open lands in adjacent areas. This new departure in federal land policy is embodied in the Housing Act of 1961.

At this writing, it is unlikely that even this new departure will lead to a large-scale federal land-grant program in the foreseeable future in any way comparable to the great land-grant programs of the last century. Yet the direct impact of federal land grants is still widespread even without new infusions. The permanent funds of the majority of the old public-land states attest to this continuing impact by their continued productive existence.

13

The Maturing Partnership and the Eastern States

The Hartford Deaf and Dumb Asylum and the Virginia military bounty program were two early examples of the beneficent impact of the public domain on every section of the nation. As the number of public-land states grew, the nationwide impact of the public domain became even more pronounced.

SURPLUS DISTRIBUTIONS AS FINANCIAL
AIDS IN NEW HAMPSHIRE

The first major federal program to apply the benefits of the public lands on a nationwide basis was the distribution of the treasury surplus among the states in 1837, which was followed by similar distributions in the 1840's. Through these surplus distributions, vital federal aid to education was furnished even to states like New Hampshire, which had shared the New England tradition of providing a common-school education for the young since the seventeenth century. Public schools supported by local school districts had been mandatory under New Hampshire colonial, then state, law since 1716. Prior to 1885, however, the state did little more than require local districts to maintain common schools with minimal state support through permanent Literary Funds, similar to the one developed in Virginia. Before these funds were created to provide what were essentially stimulatory grants to the local districts, the compulsory school laws were generally unenforced. While the laws placed primary responsibility for support of the common schools on the local districts, the majority of the localities tended to take action only in so far as

200

they were stimulated by the state government. The state government, in turn, was not prone to assume responsibility for the schools because such responsibility meant increased taxation. Thus, the state waited to be stimulated by the federal government. Though seemingly paradoxical, it is generally accurate to conclude that what has commonly been considered to be the most local of nineteenth-century functions, the New England common school, was ultimately started on the road to effectiveness (at least in New Hampshire) by means of stimulatory grants from the federal government because the state and local governments hesitated to act.

The stimulatory effect of the federal surplus distributions could be interpreted as accidental on the grounds that the distributions were not designed to be aids to education but unrestricted grants of extra money accumulated in the United States Treasury. Under this interpretation, New Hampshire's use of the funds to stimulate public education is little credit to the federal government. If the distribution was but an undirected means of ridding the federal government of a burdensome surplus of revenues, this interpretation could be taken to be the correct one. If, however, the surplus distribution was part of a planned move to aid the states in the development of services needed by each and by the country as a whole, then the use of federal funds to stimulate education in New Hampshire can be interpreted as a legitimate intergovernmental co-operative program. Abundant evidence is present to support the second interpretation.

The surplus-distribution movement arose shortly after the conclusion of the War of 1812 as part of the nationwide concern with activity in the fields of internal improvement and education. Between 1816 and 1836, a substantial number of proposals were put forward calling for the use of any revenues that might remain in the federal treasury after the war debt was repaid to construct needed internal improvements or subsidize educational activities. Some of these proposals advocated direct federal expenditures under a broad interpretation of the Constitution; others were designed to secure a constitutional amendment that would permit such federal activity. Still others wanted the federal government to grant the money, according to various formulas, to the states for specific purposes. Another group wanted to distribute the money under some general formula among the states without restriction as to use, on the grounds that it would certainly be used for either internal improvement or education in some form, depending on the needs of each state, and that an attempt

on the part of the federal government to set specific purposes would necessarily fail to include all the legitimate alternatives.

The funds to be distributed were to come from the proceeds of the
public land sales and from the tariff receipts, then the two major sources
of federal revenues. Since both of these sources were subjects of important and controversial political interests in their own right, twenty years
elapsed before a distribution formula that took these other interests into
consideration could be worked out.

Speculators and promoters of western settlement were impatient with
the policy of the federal government toward the disposal of the public
domain. Many of them wanted the public lands turned over to the states
in which they were located, where the impatient people would have a
better chance of securing tracts at little cost. These interests resisted any
permanent surplus distribution program based on land revenues because
of the vested interests it would create in favor of maintaining federal control over the public domain and federal use of the public lands to raise
revenue rather than to promote settlement. They used the states'-rights
argument to support their cause and even attracted some of the more
doctrinaire states'-righters to their camp.

The majority of the states, northern and southern, opposed any attempt to take the public domain out of federal hands. The eastern states
already felt that they were not receiving their proper share of the return
from the national domain. They were interested in a more equitable distribution, not in increasing the supposed imbalance that had resulted
from the federal land-grant programs. Thus, they tended to support proposals for surplus distribution. The issue was further complicated by the
tariff question. The southern states were generally in favor of surplus distribution but were unalterably opposed to the protective tariff. As long
as a permanent surplus distribution program meant a permanently high
tariff, they were content to do without the desired federal aid.

Yet the need for federal aid in promoting internal improvements and
education persisted. As in the case of New Hampshire, other states were
either unable or unwilling to finance the programs themselves, particularly when funds were available in the United States Treasury and the
states' main source of revenue, the property tax in its various forms, was
considered so odious by their rural, agricultural citizenry.

A compromise between the interests was developed by the middle of
Jackson's first term as President, leaving only the constitutional issue.
While unilateral federal action and relinquishment of the public lands to

the states were both rejected as extremist proposals, the case for inter-governmental collaboration had crystallized and found a spokesman in Senator Mahlon Dickerson, of New Jersey, who presented the co-opera-tive principle to the country in a series of Senate reports. In the first of these reports, prepared in 1830, Dickerson opposed unilateral action on the grounds that it would unconstitutionally interfere with the rights of the states. (This was not an argument against participation by the federal government, but only against its direct and exclusive action.) He opposed a scheme by which the public-land states would receive the lands within their boundaries after assuming an obligation to pay the federal govern-ment for them at the minimum price of $1.25 per acre as the land was sold as a threat to the independence of the states, since they would be-come so heavily indebted to the federal government through such an ar-rangement. He opposed an outright gift of the public domain to the pub-lic-land states as a violation of the compacts by which the western lands were ceded to the federal government in the first place—to be used for the benefit of the whole nation.

Perhaps Dickerson's most telling argument rested on his feeling that the federal government was better equipped to raise revenues for govern-mental activities that were in the national interest than were the states. He spent some time discussing the constitutional advantages of the fed-eral government in raising revenue by its use of the least odious forms of taxation as compared with the states, dependent as they were on land and property taxes. He concluded that rather than relinquish its sources of revenue, the federal government should use them to the advantage of the states themselves by a proper method of revenue distribution that would equalize the benefits throughout the Union in so far as possible. This would have the added advantage of maintaining national sources of revenue for use in times of national emergency to avoid the recurrence of financial difficulties such as those which faced the federal government during the War of 1812.

In the same report, Dickerson and his committee submitted a reasoned plan for a surplus-distribution program. The immediate political problem that confronted them included the development of a distribution formula that would satisfy the demands of the states without public lands for re-dress of the supposed imbalance in United States aid without discrimi-nating against the public-land states to the point that they would oppose the entire program. They also had to find a mode of distribution that would guarantee the most return for the money expended. This meant reasonable federal controls to indicate the general use to which the funds were to be put without the inclusion of conditions of the type that would alienate the states'-rights bloc. Dickerson came to the conclusion that the funds did not have to be specifically earmarked in the proposed legislation, because there was such a general consensus as to the purpose of the distribution that it was unnecessary to directly antagonize the strict constructionists. As he put it, "It is not proposed to restrict the states in the application of the funds to be assigned to them as the states may be safely trusted to make the best use of their own—to make new roads and canals —to pay the heavy debts already contracted in making roads and canals— or in establishments for the purposes of education, as their exigencies or interests may require."[1]

On June 23, 1836, the surplus-distribution measure, based on the Dickerson reports and sponsored by Henry Clay, of Kentucky, was finally enacted into law. It provided for the lending (subject to recall) of any surplus in the Treasury that exceeded five million dollars (whenever it should occur) to the states on the basis of their representation in Congress. The representational basis of apportionment provided a means of equalizing benefits, while the legal technicality of a loan provided some acceptable form of potential federal control. The uses to which the funds were to be put were not specified, but the very form of the distribution was designed to encourage their investment in some type of permanent fund that could be used for internal improvement or education, the two activities generally supported by permanent funds in that period.

Although the Panic of 1837 and the resulting drop in federal revenues forced the federal government to suspend the program entirely after the payment of three of the quarterly installments, the money received by the more populous eastern states often equaled the total amounts received by the public-land states from sale of lands granted to them for similar purposes over many years. In the ante bellum period, very little money was needed to create a permanent fund that would provide a substantial share of state and local governmental expenses. This money, invested in some manner consistent with its designated use, provided the additional support needed to expand educational, banking, and internal improvement programs to meet at least the minimum needs of the age.

[1] U.S. Senate, *Report on the President's Message as Respects the Distribution of the United States Surplus*, 21st Cong., 1st Sess. (1830), Doc. 139. This remarkable report could be used to justify any grant-in-aid program. Dickerson even discussed the problem of differentials in state tax rates raising problems for high-tax states in the attraction of industry.

New Hampshire took the first step toward allocating its share of the surplus within months after the passage of the act. As in the case of every grant-in-aid program, the state legislature had to formally accept the grant and the conditions attached to it. In its session of November, 1836, the New Hampshire General Court accepted the grant as a loan and agreed to repay it on the demand of the federal government. The legislature also provided for the distribution of the grant to the towns in the state to be used for any legitimate governmental purpose. Vesting the funds in the localities was quite in line with the general policy in New England at the time. Most governmental activities were left in the hands of the towns, placed there by state legislation which set minimum standards and provided for their general supervision on a rather casual basis.[2]

Under the terms of the act, the money was to be deposited with the towns according to a formula based on the assessment figures for taxation of each town (one half) and on the number of ratable polls in 1836 (the other half). Each town meeting had to accept the money by formal resolution, pledge the faith of the town for its safekeeping and repayment if recalled by the state "upon the requisition of the United States," and appoint an agent to receive the funds and execute certificates to the state treasurer to that effect. The state treasurer would then distribute the funds as they were received from the federal government.

In the original act, the towns were forbidden to spend the principal of the money received on penalty of double repayment to the state. They could loan the funds to individuals and corporations as they saw fit and use the interest for any legitimate purpose. This section was repealed, except for any penalties already incurred, in 1838, and was replaced by a provision that the funds received could be loaned with good security in amounts of $25 or more or appropriated for any purposes for which the towns could lawfully raise taxes.

Each town was given the option to decide whether it wanted to assume control over its share of the funds or leave their management to the state. When the state treasurer received the installments from the United

---

[2] Alexis de Tocqueville discusses this at length in *Democracy in America*, in which he concludes that local government was the predominant, if not only, form of government in contact with the great mass of citizens in mid-nineteenth-century America. His account has contributed in no small measure to the theory of dual federalism as a concomitant of the general theory of "little government." His views, which seem to be erroneous, may have stemmed from a tendency to contrast American decentralized government with the strongly centralized government that he knew in his native France; and from observing American government from the vantage point of New England, where it was far more locally centered than in the South or West.

States Treasury, he notified the towns by publishing announcements in the appropriate newspapers. If any town neglected or refused to take its share of the funds within ninety days after the last publication date, the state treasurer placed the money in the state fund, used it for lending purposes, and applied the interest received to the benefit of the towns in question. Subsequently, if the towns decided that they wanted the money, they could claim it after giving the treasurer six months' notice. In the case of unincorporated areas, the treasurer managed their shares in a similar manner, using the interest for local benefits. Upon incorporation, any such areas could claim their shares in the same manner as any other town.[3]

After the governor had officially notified the secretary of the treasury that New Hampshire had accepted the terms and conditions of the act of Congress, the treasurer of the United States made arrangements with the state treasurer for the actual transfer of funds. The funds were transferred in quarterly installments, three of which were paid before the Panic of 1837 ended the program. They were placed on deposit in various state banks by the United States treasurer in the name of the state. The state treasurer then certified to the banks that he had received the money. The banks had to accept this certification and forward it to the United States treasurer before the deposits were released to the state.

On January 30, 1837, New Hampshire received the first installment in transfer drafts, totaling $223,028.93, which were placed in the Merrimack Bank. As soon as the proportions accredited to each town had been ascertained, most of the towns began claiming their shares. Some invested the money they received in permanent educational trust funds. Others used the money for internal improvements. One town, Concord, used the funds to match a state grant in order to obtain the New Hampshire Insane Asylum for its area. The state treasurer invested the funds of the remaining towns and unincorporated areas and distributed the interest annually.

The immediate benefits of the 1837 distribution were limited, in part because of a near scandal in the incumbent state treasurer's use of the

---

[3] For a very brief description of the nationwide program for surplus distribution, see William J. Shultz and M. R. Caine, *Financial Development of the United States* (New York: Prentice-Hall, Inc., 1937), pp. 217–19. Records of the actual administrative procedures involved for the states of Virginia and New Hampshire (and others) may be found in U.S. Treasury Department, *Letters from Banks, 1837–1840;* Virginia House of Delegates, *Journal for the 1838 Session,* Document Section; and New Hampshire, *Laws* (1836), approved January 13, 1836; and New Hampshire, *Laws* (1838), chap. 375, approved July 4, 1838.

interest accumulated in the local banks, in which the state-managed funds were on deposit.[4] The program as a whole was set back ten years.

Meanwhile on the national scene, proponents of a permanent annual distribution program were seeking new legislation that would fill the gap left by the failure of the Act of 1836. As in the first attempt, Henry Clay led the fight. He had originally attempted to secure passage of a more comprehensive measure, which, although confined to distribution of the revenues earned from public-land sales, would have provided for an annual distribution based on a formula designed to satisfy both the new and the old states. Clay's plan, first submitted in 1832 and then in every subsequent session of the Congress, would have been a true cash grant-in-aid and would have specified that the states use the funds for internal improvements and education. In 1832 the plan had passed both houses and was vetoed by President Jackson, who favored surplus distribution but felt that the imposition of conditions was unconstitutional. In 1836, Clay had agreed to the successful surplus-distribution bill as a compromise in order to pass a stopgap measure. Once it was no longer of use, he returned to his original intention of creating a true co-operative grant-in-aid program.[5]

In 1841, he was able to arrange a compromise in the form of an omnibus bill that satisfied agrarian western and southern interests as well as the commercial and manufacturing interests of the eastern and border states. For the agrarian westerners, it authorized settlers to pre-empt their already settled farms on most surveyed lands for the minimum price of $1.25 per acre (excepting only the alternate sections retained by the federal government in land grants, which could only be pre-empted at the statutory minimum of $2.50 per acre). This was a great victory for the agrarian West, as it recognized settlement before purchase as a legal device and made actual settlement of the public domain the cornerstone of United States land policy rather than the former primary interest of using the lands as a source of revenue. For the public-land states, it provided land grants of five hundred thousand acres for the construction of internal improvements (see chapter xvi). This provision was to apply to all new states subsequently admitted to the Union, and it became a major

[4] New Hampshire State Treasurer, *Annual Report* (1847), pp. 68, 90–91; and *Annual Report* (1848). See also New Hampshire, *Report of the Commissioner of the Common Schools* (1847).

[5] Mathias N. Orfield, *Federal Land Grants to the States with Special Reference to Minnesota* (Minneapolis: University of Minnesota Press, 1915), pp. 98–101.

co-operative program. The public-land states were also to receive 10 per cent of the proceeds of the public-land sales within their boundaries. The remainder of the proceeds, minus administrative costs, was to be distributed among the twenty-six states without public lands and the territories on the basis of their representation in the House of Representatives. As an indication of the intentions of the grant, the funds allocated to the District of Columbia were specifically earmarked for educational purposes. No such provisions were included in reference to the states, which were allowed to use the funds as they saw fit, in order to avoid the constitutional question. Again, the issue was not fought out because it was common knowledge that the funds were for the benefit of education or internal improvement. In order to gain the support of the South, which was still afraid that the program would increase the demands for a high tariff (in order to cover government expenses and leave the public-land revenues free for distribution), the measure included a provision that the distribution would cease if the tariff rose to 20 per cent. In one short year, this provision proved to be the death of the entire program.

The Act of 1841 provided an opportunity for the governor and General Court of New Hampshire to state their formal ideological position on the question of federal aid and to contradict it immediately in practice. In his annual message for 1842, Governor Henry Hubbard announced his objections to the distribution on the grounds that money gained from public lands should be used for the common good at the national level and should not accrue to the individual states. He elaborated on this position from the more immediately practical viewpoint that the federal government was in no financial position to undertake such an allocation of a major source (one-fifth) of its revenue without increasing tariffs and taxes. After denouncing the plan as an attempt by the debtor states to have the federal government assume their debts, he continued with an orthodox description of the division of powers between the federal government and the states as outlined in the Constitution, which was based on the separatist thesis. "So long as these two political bodies shall, in their course of action, be confined within their constitutional limits, the sovereignty of the states will never be endangered by the acts of the Federal Government. The harmony of the whole system will be most happily preserved, and the Union faithfully maintained."[6] The most interesting aspect of this message is the lack of concern over the expansion of the federal government, which was implied in his statement that the

[6] New Hampshire, *Governors' Messages to the Legislature,* June 2, 1842.

money in question should be spent for common ends at the national level and that the real danger lay in crossing constitutional lines of separation.

In 1842 and 1845, the General Court went on record as being opposed to any distribution of land-sale revenues. Their views coincided more closely with the states'-rights position on federal grants than with those of Governor Hubbard and his successor, Governor John Steele. They accused the proposal of

indirectly sanctioning the principle, that the federal government might raise money for the purpose of distributing the same back again to the pockets of the people from which it had been drawn, and was thus in its consequences, calculated to make the state governments, and through them the people of the states, the mere dependents and stipendaries of the national government.[7]

Nevertheless, in 1846, the General Court passed an act in which

the treasurer of this state . . . is authorized and required to apply for and receive the portion of the proceeds of the sales of the public lands in the United States treasury, assigned to the state of New Hampshire for the use of the state.[8]

In 1847, as part of the revival of the education fund, the lower house of the General Court requested the state treasurer to report on the amount of surplus revenue as yet undistributed to the towns and what was being done with it. The treasurer, James Peverly, reported that $11,181 remained in his custody. In 1848, the General Court appropriated this fund to be used for educational purposes.[9] In addition to the undistributed funds, the state treasurer held and managed the permanent funds of 18 of the state's 223 townships. The interest from these funds, in addition to that of the $11,181 added in 1848, provided almost the full extent of the state government's contribution to the support of elementary education in New Hampshire prior to 1885. The fund itself continued to supply revenues as an independent source until 1895, when it was incorporated into the general revenues of that year and spent, principal and interest, for current needs, thus ending a program of over half a century's duration.

In 1856 the distribution was taken over by the State Board of Education through the state commissioner of common schools in co-operation with the state treasurer. The amount received by each town was determined on the basis of the number of students four years of age and

[7] New Hampshire, *Laws* (1842), chap. 31; and *Laws* (1845), chap. cclxvii.

[8] New Hampshire, *Laws* (1846), chap. 264, July 7, 1846.

[9] New Hampshire, *Laws* (1848), chap. 644, June 23, 1848.

over who were reported by the local supervising school committee to the secretary of state as having attended at least two weeks of school during the preceding year. The money could be used either for maintaining the common schools in the town or for any other educational purpose.[10]

The Literary Fund was kept formally separate from the Surplus Revenue Fund, though both benefited from federal grants. Primarily supported by a tax paid to the state by its banks for the privilege of issuing currency, the Literary Fund had been created in 1822. The funds received by the state from the federal government between 1841 and 1846 under the acts of 1841 were added to the Literary Fund.[11] In subsequent years, the state government took advantage of the fund to introduce some minimal supervision over the local educational systems. In order to qualify for the annual subventions from the Literary Fund, each town had to report annually to the New Hampshire secretary of state on the condition of its own educational fund (which had generally been established with the money received from the 1837 distribution). Out of these very humble beginnings, the state government gradually increased its role in the public education process.

BENEFITS OF THE SURPLUS IN VIRGINIA

In Virginia, it was the state's internal improvement program that benefited most from the surplus distribution of 1837. The Board of Public Works, presumably in anticipation of the distribution, set the wheels in motion for the expanded financing of the internal improvement program in its report to the General Assembly in that year. In June, 1837, the General Assembly appropriated $110,000 from the surplus to meet interest charges on loans previously contracted by the board. This was the only direct appropriation to the Internal Improvement Fund. Most of the surplus money was used to increase the banking facilities of the state to stimulate semipublic financing of internal improvement projects. A sum of $175,000 was set aside for direct loans to companies pioneering in the then new field of railroad construction. The board, working in close co-

[10] New Hampshire, *Report of the Commissioner of the Common Schools* (1859).

[11] The transfer of the accumulated funds from the federal government to the state took several years. This distribution was repealed in 1842 when the tariff came to exceed the 20 per cent level. See Richard B. Morris, "Federal Land Legislation and Policy Since 1789," *Encyclopedia of American History* (New York: Harper & Bros., 1953), p. 438, for a short summary of the history of the act and its provisions.

operation with the major railroad companies, which were at least partly state-owned, helped some of them secure these loans.[12]

This use of the federal surplus distribution, by no means restricted to Virginia, was a formal indication that the era of roads and canals was giving way to a new era of railroads. This revolutionary change in the transportation system forced corresponding changes to be made in the governmental programs designed to improve transportation. The change from roads and canals to railroads as the primary means of internal communication, coupled with the abandonment of mercantilist capitalism in favor of laissez faire and the nationwide readjustment brought by the Panic of 1837, caused the abandonment of the older co-operative programs as the basic forms of intergovernmental collaboration. That is, although those programs of continuing value, such as the Dismal Swamp Canal, were continued, programs whose value had declined, such as the east-west canal projects that were soon replaced by railroads, were tapered off, and no new ones were started. The change was not uniform around the nation. The South continued to rely heavily on government participation, particularly on the state level, until the Civil War. The West remained very dependent on governmental activity, particularly on the federal level, for some time. But it was the political persuasion and economic approach of the dominant Northeast that was superimposed on all sections of the country.

In this respect, the growth of the railroads was symbolic of the entire age. The new, highly competitive, free-wheeling private enterprise, which reached its highest development in the railroad corporation, changed the value of the old forms of intergovernmental co-operation. As in the case of banking, forms that had brought about beneficial co-operative programs in an economy heavily influenced by governmental activity became inapplicable in a situation in which many competing private groups vied for the favors of government-aided programs. Continued use of the old system actually became inequitable, since it favored some private groups to the detriment of others. A joint-stock company to construct a canal could be a legitimate federal-state project in light of American values because the project was a quasi-monopoly primarily in government hands which would provide equal opportunities for private investors to

---

[12] Virginia Board of Public Works [hereinafter referred to as BPW], *Twenty-second Annual Report* (1838); also, Lieutenant Governor to Auditor's Office, July 19, 1837. By far the largest of these loans was to the Richmond and Petersburg Railroad, which received $98,065.83 by Act of the General Assembly of March 25, 1837.

participate alongside the governments involved. With the development
of railroads, however, many competing companies were striving to serve
the same territory. Anyone who could raise the money and hire the manpower could construct a railroad, whereas canals depended on monopo-
listic control of a water supply. In such cases, if governments invested in
railroad joint-stock companies, they would be competing, at a great advantage to themselves, against private individuals.

Situations like this actually occurred, in which the application of co-
operative devices developed for the mercantilist period led to the favoring of the lucky group of private investors that had secured government
support over their rivals. With the free-enterprise persuasion the order
of the day, the country would not stand for this; and there was a strong
movement to eliminate potential favoritism by eliminating government,
state as well as federal, from any positive role in the economy.

Virginia, as a southern state, was one that continued to participate in
the internal improvement field until 1861, though not nearly to the extent
of some of the others, such as Georgia, which constructed its own wholly
state-owned railroad. Railroad construction in Virginia involved both the
federal and state governments perhaps to a greater degree than in most
of the states without public lands. As in the case of the turnpike and
canal companies, Virginia owned large shares of the major railroad companies operating in the state, control of which was vested in the Board
of Public Works. For example, the state owned $160,000 worth of stock
in the Petersburg Railroad, which had a total capitalization of $605,-
500.[13] In addition, major loans were made to the Petersburg Railroad
and the Richmond, Fredericksburg and Potomac line from the surplus
distribution funds. Revenues received from those railroads as interest
payments on the loans went to the board to pay interest on the Internal
Improvement Fund. In 1838, out of a total interest on the fund of
$31,504.05, the railroads' interest payments supplied $12,166.06, the federal surplus provided $9,947.87, and ordinary revenue (including the
earnings of the federal-state joint-stock companies) provided the remaining $9,390.12.[14]

The federal government entered the field of railroad development directly in the states without public lands through a system of subsidies

[13] Virginia Legislative Documents (Virginia State Archives), 1838, pp. 238 f.

[14] Ibid., p. 380 (Report of the Second Auditor on BPW Accounts). The remainder
of the $110,000 appropriated for the board by the General Assembly from the United
States surplus was used for current expenses.

paid to railroads for carrying the mail. Such a program of mail subsidies was not new in the 1830's, when the railroads first began to qualify as recipients. Subsidies had been available to stagecoach companies for the same purpose for many years primarily in the form of contracts for carrying the mail over specific routes. These contracts were prizes eagerly sought, which often provided the initial capital needed to establish the companies that received them and enabled their owners to build transportation empires based on mail deliveries. As such, they were also extremely important in the economies of large parts of the United States.[15]

Whether by design or through force of circumstance, the federal government developed different patterns for aiding railroads depending on whether they were designed to connect previously settled territories or to open up new ones for settlement. The former were aided primarily through the mail subsidy and also by federal services-in-aid granted through the Army Engineers. The latter received grants of land and material from the public domain. The American value system has recognized pioneering as grounds for government aid since the establishment of the Republic. Since both types of railroads were engaged in pioneering ventures, both were "entitled" to governmental aid on these grounds; but the railroads that opened the West served the cause of the advancing frontier of settlement, then considered to be the most important frontier, and were given even more aid as a consequence.

The Virginia railroads had contracted to carry the mail and receive the subsidy by 1837. While the relationships that developed between the railroad companies and the United States Post Office rarely involved any

---

[15] An outstanding example of the importance of such mail contracts is furnished by the career of James R. Powell, of Alabama. In 1837, Powell was awarded the contract for thrice-weekly hack service between Montgomery and Talladoga, Alabama, through the intercession of his Alabama congressman and the congressman from his former place of residence in Virginia. His goal was to establish a stagecoach company, and he sought the mail contract in order to receive the necessary financing. The post office subsidy was sufficient to enable him to start his stagecoach service, which commenced on July 1, 1838. From this small beginning, he increased his operations, often through the acquisition of additional mail contracts, to cover the greater part of Alabama. When the Civil War broke out, he had stagecoach lines operating in five states, which employed over one thousand men and used five thousand horses. He was even planning to open a southern overland route to California. The war ended his private operations, when he was persuaded by the postmaster-general of the Confederate States to establish and direct the mail service to Texas. For a description of his activities, see *Alabama Review*, X (January, 1957), 62–69. This is a prime example of the impact of federal mail contracts. Powell's story was repeated in most states in one way or another.

state agencies directly, the railroad companies themselves, as creatures of the state, had to report every activity to the state through the Board of Public Works. The amount of the subsidy to be paid to the railroads for carrying the mail was based on mileage, and varied from $150 to $300 per mile. In return, the United States Post Office had considerable control over train schedules. On one hand, this arrangement was beneficial to the state, since it added federal funds to those of Virginia for the development of the railroads. On the other hand, federal control over scheduling to expedite the mails often conflicted with the state's goals of increasing passenger traffic. When conflicts arose, the railroads always brought matters to the board's "particular attention."[16]

The state was not unwilling to use its ownership of the railroad companies for purposes of influencing federal policy when it felt justified in doing so. Its proxies on the boards of directors of the various railroads were active in dealings with the Post Office and often took the lead in these matters. In 1855, the mail contract with the Richmond and Petersburg Railroad was due for one of its periodic renewals. The company (of which the state owned 3,856 out of 8,457 shares, worth slightly more than half of the company's capitalization[17]) wanted to make use of its opportunity to revise the payments upward on the basis of the increased expense involved in transporting the mail, particularly in view of schedule limitations imposed by the Post Office, which lessened passenger revenues. A resolution was drafted, and "at the suggestion of Mr. William F. Watson, state proxy," was adopted unanimously, instructing the company officials to cease transporting the mail until the rate of payment was adjusted and arrangements were made by the Post Office to adjust the schedule of its mail car so as not to interfere with the passenger travel of the Richmond and Petersburg and its connecting lines.[18]

[16] Although the writer has been unable to examine the records of the Post Office Department to ascertain the facts of the matter, it would seem quite likely that the board's attention was invited so that it would either contact the state Congressional delegation, or support the railroad when it should do so, to present the company's case to the postmaster-general and secure a modification or change in post office policy and actions. Some evidence for this view exists in paragraphs of the 1840 and 1843 reports of the Petersburg Railroad to the board, which refer to the Post Office's refusal to pay certain claims made by the railroad and the company's attempt to bring the matter before Congress. BPW, *Twenty-fourth Annual Report* (1840), p. 65; and BPW, *Twenty-eighth Annual Report* (1843), p. 101.

[17] The total value of the stock was $766,100, while the value of the state's shares was $385,000. There were evidently two types of stock issued.

[18] BPW, *Thirty-ninth Annual Report* (1855), p. 63.

Despite these occasional conflicts between established railroad companies and Washington, the newer railroads recognized that mail contracts were vital subsidies, and said so in their stockholders' reports. In 1843, President Walter Gwynn, of the Portsmouth and Roanoke Railroad Company (of which the state owned 5,133 out of 12,833 shares), reported that "The first quarter's instalment is now due by the government for transporting the mail, which amount would enable us to lessen our individual debts $2000 more."[19] If this was an odd and indirect form of intergovernmental collaboration to create a railroad system, it was a very important and successful one, nonetheless.

Although it would be inaccurate to conclude from the evidence submitted above that railroad construction in Virginia was undertaken through the formal co-operative endeavors of the state and federal governments, it is indicative that, even where no formal provisions for such co-operation were made, a high degree of contact in some form or another was made inevitable because the interests of both were involved. Since railroads were one of the major governmental and private enterprises of the mid-nineteenth century, the interests of the two levels of government could not possibly have been prevented from coinciding, just as the public and private interests could not fail to overlap.

Virginia, never a great railroad state, had a minor role compared with her neighbor, Maryland. The latter state was the home of the first, and for many years the major, railroad in the nation, the Baltimore and Ohio. That road, which in the twentieth century has boasted that it was constructed entirely by private enterprise, was partly owned by its home state, which purchased $500,000 worth of stock by legislative enactment in 1828. Its route was surveyed and located by the United States Topographical Engineers, who were detailed by the War Department to serve the company and supervise some of the construction on the ground that this was part of its services as a national planning body.[20] A Congressional measure providing for the United States to purchase $1,000,000 worth of the company's stock failed by a narrow margin, "principally through the opposition of the President of the Chesapeake and Ohio Canal Company, who at that time was Chairman of the Committee of

[19] BPW, *Twenty-eighth Annual Report* (1843), p. 92.

[20] U.S. War Department, "Report of Lieutenant Colonel S. H. Long, William Howard, and Captain William McNeill on the Preliminary Survey of the Route of the Baltimore and Ohio Railroad, 1827," National Archives, Baltimore and Ohio Railroad file.

Roads and Canals of the House of Representatives." And, not least important, the right of way through Virginia was set at Harpers Ferry, with one terminus of the railroad to be at Wheeling, by act of the Virginia General Assembly (permission had to be secured from the state legislature to build through the state and sell stock within its boundaries); and the right of way at Harpers Ferry was obtained as a grant from the federal government.[21] This was more typical of the "hidden" forms of federal subsidy and federal-state collaboration that played an important role in the creation of many of the eastern railroads.

RAILROADS IN NEW HAMPSHIRE

If railroad construction did not become a co-operative endeavor in New Hampshire, it was not for lack of willingness on the part of the federal government. It was the state that decided, for reasons not related to the legality or validity of intergovernmental co-operation, not to participate in the construction of railroads within its boundaries. By its decision to leave the construction of railroads to private enterprise, the state also left the major governmental role to the federal government, which continued to participate through the postal service subsidies, as it had been doing in Virginia and other states.

Despite the pressure of the laissez faire persuasion and the absence of positive participation on the part of New Hampshire in the railroad development boom, it was still impossible to eliminate all vestiges of state activity in the railroad field and, as a result, to eliminate all vestiges of intergovernmental collaboration. In 1844, the legislature passed the Railroad Corporation Act to regulate the public aspects of the new railroads. This act declared that the railroad corporations were to be considered as public corporations in certain cases. To govern this aspect of their existence, the state was to appoint commissioners, who were to report to the governor and Executive Council, and who were removable by them. The railroads could petition these commissioners to survey routes and, on application, to lay out the roads, which indicated that in respect to the location of rights of way, the railroads were to be considered public highways and were to be subject to the consequent state regulation.

[21] A History and Description of the Baltimore and Ohio Rail Road by a Citizen of Baltimore (Baltimore: John Murphy & Co., 1853). See also Edward Hungerford, The Story of the Baltimore and Ohio Railroad, 1827–1927 (New York: G. P. Putnam's Sons, 1928).

The governor and council could lease property and land to the rail-roads. In return, railroad corporations were bound to the state in different ways. For example, any excess profits (over 10 per cent) were to be paid to the state treasury. This provision was actually implemented and the funds received were added to the state Literary Fund, where they matched certain federal funds and provided the state's contribution to the support of public education.

The act also required the railroads to carry soldiers and military supplies of the state and the federal government and the United States mails, when required to by the federal government or its authorized agents, "at such rates and on such conditions as the governor and council of this state shall allow and impose, in case the United States and such corporation cannot agree upon the same, and the United States shall consent to submit the matter to the decision of the governor and council as aforesaid." This served to ratify and reinforce Congressional provisions on the same matter and placed the state on record as willing to serve as arbitrator between the federal government and the railroads should the need arise.[22]

"UNTIDY" PATTERNS OF COLLABORATION IN THE EAST

Federal-state co-operation in the states without federal lands was not as apparent as were the more visible programs in the states that benefited directly from federal grants-in-land. Nevertheless, lack of "tidiness" did not reflect an absence of collaboration, but only served to obscure it. Even the most casual probing beneath the shiny surface that reflected the image of separation reveals a degree of intergovernmental collaboration not significantly less than that found farther west.

It has already been shown how intergovernmental collaboration in the East was developed in the mercantilist period. Consequently, the forms of co-operation had to undergo some sweeping changes in order to fit into the period of laissez faire economics. These changes were brought about at least partly through the direct and indirect impact of the public domain.

The states without public lands were able to share the federal benefits because of two factors in the American value system that operated in their favor. On one hand, their national representatives could make a

[22] New Hampshire, *Statutes* (1844), chap. 128, December, 1844.

strong case for equalization of federal benefits among all the states. However, their case would not have been sufficient to overcome the states'-rights argument without support from another aspect of the American value system. The ancient and honored principle of aid to pioneering ventures provided the additional factor needed. Though pioneering a new technology in the East was not considered to be as important as pushing back the land frontier in the West, it had considerable support in Congress in its own right. Consequently the federal government found ways to support eastern pioneering ventures through use of the public domain and by other means in areas where it did not have public lands to grant. The states themselves had the power to determine to what degree they would participate in these programs. In the field of railroad developments, some, like Georgia, were deeply involved in co-operative programs. Others, like Maryland, participated with less intensity. Virginia became a partner rather reluctantly, but no less actively. New Hampshire, on the other hand, elected to participate only minimally. In any case, the choice was the state's, and in no case could intergovernmental collaboration be entirely avoided.

14

Land Grants and Higher Education

FEDERAL AID TO UNIVERSITIES

The federal government adopted a policy of aiding the public-land states in the establishment and support of colleges and universities in the late eighteenth century at the same time that it promised support for the development of common schools. During the ensuing years, this policy was extended to the newly created states through periodic individual grants. In 1862, it was made a uniform national policy by the Morrill Act, which provided for the establishment of colleges of agriculture and the mechanic arts in every state and territory.

Though the Morrill Act is often considered to be the first federal grant-in-aid and an early, isolated example of the grant-in-aid idea as embodied in later years, in fact it was not a new departure but the culmination of a long series of experiments in support of higher education, the outgrowth of grant-in-aid principles and programs extending back over seventy-five years. It has been remembered, while similar programs were forgotten, because of its uniform nationwide application and its extraordinary success. It was the first major grant-in-aid program to be applied uniformly to all states and territories at the same time; and while many of the land-grant programs fell short of what had been expected of them, the land-grant colleges exceeded the fondest hopes of all but a few visionaries to become major centers of public higher education and research in the United States.[1]

As in the case of most of the land-grant programs, the precedents for

[1] For a history of the land-grant colleges, see Edward D. Eddy, Jr., *Colleges for Our Land and Time* (New York: Harper & Bros., 1956). This study will concentrate only on those aspects of the program of significance in the evolution of American federalism.

university grants were set in colonial times.[2] The New England colonies had taken the lead, commencing with grants to Harvard College in the seventeenth century. By the end of the Revolutionary War, ten of the original thirteen states had granted what were considered crown lands for the establishment and support of institutions of higher learning, in general to private colleges holding charters granted by their state governments. When the federal government acquired title to the western lands, it inherited this policy of government support and expanded it into the land-grant programs of the nineteenth century and, from them, into the grant-in-aid programs of the twentieth.

Colonial land-grant policy had reached its highest development in New England; and men from New England were the leading authors of the policy of the new federal government to grant lands to new states for common schools and colleges. As a result of the efforts of a group of New Englanders led by Manasseh Cutler, who had organized the Ohio Company to purchase western lands from the Congress and market them, the Northwest Ordinance of 1787 included provisions for grants of land for universities as well as for common schools. The men of the Ohio Company not only intended to sell the lands they had obtained from Congress, but many of them also wanted to settle in the West. This meant that they were personally concerned with the need to extend New England standards of education to the frontier. Many of them were Harvard graduates. They would settle for no less than a college education for their children. Congress was initially reluctant to provide lands for higher education; but the federal government needed the revenues from the public lands and only the Ohio Company was prepared to market them, so the legislators acceded to the demands of the company. Thus, the inclusion of lands to be reserved for higher education, which became an established feature of American policy, was the result of a hard bargain driven by local or special interests in negotiations with the federal government.[3] It was not a policy developed in Washington and handed down to the nation, no more than any of the other grant programs have been, almost all of which have originated from the action of local and special interests.

A few weeks after this first precedent for federal aid to higher educa-

[2] Mathias N. Orfield, *Federal Land Grants to the States with Special Reference to Minnesota* (Minneapolis: University of Minnesota Press, 1915), pp. 18–24.

[3] *Ibid.*, pp. 38–40, 53–55. Orfield describes Cutler's role in the adoption of the Northwest Ordinance of 1787 in a manner that is illustrative of the thesis of this study.

tion was established, Congress sold a large tract of land to John Symmes, who asked for, and was granted, one township for higher educational purposes. These two grants, though made in conjunction with sales of land to private land companies, were actually grants to the future state of Ohio, since Congress expressly provided that the lands were "to be applied to the intended object by the legislature of the state."[4] Ohio thus received three townships for university purposes when it entered the Union. The land grant secured by Symmes was used as the basis for the founding of Miami University in 1809, one of the first state universities in the United States.[5]

What had originally been a program forced upon a reluctant Congress soon became generally accepted national policy. In 1804, Congress directed the secretary of the treasury to locate a township for the use of a seminary of learning in each of the three land districts of what was then Indiana Territory, which ultimately became the states of Indiana, Illinois, and Michigan. After that, no state was admitted to the Union without receiving a university land grant in some form. At first, no conditions were attached to the university grants other than that they be used for purposes of higher education. As in the case of the other land grants, the federal government imposed few specific regulations on state management or sale of the lands until experience demonstrated the need for them. This did not mean that there was no policy to be followed by the states in regard to the use and disposition of the grants. As specific issues arose and were handled by Congressional action, an implied policy was made increasingly explicit. This policy can be essentially stated in the following manner: Every new state was entitled to receive grants of land for university purposes. These grants could be used for either public or private universities (until 1889, when Congress required that all subsequent grants be used only for state institutions). With a few exceptions, university lands were reserved in the act creating a territory, but were not granted until the territory achieved statehood. (The federal government did not entrust the management of university lands to territorial governments on principle.)

Until 1827, selection of the lands was left to federal officials. Between 1827 and 1850, the new states all received lands that had been selected

[4] I Stat. 573 (1787).

[5] Walter Havighurst's *The Miami Years* (New York: G. P. Putnam's Sons, 1958) has a full account of the role of the land grant in the founding and development of Miami University.

in territorial days, necessarily by federal officials. After 1850, the states were empowered to make the selections, with the federal government designating the state official or body to do the job. Until 1861, the task was entrusted to the governor. From 1861 to 1910, the state legislature was the designated body, and after that year, a board of state officials was given the task. The federal government prescribed the minimum size of tracts to be selected. This minimum was progressively reduced to enable the states to choose smaller parcels of land with greater value, such as watered lands in the West. Leasing regulations were left in the hands of the states until 1888, when the federal government introduced national leasing regulations which the states had to apply.

Congress did not require the creation of permanent university funds in the early years, though it indicated its intentions in that regard when it gave the territory of Florida permission to sell part of its university grant on condition that the money not used for buildings and apparatus be invested in a permanent university fund. The permanent-fund provision was not incorporated until the university land-grant program as a whole was restricted to state institutions in 1889, in order to give the states a free hand in making the best possible use of the lands under local conditions. When it was determined that this earlier approach was not a good one, provisions for permanent funds were unhesitatingly added.

The university land grants thus set a general precedent for the land grants under the Morrill Act, though they represented a separate program that continued to exist alongside the Morrill Act grants, even in cases in which the same state university was the recipient of both forms of federal aid.

The history of the passage of the Morrill Act is illustrative of the way in which formal collaborative activities were accepted in mid-nineteenth-century American politics. First introduced in 1857 by Representative Morrill of Vermont with considerable popular support, it was designed to extend the benefits of federal aid for higher education to all the states in proportion to their populations, with specific reference to the promotion of "agriculture and the mechanic arts." This was the first successful attempt to combine the needs of higher education with the encouragement of internal improvement, a combination that contributed greatly to the ultimate success of the measure.

Despite the opposition of states'-rights southerners, who were to take the South out of the Union only three years later, the measure was passed in both the House and Senate, only to be vetoed by President Buchanan in a display of the strict-constructionist tendencies that would later lead him to permit secession rather than make any moves toward the "coercion" of "sovereign" states. In an attempt to override the veto, the House repassed the bill by a vote of 105 to 96. While this was short of the necessary two-thirds majority, it is surely an indication that at the height of the ante bellum period when the states'-rights doctrine was considered to be at its peak and the South was represented in the halls of Congress by its most extreme states'-righters, a bill such as the Morrill Act could be passed and even repassed (albeit with less than the requisite majority) despite a presidential veto. Its successful passage in 1862 cannot, then, be solely attributed to the tide of nationalism that had arisen during the Civil War, as some have claimed.

Under the terms of the act, the federal government granted to each state (originally to the loyal states, but after the Civil War ended, to the states of the former Confederacy as well) thirty thousand acres of public land for each senator and representative then in Congress for the establishment and support of an agricultural college. The states could select only lands previously surveyed by the federal authorities in tracts no smaller than quarter sections to simplify administration. In so far as possible, the lands were to be selected within the boundaries of the selecting state. For states which did not have enough land available within their boundaries, or for states with no public lands, the secretary of the interior would issue scrip to cover the number of acres deficient or appropriated, which the states could then sell to individuals for location in a public-land state, and obtain the money for the colleges in that manner. No state government was to select lands in another state or territory, since it was reasoned that this action might infringe upon the sovereignty of the latter. The legislators wisely foresaw that it would very likely create political conflict if one state should own large tracts of land in another. Only a state's assignees, the purchasers of its scrip, could do so as private individuals, and even they were restricted by the provision that no more than one million acres could be located by assignees in any one state. This was, of course, a provision that was demanded by the public-land states to protect their control over their own internal affairs.

The legislation itself indicates that there was no question in the minds of congressmen as to the monetary equivalent of the land grants. The selling price of each acre was placed by statute at a minimum of $1.25, which was the standard price for public lands subject to sale and entry (those lands to which the grant was confined). This meant that the acreage granted for each senator or representative was worth $37,500 under normal conditions. New Hampshire, for example, with two senators and three representatives, was to receive land equal in value to no less than $187,000. Congressional thought on the matter was further clarified by the stipulation that if the state selected lands adjacent to lands granted for railroad construction, the selling price of which was doubled (to $2.50) by statute because of their proximity to the railroad, each selection was to be counted as a double one and the total amount of acreage decreased accordingly. Since each selection had to be approved by the General Land Office, that agency could adjust the total amount of land credited to each state in the normal course of its business.

Still another co-operative routine was established as part of the attempt to guarantee proper supervision of the grant. The governors of all states receiving scrip from the secretary of the interior in place of lands were required to report to Congress annually on all sales of their scrip, indicating the amount of money they had received and accounting for its use. The report was to be made annually until all the scrip was sold. Thus, the governor was made the agent of Congress as well as of his state in the disposal of the scrip.

The Morrill Act grants included, as did most of the land grants, rudimentary matching provisions that were in the process of becoming more sophisticated. In this case, the state was charged with the administrative costs of the program. The federal funds were to be kept available in their entirety for the college trust fund that was to be established. All expenses of the management and supervision of the lands prior to their sale and of the fund thereafter were to be borne by the state and paid out of its treasury, so that neither the principal nor the interest accruing to it would be spent for any purpose other than that designated in the original grant. The state was also required to "erect, preserve, and repair" the buildings for the college.

The proceeds of the land sales were to be invested, safeguarded, and used in a manner prescribed by the act. United States or state stocks were indicated as being preferable, though any safe stock yielding not less than 5 per cent interest on its par value annually was acceptable. The fund was to be perpetual with undiminished capital, except for the amount specified by Congress for use in acquiring the site and establishing the college. If any of the fund should be lost through poor investment, the state was required to replace the amount from its own resources in order to maintain the principal undiminished.

Up to 10 per cent of the federal grant could be expended for the acquisition of a site for the college or an experimental farm. The state was required to establish at least one college within five years of the date of passage of the act or forfeit its grant, with the proviso that it would have to repay any money received from the sale of the lands in the interim. The curriculum of the college was to include studies in agriculture, the mechanical arts, and military science, as well as studies in the other sciences and arts (including classical studies, which were specifically mentioned). This is perhaps as close as Congress has ever come to prescribing the curriculum and the educational policy of the educational institutions aided by the federal government.

These elaborate provisions were designed in the spirit of the nineteenth century; some of them are familiar in twentieth-century grants, while others are not. The unfamiliarity of some of these provisions has obscured the binding character of the entire land-grant measure on the states. In a day before the elaborate administrative procedures of the twentieth century, these provisions were enforced by the courts rather than through the administrative process, except in certain specified cases. This did not mean that less strict enforcement was intended, but that more cumbersome procedures were involved. When enforcement through the courts proved to be too cumbersome, provisions for administrative enforcement were incorporated into grant-in-aid measures.[6]

[6] An analogous situation prevailed in the rise of railroad regulation by regulatory commissions. As an examination of railroad-regulation legislation will demonstrate, the states did not leave the railroads unregulated prior to the 1870's and 1880's. The regulatory provisions were there, but had to be enforced through the courts. The creation of regulatory commissions was the necessary result of experiences that indicated that recourse to the courts was an unsatisfactory way to regulate institutions such as railroads effectively. It was not regulation that was established by the creation of regulatory commissions, but enforceable regulatory procedures. The same might be said in regard to federal grants-in-aid. As experience was accumulated in regard to their proper administration, beginning with the first land grants in 1787, new and better enforcement procedures were added. However, it is questionable whether, even with the strict enforcement procedures included in mid-twentieth-century grants, a state can be made to forfeit its share of a grant program, except in rare cases, given the locally oriented nature of the American political system.
A recent example of the effectiveness of the conditions embodied in the land-grant programs was provided in the 1956 decision of the Montana Supreme Court, which held that funds obtained by the state of Montana from a federal land grant for the erection of the state's public buildings (a program inaugurated nationally in 1816) could not be used for repair or maintenance of those buildings under the terms of the grant. In order to use the money remaining in its Public Building Fund, which had been idle for half a century since the buildings were completed, the state had to secure an act of Congress releasing the funds (Pub. L. No. 411, 85th Cong., 2d Sess.).

The importance attached to the exchange of information by those responsible for higher education at that time is made clear by another provision of the act, which made mandatory the exchange of reports. Each college was required to make an annual report of its progress, emphasizing improvements made and experiments undertaken and including information as to their cost and results. Pertinent information on the industry and economy of the state it served was also to be included, with relevant statistics. This report was to be sent free of charge to every other land-grant college, and one copy was to be sent to the secretary of the interior.

It is clear from this provision and its subsequent applications that one of the major goals of the Morrill Act was to create and make available to the entire nation a body of research and experience in the agricultural and mechanical sciences and in the field of higher education. With some notable exceptions, there was little governmental activity in applying the results of its own research in this period. However, the idea of government responsibility for the dissemination of information for use by interested citizens was already an important one. Since then, of course, programs for both dissemination of information and use of research results have expanded with the general increase in the velocity of government.

While the Morrill Act grant-in-land was designed to develop a nation-wide body of knowledge, its equally important though unstated goal was to strengthen the states, a goal certainly achieved by the establishment of centers for research and education where none or deficient ones had previously existed. The reaction of the states to the entire program demonstrates at least an implicit appreciation of both goals. Politically, their acceptance had the effect of establishing an ongoing and formally routinized system of co-operation between the federal government and the states and among the states themselves. The educational effects of this act were widespread to say the least. Only seventeen state universities existed before 1862; the Morrill Act was responsible for the creation of sixty-nine additional ones.[7]

THE UNIVERSITY OF NEW HAMPSHIRE

New Hampshire responded to the passage of the Morrill Act with great interest and appreciation. On July 8, 1862, six days after the act was ap-

[7] Richard B. Morris (ed.), *Encyclopedia of American History* (New York: Harper & Bros., 1953), pp. 439, 557.

proved in Washington, the General Court resolved that "the State of New Hampshire hereby gratefully accepts the benefits of the act of Congress of the United States, passed at the present session thereof, entitled 'An Act donating Public lands to the several states and territories which may provide colleges for the benefit of Agriculture and the Mechanic Arts.' "[8]

The following year in its formal acceptance of the terms of the grant, the New Hampshire General Court provided for the implementation of the conditions set down by Congress. The governor was instructed to notify the secretary of the interior or "other proper official of the United States" of the state's acceptance. He was also authorized to receive, "by himself or his order," all land scrip due the state from the secretary of the interior or any other federal officer authorized to issue it. In co-operation with the Executive Council, he was authorized to appoint a commissioner to take charge of the scrip. This commissioner was to sell the scrip and transfer it to purchasers approved by the governor and council, according to the legislative provision that no scrip was to be transferred until paid for in full and the money deposited with the state treasurer. The commissioner was required to report to the governor and council every six months.

The state treasurer was given the responsibility of holding the money received and investing it "in accordance with the provisions of the fourth section of the before mentioned act of Congress." The money was to be invested through a "separate and perpetual fund," and the interest was to be used "as the Legislature will prescribe, in accordance with the act of Congress." The treasurer was also required to make an annual report on the fund.

In providing for the actual establishment of a college, the General Court sought to include representatives of the local governments, no doubt because of the competition that was bound to arise over the location of the new institution.[9] The General Court instructed the governor

[8] New Hampshire, *Laws* (1862), chap. 2649, July 8, 1862.

[9] The role played by state institutions in the local economies in the nineteenth century was much like that in the twentieth. Such institutions were much sought after by local communities. Certainly the evidence gathered in the process of preparing this study indicates that a high degree of competition existed in each of the states studied. The division of the state institutions among all sections of the state was a matter of prime political concern, which, in itself, attests to the economic role played by such institutions. The pronouncements of local leaders engaged in the struggle to secure institutions for their communities quite openly refer to the economic benefits involved.

and council to appoint a committee of ten, one representative from each county, to "prepare a scheme for the establishment of a college for education in agriculture and the mechanic arts" and to submit a printed report on the matter by June of 1864.[10] One year did not prove sufficient for the preparation and acceptance of a plan. It was not until June, 1866, that Governor Frederick Smyth proposed a definite plan of action, warning the legislature that immediate action was necessary since the act of Congress specified that the offer would expire on July 2, 1867, if a college were not in existence by then. He reported that the state had received scrip for a total of one hundred fifty thousand acres, which he valued at sixty cents per acre. This pessimistic estimate led him to conclude that no more than $100,000 would ever be raised from the grant, and that that amount was not sufficient for the establishment and equipment of an independent college without imposing "an onerous burden upon the taxpayers."

In order to avoid such an "onerous burden" yet retain the grant and the public college, Governor Smyth suggested partial affiliation with Dartmouth (the famous private college in the state, which had been founded partly through a colonial land grant), whereby the two institutions would share certain facilities and maintain other departments separately. This arrangement was adopted and implemented for the first quarter-century of the land-grant institution's existence.

The Governor also proposed that the board of trustees of the new college serve as a board of agriculture for the state to administer an experimental farm and otherwise promote the cause of scientific agriculture.

I am satisfied that in this way scientific agriculture can be instilled into the minds of our youth, and spread abroad among the people; and that at the same time those admirable rules of farming which have been derived from long experience may be definitely laid down and connected with the results of scientific research for the mutual benefit of the practical workman and scientific explorer.[11]

The General Court immediately responded by passing an act incorporating the New Hampshire College of Agriculture and the Mechanic Arts.[12] The first paragraph of the act was copied almost verbatim from the original act of Congress. Government of the college was placed in the

[10] New Hampshire, *Laws* (1863), chap. 2732, July 9, 1863.

[11] New Hampshire, *Governors' Messages to the Legislature,* June, 1866.

[12] New Hampshire, *Laws* (1866), chap. 4216, July 7, 1866.

hands of a board of trustees, which would also appoint the faculty. The board was to make an annual report to the legislature, which would also be used for distribution to the other land-grant colleges and the secretary of the interior, as prescribed by Congress. The college was located in Hanover, adjacent to Dartmouth, and the legislature granted it permission to be connected with the latter institution in the use of facilities and faculty. Indigent students were granted free tuition, and arrangements were to be made for free public lectures on agriculture and the mechanic arts to be given in various parts of the state. The Land Grant Fund was to be invested in registered bonds of New Hampshire or the United States, which would be held in the custody of the state treasurer, who would transmit the income of the fund to the treasurer of the college.

This was merely the beginning. The wider stimulatory effect of the original grant became evident in 1869, when the General Court appropriated $15,000 for the erection of a building for the college to match a Dartmouth appropriation of $25,000. Both schools were to use the building, and the legislature set down detailed provisions as to how it was to be divided.[13] In 1872, the year in which the building (Culver Hall) was completed, Governor E. A. Shaw reported that $80,000 had been derived from the sale of the land scrip since the inception of the program, an experimental farm of 163 acres had been established, and the Honorable John Conant had donated $60,000 primarily to endow scholarships.[14]

The next fifteen years were years of both progress and disappointment. On one hand, the college was gaining its independence. In 1877, its professorships were made distinct from those of Dartmouth; and a superintendent was appointed to manage the experimental farm.[15] Yet the complaint arose that the college was too far removed from the people it was designed to serve. In 1883, a movement to increase the percentage of farmers on the board was successful; and in a few years, it was made mandatory that a majority of the board be practical farmers.[16] Still, in 1885, the Governor was led to protest that the Agricultural College had failed to become important in the life of the state. It had too few stu-

[13] New Hampshire, *Laws* (1869), chap. 51, July 9, 1869.

[14] New Hampshire, *Governors' Messages to the Legislature*, June, 1872. The latter grant was matched by another appropriation of the General Court (New Hampshire, *Laws* [1872], chap. 57, June 25, 1872).

[15] New Hampshire, *Governors' Messages to the Legislature* (Benjamin F. Prescott), June, 1877.

[16] *Ibid.* (Samuel W. Hale), June, 1883.

dents (only ninety-two had graduated by that year) and was not being utilized properly as an experiment station despite its general good management.[17]

The instrument that brought about the transformation of the college was another federal grant. By 1887, Congress was prepared to take the next step on the road to enhancing the effectiveness of the land-grant colleges. By that time, however, the valuable lands of the public domain had diminished to such an extent that they could no longer provide for a nationwide land grant. Thus, Congress was compelled to take a step rejected some sixty years earlier and, through the Hatch Act, provide for annual grants of cash. The Agricultural Experiment Station Act was the first of the modern annual grants-in-aid.

Governor Sawyer commented on the new grant-in-aid program in his message of June, 1887:

By an act of Congress passed at its last session each state is entitled to receive the sum of $15,000 annually for the establishment and support of an agricultural experimental station. Should the conditions upon which this grant is made be such that it can be used in connection with the college and its experimental work, it must favorably affect the future success of the institution.[18]

Since the terms of the act were definitely designed to link the experiment stations with the colleges, it was not long after the act was formally accepted by the General Court that the Governor could report:

The establishment of the Agricultural Experiment Station has increased the number of specialists and greatly added to the value of the agricultural course. At the same time the mechanical engineering course, with its workshop instruction in the manufacture and use of tools and machinery, bears directly upon some of the greatest industries of New Hampshire. . . .[19]

And, two years later, Governor Hiram A. Tuttle could add:

Students may derive much benefit from the trained corps of specialists of the Experiment Station, a branch of the college which is provided for by the national government at an annual expense of $15,000.[20]

Urging more state financial support for the institution, he continued:

The Agricultural College and the Experiment Station, in addition to the work for students, render much aid to agriculture through their bulletins and publications, and the lectures of specialists.

[17] *Ibid.* (Moody Currier), June, 1885.
[18] *Ibid.* (Charles H. Sawyer), June, 1887.
[19] *Ibid.* (David H. Goodell), June, 1889.
[20] *Ibid.* (Hiram A. Tuttle), June, 1891.

Never in the history of the state have such active and systematic efforts and such liberal expenditure of money been made as at the present time for the promotion of agriculture and kindred interests.

Meanwhile, Congress had passed the second Morrill Act, increasing federal monetary support for the land-grant colleges.[21] The General Court accepted the grant through the normal legislative process in its next session and provided for its administration according to the procedures established for the earlier ones. In the second Morrill Act, Congress was quite specific about the subjects for which it should be applied:

Only to instruction in agriculture, the mechanic arts, the English language, and the various branches of mathematical, physical, natural, and economic sciences, with special reference to their application in the industries of life and the facilities for such instruction.

The act of the legislature embodied this quotation from the act of Congress, with the state's "assents to its purpose."[22]

In 1890, the college severed its last formal connections with Dartmouth by moving to a new site at Durham.[23] In order to prepare the new campus, the General Court had to appropriate funds for building purposes. By January, 1897, $150,000 had been spent in construction of facilities on the new site. As the new century began, the $80,000 trust fund established under the original Morrill Act remained intact in the hands of the state treasurer, and the New Hampshire Agricultural and Mechanical College (now the University of New Hampshire) was firmly established.[24]

HIGHER EDUCATION IN COLORADO

The University of Colorado, though authorized by the territorial legislature much earlier, did not open its doors until September 5, 1877, after Colorado had been admitted to the Union and had been granted the customary seventy-two sections of land to finance a university under the University Land Grant Program. The federal grant was matched by a state tax levy of one-fifth of a mill on the assessed valuation of property

[21] August 30, 1890.

[22] New Hampshire, *Laws* (1891), chap. 2, February 13, 1891.

[23] New Hampshire, *Governors' Messages to the Legislature* (John B. Smith), January, 1893.

[24] *Ibid.* (George R. Ramsdell), January, 1897.

within the state and a special appropriation of $15,000 made in 1876 to provide funds to support the university until the land grant could be claimed and its permanent fund begin to produce revenue. In addition, the city of Boulder, which as early as 1860 had lobbied to be selected as the school's site, contributed some money and land, thereby securing the institution.

Location, selection, and acquisition of the university lands followed the same pattern as the other land grants and involved the same administrative and political relationships between federal, state, and local officials and private citizens. By 1885, the Permanent University Fund amounted to $28,340. Of the 46,080 acres included in the United States grant, 44,841 had been selected and confirmed to the state. Nearly 31,000 of these acres had been sold, at an average price of over $2.00 per acre;[25] 3,680 acres had been leased, though for the very small annual rental of $239.[26] In 1887, the Permanent Fund reached $55,344.[27] The fund has continued to grow in the twentieth century. Table 8 shows the Permanent University Fund's 1954–56 income from previously unalienated lands.

The Colorado Agricultural College (later to become Colorado State University) was founded as, and has remained, an institution independent of the state university. The first Morrill Act and subsequent federal agricultural college grants were allotted to it. The college itself was founded by citizens of Fort Collins, who donated lands for it before 1872. Although the Morrill Act was not directly responsible for its establishment, its provisions were commonly known and, according to accounts of participants at the time, influenced and encouraged the state legislators to appropriate $1,000 for buildings, an amount which was matched by the trustees of the school in 1874, and to place it under state jurisdiction in 1876, when Colorado was admitted to the Union. In 1877, the college was placed under the newly created State Board of Agriculture, and its aims were stated in terms almost identical with those in the Morrill Act.

The intention of the General Assembly to claim the ninety thousand

[25] In 1883–84, 22,445 of these acres had been sold as part of the changed land policy discussed in chap. xvi, p. 383, and were not, as yet, included in the Permanent Fund.

[26] Colorado, *Governors' Messages* (James B. Grant), 1885. This situation improved considerably over the next biennium, so that by November 30, 1886, the leased lands were bringing in $4,538 (*ibid.* [Ben H. Eaton, 1886]).

[27] *Ibid.* (Alva Adams), 1887.

acres due Colorado under the terms of that act for the college was clear. In 1879, that body passed an act amending the State Board of Agriculture Act of 1877 to give that board "general control and supervision over the . . . lands which may be vested in the college by state or national legislation," and another accepting the provisions of the first Morrill Act.

In 1884 the lands were made available by the federal government and were then located, selected, and disposed of in the standard manner, with the proceeds and income establishing a permanent Agricultural College Fund. There seems never to have been any question as to the co-

TABLE 8

CASH RECEIPTS OF THE UNIVERSITY PERMANENT FUND AND THE UNIVERSITY INCOME FUND IN COLORADO*

SOURCE	PERMANENT FUND		
	July 1, 1954, to June 30, 1955	July 1 1955, to June 30, 1956	Total for Biennium
Sales			
Lands.........................	$ 17.04	$ 54.48	$ 71.52
Rights of way..................	128.32	....	128.32
Timber from state forests†........	4,011.33	3,315.60	7,326.93
Rentals			
Oil and gas.....................	2,914.50	2,126.39	5,040.89
Oil and gas (state forest).........	....	1.13	1.13
Mineral........................	4.51	....	4.51
Mineral (state forest).............	54.75	14.02	68.77
Royalties			
Mineral (state forest).............	....	.12	.12
Total.........................	$7,130.45	$5,511.74	$12,642.19
	INCOME FUND		
Land rentals (surface)..............	$2,083.87	$2,396.72	$ 4,480.59
Interest on certificates of purchase...	66.96	197.52	264.48
State forest			
Grazing........................	547.97	392.16	938.13
Term permits...................	9.45	18.90	28.35
Telephone......................	3.15	9.45	12.60
Total.........................	$2,709.40	$3,014.75	$ 5,724.15

* Colorado, *Report of the State Board of Land Commissioners*, 1954–56, p. 10. Total lands granted: 45,844.43 acres (total statutory grant, 46,080 acres)—patented, 41,658.47; remaining state property, 4,265.96.

† Some years ago, the SBLC exchanged isolated state lands within national forests for other forest lands under a plan developed by the General Land Office and the SBLC to consolidate state holdings into a compact and more readily usable group. As a result, a state forest of 70,819 acres was created in Jackson County and linked with the Routt National Forest to create a broad public forest zone in the north central part of the state. This state forest, the only one in Colorado, is composed of lands due the Agricultural College Fund, the Permanent University Fund, and the Internal Improvement Fund. Revenues from timber logged in the forest and from grazing are distributed between these three funds proportionately (Colorado State Planning Division, *Yearbook of the State of Colorado, 1956–1958* [Denver, 1958], p. 449).

operative nature of the agricultural education program. In 1887, in his message to the General Assembly anticipating Congressional passage of the Hatch Act, Governor Eaton talked of the local authorities establishing experimental farms to be placed under the general direction of the agricultural college, which he hoped would receive federal aid.[28] In 1888, the Hatch Act experiment station was attached to the college and a Congressional appropriation of $15,000 was made, specifically earmarked for that institution.[29] A station was immediately established with three branches covering the major agricultural regions of the state. The annual appropriation of $15,000 could only be used for agricultural experimentation by the terms of the federal law; but since the president and all the members of the faculty were also automatically on the faculty of the experiment station, the funds actually furnished a significant means of support for the college.

While the state legislature continued to appropriate funds for new buildings and increase the tax levy for the college, the federal government once again stepped in to provide an additional annual income. The passage of the second Morrill Act on August 30, 1890, brought the institution $15,000 for the first year and an annual increase of $1,000 until a total annual appropriation of $25,000 was reached.[30]

In Colorado, as in the other states, the ease of transition from land to cash as the medium for federal grants-in-aid was nowhere more clear than in the promotion of education in agriculture and the mechanic arts.

[28] *Ibid.* (Ben H. Eaton), 1887. His tone indicates his interest in the matter and points to the already obvious role the states had in securing this legislation.

[29] By the time Congress acted, the General Assembly had adjourned for the biennium, so that it was not until 1889 that it could enact the necessary measure to accept the grant (Colorado, *Statutes,* Act of March 25, 1889). Meanwhile, temporary co-operative administrative arrangements had preceded passage of the state law, so that the college was not denied its appropriation for the first year of the program (1888). While this could not continue once the legislature had convened, the existence of previous administrative relationships between the United States agencies and the State Board of Agriculture through the land-grant program undoubtedly helped in the development of this quasi-formal arrangement by the administrators involved on both levels of government.

[30] The provisions in the first Morrill Act requiring military training at the land-grant colleges provided an additional, if minor, form of federal aid. The Agricultural College cadets were placed on the same footing as the Colorado National Guard in regard to the supply of arms, ammunition, and camp and garrison equipment. This entitled them to receive supplies (except clothing, which was specifically excluded) from the U.S. Army militia program through the state (Colorado, *Statutes,* Act of April 4, 1887). The provisions of the Morrill Act were referred to specifically in the bill that was passed to implement them.

The fact that the congressman who had initiated the original agricultural-college land grant was also able to be one of the instruments of that transition only serves to place the ease of transition in greater relief. Once the issue was faced squarely, there was little doubt as to the outcome. The majority of the representatives of the states in Congress realized that once the public lands were exhausted, federal monetary aid was necessary to the continued progress of the country along the lines they wanted to direct that progress.

As the century drew to a close, Governor Adams reported that the annual cost of the agricultural college was $83,000, of which $66,000 was for the school proper and $17,000 for the experiment station. Aside from the income of the permanent fund based on the land grant, the federal government furnished $43,000, or over half of this amount, in cash grants —the entire $17,000 needed for the experiment station and $26,000 for the school proper.[31]

Selection of the lands involved in the grant continued through the administrative apparatus of the State Board of Land Commissioners. Table 9 shows how the lands granted to Colorado for the agricultural college are being used as sources of revenue in the mid-twentieth century and gives the status of the acreage granted by the federal government to the state under the first Morrill Act. Virtually all the lands to which the state was entitled were transferred to Colorado; over two-thirds of them have since been sold. As in the case of the common-school lands, there are two funds, one for the income from the lands themselves and the other for the proceeds from the invested funds. Sales, rentals, and royalties make up the primary sources of income for the funds.

Co-operative relations with the federal government extended in less comprehensive ways to the other state-supported institutions of higher education in Colorado. The Colorado School of Mines, at Golden, became the meteorological reporting center for the state, commencing with 1874. As early as 1876, William H. A. Loveland, president of the board of trustees, reported:

The meteorological register kept is carried out strictly under the rules and directions of the chief signal officer of the U.S. Army. It is sent monthly to the signal office at Washington, and I have the pleasure to state . . . that the humble part we have here in Colorado taken to illustrate and work out the intricate problems of temperature, rainfall, storms, etc., and of all natural and periodical phenomena generally is fully appreciated . . . abroad as well as at home, the

[31] Colorado, *Governors' Messages* (Alva Adams), 1897.

Signal Service and "voluntary observers" of the United States, having at Paris last spring received from the assembled science of the world, the compliments of extraordinary merit, and the acknowledgement of superior unexcelled skill, and success in the department of meteorology.

Weather reporting soon led to co-operative research projects into the nature of the physical universe. A co-operative project of observations into the nature of ozone was begun in 1876,[32] laying the foundations for scientific co-operation between Colorado's state universities and the federal government.

[32] Colorado School of Mines, *Annual Report* (1876).

TABLE 9

CASH RECEIPTS OF THE AGRICULTURAL COLLEGE PERMANENT FUND
AND THE INCOME FUND IN COLORADO*

SOURCE	PERMANENT FUND		
	July 1, 1954, to June 30, 1955	July 1, 1955, to June 30, 1956	Total for Biennium
Sales			
Lands...................	$ 1,821.31	$ 2,319.32	$ 4,140.63
Rights of way.............	41.00	....	41.00
Timber..................	137.97	....	137.97
Timber (state forest)...........	3,438.30	2,841.95	6,280.25
Rentals			
Oil and gas...............	8,873.73	10,739.58	19,613.31
Oil and gas (state forest)	....	.97	.97
Mineral..................	1,795.72	1,642.50	3,438.22
Mineral (state forest)..........	46.94	12.01	58.95
Coal....................	....	93.15	93.15
Royalties			
Coal....................	....	576.00	576.00
Mineral..................	326.93	270.00	596.93
Mineral (state forest)..........	....	.11	.11
Total.................	$16,481.90	$18,495.59	$34,977.49
	INCOME FUND		
Land rentals (surface).............	$ 5,492.26	$ 6,490.84	$11,983.10
Interest on certificates of purchase..	841.82	808.36	1,650.18
State forest			
Grazing..................	467.97	336.15	804.12
Term permits..............	8.10	16.20	24.30
Telephone.................	2.70	8.10	10.80
Total.................	$ 6,812.25	$ 7,659.65	$14,472.50

* Colorado, *Report of the State Board of Land Commissioners,* 1954–56, p. 8. Total lands granted: 89,999.65 (3,812.13 acres of this figure represent acreage exchanged with the United States for 3,820.37 acres now a part of the state forest)—patented, 63,305.00; remaining state property, 26,694.65.

Not surprisingly, the School of Mines also collaborated with federal agencies in the field of geology. The school received all the publications of the United States Geological Survey. Information was exchanged between its faculty and their colleagues in the federal service. Some expeditions were undertaken co-operatively, though Colorado did not reach the state of formal co-sponsorship of scientific expeditions, as did the University of Illinois.[33]

In 1889, a state normal school was established to train teachers. By act of the General Assembly, it was officially incorporated into the state public school system so that it could receive support from the Permanent School Fund as a state high school. Since it was not part of any local school district, the overwhelming part of its support was from that federal-state fund.[34]

One other school was founded through the aid of the federal government, a junior college with the impressive title of Fort Lewis School of Agriculture, Mechanic, and Household Arts. Located in Durango, its site and buildings were the remnants of an army post founded in 1880 to protect the area from the Ute Indians. In 1892, the Utes were confined to reservations, the garrison withdrawn, and the post was converted into a federal Indian school. In 1910, the 6,300-acre post was turned over to the state of Colorado to be part of its land-grant college system and was attached to the agricultural college at Fort Collins, with the proviso that "Indian pupils shall at all times be admitted to such school, free of charge for tuition, and on terms of equality with white pupils."[35]

By the end of the nineteenth century, the state of Colorado, despite its relative youth, had founded or acquired four institutions of higher learning, which provided its citizens with educational opportunities in the liberal arts, the fine and applied arts, and the agricultural, geological, and meteorological sciences—opportunities which were even extended to the Indians within its boundaries. Three of these institutions owed their existence and continued support to the federal grant-in-aid programs. The fourth reaped its federal benefits in the form of scientific collaboration and stimulation. Two thousand miles to the east, the state of New Hampshire was following substantially the same path.

[33] William Culp Darrah, *Powell of the Colorado* (Princeton, N.J.: Princeton University Press, 1951), p. 81.

[34] Colorado, *Statutes*, Act of April 1, 1889.

[35] Wilbur Fisk Stone (ed.), *A History of Colorado* (Chicago: S. J. Clarke, 1918), I, 618, and Colorado Writers' Project, *Colorado* (New York: Hastings House, 1941), p. 344.

15

The Expanding Range of Government

After a decade of readjustment in the 1840's, during which the machinery of American government began its reorientation to serve a free enterprise, rather than a mercantilist, economic order and an expanding urban-industrial society, American governments entered a period of expansion that continued without interruption for two generations. Between 1837 and 1847, the previous course of governmental expansion was halted and even reversed. After the end of the Mexican War, new governmental vistas were opened, slowly at first, but with the impetus of the Civil War, rapidly enlarging in scope until World War I.[1]

Among the major areas of governmental expansion, aside from those previously treated as parts of the great grant programs, were the creation of a new national banking system, raising educational standards, land reclamation, activities in scientific fields, increasing social services, and reorganizing veterans' assistance.[2] Aspects of these activities will be explored in this chapter.

A NEW NATIONAL BANKING SYSTEM

The Civil War brought the next major change in American banking. The last vestiges of the earlier forms of federal-state collaboration in the

[1] At that time, another decade of readjustment reoriented American government to welfare capitalism and an urban society, a subject outside the scope of this study.

[2] The full range of governmental activity after 1847 is so great that it is hard for those schooled in the traditional view of nineteenth-century limited government to actually grasp it in its entirety. Too many years of budgetary and personnel comparisons with post–World War II America have left us with a picture of small government that only constant exposure to nineteenth-century data can alter. The cases presented here are but selections from the whole. It is encouraging to note than an increasing amount of published material, some of which is cited here, has appeared in recent years to open up the history of specific fields of nineteenth-century governmental activities.

field had disappeared by 1850, and a chaotic, unstable "system" of wild-cat banking had become the norm in most of the states. The Panic of 1857 demonstrated the need for some type of nationwide banking and currency system. The difficulties that arose in financing the Civil War through state banks provided the necessary impetus that led to the passage of the National Banking Act of 1863. The new act provided for fed-eral-chartered banks subject to sufficient federal supervision to create a national currency and a market for United States bonds. Individual banks could opt to recharter as national banks or remain under state charter. At first the system did not expand as rapidly as intended. The state-chartered banks were opposed to the idea of federal (meaning more strict) control, particularly control over issuance of bank notes. In 1865 Congress enacted a 10 per cent tax on notes issued by state-chartered banks, removing all chance of profit from their issuance. This, in effect, forced the major state banks, which had served as banks of issue, to recharter under the federal act or perish.[3]

After passage of the National Banking Act, most of the states enacted measures aimed at facilitating the transition from state to federal charters without forcing existing banks to lose their corporate identity in the process. New Hampshire enacted such a measure in July, 1863, which provided for certification of change-overs by the state banking commissioners.[4] The operation was carried on with little difficulty throughout the country mainly because of the abilities of Hugh McCulloch, formerly president of the Indiana State Bank (which was state-controlled until the Civil War) and the first federal comptroller of the currency. A man experienced in the governmental banking field, he was able to combine his experience in managing a state central bank with an understanding of the politics of federalism, and bring both to bear on the problem of creating a national currency and a nationwide banking system.[5]

[3] William J. Shultz and M. R. Caine, *The Financial Development of the United States* (New York: Prentice-Hall, Inc., 1937), pp. 317–18.

[4] New Hampshire, *Laws* (1863), chap. 2714, July 3, 1863.

[5] Shultz and Caine, *op. cit.*, p. 319. McCulloch acquired the position in a most curious manner. Sent to Washington on behalf of the state banks to lobby against the National Banking Act, he was asked by Secretary of the Treasury Salmon P. Chase after the act was passed to assume the task of implementing it. Evidently he was converted to the view that it was a necessary device, because he accepted the position of comptroller in March, 1863. He successfully fought Chase's plan to require all state banks changing to national charters to adopt numerical designations on the eminently sensible grounds that the prospect of losing their names as well as their

Though in the separatist spirit of the times the national banking program was inaugurated entirely under the direction of the federal government, the inner logic of the federal system soon gave it a collaborative
aspect of some proportions. New Hampshire is a case in point. In 1864,
New Hampshire extended all state laws relative to the duties of officers
of state banks and all state banking taxes to the national banks operating
within its boundaries.[6] This measure, enacted just prior to the great
shift, provided for a measure of dual control over the new national banks
at a time when it was thought that state-chartered banks would disappear
entirely. It was Secretary Chase's desire that state banks disappear, and
for a decade, it appeared that they would. The number of state banks in
New Hampshire declined from fifty-two in 1863 to two by 1869, while
the number of national banks rose to twenty-six. In 1873, only one state-
chartered bank remained.[7]

Contrary to predictions, however, the federal banking program did not
usurp the banking field entirely. While it replaced the state banks as
banks of issue, it stimulated new and more secure state banking activities.
In New Hampshire, the first state banking institutions to benefit from
the federal return to the banking field were state savings banks which
grew in number from twenty-seven in 1863 to sixty-six in 1878. By the
mid-1870's, even state banks in the general banking business were being
revived. By 1878, New Hampshire had chartered nineteen banks, as compared with its twenty-seven national banks.[8] By 1890, the number of
state-chartered banks had passed the number of national banks in the
state. The decline and subsequent revival of the state banks was a nationwide phenomenon, as indicated in Table 10.

This unanticipated reversal of Chase's policy developed because the
highly conservative organization of the national banking system opened
marginal areas of financial activity that demanded a banking system
with greater flexibility. The new state banks were needed in smaller
communities since state laws did not require them to meet the minimum
capital requirement of $50,000 to obtain a charter, which was required

------

freedom would keep many banks out of the system that would otherwise be persuaded
to enter it. His good relations with the leaders of the state banks were instrumental in
the success of his task. See *Dictionary of American Biography*, Vol. XII.

[6] New Hampshire, *Laws* (1864), chap. 2872, July 16, 1864.

[7] New Hampshire Bank Commissioners, *Annual Report*, 1865, 1866, 1869, 1873.

[8] *Ibid.*, 1878.

of national banks. If they could no longer profit from issuing bank notes, they could benefit from the more liberal reserve requirements under state laws to keep their assets in wide and profitable, if more hazardous, use, such as extending rural credit, taking farm mortgages, and making intermediate-term crop loans. Indeed, the mode of operation of the national banking system inhibited closer state regulation of its banks, since there were always potent forces working to prevent the closing-off of institutions providing easy credit.[9] Though the greatest development of the new state banking movement took place in the South and West, New Hampshire did not lag behind.[10]

TABLE 10

NATIONAL AND STATE BANKS IN THE
UNITED STATES, 1865–1955*

Year	National Banks	State Banks
1865.............	1,600	300
1868.............	1,700	200
1875.............	2,100	550
1885.............	2,700	975
1890.............	2,500	2,100
1955.............	4,700	9,000

* The statistics, given in round numbers, are from New Hampshire Bank Commissioners, *Annual Report*, 1878, pp. 348, 419; and U.S. Comptroller of the Currency, *Annual Report*, 1955.

Not only did the new system stimulate the growth of state banks, but it also created new co-operative relationships between the federal government and the states. A prime source of these new relationships was found in the combination of federal-chartered general banking institutions and state-chartered savings banks under the same management. This was a normal occurrence in New Hampshire, for example, where both national and state banks maintained savings banks in order to provide a full banking program. Each of these three types of institutions had its own regulations to follow and each was subject to its particular form of state inspection. In cases in which a state bank operated a savings bank, there was no particular problem, since both institutions were inspected annually by the same state board. In cases in which a national bank maintained a savings bank, the situation was a different one, since

[9] Shultz and Caine, *op. cit.*, pp. 347–48.

[10] New Hampshire Bank Commissioners, *Annual Report*, 1878, 1890.

the former institution was inspected by the federal government and its
subsidiary by the state.

In their report for 1873, the New Hampshire Bank Commissioners
indicated how they had arranged to solve the problem of dual inspection:

It is evident that where the same man is Cashier of a National Bank, and
Treasurer of a Savings Bank, that the examination of either might be made
a farce inasmuch as a dishonest officer might produce the securities of either
bank as the property of the other. Hence, the Commissioners made an arrangement with the National Bank examiner that wherever National Banks and
Savings Banks had the same Cashier and Treasurer, they should be examined
together and produce all the securities of both banks at the same time, and
the examination of such banks was made in this way. The plan was satisfactory
to the National Bank Examiner, and the several treasurers who offered every
facility for its accomplishment.[11]

This system proved so satisfactory that it was enacted into law at the
next session of the General Court, with a provision for semiannual inspections:

Where the savings bank is operated . . . in the same office with a national bank,
the treasurer . . . shall procure . . . a certificate, made under oath by a committee of the directors of the national bank, that they, upon the same day and
. . . time of the examination of the savings bank . . . did make an examination
of the . . . national bank, and found it to be correct.[12]

If the treasurer failed to comply with this provision, the savings bank
was to be removed from the office of the national bank. If the treasurer
was also the cashier of the national bank, he was to be removed from
his position as treasurer.

The twenty-four largest of the sixty-six savings banks in New Hampshire in 1878 were connected with national banks, only three of which
did not have savings banks attached.[13] As a consequence, the joint examination program was one of considerable importance in the field of
banking regulation.

Close examination of the consequences of the National Banking Act
reveals no great centralization of the nation's banking system in the
hands of one government. In the western states, the impact of the Na-

[11] *Ibid.*, 1873, p. 85.

[12] New Hampshire, *Laws* (1874), chap. 71, July 8, 1874.

[13] New Hampshire Bank Commissioners, *Annual Report*, 1878.

tional Banking Act was small, since most of the states were too young to have experienced many years of an exclusively state-regulated banking system. In Minnesota, the first bank in the territory was created in 1852. Although perhaps twenty banks were in existence in 1857, the panic of that year closed nearly all of them. Consequently, the few banks operating successfully in the state in 1863 were relatively new institutions with minimal importance on the money-short frontier.[14] The state's permanent banking system developed after the federal government instituted the national banking system. In the case of Colorado, the territory did not even become a state until the National Banking Act had been in operation well over a decade. In both states, co-operative regulatory features similar to those found in New Hampshire were developed almost from the outset.

In the East and South, the National Banking Act gave federal recognition to the centralizing trend in banking that had been taking place privately for twenty years or more by providing a less comprehensive return to the idea of federal responsibility for national finance, which had been virtually abandoned in theory, if not entirely in practice, in the days of Andrew Jackson. Though designed as a program that would not only operate separately from, but would replace, that of the states, it became by virtue of the ways of American politics and the nature of American institutions a stimulant to the growth of state banks. As a result, not only did informal co-operative relationships arise between the banks (which were in private hands), but similar relationships arose between the federal and state bank examiners, relationships that were even written into law.[15]

PROFESSIONAL EXCHANGES IN EDUCATION

Intergovernmental co-operation in the field of education was not limited to the financial aid provided by the surplus distributions. The promotion of education has always been a matter of concern around the nation, and this concern has continually manifested itself at all levels

[14] Theodore Christianson, *History of Minnesota* (Chicago: American Historical Society, Inc., 1935), I, 307–8, 321.

[15] For a brief presentation of the political struggle involved in the passage of the National Banking Act, its successes and its failures, and an analysis of its achievements from the viewpoint of political economy, see Bray Hammond, *Banks and Politics in America* (Princeton, N.J.: Princeton University Press, 1957), pp. 718–34.

CO-OPERATION IN THE MATURING REPUBLIC

of government. From the beginning, the real question was not whether the federal government and the states should both participate in the development of educational systems, but what their respective roles should be. It is true that the formal debates revolved around questions of states' rights and federal interference into local affairs, but what was really being discussed was the extent of the federal government's direct activity in the educational field and, in particular, its control over educational policy. Exclusion of the federal government from either direct activity or any form of control over local educational policy was a principal established quite early in American history. At the same time, the federal government was quietly given a role as the stimulatory agent in the promotion of public education throughout the country. The history of government and education in the United States is, in great part, a history of the development of federal stimulatory activities with the simultaneous limitation of the possibilities for federal control. As each new era presented new problems in education, the battle had to be refought and a new system of federal stimuli without concomitant controls had to be developed.

In 1847 New Hampshire established the office of commissioner of common schools. In 1851 this embryonic state office of education was expanded to include a state Board of Education, of which the commissioner was ex officio executive officer. In 1854, the New Hampshire State Teachers' Association was founded.[16] Meanwhile, cognizance of the need for intergovernmental co-operation had been indicated at the legislative level. In the act establishing the office of common-school commissioner, the General Court authorized the commissioner to exchange educational reports with the federal government and the other states. This authorization was often repeated in subsequent legislation.[17] In an era when professional conferences in the field of education were virtually nonexistent, particularly on a regional or national scale, this mode of communication provided the major means for the interchange of ideas so necessary for the growth of the new public education system in the nation as a whole. The new professional educators eagerly sought the ideas of their colleagues around the nation from the very beginning. The privilege of exchanging reports was one well used by them.

In time, the exchange of educational information and experience

[16] New Hampshire, *Report of the Commissioner of Common Schools,* 1847, 1851, 1854.

[17] New Hampshire, *Laws* (1847), chap. 532, June 28, 1847; (1848), chap. 655, June 24, 1848; (1849), chap. 760, January 3, 1849.

reached a point at which it became patently clear to a majority in Congress that it was of sufficient scope and importance to justify a federal center to facilitate it. This awareness led to the establishment in 1862 of the Office of the United States Commissioner of Education, later to become the United States Office of Education.

Not the least potent influence in the establishment of a federal agency for education were the state offices of education, which campaigned vigorously for such an agency. For example, in 1861, J. W. Patterson, secretary of the New Hampshire Board of Education, suggested, in the name of the board, that the federal government might have to establish a "department of public instruction," if necessary by constitutional amendment, to preserve the nation. In advancing reasons as to why this might be necessary, he also presented a contemporary view of federal aid to education:

The Federal Government has from time to time made princely reservations of public lands for educational purposes, but the dispositions of the proceeds of these lands and the work of devising and maintaining educational systems have been reserved exclusively to the states.[18]

He said that some states had done this well, and others not so well. Consequently, the federal government might have to intervene to provide equal educational opportunities for the whole country, not only to secure full development of the nation's natural resources, but also to eliminate the need for a standing army (to maintain domestic tranquillity?) and "avert the evils predicted by European statesmen."

In 1867, the board hailed the development of the federal education agency in a special section of its annual report entitled "National Education":

In accordance with the wishes of this Board, and of the Boards of other states, a National Department of education has been established at Washington and Hon. HENRY BARNARD [sic] has been appointed Chief, whose reports we may hope to obtain in due time.[19]

[18] New Hampshire, *Report of the State Board of Education*, 1861, p. 13.

[19] New Hampshire, *Report of the State Board of Education*, 1867, p. 24. Aside from illustrating the desires of the state boards of education for federal participation, the above paragraphs indicate something of the scope of the federal land-grant program in support of public education. In this vein the board commented on the extension of general education throughout the United States:

Generous benefactions, also for the education of the people, have been made to some sections of the country, and some states enjoy large school funds. The reports from other states teach us the importance of seeking more ample funds and more generous annual appropriations.

Concern over New Hampshire's need to maintain its high educational standards in order to retain its influential position in the Union led the board to request the federal government to grant their state public lands for education:

The government is as bound to take care of the education of the people, as to attend to many other matters which claim attention. And common schools for all the people are as worthy of grants of public lands, as agricultural colleges, which at the most can reach only a limited class. No exact statistics are accessible to show how much land has been granted to each of the newer states, for schools, but probably the report of the Chief of the National Department of Education will give us the facts, as that was one of the first objects had in view in his appointment.

Despite this interest, however, the immediate course of federal-state relations in the realm of the common schools was to move further toward co-operation among professionals and further from federal aid, particularly as the public-land states claimed the lands due them under the land-grant programs and ceased to receive additional aid from the federal government.

The increased co-operation among professionals manifested itself in various ways. Reports and communications continued to be exchanged. The United States Commissioner of Education developed and co-ordinated activities designed to publicize education in the nation both at home and abroad. (For example, New Hampshire's participation in an exhibit showing the progress of education in the United States that was to be held at the Vienna International Exposition was discussed by the United States commissioner and the state superintendent in 1872 and 1873.[20])

Another matter of interest was the securing of exemption for educational institutions and personnel from the internal revenue stamp tax. Since no fixed policy had been announced by the federal government, the individual towns (which were responsible for the sale of the stamps to some extent) developed different policies on the matter, "some using them on all their school documents, others using them on some, and others not on any, and the majority using them on teachers' certificates." In response to Roger M. Sargent, secretary of the state Board of Education, the commissioner of internal revenue in Washington wrote (September 24, 1866) that certificates of qualification of teachers, certificates

[20] New Hampshire, *Report of the State Board of Education*, 1873.

of the returns of teachers' registers, and copies of the district superintending committees' reports, which were required to be filed with the
town clerk and the secretary of state, were exempt. Sargent then notified
the county commissioners and, through them, the superintending school
committees of the ruling.[21]

The New Hampshire State Library also began its history in co-operation with the governments of the United States and other states. In this
rather small example, the principle of simultaneous interest on all levels
is again in evidence. It was generally conceded that every government
should have a small library at its disposal, consisting primarily of reference works and governmental reports. The best way to assemble such a
library was through an exchange of documents, whereby each state and
the federal government would make its relevant publications available to
the others, thus providing complete collections of the laws, administrative reports, and scientific publications for each government. This exchange was generally handled through several agents on the federal end:
the Library of Congress, the Smithsonian Institution, some federal agencies, and members of Congress who distributed various documents.

These exchanges were made formal by law. Table 11 summarizes the
major continuing exchange programs established in New Hampshire between 1843 and 1891. As part of a general reorganization of the state library in 1891, the state librarian was placed in full charge of the distribution and exchange of all state publications sent outside of New Hampshire. The secretary of state, who was in charge of the publication of
state documents, was directed to furnish the library with all publications
that could or had to be distributed. The reorganization act also provided
for the suspension of distributions to any "state, government, department
of government, institution, or official" not "making fair or reasonable
return" of its publications to the state library. The decision to suspend
or resume the exchange was to be made by the trustees of the library.
The trustees were also given the power to "designate states, governments, institutions, libraries, officials and persons to be recipients" of
the state's publications.[22]

Thus, before 1891 and the reorganization of the state library as an in-

---

[21] New Hampshire, *Report of the State Board of Education,* 1867, p. 29.

[22] New Hampshire, *Laws* (1891), chap. 7, February 25, 1891. Less than two months
later, the legislature instructed the New Hampshire Congressional delegation to press
for Congressional aid for libraries—sixty years before a formal aid program was
enacted (*ibid.,* chap. 126, April 11, 1891).

stitution of broader activity, its services and acquisitions revolved around
the documents and publications obtained through exchanges, particularly in the legal, governmental, and scientific fields. These exchanges
were facilitated by the federal government, which used this method as an
inexpensive way in which to spread scientific information throughout the
country. It involved an ongoing, if small, correspondence between fed-

TABLE 11

MAJOR EXCHANGE PROGRAMS ESTABLISHED IN NEW HAMPSHIRE, 1843-91*

Material Exchanged	Date Initiated	Recipient	Statutory Authorization	Remarks
State judicial reports†..	1843	U.S. and states	Chap. 9, Act of June 21, 1843	
State geological and min-eralogical survey‡....	1844	U.S. and states	Chap. 178, Act of December 21, 1844	
State school commission-er annual reports....	1847	U.S. and states	Chap. 532, Act of July 28, 1847	Initiated on es-tablishment of N.H. Office of Education
Journals and acts of the General Court.......	1851	Smithsonian In-sitution	Chap. 1154, Act of July 5, 1851	In exchange for publications of Smithsonian Institution
Session laws of General Court.............	1877	U.S. Dept. of Justice	Chap. 100, Act of July 14, 1877	
N.H. state manual and public statutes.......	1891	Judges and clerks, U.S. Circuit and District Cts. in N.H.; clerk, U.S. Sup. Ct.; fed. executive depts.; librari-an of Congress; states	Chaps. 34 and 87, Act of April 4, 1891	

* In response to the federal policy of setting aside copies of its publications for each state, provided that state would cover the expenses involved in transporting them from Washington, the state librarian was authorized in 1862 to order any books from any of the federal departments that had been set aside for distribution to New Hamp-shire. Money for their shipment was to be paid from the state treasury (New Hampshire, *Laws*, chap. 2400, July 3, 1860).

† In 1860, the governor was authorized to trade for or purchase any judicial reports of the United States or the individual states missing from the state's collection that had not been acquired in the previous exchanges of docu-ments (*ibid.*).

‡ After the Civil War, a new geological survey was prepared with help from the U.S. Coast Survey, and copies of the report that emerged were ordered sent to the Smithsonian Institution and the Library of Congress, among others (*ibid.*, chap. 46, July 3, 1873).

eral and state officials and some matching of federal grants with state funds. The importance of the documents thus received is indicated by the frequent references to them made by state legislative, administrative, legal, and scientific personnel.

FORESTRY EFFORTS IN MINNESOTA

One of the earliest conservation activities in the United States was in the field of forestry. Initially an attempt to provide trees for the treeless prairies, the forestry movement had become, by the end of the nineteenth century, the first nationwide conservation effort designed to preserve existing forests as well as to create new ones. The program developed initially from the efforts of spontaneous organizations of individuals in several states and localities to develop tree-culture programs. They soon turned to government for aid, and in doing so, they turned to both the federal government and their respective states.

The Minnesota State Forestry Association was the first one founded in the United States. It was organized in 1874 as a private association composed of leading figures in the state. In 1876 it was reorganized under state law, with a charter granted to it by the legislature.[23] This made the association virtually an arm of the state, charged by the legislature with the responsibility of stimulating tree-planting by giving awards and premiums and promoting the observance of Arbor Day.

The creation of the association coincided with the passage of the federal tree-culture acts, which, in turn, coincided with the passage of acts by the state granting premiums for tree-planting. The federal and state acts were quite similar. Both provided that settlers on the treeless plains could claim specified additional acreage (federal) or receive cash premiums (state) on condition that they plant trees on their homesteads according to patterns set down by law.

The conditions of the acts were specific and detailed, indicating the exact methods and times of planting, and the quantities of trees to be planted per acre. In fact, they were so detailed that they did not work. The provisions in them had been drawn up for climates and soils other than those of the trans-Mississippi plains, and trees planted according to these eastern specifications did not survive. One of the first tasks of the

---

[23] November 23, 1876. Even prior to the reorganization, the legislature appropriated $2,500 to promote the objects of the association (March 2, 1876).

Minnesota State Forestry Association was to secure the revision of both the United States and the state laws to meet the conditions imposed by nature. The secretary of the association, Leonard B. Hodges, one of the pioneer professionals in American forestry, drafted a revised measure on behalf of the association. As a result of this work, no doubt coupled with that of other interested people around the nation and in Congress, the federal act was revised to meet virtually all the association's objections. Indeed, the revised act was almost identical with the draft the association submitted. Shortly thereafter, the state law was also changed to conform with the association's draft and the federal act.[24]

The association did not confine itself to promoting legislation. It became the co-ordinating agency that brought the federal and state programs into harmony and made them easily available to the settlers. This work was aided by the association's status as a state agency and by the fact that officers of the local United States land offices were to be found among its charter members. Two particular methods were used to achieve co-ordination of the programs. The association's secretary answered specific requests; and a manual was published and distributed around the state to provide general information. The manual was first issued in 1874 as *Practical Suggestions on Forest Tree Planting in Minnesota* and was edited by Hodges. The title was shortened and the manual broadened in 1879 to become *The Forest Tree Planter's Manual*. Between 1879 and 1896, twelve editions of the manual were issued.

The association also assumed the role of integrating private activities into the general pattern of the government-supported programs. In co-operation with the land-grant St. Paul and Pacific Railroad, it printed guides to help farmers acquire federal land and state bounties for tree planting and to fulfill the forestry requirements on the federal lands. These guides were distributed free of charge throughout Minnesota at the request of the state legislature.[25] People interested in forestry, like

[24] Information from the Minnesota State Forestry Association records, St. Paul, Minnesota.

[25] The railroad was interested in this because it wanted to attract settlers to its hinterland and make them prosperous. Although this co-operation between the governments and the railroads was common along most of the Western frontier (which was opened up by the rails), it was carried to its highest form in the northern tier of states stretching westward from Lake Superior—the empire of the Great Northern and Northern Pacific railroads. The St. Paul and Pacific was the forerunner of the Great Northern and provided the basis for its establishment by James J. Hill, who believed strongly in the role of the railroad to promote settlement and advance the region in which it was located.

those interested in similar programs before and after them, were not particularly concerned with the level of government giving them support.
On the contrary, they wanted to involve all three levels and private
sources as well.

The year 1876 saw the inauguration of the co-operative forestry program in Minnesota under the auspices of this quasi-governmental state
forestry agency. During the next twenty years, the scope of that agency
expanded to include such activities as providing aid to sufferers from the
grasshopper plagues that infected Minnesota during the 1870's and 1880's,
which would enable them to maintain their federal grants; distribution
to farmers and others of tree seedlings given them by the United States
Department of Agriculture (USDA); distribution of federal forestry
publications; establishment of a state fire warden system to protect the
federal grant of land surrounding the headwaters of the Mississippi River
to Minnesota for a state forest (now Itasca State Park); and promotion
of Arbor Day in conjunction with the Forestry Division of the USDA.[26]

In addition to these more or less administrative activities, the association engaged in educational and lobbying campaigns that contributed
significantly to the establishment of the national forest system in 1891
and the state forest system, based on the aforementioned federal grant,
short years later. Both endeavors, in turn, led to further co-operative activities.

The development of the forestry movement in the United States as a
whole followed closely along the lines developed in Minnesota. From the
outset, partnership between governments and with private agencies was
the key. Minnesotans were pioneers in the movement. Thus, the partnership as it evolved in Minnesota was perhaps more refined than in some
of its sisters. The impact of the Minnesota Forestry Association on federal legislation was perhaps greater than that of other state associations.
However, the main outlines of intergovernmental collaboration were
nearly universal. The state agencies served as keystones in the governmental arch. They brought together the diverse programs—federal, state,
local, and private—into one package for the benefit of the citizenry. They
did this because it has traditionally been the role of state associations and

[26] Arbor Day is an excellent example of a holiday that was promoted and developed
through these processes of government, involving continuing co-operation between
private forestry associations and all levels of government. See Minnesota State Forestry Association records for correspondence between the Forestry Division of the
USDA and the state forestry association on the promotion of Arbor Day. Thanks-
giving Day has a similar origin in the processes of co-operative federalism.

agencies to do so. The federal agencies involved, the General Land Office and the Department of Agriculture, were assigned their roles by Congressional enactments, which, in turn, were the products of local pressures. The federal agencies served to stimulate state and private endeavors. They filled this role because it has traditionally been the federal task
to stimulate, just as it has been the state's task to co-ordinate.

LAND RECLAMATION IN COLORADO

From the earliest days of the state's settlement, reclamation was an important issue in Colorado. In view of its place among the state's problems
—and in light of the general rule that a major concern of one government
in the United States soon becomes a major concern of all—it would indeed have been unusual not to find intergovernmental co-operation in the
reclamation field. The problem was not how to establish such co-operation, but how to direct it into effective channels.

The principle of intergovernmental co-operation in the reclamation
field was not a new one by the latter part of the nineteenth century. In
the arid West, however, its nature had to undergo a radical change. East
of the ninety-eighth meridian, the problem was one of reclaiming lands
that had an excess of water. In order to accomplish this, federal swamp
and overflowed land grants were made to the states, with varying degrees
of success in the actual reclamation of land. West of the ninety-eighth
meridian, the problem was lack of water. There were no swamp lands to
be granted, but there was even greater necessity for some type of federal
aid to bring water to the arid lands.

Westerners were not slow to perceive the essential sameness of the
problem and to request some new form of federal aid in place of the
swamp land grants. John L. Routt, first governor of the state of Colorado,
in his first message to the General Assembly stated that

the expense of irrigating dry areas on a sufficiently large scale is too great to be
undertaken by the state at present or by individual enterprise, and as the federal government has made to other states large grants of swamp lands, which
by labor and expenditure of money have become very valuable, why should not
we, with our vast unproductive plains, ask the government to assist us in like
manner by a grant of lands which would enable the state to accomplish this
most desirable object?[27]

[27] Colorado, *Governor's Messages* (John L. Routt), 1876.

He recommended that the General Assembly memorialize the state's Congressional delegation to secure the desired aid.

The General Assembly agreed with Governor Routt; and the state, in conjunction with other western areas and interests, embarked on a long campaign to secure the enactment of the necessary legislation, which was to bring limited success in 1894 with the passage of the Carey Act, and to be adopted as national policy, albeit in a different form, in 1902 with the passage of the Reclamation Act.

At first, progress on the national level was slow, since the greater part of the nation did not understand the western need. In the meantime, the states had to provide such governmental aid as was available from resources at hand. To do this, Colorado turned to the Internal Improvement Fund. State lands were sold primarily to encourage irrigation. Appropriations were made from the proceeds of the fund for reservoirs and irrigation canals. Governor Adams, in his proposal to have Congress release the Internal Improvement Fund from its prescribed uses, stated that if Congress would not do so, it should at least permit the fund to be used for the promotion of irrigation works. By 1891, $209,500 had been appropriated from the proceeds of the Internal Improvement Fund for irrigation purposes.[28] State lands were sold at minimum prices to irrigation companies in alternate quarter-sections, with rights of way granted over other lands retained by the state, for the construction of irrigation ditches.

Though these grants were made primarily to promote construction of irrigation facilities, the State Board of Land Commissioners modeled the program after that of the federal government to enhance the value of the state-retained lands. Although the ditches were generally constructed and furnished the major part of the small irrigation program for many decades, the state did not earn the money it had hoped to, since the irrigation companies generally were able to acquire the other lands either at the same minimum sale prices or for trifling rentals. As a result, many of the irrigation projects that were recorded as financed by private enterprise were actually products of this often unintentional but necessary federal-state subsidy.

The policy of the state was to subsidize private companies for the smaller projects and undertake directly only those projects too costly or

[28] *Ibid.* (Job A. Cooper), 1891.

too large for even subsidized private enterprise to handle.[29] Very often, they were too large for even the state to handle, with the relatively limited amount of money available from the Internal Improvement Funds. Thus, they were registered as failures until the federal government stepped in to take a more directly active role.

After nearly twenty years of agitation by the western states, including memorials from state legislatures and hard work by western Congressional delegations, the compromise Carey Act for reclamation of arid lands in the West was passed in 1894. Under the terms of this act, a state could receive up to one million acres of desert land, provided it then reclaimed, irrigated, and settled the lands. The states had originally requested that the lands be turned over to them in a grant to be disposed of under general conditions similar to those accompanying the previous internal improvement grants. Congress, however, had long since abandoned such unrestricted grants and wanted the federal government to exercise more direct control over the diminishing public domain. The compromise that was effected authorized the secretary of the interior to enter into agreements with each of the desert-land states to set aside up to one million acres of land, which would be patented to the state as it was reclaimed and settled. In this way, the states were required to improve the land in tracts before receiving any of it. The tracts could then be sold only to bona fide settlers, no more than one hundred sixty acres per person. Any surplus that was received from the land sale, above the cost of reclamation, was to be placed in a permanent fund to be used for reclamation of other desert lands in the state. In order to qualify for the grant, a state had to submit a request to reserve a specific tract and present a plan for its reclamation. If approved by the Interior Department, the land would be reserved for a ten-year period, during which time the project had to be completed.[30]

While this final land-grant program did accomplish some of the things for which it was designed, the basic problem of desert land reclamation was too great for it to solve. It could do little more than had been done with the Internal Improvement Fund and lands in Colorado. In that state, the State Board of Land Commissioners was made responsible for selecting the lands to be gained under the program, with the co-operation of the state engineer, who prepared the plans that were then submitted

[29] *Ibid.* (Davis H. Waite), 1895.

[30] Mathias Orfield, *Federal Land Grants to the States with Special Reference to Minnesota* (Minneapolis: University of Minnesota Press, 1915), pp. 110–11.

to the General Land Office. By 1918, lands had been withdrawn in Colorado for twenty-three projects, only one of which had been completed successfully. This lack of success stemmed from several causes: difficulty in preparing acceptable plans, difficulty in raising adequate funds to do the work, the time lag between construction and reimbursement through sales, and, most important, the high cost of construction at a time when better-watered communities still offered opportunities to prospective settlers at less cost. It was only after all the better-watered lands were exhausted and the federal government was willing to pay for the large installations needed to bring water to the less favored areas that the reclamation program really became a big one. And that was not until the third decade of the twentieth century.

TWO SCIENTIFIC PROJECTS IN THE EAST

Federal-state collaboration in the field of science dates from the earliest days of the Republic, when the science-minded founding fathers inaugurated the first governmental programs of a scientific nature. Federal and state interests in the realm of science soon opened up areas for intergovernmental collaboration that were not inhibited in form by the pre-Constitutional or post-Constitutional origins of the various states (as were the land-grant programs), presaging the collaborative orientations of the twentieth century.

In 1807, Congress had been prevailed upon, through a combination of fortuitous circumstances, to establish a general geodetic survey of the United States seacoast. After an initial eleven years of haphazard action, the Coast Survey, as the agency was then called, was allowed to languish until 1843, when its vigor was renewed under a new director, Alexander Dallas Bache. Although the previous director, Ferdinand R. Hessler, had been an excellent scientist, he was no politician; and he had done a thorough job of alienating Congress. Bache was of a different stripe. A capable scientist, he was also a West Point graduate with connections in influential political circles. He redesigned the survey so that its worth was easily demonstrable to the most locally minded or economy-minded members of Congress, and involved the coastal states in the enterprise by showing how the work of the survey would benefit them commercially.[31]

---

[31] The Coast Survey, now the U.S. Coast and Geodetic Survey, was one of the pioneer scientific agencies of the federal government, one which collected under its

New Hampshire responded to the new approach with considerable interest, enacting a broad Coast Survey Act to provide for the activities of the United States Topographical Engineers, who were conducting the survey work in the field. The most significant feature of this act was its provision for utilizing the machinery of local government to implement a "purely federal" program. The Topographical Engineers were granted the right to enter into and use land in the state for the erection of stations and other structures needed for survey work. If, after doing so, they were not able to secure an agreement with the landowner for damages, either side might petition the court of common pleas in the county in which the land was situated for an appraisal of the damages. The court would then refer the matter to the county road commissioners, who would hear both parties and submit a report in the same manner as was done for land taken for highway construction (the road commissioners seem to have been an embryonic administrative tribunal); the court would then render judgment upon this report, with both parties retaining the right of appeal to a jury. In addition, the measure provided that any person damaging the federal installations was liable to be fined $50 plus damages for each offense.[32]

Although this act and its subsequent implementation provided for state aid to the federal project in a limited sense only, it was the forerunner of an act that came three decades later, which provided for routinized cooperation at the administrative level. In June, 1872, Governor E. A. Straw raised the issue in his annual message:

The triangulation of the state is now being carried on by the United States Coast Survey, under the authority of a recent act of Congress. In order to secure to the state the greatest benefit from this triangulation, the cooperation of the authorities of the several towns in the state to aid in the erection of signals upon the most prominent hills will be necessary. It seems, therefore, important that such legislative action be taken as will secure this cooperation

---

wing and otherwise stimulated many areas of scientific research that would otherwise have been neglected. In the long perspective of history, it may be more significant than many an endeavor given much more space in the ordinary history books. For an excellent description of its political history and activities, see A. Hunter Dupree, *Science in the Federal Government* (Cambridge, Mass.: Harvard University Press, 1957), pp. 29–33, 52, 53, 64–65, 100–105, 202–3; and Leonard D. White, *The Jacksonians* (New York: Macmillan Co., 1954), pp. 488–91. For a discussion of Bache's approach to Congress and the reasons for its success, see Dupree, *op. cit.*, pp. 100–105.

[32] New Hampshire, *Laws* (1876), chap. 37, June 30, 1846.

and not leave so important a matter to the uncertain action of the several town authorities.[33]

The Governor's message had its intended effect and resulted in a legislative enactment to stimulate state participation in the survey, which provided that

the acting assistant, in charge of the triangulation now being carried on in this state by the United States coast survey, is hereby authorized to set such signals as may be necessary to render this survey complete, for future use in the construction of a map of the state, at an expense not exceeding twenty dollars in any town or city of the state, and to draw upon the state treasurer for the sums so expended.[34]

Under the terms of this act and the relevant acts of Congress, the United States Coast Survey and the state survey worked together to prepare accurate records of the geography, topography, and geology of the state. The United States acting assistant in charge of New Hampshire operations drew money from the state treasurer for the signal stations after 1872.[35] The Coast Survey loaned instruments to the state geological survey during the 1860's and 1870's as an informal part of the co-ordinated mapping effort.

Another responsibility that was placed in the hands of the Coast Survey, primarily because of the scientific qualifications of its first two directors, was supervision of the nation's standard weights and measures. The power of the federal government to fix the standard weights and meas-

[33] New Hampshire, *Governors' Messages* (E. A. Straw), June, 1872, p. 16. The last sentence of this message again illustrates the important point in the history of federal-state relations in the United States that, rather than usurping powers of the states, the programs of the federal government have generally stimulated their activity and increased assumption of the powers they possessed. It was the stimulus of the federal survey that put the state of New Hampshire in the survey field, rather than "leave so important a matter to the uncertain action of the several town authorities." It may even be said that this action, in turn, stimulated the local governments to assume their responsibilities by providing standards, guidance, and financial aid. All this was possible because the entrance of the larger governmental unit into the field was not designed in such a manner as to eliminate the smaller units but, on the contrary, to stimulate them. In this way, the total velocity of government was increased, not that of any single level alone.

[34] New Hampshire, *Laws* (1872), chap. 29 (July 3, 1872). In 1878, this act was amended to give the state a greater role in the survey by establishing the location of its signals (New Hampshire, *Laws* [1878], chap. 25, July 25, 1878).

[35] New Hampshire State Treasurer, *Annual Report*. Annual expenditures were made in 1873, 1874, 1875, 1876, 1877, 1879, 1880, 1883, varying between $280 and $1,300 per year.

ures for the nation was specifically enumerated in the Constitution. Although on first examination this might seem to be a trivial program, it actually represented an activity that lay at the base of all subsequent scientific and technological progress (which is why it was mentioned in the Constitution in the first place). Under a Congressional enactment of 1836, it was the responsibility of the director of the Coast Survey to prepare sets of standard weights and measures, based on the national standard, for each state and to arrange for their proper distribution and preservation within the states.

Bache was the first of the directors to actually undertake the distribution of the sets. He initiated correspondence with the governors of the several states, informing them of the availability of sets of standard weights and measures and describing the conditions established by Congress and his agency for their protection and use.

New Hampshire was quite willing to do its share to obtain these sets of weights and measures and to use their acquisition as a means of implementing higher standards of accuracy in the counties. The state treasurer was made custodian of the sets and handled the administrative procedures for their acquisition and subsequent maintenance. The legislature enacted a measure in 1848 requiring all county sealers to present the standard weights and measures of their respective counties at the state Treasury Office to be "proved" by the standard weights and measures received from the federal government.[36]

The distribution to New Hampshire was not completed until 1877 when Solon A. Carter, the state treasurer, discovered that although the state had received the complete set of United States standard weights and measures, it had not received the scale beams or balances necessary to compare the accuracy of county or private sets. (Since there is evidence that county standard sets were examined in the 1850's, it is more than likely that the original scale beams and balances had been lost.) This deficiency was remedied by the United States Coast Survey, which provided the state with a full set of standards for both the American and the metric systems, together with balances required "for their practical operation." As a consequence, the state set aside a specially equipped room to house them.[37]

With the completion of the sets serving as an impetus, Carter began to enforce the laws governing the county weights and measures again.

[36] New Hampshire State Treasurer, *Annual Report,* 1849, p. 451.
[37] New Hampshire State Treasurer, *Annual Report,* 1877, p. 29.

In 1878 he was able to report that all vacancies in the position of county sealer had been filled. All county sealers had their standards examined during the year and checked against those of the state, their deficiencies had been corrected and any missing pieces supplied. In this way, the purposes of the federal grant were fulfilled.[38]

The weights and measures program continued past the original distribution, serving to set standards for the states and to keep them abreast of the latest measuring instruments. The rise of the new technology of the post-Civil War period led to the establishment of a separate Office of Weights and Measures in the United States Coast and Geodetic Survey (1897). As the twentieth century was ushered in, this task was removed from the survey entirely and given to the new National Bureau of Standards (1901), an agency with powers sufficient to cope with the new age that was dawning but still designed to continue the service to federal, state, and local governments provided for in the Constitution and implemented for almost a century by its predecessor bureaus.[39]

VETERANS' WELFARE: THE SOLDIERS' HOME GRANTS

The second modern cash grant-in-aid program was established in 1887 to help the states support aged and infirm veterans of American wars. In order to stimulate the creation and maintenance of state soldiers' homes, Congress provided for annual payments of $100 per inmate to states founding such institutions. As a direct result of the federal legislation, New Hampshire established a soldiers' home in 1889.[40] The home was governed by a board consisting of the governor (ex officio chairman), the department commander of the Grand Army of the Republic, and five appointed members. (One of the appointed members, Charles E. Tilton, purchased a farm and donated it to the state for the site. This donation was vital to the establishment of the home, since the board did not have sufficient funds to purchase any of the other prospective sites that had been examined.)

On December 3, 1890, the home's first building was dedicated. The General Court had appropriated $30,000 for the construction of the building, but this proved insufficient. The Women's Relief Corps (the

[38] Ibid., 1878, p. 32.

[39] Dupree, op. cit., pp. 271–77.

[40] New Hampshire, Laws (1889), chap. 76, August 16, 1889.

GAR auxiliary) undertook to furnish it, contributing approximately $5,000 in the course of the work. The legislature then appropriated $10,000 for its maintenance, with the expectation of partial reimbursement by the federal government. As the secretary of the Board of Managers reported:

Under the laws of Congress the United States will reimburse us to the extent of $100 per year for each veteran soldier maintained in the home, a provision which will go far towards the support of the inmates, especially when the numbers become considerably larger than now.

Even at the outset the direct federal subsidy covered 40 per cent of the state's contribution to the operating budget. (The home had forty residents when it officially opened, which gave the state $4,000 in federal funds). Furthermore,

if the applicant is a United States pensioner, he will not be admitted until he shall have filed his pension certificate with the board of managers, to be retained by them while he remains an inmate of the home, with an agreement to transfer his pension to the board subject to such disposition as to them may seem proper in each particular case.[41]

Under this provision, control of the federal pensions was turned over to the board. The board allotted the money so that each pensioner received two dollars per month for his personal use. The remainder was used for the support of any dependent relatives and, if there were none, for the support of the home. This system was put into operation in July, 1891. Initially, it raised a great deal of opposition, including an uproar in the press. Some of the residents even left the home because of it. But by 1892 the issue had quieted down, leaving the system intact except for one rather significant change. Apparently, many states were taking control of residents' pensions in a similar manner, thereby informally increasing the amount of federal support for their institutions. Congress reacted to this by passing an act (August 5, 1892) diminishing federal payments to the state institutions by half of the amount collected from pensions. In 1892, for example, the board collected $720.50 in pensions and lost $360.25 through federal deductions.[42]

The state soldiers' homes were inspected periodically in the same man-

---

[41] *Report of the Board of Managers of the New Hampshire Soldiers' Home*, 1889–1890.

[42] *Ibid.*, 1891–92.

ner as the National Military Home in Washington by the inspector of national military homes and state soldiers' homes. In 1892, General W. W. Averill, the inspector, commended the home for fulfilling "all the promises and predictions regarding its development in the most satisfactory manner" since his first inspection.[43]

The financial record of the biennium January 1, 1891–January 1, 1893, illustrates the role played by the federal government in supporting the home. Receipts for that period included $20,000 appropriated by the General Court, $220 earned by the home's farm, $7,187 granted by the

TABLE 12

FEDERAL AND STATE AID TO THE NEW HAMPSHIRE SOLDIERS' HOME

	1893–94	1895–96	1898–99	1899–1900
Receipts				
Unexpended balance . . .	$ 3,130.22	$ 2,770.09	$ 826.04	$ 2,158.72
State appropriation. . . .	15,000.00	25,000.00	20,000.00	20,000.00
U.S. grants.	10,200.45	13,390.50	13,889.35	13,935.87
Pensions*.	2,851.24	4,032.00	4,737.67	4,936.35
Other.	. . . .	. . . .	400.00	50.00
Total.	$31,181.91	$45,192.59	$39,493.06	$41,080.94
Disbursements				
State share.	15,360.13	16,944.05	19,212.11	20,525.83
U.S. share.	13,051.69	17,422.50	18,627.02	18,872.22
Total.	$28,411.82	$34,366.55	$37,839.15	$39,398.05

* Actually, the board received more pension money from the federal government than indicated in the table, which only includes that part used for maintenance of the home itself. (Incidentally, the pension money was also channeled through the state treasury.) The rest of the pension funds were used by the board to support the pensioners' dependents (see Table 13).

federal government, and $806 from federal pensions. The total maintenance costs for the same period show an even more striking balance in favor of the federal government. Of the $21,616.23 expended, $13,623.07 was paid by the state and $7,993.26 by the federal government.[44] The federal share increased even more in the next biennium.[45] By 1895–96, the federal government was contributing more than half of the total costs.[46] Tables 12 and 13 illustrate the expanded federal role in supporting the home.

[43] *Ibid.* The board regularly received copies of the inspectors' reports.

[44] *Ibid.*

[45] *Ibid.*, 1893–94.

[46] *Ibid.*, 1895–96, 1897–98, 1899–1900.

The creation and maintenance of the Minnesota Soldiers' Home followed a similar pattern. The Minnesota department of the Grand Army of the Republic initiated intensive lobbying for the creation of such an institution by the state in 1886 in conjunction with the efforts of the G.A.R. on the national level to secure a federal grant for the purpose. The thirty thousand veterans in the state formed a powerful group and secured immediate support from their public officials. Governors Hubbard and McGill included the request in their messages to the state legislature, which enacted a measure creating "a home for honorably discharged soldiers, sailors and marines who by reason of wounds, disease, old age or infirmities are unable to earn their living and have no adequate means of support" in 1887. The city of Minneapolis, eager to have the institu-

TABLE 13

FEDERAL AID TO PENSIONERS IN THE NEW HAMPSHIRE SOLDIERS' HOME

	1893–94	1895–96	1897–98	1899–1900
Amount received by board..	$5,923.57	$9,806.92	$12,230.57	$11,915.00
Amount paid to pensioners and dependents.........	3,072.33	5,774.92	7,492.90	6,978.65
Amount used for home.....	2,851.24	4,032.00	4,737.67	4,936.35
Monthly aggregate........	$ 490.00	$ 540.00	$ 550.00	$ 500.00
Number of pensioners in home.................	50	56	55	55
Total number of residents...	83	92	85	86

tion located within its boundaries, made available fifty-one acres near Fort Snelling, which a group of citizens had purchased at a cost of $55,000. The site was immediately accepted by the institution's trustees; and the home was opened in temporary quarters in November, 1887, to take advantage of the first year of the federal grant. The legislature initially appropriated $50,000 for permanent buildings and continued thereafter to provide the balance in cost of maintenance over and above the annual federal grant.[47]

The soldiers' home program was typical of the new co-operative programs of the post-Civil War period. Similar institutions, founded along the lines of the ones in New Hampshire and Minnesota, were established in every state except those of the former Confederacy and were similarly supported by federal grants. Most of these institutions have continued to exist to serve veterans of the nation's subsequent wars.

[47] For a brief account of the establishment of the Minnesota Soldiers' Home, see Theodore Christianson, *op. cit.*, II, 168–70.

THE SUM OF CO-OPERATIVE FEDERALISM

Every aspect of later forms of intergovernmental co-operation is already identifiable in the seven programs analyzed in this chapter. With the exception of the two scientific programs and the system of national banks, these programs originated as a result of what is usually termed "grass-roots" pressure that had been developed in each case through organized pressure groups (of educators, veterans, or conservationists). The pressure exerted by these groups was applied simultaneously to the federal and state governments, and their successes with each were equally simultaneous. In the case of the national banking program, similar local pressure groups succeeded in shaping and modifying legislation proposed by the chief executive to meet a national emergency. The two scientific programs exemplify the occasional deviant cases in which lack of concern at the grass roots allows pressure groups within government to establish programs in which they are interested—programs which are subsequently fitted into the system of sharing.

Of the seven programs discussed, four were formally designed to be intergovernmental at the outset. The reclamation, weights and measures, and soldiers' home programs involved federal grants-in-aid, whereas the educational exchange program was based on federal-state sharing of intelligence. The forestry program was not made a formal co-operative endeavor at first, though the pressure group behind it intended to co-ordinate federal, state, local, and private actions from the beginning and did so successfully. The topographical survey program was designed as an all-federal activity under specific Constitutional authorization. It soon became apparent that federal-state co-operation would lead to the most widespread benefits obtainable for the money and effort to be expended, so the originally ad hoc administrative agreements for collaboration were shortly thereafter written into the law.

The national banking program was the only one of the seven expressly designed to nationalize a function previously in the hands of the states. In this case, not only was the federal government involved in a field considered to be theoretically within the scope of state powers (though not reserved powers) as described in the Constitution, but it also was making an earnest attempt to totally usurp powers then being exercised (albeit inadequately) by the states. This example, brought on by the Civil War, is one of the few actual attempts made by the federal government to exercise its strength to nationalize fully an activity already in state hands. Initiated in response to the greatest crisis ever to face the American federal system, the national banking program was implemented by the federal government with the utmost force that it could politically afford to apply. Yet the net result was a temporary nationalization of American banking followed by a resurgence of state participation in the banking field and, ultimately, by the establishment of formal devices for federal-state co-operation in the regulation of banking operations in which both levels of government were involved.[48]

As these programs became formally co-operative, provisions for federal supervision were developed for each along lines already traditional, although in some cases expanded. For the first time, federal inspectors involved in routinized tasks of supervision and inspection are encountered. More formalized administrative tribunals and more active professional associations appear with greater frequency. Perhaps the least revolutionary of these new developments was the expanded use of monetary grants and the decline in significance of special programs for the public-land states. None of the above devices were new in the period following the Civil War, but all were expanding under pressures of a new age and its new frontiers.

[48] Similar attempts to utilize a period of national crisis to centralize governmental functions were made during the period of the New Deal. They generally failed, much as this attempt did and for similar reasons. See Morton Grodzins, "American Political Parties and the American System," in *Western Political Quarterly*, Vol. XIII (December, 1960), for an analysis of several examples of such attempts and the reasons for their failure.

16

Internal Improvements for Local Purposes

While the role of the federal government in the promotion of internal improvements of interstate value was often taken for granted in the nineteenth century, few people realized the extent of federal aid available for the construction of internal improvements designed to meet "purely local" needs. The federal government provided a variety of internal improvement aids, ranging from joint-stock companies and the great grant programs for improvements in the national interest to river and harbor appropriations and swamp land grants to aid the states and localities in specifically local development.

FEDERAL AID FOR RIVERS AND HARBORS

Part of the accepted myth of nineteenth-century dual federalism is the idea that only recently did the federal government begin to deal directly with the cities, creatures of the states, in programs of substantial scope that include federal grants. The historical record belies this view.

In the nineteenth century, the most important developmental task facing American cities was to secure a firm place in the stream of American commerce and development. In almost every case, this meant developing lines of communication—first with the potentially valuable hinterland and then with the rest of the country, or the world—in order to provide the facilities that would attract population and commerce necessary for growth. This is the reason the cities participated in the internal improvement boom along with the states and the federal government. In Virginia, connections with the interior were developed through federal-state-local co-operation; while ports to link the cities with the nation and the world were made possible by federal river and harbor improvement appropriations in direct co-operation with local interests.

So much has been written of the "pork barrel" aspects of river and harbor appropriations that the necessity and value of much of the work done has been obscured. Comparison of the importance of river and harbor improvements for the major cities of the nineteenth century with the importance of superhighways for those of the twentieth would not be amiss. Whereas the strict constructionists could limit the amount of aid given by the federal government in other fields, Congress had a constitutional right and obligation to improve navigation by direct action. The first omnibus Rivers and Harbors Act was passed in May, 1826. In the following decades, it and its successors secured a firm place in the affections of the nation. Ostensibly a solely federal program, it soon became a federal-local co-operative activity because of the exigencies of the federal system. All projects had to be initiated at the local level. Local communities developed and proposed projects through their Congressmen, who would then secure a place for them in a rivers and harbors act. Then, when the United States Army Engineers were ready to commence work, the locality would furnish aid in various forms to either hasten completion of the work or maintain the rate of progress after federal funds had been expended and while new appropriations were still pending.

On August 30, 1852, a new omnibus bill "making appropriations for the improvement of certain rivers and harbors" was approved by Congress. Under its terms, the United States Army Corps of Engineers was assigned the responsibility for almost all works and surveys on the Atlantic coast and the rivers emptying into it and on the Gulf Coast (except for the Mississippi River above its mouth). To carry out this assignment, the secretary of war established a Board of Engineers of River and Harbor Improvements to oversee the work from a national point of view and dispatched officers to the various localities to take charge of local projects. Among the major works designated in the bill was the improvement of the James River below Richmond and the Appomattox River below Petersburg.[1]

The reaction of the Virginia cities was one of pleasure and eagerness to get on with the work. On October 6, 1852, a committee of the Rich-

---

[1] U.S. War Department, *Annual Report of the Chief Engineer, 1852.*

mond Common Council wrote to the chief of engineers in Washington to inform him that they were "pleased to hear that the improvement of the James River, which is of such interest to Richmonders has been given to the Department." In the name of the Common Council, they expressed a desire for the dredging work to begin even before the survey had been made and offered to furnish any aid or information to the officer in charge of the work that they might be able to supply. Since the city was applying to Congress for additional appropriations to be made in the next session, they felt that any work started by then would help them secure favorable consideration for future aid.[2]

Lieutenant Colonel R. E. DeRussy was sent to supervise the work on both the James and Appomattox rivers. In 1853 he reported to General Totten that he had received help from the cities of Richmond and Petersburg in the dredging operations. With the encouragement of the Richmond city fathers, he reiterated a suggestion previously advanced by Colonel Mansfield, his colleague in charge of the Appomattox River project, to purchase the dredging machines rather than continue the policy of leasing them for the duration of each project.[3]

I am satisfied that the City Council of Richmond would prefer the adoption of the mode asked for, as they would be willing to continue the improvements, with their own means, after the balance of our appropriation is expended, with the machines used by the Department.

Totten was either unwilling or unable to accept DeRussy's suggestion, previous department procedure having always been to contract for the dredging machine and its handlers from among the local population.[4] The problem was solved, however, by the city of Richmond's purchase of a steam dredging machine, which was then leased to the United States engineer in March, 1854. It seems that the cost of the dredge was paid

[2] Letter from Joseph R. Anderson, Thomas W. McCaine, and Richard O. Haskins, Committee of the Common Council of Richmond, to Brigadier General Totten, Chief of the U.S. Army Corps and Engineers, October 6, 1852, National Archives, Record Group 77.

[3] Letter from Lieutenant Colonel R. E. DeRussy to Brevet General J. G. Totten, May 15, 1853, National Archives, Record Group 77.

[4] U.S. War Department, *Annual Report of the Chief Engineer, 1853*, pp. 298–99. It is quite possible that this policy of contracting for dredging machines with private firms was the result of Congressional interest in the matter based on a desire to have as much of the federal appropriation as possible expended in the locality. Such an approach is not unknown in other, similar, situations.

from the contract fees of the federal government, thus fulfilling the spirit
of the original suggestion, albeit somewhat indirectly.[5]

By 1856 the Congressional appropriation had been exhausted, but the
work was continuing under a new arrangement. The city of Richmond
furnished the means, and the direction was supplied by the United States
engineer, who was still on assignment there for that purpose.[6] There
seems to be little question that whenever possible, the executive departments attempted to increase this type of co-operation when Congressional authorization of funds expired. Of course, the local Congressmen,
who might not be able to obtain more money for the improvements of
their areas, could certainly band together to protect such grants of services. The James River improvements were carried on for many years under one arrangement or another, sometimes with federal funds and sometimes without. At the time of this writing (1962), the Army Engineers
are still there.

The situation on the Appomattox River was somewhat more complex.
With the passage of the Act of 1852, the secretary of war dispatched a
survey team under the direction of Colonel Mansfield to examine the
channel where the improvements were to be made. On December 14, the
secretary joined the chief engineer in approving the report of the Board
of Engineers for River and Harbor Improvements initiating the project.
Colonel Mansfield remained at Petersburg to begin the operation. On
February 5, 1853, he forwarded a resolution of the city council of Petersburg to the secretary of war, which offered the city's assistance in the
work.

On November 11, 1854, the War Department was notified by the Petersburg city council that their committee had been authorized to procure
a dredge to be leased to the United States engineers for the project.
Meanwhile, the command had passed to Brevet Colonel J. C. Smith. In
1855, he had to report little progress other than "thorough digestion of
the mode of operating that it would be most advantageous to pursue"
and negotiations over methods of procedure (seemingly with the city),
which were unfortunately interrupted although there was "no material
disagreement between the parties on either side." He reported that, "The
mode of operation now determined on is to provide a dredger capable of
raising 2000 cubic yards a day with the requisite number of discharging
lighters at the expense of the City of Petersburg." A competent dredge

[5] *Annual Report of the Chief Engineer, 1854*, p. 413.

[6] *Annual Report of the Chief Engineer, 1856*, pp. 51, 54.

constructor had been engaged to construct the machine for the city according to plans drawn up by the United States engineer, who also drew up the plans for the lighters to be constructed with it. "All that has been done in regard to this work has been with the concurrence of the authorities of the City of Petersburg. They are resolved that the Improvement shall be completed and will furnish the fund required for it if not assisted by the Government." Nevertheless, he asked for an appropriation of $50,000 for the fiscal year 1857.[7]

In 1857, the dredge was completed and work resumed. Work was continued under the contract with the city until September 22, 1858, when the federal funds were exhausted. In most river and harbor projects of the period, Congress would appropriate sufficient funds to initiate a project but not to complete it. The locality benefiting from the project would then be called upon to continue the work using its own financial resources until local initiative could secure another appropriation; the United States engineers continued their field direction of such projects as long as funds for their salaries were included in the War Department's budget. The Civil War disrupted the work on the James and Appomattox rivers, but once the war was over, the United States engineers were back, continuing the work to whatever degree their services were needed.[8]

River and harbor improvements almost always involved direct federal-local co-operation. (In some cases, when the state government was sufficiently interested, it also participated.) Projects were initiated by local interests, who steered their proposals through Congress. Implementation was in the hands of the United States engineers, who would develop co-operative administrative relationships with the local governments in the areas to be served. The projects would then be continued on a partnership basis, which, particularly in the later stages of the work, often included joint financing.

[7] Report of Brevet Colonel J. C. Smith, U.S. Army Corps of Engineers to General J. G. Totten, Chief Engineer, on the James and Appomattox rivers improvements, October 15, 1855, National Archives, Record Group 77. Smith was in over-all charge of both river improvement projects, with local engineers directing the specific dredging operations under his general supervision. For example, on the James River, the city engineer of Richmond was directing the actual work, using federal funds, and reporting to Smith. Smith enclosed a copy of that engineer's report with his own to Totten.

[8] The Appomattox River material is taken from the records of the U.S. Army Corps of Engineers, DeGrange Index of River and Harbor Improvements, Box 1, in the National Archives, Record Group 77.

LOCAL IMPROVEMENTS IN COLORADO

The greater part of the internal improvement work undertaken by the state of Colorado and its subdivisions was financed by funds from federal land grants. Aside from the railroad grants, the major source of federal aid was the Internal Improvement Land Grant of 1841, which extended five hundred thousand acres to Colorado upon its admission to the Union. After the United States survey, the state had to locate, select, and file for every acre transferred to it by the General Land Office. The State Board of Land Commissioners (SBLC) then had to sell or lease the lands and manage the accumulated funds. Other federal sources of support for local improvements included two grants for public buildings (for the state capitol and the penitentiary), both of which had to be administered as separate funds under the terms of the grants. Finally, there was the Five Per Cent Fund, which required only the administrative arrangements necessary to secure its transfer to the state each year and its subsequent use.

The methods of location, selection, and claiming of these lands followed the standard land-grant pattern. After Congressional authorization and state acceptance, the SBLC was entrusted with the administration of the three land-grant programs. It sent its agents into the field to select blocs of land that were as well watered as possible, which would enhance their value. As the agents submitted their selections, the SBLC would examine them for conflicting claims prior to filing with the United States land office.[9] The receiver of the United States land office would then check the list to ascertain whether the selections were open. If some were not, he would notify the SBLC to make other choices and submit a revised list. If all the lands listed were available, he kept one copy of the list, returned one to the SBLC with his certification, and sent the third one to the General Land Office also with his certification that the lands were open and available. The General Land Office would then approve the list and send patents to the SBLC transferring title to the state and notifying the local United States land office of the transfer. In case of conflicting claims, the commissioner of the General Land Office would make a decision, subject to appeal to the secretary of the interior.

[9] Filing meant the submission of a list of the lands selected by the state (in triplicate) with filing fees to the United States land office in whose district the lands were located, accompanied by an authorization to make the selections based on the particular land-grant program in question.

Once the state board took possession, it would either sell the lands according to the terms of the federal grant or lease them. If they were to be sold, the sale was public (under the terms of federal and state law), advertised in the newspapers (state law), and sold for no less than a set minimum price (federal and state law) with the terms of payment arranged according to state law. If they were to be leased, all this was done under state law. The money received from sales was placed in the appropriate fund, held by the state treasurer, to be invested by the SBLC under the direction of the General Assembly. The money received from the leases was deposited with the state treasurer until appropriated by the General Assembly. The earnings of the permanent funds were appropriated for roads, bridges, irrigation projects, state and other public buildings, and public institutions—projects running the gamut of the internal improvement field.[10]

Between 1880 and 1902, the General Assembly used the Internal Improvement Fund by dividing it among the counties for specific projects. This led to competition between the various counties for aid in constructing their projects not unlike that associated with rivers and harbors legislation on the national level. In fact, very similar charges of "pork barrel" politics were made; but, in general, the fund was used for legitimate, if not always successful, improvements that were constructed economically.[11]

Grants for improvements were generally made on a matching basis, with the state furnishing its share from the fund and the county adding its contribution under the terms of the applicable state law. The improvements so constructed were intended to last; and most of the successful ones continued to be in use until the advent of the highway construction boom of the 1920's and afterward, when they were replaced by improvements more suited to the automobile age.

Here again, federal funds provided a means for strengthening state control over programs that had previously been considered to be local responsibilities. For example, in the appropriation for the construction of a very important bridge over the Grand (now Colorado) River near Grand Junction, Mesa County had to provide $15,000 in order to qualify for

[10] Records covering the location, selection, patenting, selling, and leasing of internal improvements lands are on file in the Colorado State Archives, Board of Land Commissioners Records. Since the creation of the State Highway Department, the income from these funds has gone directly to it.

[11] Wilbur Fisk Stone (ed.), *A History of Colorado* (Chicago: S. J. Clarke, 1918), I, 579.

$25,000 from the Internal Improvement Fund. In addition, a board of construction was established to supervise the project, consisting of the governor, the state engineer, and the chairman of the Mesa County Board of Commissioners. The state law provided for advertisement for bids and preparation of plans that would meet state standards. The bridge was made a free highway, important in a day when private roads were considered reasonable profit-making ventures in Colorado; and Mesa County was made responsible for its maintenance.[12]

Similar conditions were imposed in other projects. An appropriation for $7,500 to straighten the channel of the Rio Grande River and build a levee near Alamosa did not formally require matching funds from Conejos County, but a similar board of construction was established. The board was required to examine the river and have the plans and specifications for the work drawn up. It was given the authority to select the best plan submitted within the range of the appropriation and to let the construction contract to the lowest bidder. It had to approve the completed project before issuing the warrants for payment.[13] In actual practice, it was the state engineer, or his deputies, who worked with the county commissioners on the project, so that the state actually provided the professional supervision.

Wagon roads were also constructed from Internal Improvement Fund appropriations. For example, the road that opened up the Sangre de Cristo Range near Stonewall, just north of the New Mexico border and west of Trinidad, was constructed with $15,000 appropriated from the fund in 1889 under conditions and supervision identical with the projects described above.[14] Irrigation canals were also considered to fall into the category of legitimate internal improvements and received state aid in this fashion. In such cases, the appropriations were contingent on surveys conducted by the state engineer, which had to show that the project was practical. If it proved to be so, then the same conditions and procedures applied as in the other cases.[15]

Aid from the Internal Improvement Fund was not confined to small towns or rural areas. In 1889, the General Assembly appropriated $25,000

[12] Colorado, *Statutes*, Act of April 6, 1885.

[13] *Ibid.*, Act of April 4, 1887.

[14] *Ibid.*, Act of April 24, 1889.

[15] *Ibid.*, Act of April 23, 1889. For a discussion of the importance of irrigation and land reclamation in nineteenth-century Colorado, see chapter xv.

from the fund for the construction of the Fourteenth Street viaduct in Denver to connect the east and west banks of the South Platte River at a level high enough to be above the flood plain. In this case, the professional services and supervision of the state engineer were not considered to be necessary, since a city body, the Fourteenth Street Viaduct Association, was responsible for the project and had its own competent help; consequently, only the governor was included on the Board of Construction as a representative of the state. Once again, the feasibility of undertaking the project within the amount of money appropriated had first to be ascertained before the appropriation took effect. The completed structure was given to the city to maintain.[16]

Irrigation projects for the diversion of water and for reservoirs were also authorized by the General Assembly to be paid for out of the fund. Most of them, however, did not prove to be practical with the limited amount of money available for their construction. Despite much talk and many attempts to meet the water needs of the area, it was not until after the passage of the United States Reclamation Act of 1902 that any substantial progress was made by government in this field. The appropriations bills for water projects are interesting, though, for what they reveal about the greater willingness of the state to assume control over such projects on the basis of control over the funds than over the road projects. For example, a measure appropriating $3,000 for a preliminary survey of the Grand, Laramie, and North Platte rivers to ascertain the possibility of diverting part of their flow to the South Platte and Arkansas Rivers (a mammoth project that would have called for crossing the continental divide at its highest point, which was not even partially achieved until the Big Thompson Diversion Project was completed in 1958 by the Bureau of Reclamation) included the provision that all works constructed and water flowing through them would be the property of the state of Colorado and would be used to supply water deficiencies according to priorities established by the state engineer and his deputies. Since this would undoubtedly have led to legal complications, the attorney-general of the state was included along with the governor and the state engineer in the survey board.[17]

The state government generally took the lead in such irrigation projects, even when its grant had to be matched by private donations. In the

[16] *Ibid.*, Act of April 19, 1889.
[17] *Ibid.*, Act of April 19, 1889.

case of the Coal Creek Reservoir in Arapahoe County, the state was willing to appropriate $20,000, provided that private funds would supply
whatever additional money was needed to complete the job. The Board
of Construction was to consist of the governor, the attorney-general, and
the state engineer, with the latter responsible for preparation of the
plans.

The problem of investment of the proceeds of the land sales had been
considered prior to 1885, since the money often remained in the state
treasury without earning interest for lack of suitable investment opportunities. In that year, Governor Grant suggested that the funds be invested in state warrants, which had previously been sold to banks. Such

TABLE 14

STATUS OF THE THREE FUNDS FOR LOCAL IMPROVEMENTS
IN COLORADO IN 1885

Fund	Original Grant (Acres)	Acres Con-firmed	Acres Sold	Average Price per Acre	Acres Leased	Annual Rental	Fund Total
Internal improve-ment.........	500,000	492,360	191,680	$1.45	115,126	$6,011	$140,038
Capitol building..	32,000	29,146	19,914	2.25	2,400	104	20,063
Penitentiary*....	32,000	25,227	7,761	1.36	3,661	114	4,085

* Figures from Colorado, *Governors' Messages* (James B. Grant), 1885. The penitentiary was in operation using buildings granted to the state for the purpose by the federal government, in addition to the land grant, and was housing United States prisoners at the standard fees.

a step would provide the state with cash for use in governmental activities not supported by permanent funds, provide revenues for the permanent funds through the interest on the warrants to be paid by the
state, and save the state money because instead of paying the interest to
the bankers, it would be transferring money, as it were, to other state
programs.[18] This proposal was ultimately adopted and became a major
"fringe benefit" of the federal grants. By 1887, $575,047.92 was invested
in state warrants, covering over two-thirds of those outstanding. Governor Adams was moved to comment "that over two-thirds of the interest
paid returns again to the people through the school and other channels."
He could see no reason why the remainder should not be similarly invested.[19]

[18] Colorado, *Governors' Messages* (James B. Grant), 1885.

[19] *Ibid.* (Alva Adams), 1888.

Despite the success of this "revolving fund" device, Governor Adams recognized some of the unfavorable consequences of the permanent funds that have traditionally been associated with federal grant-in-aid programs:

Unfortunately the plethoric condition of our treasury is due to special funds dedicated to particular uses, that cannot be diverted to the payment of general debts or demands upon the general fund. If these funds could be transferred as needed, then would our debt problem be solved and our financial difficulties vanish in the delights of a complete liquidation.[20]

He followed this with a specific recommendation:

. . . The Internal Improvement Fund I believe will do Colorado more good by being turned into the General Fund . . . than it will ever do by being expended as directed by the law which created the fund. I would, therefore, suggest that the General Assembly memorialize Congress, asking for a law that will permit such a transfer of this fund.

No transfer was ever requested and the fund continued to be directed toward uses in line with the purposes for which it was created. On several occasions, other states requested and received permission to divert one permanent fund to another in the light of differing local conditions. However, it seems clear why most Coloradans were not anxious to have the law changed. In Colorado, the legislators and their constituents wanted a fund for the construction of internal improvements throughout the state. They agreed with the federal government on the purpose for establishing the fund in the first place. Indeed, the fund would not have been established had not this feeling been general throughout the United States. Furthermore, they wanted an earmarked fund that would provide a permanent monetary basis from which to appropriate at every legislative session. While the Governor's words, taken at face value, might imply a conflict between the state and the federal government, in reality they were directed toward differing interests that cut across both levels of government. On one side, there were advocates of the "earmarking principle" in both the state and federal governments. They were opposed, in both governments, by those who stood with the Governor. The conflict was between advocates of differing theories of public finance, not between "centralists" and "states'-rights" supporters.

[20] *Ibid.*

FEDERAL AID AND LOCAL NEEDS

The Virginia and Colorado experiences with federal aid to localities represent the two extremes in form that such aid took in the nineteenth century, ranging from direct federal-local collaboration to state-local projects financed by federal grants. The record reveals that virtually every local community of any significance in the United States received federal aid in one form or another in this period.[21] In almost every case involving river and harbor improvements, the localities were directly involved in partnership with the United States Army Engineers, and in many of them, the states were involved as well.[22]

In the period between 1826 and 1912, the four states examined in this study received substantial federal aid for local improvements. Indeed, all four benefited from the rivers and harbors program. Colorado benefited least since the Corps of Engineers undertook only one survey of reservoir sites within its boundaries at a cost of $5,000.[23] New Hampshire, with few rivers and a short coastline, still managed to benefit from work done on ten rivers and six harbors at a cost to the federal government of $1,258,-285.[24] Virginia and Minnesota, both with many miles of navigable waters, benefited exceedingly. Seventy-four rivers and waterways as well as twenty-one bays and harbors were improved in Virginia, including the James and Appomattox river projects and the direct appropriations for the Dismal Swamp Canal, with a total federal expenditure of $14,819,-955.[25] The state of Minnesota was covered by the Army Engineers from end to end. Twenty-six lakes and rivers and thirteen ports, bays, and harbors were surveyed and improved. The federal government spent $17,230,785 in this work, exclusive of several millions for general im-

[21] One record available is the *Index to the Reports of the Chief of Engineers, U.S. Army, 1866–1912*, Vol. I, Rivers and Harbors (Washington, D.C.: Government Printing Office, 1915). The list of improvements, expenditures, and surveys included in the Index reaches into every corner of the United States.

[22] *Ibid.* The numerous references to state activity are listed by project.

[23] *Ibid.*, p. 1061.

[24] *Ibid.*, pp. 23–104. This figure includes expenditures for some interstate projects involving Maine and Massachusetts.

[25] *Ibid.*, pp. 329–450. This figure includes expenditures for some interstate projects involving the District of Columbia, Maryland, North Carolina, Tennessee, and West Virginia.

provements and maintenance of the upper Mississippi River between St. Paul and the mouth of the Ohio.[26]

Following the traditional theory of American federalism, the rivers and harbors program was designed as an exclusively federal one, while the construction of local bridges, county roads, and irrigation ditches was certainly meant to be the exclusive concern of the localities involved. In neither case was intergovernmental co-operation intended or anticipated by the founders of the Republic, and in both it became vital. Hindsight indicates that the assimilation of both activities into the American partnership could have been expected. The fact that both became shared activities almost from their inception is testimony to the pervasiveness of the partnership in practice in the nineteenth-century United States.

[26] *Ibid.*, pp. 1067–1226, 1231–1294. This figure includes expenditures for some interstate projects involving Iowa, North Dakota, South Dakota, and Wisconsin.

17

The Impact of Co-operative Federalism

The real import of co-operative federalism can best be understood when the full impact of federally-aided programs in a particular state is assessed as a unified whole. In this chapter, the scope of intergovernmental collaboration in the state of Minnesota will be subject to this type of scrutiny.

MINNESOTA: AN OVERVIEW

Federal land-grant programs encompassed almost every field of governmental activity in Minnesota (see Table 15). There were grant programs for education (common-school, university, and agricultural and mechanical college grants), internal improvements (general internal improvements, railroad construction, river and harbor improvements, and public-buildings grants),[1] welfare (salt spring and public-institutions grants), reclamation (swamp and overflowed land grants), and conservation (Itasca State Park grant). In addition, funds from the federal land grants that were not earmarked for specific projects were instrumental in the founding and maintenance of virtually every state institution.

Despite the supposed general absence of cash grants, Minnesota received money for internal improvements (from the Five Per Cent Fund), welfare (for support of the Minnesota Soldiers' Home), defense (militia

[1] The Minnesota territorial legislature was instrumental in securing the construction of approximately one thousand miles of roads by the Army Engineers at federal expense on grounds of national security. These roads were completed after statehood and became co-operative enterprises in the process. When completed, they were transferred to the state for maintenance purposes, though they were ostensibly military roads. They furnished the earliest means of access into the interior of Minnesota. For a history of the program, see W. Turrentine Jackson, *Wagon Roads West* (Berkeley: University of California Press, 1956).

278

funds), and education (the Hatch Act and the second Morrill Act). Goods and materials were granted to the state for programs in science (weights and measures, specimens from United States scientific expeditions), agriculture and conservation (seed distributions, fish stocking), and education and welfare (distribution and exchange of documents for libraries, schools, and public institutions). Co-operative activities involving co-ordination of services included the fields of education (exchange of information), science (meteorological reports, geological surveys), law enforcement (hunting and jailing of federal offenders), conservation

TABLE 15

GRANTS OF LAND, EXCLUDING GRANTS FOR RAILROADS, MADE BY THE
FEDERAL GOVERNMENT TO THE STATE OF MINNESOTA

Grant	Date	Statutory Authorization	Acres
Internal improvement...	September 4, 1841	5 Stat. 453, chap. 16	496,482.29
First university.........	February 19, 1851	9 Stat. 568, chap. 10	45,206.49
Common school.........	February 26, 1857	11 Stat. 166, chap. 60 (secs. 16 and 36)	2,443,753.41
Indemnity school........	February 26, 1857	11 Stat. 166, chap. 60	532,701.23
Public building..........	February 26, 1857	11 Stat. 166, chap. 60	6,397.07
Salt spring lands........	February 26, 1857	11 Stat. 166, chap. 60	46,080.00
Swamp lands*..........	March 12, 1860	12 Stat. 3, chap. 5	4,709,038.18
Agricultural college......	July 2, 1862	12 Stat. 503, chap. 130	119,986.80
Second university.......	July 8, 1870	16 Stat. 196, chap. 227	46,317.60
Total.............			8,445,963.07

* In the Minnesota state auditor's report for 1905–6 (p. 20), reference is made to 5,528,129.62 acres of swamp lands inuring to the state by selections of the U.S. surveyor-general. In the report for 1935–36 (p. 43), 4,777,223.76 acres of swamp lands are shown as patented to the state. This means there were 750,905.86 acres still due the state in that biennium.

(protection of forests), land settlement (homestead and tree-culture programs), and agriculture (co-operation in grasshopper eradication, exchange of experiment-station research reports, exchange of information).

The financial impact of these programs on the state of Minnesota was generally greater than that of the mid-twentieth-century grants-in-aid. In the last third of the nineteenth century, a greater portion of the state's revenues came from federal sources than in any subsequent period. At times, federal sources comprised over 50 per cent of the total state revenues, and after 1865, never fell below 20 per cent. Table 16 gives the gross amounts of federal aid from all sources as compared with total state receipts from 1862 to 1900, with an additional comparison of the analogous, and lower, percentage of federal aid in 1959.

In the nineteenth, as in the twentieth century, federal aid stimulated matching state contributions. In some cases, there were formal matching requirements attached to the federal grants. For example, the first Morrill Act required the states to appropriate funds for construction of buildings for their agricultural colleges. In this way, grants originating on the federal level involved state funds in the development of joint collaborative programs. Table 17 illustrates the degree to which Minnesota's expenditures were used to support formal collaborative programs. Between 1862 and 1900, formal collaborative programs claimed an average of 50 per cent of the state's total expenditures. Table 17 includes only pro-

TABLE 16

FEDERAL FINANCIAL AID TO MINNESOTA IN SELECTED YEARS, 1860–1900 AND 1959*

Fiscal Year	Total Receipts	Direct Federal Payments†	Funds Originating from Federal Grants‡	Total Federal Aid	Per Cent of Federal Aid
1860...........	$ 139,523	$ 24,805	$ 101	$ 24,906	17.9
1863...........	632,954§	207,207	149,058	356,265	56.3
1864...........	488,769§	1,398	174,024	175,422	35.9
1866...........	528,428§	7,096	191,756	198,852	37.6
1875...........	980,604	9,452	363,513	372,965	38.0
1880...........	1,563,026	5,445	598,231	603,676	38.6
1885...........	2,077,664	66,183	801,885	868,068	41.8
1890...........	3,940,064	10,302	863,647	873,949	22.2
1895...........	5,426,936	92,985	1,565,545	1,658,530	30.6
1900...........	6,903,296	66,235	1,754,487	1,820,722	26.4
1959...........	570,769,000	129,075,000	15,289,000‖	144,364,000	25.3

* Sources: Minnesota State Auditor, *Biennial Reports;* and U.S. Bureau of the Census, *State Government Finances in 1959.*

† Federal funds paid directly to the state or its institutions as continuing grants-in-aid, reimbursements, or special grants.

‡ State receipts from federal land grants and the permanent land-grant funds.

§ United States direct tax collections have been subtracted.

‖ Includes income from matching state funds.

grams designated by law as collaborative and the direct expenses of agencies administering specified collaborative programs. Since the terminology of collaboration in the nineteenth century was somewhat veiled, most of these were not labeled collaborative in the records, as similar programs are labeled in the twentieth century. The table does not measure the impact of these collaborative programs, only their cost. It also omits the amounts expended in informal collaborative arrangements and the general expenses of elected officials, such as the governor, who were directly involved ex officio in the administration of co-operative programs to a much greater extent than they are in the present era of "big government."

The impact of federal aid was state-wide and federal funds penetrated into every county. Table 18 shows the scope and distribution of federal funds expended annually either through direct federal grants or through the earnings of a permanent trust fund distributed to the counties by the state. The state's major activities are shown to have been clearly dependent on federal aid. Minnesota's military establishment, important in defending the state's settlers against marauding Indians, relied heavily on federal funds. State and local internal improvements were almost entirely federally supported. The role of the federal government in the development of the railroads has been demonstrated earlier. The major wagon roads were constructed by the Army Engineers even prior to statehood, and the federal Five Per Cent Fund furnished most of the money for

TABLE 17

MINNESOTA STATE EXPENDITURES IN SELECTED YEARS, 1862–1900*

Fiscal Year	Total State Expenditures (All Sources)	Expenditures† in Federally Aided Programs	Investment of Federally Aided Permanent Funds	Total Expenditures Matched by Federal Funds	Per Cent of Total Expenditures
1862‡	$ 221,091	$ 105,259	....	$ 105,259	47.6
1864‡	402,952	94,395	$ 134,335	228,730	56.8
1866	461,265	117,698	109,000	226,698	49.1
1875	1,033,510	351,875	109,872	461,747	44.7
1880	1,420,904	385,437	359,700	745,137	52.4
1885	2,400,314	727,833	502,494	1,230,327	51.3
1890	3,479,874	1,592,786	150,000	1,742,786	50.1
1895	5,791,518	1,950,245	617,079	2,567,324	44.3
1900	6,801,074	2,099,598	1,166,806	3,286,404	48.3

* Source: Minnesota State Auditor, *Biennial Reports.*

† Includes formal co-operative programs, federally aided programs, and state "matching funds" for permanent fund programs established by federal grants.

‡ Includes some Civil War expenditures.

county roads and bridges before the advent of the automobile. Minnesota's school system benefited greatly from the semiannual subsidy distributed from the earnings of the common-school land grant. In addition, the Permanent School Fund was used as a revolving fund to provide capital loans for the construction of elementary- and high-school buildings in every school district and town in the state. The state university's operating costs, including the budgets of the agriculture experiment station and the state geological survey, were almost entirely borne by the earnings of the university land grants and direct federal appropriations. A major proportion of the operating costs of the Minnesota Soldiers' Home also came from direct federal matching grants. Not shown in the table is the intermittent but vital aid given to the state normal schools and public institutions from the various permanent funds and land grants.

TABLE 18

IMMEDIATE USES OF FEDERAL AID IN MINNESOTA IN SELECTED YEARS, 1866–95*

USE AND SOURCE	1866 Amount	1866 Purpose and Distribution	1875 Amount	1875 Purpose and Distribution	1885 Amount	1885 Purpose and Distribution	1895 Amount	1895 Purpose and Distribution
Indian war (federal reimbursement)	$ 9,093	Military expedition						
Indian war relief (federal reimbursement)	1,345	Individual relief						
National Guard (federal reimbursement)	11,880	State fund					$ 5,322	National Guard arms and equipment
Internal improvements (direct federal grant)	89†	Mower Co.	$ 13,733†	21 bridges 4 roads 1 river improvement 1 canal survey in 20 counties	$ 53,819†	45 bridges 5 roads 1 river improvement in 38 counties		
Internal improvement (federally endowed fund)							3,268 4,028	Kandiyohi Co. 9 bridges 2 roads 1 drainage project in 9 counties
Support of common schools (federally endowed fund)	81,472‡	42 counties (50,564 students in school-age population of 87,244)	191,579‡	All counties	350,782‡	All counties	1,075,544‡ 224,906	All counties (276,000 students) Loans to 249 school districts in 72 counties
Support of state university (federally endowed fund from direct federal grants)			30,000§	State university	72,140§	State university	262,962§ 39,750	State university State university
Repayment of railroad bond debt (federally endowed fund)					70,700	Bondholders		
Board of United States convicts (federal reimbursement)			4,384	State prison	1,767	State prison		
Veterans' care (direct federal grant)							34,812	State soldiers' home

* Source: State Auditors' *Reports*. Statistics include only earmarked funds, not full amount of federal aid.

† Entire state contribution to non-railroad internal improvements.

‡ Entire state-distributed support to common schools and high schools.

§ Entire state support for university's general operation.

MINNESOTA IN 1860

In 1860 Minnesota entered its third year of statehood. The transition from territorial status was almost completed, and the Civil War was still over the horizon. The United States census for that year showed that the state had a population of 172,023. Thus, both the time and the manpower were available to enable the state government to turn its attention to claiming and administering the several grants-in-land that had accrued to Minnesota but were, as yet, unexploited.

Accordingly, Governor Alexander Ramsey's concern over land grants was not confined to railroads (see chapter xi) in 1860. In his message of that year to the legislature, he was able to report that four other land-grant programs were also under way. His office had already begun to se-lect lands for common schools, the university, public buildings, and what he termed general use (swamp lands), or at least to discuss the means of their selection and disposition. He reported that the state would receive 2,888,000 acres under the common-school program, 46,070 for the uni-versity-to-be, 6,400 for public buildings, and 5,000,000 for general use, aside from the 4,399,141 for railroad construction. Ramsey had great hopes for this land if it were properly managed. He felt that the grants should raise the level of the educational system of the state above that of any of the others without additional taxation, "complete a broad and liberal system of public charities, asylums, hospitals, and prisons," pay the public debt, encourage public works, erect public buildings, and am-ply endow the proposed university and normal schools.

Ramsey understood both the direct financial and the stimulatory bene-fits of the grants and wanted his state to exploit both fully. This led him to show a great concern over the manner in which the permanent funds, to be created by the sale or lease of the lands, would be managed. In placing the issue before the legislature, he talked in terms of the Con-gressional requirement that the money received from land sales or leas-ing be placed in permanent funds and that only the interest be used for the support of the designated programs. He emphasized the federal re-quirements to bolster his own position against squandering the money to meet immediate needs.

The Governor was aware of the experiences of other states, where lands that had been granted for the same purposes had been sold at too low a price for the benefit of influential local citizens, or where the proceeds of land sales had been poorly invested and subsequently lost. Since it was relatively easy to violate the spirit of the grants without violating the legally binding terms of the acts of Congress, he was concerned about preventing this in Minnesota. He particularly called to mind the experience of Iowa, Minnesota's southern neighbor, where the various land grants had been turned over by the state to the counties and townships, under the auspices of which untrained local officials had lost a princely inheritance. His subsequent success in preventing Minnesota from following the same path not only places him high on the list of founders of the state's large permanent fund system, but gives him at least a small place among the builders of American federalism.[2]

Over the next forty years, the exploration, appraisal, surveying, patenting, advertising, selling, leasing, and investment of the proceeds of these grants-in-land occupied a major share of the interest and energy of the state government with consequent state-wide benefits, as illustrated in Table 19. The administrative processes involved in the selection of these lands also cost money. Between 1862 and 1900, the state spent a total of $463,476 for land selection and management.[3]

While selection procedures were clearly prescribed in detail for the other grants, the act of Congress authorizing the swamp land grant had left the administrative details to the discretion of the Department of the Interior. In correspondence beginning in May, 1860, between the commissioner of the General Land Office and Governor Ramsey, the Interior Department offered the Governor a choice between two alternate modes of selection.[4] The state could either undertake its own survey of the public domain within its boundaries and lay claim to every section of land it considered as falling within the federal definition of swamp and overflowed land or accept the field notes of the federal surveys. In the first case, the state would not only incur the expenses of the survey but would

[2] *Ibid.*, pp. 10–39. The Governor's message of that year was twenty-nine pages long, of which fifteen were devoted to land-grant matters.

[3] Minnesota State Auditor, *Biennial Report 1899–1900*, p. 128.

[4] This correspondence had begun in a letter of May 21, 1860, when the commissioner had written to the Governor, sending him a copy of the act of Congress that had granted the lands and had assigned to the secretary of the interior the duties of making an accurate plat and list of the lands, transmitting the plat and list to the governor, and, at the latter's request, issuing patents for the lands. In that letter, the commissioner posed the two alternative methods of selection, suggesting that the state accept the federal field notes so that it would receive the lands at no cost to itself. This was a form letter sent to both Minnesota and Arkansas, since the grant had been extended to both in the same act of Congress.

TABLE 19

PROCEEDS OF FEDERAL GRANTS-IN-LAND FOR
STATE PERMANENT FUNDS, 1862–1900,
IN MINNESOTA

Program	Number of Acres	Money Earned	Average Price per Acre	Total
School lands				
Sold......................	1,561,340	$9,417,721	$6.03	
Forfeiture of rights of way...		169,908		
Timber sales..............		2,178,673		
Mineral leases.............		124,130		
Iron ore royalties..........		294,527		
Bond sale profits...........		361,570		
				$12,546,529
Agricultural college lands				
Sold......................	94,399	$ 559,158		
Forfeiture.................		10,408		
Right of way..............		770		
				$ 570,336
University lands				
Sold......................	34,906	$ 201,347		
Forfeiture.................		3,109		
Right of way..............		183		
Timber sales..............		465,125		
Mineral leases.............		26,325		
Miscellaneous.............		102,443		
				$ 703,532*
Internal improvement lands				
Sold......................	471,521	$2,638,951	$5.59	
Forfeiture.................		20,077		
Timber sales..............		108,521		
Right of way..............		862		
Mineral leases.............		625		
Transfers.................		2,119,225		
				$ 2,769,037*
State institutional lands				
Sold......................	10,352	$ 59,859	$5.78	
Forfeiture.................		46		
Right of way..............		466		
Timber sales..............		58,091		
Mineral leases.............		22,075		
				$ 140,538
Total..				$16,729,972
Total state receipts, 1862–1900................................				$96,294,057
State receipts minus income from land†........................				$79,564,085

* Minus deductions.
† Land income does not include earnings of the invested permanent funds.

also have to justify any selections challenged by the General Land Office. Under the second alternative, the state ran the risk of losing some lands because of a less liberal definition of swamps and overflowing on the part of the federal surveyors.

Letters covering the technical aspects involved in the administration of the new program continued to pass between the commissioner and the Governor during the summer of 1860. The federal law specified that the selections had to be made during the two-year period after the passage of the act or within two years after the survey of townships that had not yet been surveyed, commencing from the date of adjournment of the next session of the legislature (to give that body time to accept the grant). The dates of that session, if fixed by law, had to be forwarded to the commissioner, so that he might establish proper enforcement procedures under the time limit. The Governor, on the other hand, wanted to know who was responsible for the decision on the mode of selection, he or the legislature. The commissioner informed him that under the regulations of his office, the action of the executive was sufficient. If the state abided by the federal field notes, Governor Ramsey wanted to know whether the federal government also would. That is, if lands designated as swamp lands by the federal surveyors later turned out not to be, and patents to the state had already been issued, would the state be able to keep them? The commissioner replied that "the federal government reserves to itself the right to supervise the selections, and hold them subject to its control, until they shall have been approved and patented to the state," after which they would not be revocable under ordinary circumstances.

In order to make a decision in accord with the best interests of the state, the Governor took the matter before the state legislature in a special message on swamp lands. He had previously requested the United States surveyor-general for Minnesota to furnish him with the amount and location of swamp lands in the part of the state already surveyed (according to the federal field notes) for use as a standard of comparison.

In the end, the state decided to accept the federal field notes and save the additional expense. The swamp land program netted Minnesota just under the five million acres anticipated by Governor Ramsey.[5] These lands were subsequently granted by the state to numerous railroad and

[5] Minnesota, *Executive Documents*, 1860, Special Message to the Legislature and Attached Documents, January 26, 1861.

wagon-road corporations, to a local industrial development project, and
to the majority of the state's health and welfare institutions, thus extending the impact of the federal grant into every corner of the state's public
economy.

MINNESOTA IN 1876

By 1876, Minnesota had become a state with a stable governmental base
upon which to anchor a growing economy. The state census of 1875 (designed to supplement the decennial federal census in the rapidly grow-

TABLE 20

RECEIPTS IN MINNESOTA FROM FEDERAL SOURCES IN 1876*

Source	Amount
Boarding of U.S. convicts............................	$ 1,931.17
School land sales....................................	51,823.69
Agricultural college land sales.....................	4,874.66
Internal improvement land sales....................	511.88
Sale of pine timber on school lands................	21,439.51
Sale of pine timber on university lands.............	8,185.74
Sale of pine timber on Internal improvement lands...	19,815.34
Interest from the Permanent School Fund..........	203,294.02
Interest from the Permanent University Fund.......	19,815.34
Interest from the Internal Improvement Land Fund..	3,035.08
U.S. Internal Improvement (Five Per Cent) Fund....	3,940.82
Total.....................................	$338,668.25

  * All of these funds were earmarked for specific purposes by the terms of the original federal
grants.

ing state) showed a population of 597,407. Railroads were advancing and
settlers were following them out of the woods and onto the prairies. New
activities in the economic and social realm brought about added responsibilities for government and new needs for intergovernmental collaboration. In 1876, total receipts of the state government came to $1,021,404.50,
of which $338,668.25 (approximately one-third of the total) were re-
ceipts from federal sources. The diversity of these sources is indicative of
the widespread character of co-operative federalism in the period. (See
Table 20.)

Fifteen prisoners of the United States were being held in the state
prison in 1876 under a co-operative arrangement. These included military
prisoners as well as civilians. When the federal penitentiary at Fort
Leavenworth, Kansas, was completed shortly thereafter, the military pris-

oners were no longer housed in the state penitentiaries,[6] except in the process of apprehension and in transit to Leavenworth.

Control of the state lands and the federal land-grant administrative procedures was vested in an ex officio State Land Board, headed by the governor and composed of the elected executive officers of the state.[7] The state auditor, as secretary of the board, submitted an annual report giving records of all the land granted and transferred to the railroads, the expenses of the state land office, and the land sales and income from the other grants.[8]

In Minnesota, the state superintendent of public instruction was also involved in the land-grant program through the school land grants and as an ex officio member of the State Land Board. Though the federal grant of two sections per township was no longer made with reference to particular townships, but was channeled directly to the state, the program was designed so that each locality would receive the benefits of the lands allotted within its boundaries to as great an extent as possible. The superintendent was responsible for the selection of lands of high quality in order to provide the best endowment for the Permanent School Fund, and was also in charge of the semiannual distribution of the earnings from the lands for the support of the local schools. In 1876, 12,989 acres of school lands were sold for an average price of $5.71 per acre.

Aside from the intergovernmental relations involved in administering the land-grant programs, the proceeds of the Five Per Cent Fund also had to be transmitted to the state. A draft for $3,940.82, the distribution for fiscal 1876, was sent to the governor from the first comptroller of the treasury on the order of the commissioner of the General Land Office. The governor received all such drafts as chief executive of the state and transmitted them to the state treasurer for deposit.[9] The money received was subsequently appropriated by the state legislature to the counties for construction of local bridges and roads.

In addition to the formal federal financial grants were the various grants of goods and services, which do not appear in the state's fiscal balance sheets but which contributed heavily to the wide range of intergov-

[6] *Ibid.*, 1876, "Report of the Warden of the State Prison," pp. 222–24; Also Minnesota Governors' Archives, file 355, General Terry, U.S.A., to Governor.

[7] The importance of the State Land Board is perhaps best revealed by its composition, which was identical with that of the State Executive Council.

[8] Minnesota, *Executive Documents*, 1876, pp. 315–36.

[9] Minnesota Governors' Archives, file 378.

ernmental activities. Like New Hampshire, Minnesota was entitled to a complete set of weights and measures. In 1876, a set of metric standards was delivered to the state by the Bureau of Weights and Measures under the terms of the Joint Congressional Resolution of July 27, 1866, which directed the secretary of the treasury to furnish each state with a set to fulfill the requirements of the recent act legalizing the metric system in the United States.[10]

The militia program and its peripheral activities produced their normal quota of intergovernmental relations in 1876. The problem of Civil War bounty reimbursement was of particular importance. Minnesota, like the other states, had assumed the burden of paying out bounties for enlistments in its United States volunteer regiments, subject to postwar federal repayment. The repayment program covered almost three decades after the war in the pattern of earlier collaborative bounty programs.

In 1876, the federal program of exchanging documents was broadened into the document depository system that has became a standard feature in twentieth-century university and library circles.[11] The program, as outlined in 1876 by the secretary of the interior, was considerably broader than in later years. Copies of all Congressional documents were to be sent to each state (or territory), one to the executive department and one to the legislative branch; to each university or college in the state; and to the state historical society. In his form letter to the governor, the secretary requested that his department be furnished with a complete list of all colleges and universities in the state, so that the documents could be sent to them directly.[12]

Co-operation on banking reports was as standard in Minnesota as in New Hampshire. On October 28, 1877, the comptroller of the currency of the United States Treasury Department made his annual request for "the last official report containing a statement of the condition of the banks organized under the laws of your state" from the governor, so that it might be published in the comptroller's annual report to Congress.[13] Evidently, there was some slipshod handling of the 1876 report on the part of the state, because on January 30, 1877, the comptroller again wrote to the governor to tell him that while the state auditor had transmitted the returns of only ten banks, sixty-five banks and private bankers had re-

[10] Ibid.; and Minnesota, *Executive Documents*, 1876, p. 154.

[11] Minnesota Governors' Archives, file 377b.

[12] Ibid., file 377d.   [13] Ibid.

ported to the commissioner of internal revenue. In order to facilitate the state's reporting, the comptroller sent the governor a copy of a model act "providing for obtaining and publishing reports of banks organized under the state laws," which his office had prepared. If such legislation were needed in Minnesota, the governor was asked to transmit the act to "some influential members of your State legislature" to secure its passage.[14]

Indian affairs also came into the scope of intergovernmental relations in 1876. That year, settlers in western Minnesota, along with the rest of the northwestern frontier community, were terrified by the Sioux uprising on the Great Plains that had culminated in the Custer disaster on the Little Big Horn. While, at first glance, the distance between the scene of combat and the Minnesota border seems great enough, sufficient numbers of Minnesotans remembered their own experiences in the great Minnesota Valley Sioux Uprising of 1862 to be alarmed at the mere suggestion of an Indian menace on an unprotected frontier. They appealed in large numbers to their governor to seek federal protection. Governor Pillsbury understood better the ephemeral relationship of the Sioux War to the Minnesota frontier and did not press the United States for troops that were being put to better use in the Dakota Territory, Montana, and Wyoming. But when the Chippewa Indians living in the northern part of the state began to leave their reservations, he took prompt action to avert potential conflict on Minnesota's own frontier. A three-cornered correspondence ensued between the Governor, the United States commissioner of Indian affairs, and the United States Indian agent at the Leech Lake Reservation until it was established that the Indians were not on the warpath but were seeking game for food; in a situation already too familiar, the federal government had neglected to live up to its treaties with the Indians to provide those necessities.[15]

In 1876, the grasshopper plague that had infected the plains states for several years was at its peak. In Minnesota, as in the other states of the northern plains, counties memorialized Congress, the state legislatures, and their governors in an effort to secure federal financial aid. Governors consulted among each other to the same end, but to no immediate avail. It was a sign of the times, though, that before the plague had ended, the United States Department of Agriculture was able to render the vital services necessary to curb it, even though no direct federal relief appropriations were forthcoming.

[14] *Ibid.*, file 378.   [15] *Ibid.*, file 377d.

A minor flurry of intergovernmental activity, unique in 1876, fittingly capped the nationwide effort to celebrate properly the first century of American independence. The centennial year brought forth an exhibition in Philadelphia in which the federal government and the states co-operated to illustrate the progress of the nation during the preceding one hundred years. A national centennial commission, which included representatives of the several states, was established and financed by Congress. The commission organized and arranged nationwide observances, including the governmental share of the Philadelphia exhibition, and advised the states and localities on ways to observe the occasion.[16] As the United States developed over its first century of existence, so did the activities of its governments, ranging from the absolutely vital construction of railroads to the joining-together to observe one hundred years of prosperous independence. In this sense, it was entirely fitting that the latter should also have been a co-operative effort.

THE GROWTH OF CO-OPERATION IN MINNESOTA

Intergovernmental collaboration in Minnesota antedated statehood; yet after 1858, it did not diminish in either extent or intensity. On the contrary, collaboration between governments expanded with the expansion of governmental activities in general as the state matured. While the number and variety of governmental activities and co-operative contacts in 1876 were still less than in 1916 or 1933 or 1960, both were considerably more extensive than in 1860. In short, as the role of government expanded, so did the process of sharing between governments. The proportions remained relatively the same.

The types of co-operative activities and the means of their administration in Minnesota are familiar. Little was found that was new or unique in its broad outlines. All the land-grant programs, except those designed to aid in the reclamation of arid lands, were found to be in operation in familiar patterns. Direct federal aids to individuals and groups were subject to state influences much as previously described elsewhere. Co-operative exchanges of goods and services in Minnesota were recognizable as parts of the national pattern. So were the paraphernalia of administration—an ex officio State Land Board and its agents, the General Land Office and its local land officers, local school and county officials, all played

16 *Ibid.*

their routine and routinized roles in the sharing process. Indeed, it seems that very few federal and state offices in Minnesota were exempt from intergovernmental co-operative procedures. This, too, is as familiar as were their activities.

If the scope of co-operative programs and the administration of sharing were no different from the standard nationwide pattern, it should be reasonable to project the Minnesota pattern of fiscal sharing onto other states as well. This does not mean that all states benefited equally from federal financial support. As in the twentieth-century grant-in-aid programs, federal aid provided a proportionately larger share of the budgets of the smaller states, the newer states, and the poorer states. Minnesota, with its land frontier still not fully conquered, probably received a greater share of its budget from federal sources than did New Hampshire or Virginia. (The differences between states may have been less pronounced than in the twentieth century, however, because of state reluctance to finance local programs with tax money obtained locally.) In turn, Colorado apparently received more federal funds than Minnesota. The proportionate role of federal funds in the Minnesota budget has remained relatively constant, although the federal government actually provided proportionately less in 1959 than in the decades under consideration above.

The politics of sharing in Minnesota during this period are also familiar. The role of the governor was central, not only because of his duties as chief executive of the state but through his role as the political head of state. There is considerable evidence in this and previous chapters that the governor's influence waxed and waned in relation to his political position. In general, the governor served as the major political broker in the state's relations with the federal government.

The central fact that emerges from an analysis of the development of sharing in a single state over several decades is the sheer weight of political time devoted to intergovernmental co-operation. Not only were the administrators heavily involved in co-operative activities, but the programs that were most highly developed as shared programs also pre-empted the bulk of the policy-makers' time. Minnesota governors and legislatures together were preoccupied with the co-operative programs throughout this entire period. The already enumerated programs should indicate why this was so, since no aspect of internal improvements, education, or general disposition of the public domain in the state escaped involvement in the sharing process. Furthermore, even defense against the Indians and the recruitment of an army for the defense of the Union became shared functions. By the end of the second decade of statehood, the regulatory functions of government were also being shared, partly because the fields of regulation were tied to already co-operative programs (as in the case of railroad regulation) and partly because it was just more convenient to co-operate (as in the case of regulating state and national banking institutions). A survey of the governors' messages, the legislative journals, the statute books, and the attorney-generals' opinions reveals the extent of this concern with programs that were co-operative in character. This concern on the part of the policy-makers was not over the processes of collaboration but over other aspects of the program. Indeed, collaboration itself seems to have been taken for granted. Federal-state co-operation was a fact of life, hence the policy-makers rarely referred to it directly in their deliberations. The system of sharing is all the more impressive because of its implicit acceptance as part of the process of government.

Part III

Co-operative Federalism in the Context of American History

18

The Scope of Co-operation

Through a series of overlapping case studies, Parts I and II of this volume have developed the general thesis that the American federal system has been fundamentally a co-operative partnership of federal, state, and local governments since the early days of the Republic. Within a dualistic structural pattern, the governments of the United States have developed a broadly institutionalized system of collaboration, based on the implicit premise that virtually all functions of government must be shared by virtually all governments in order to fulfill the demands of American democracy for both public service and private access. More specifically, the evidence presented in the preceding pages indicates that the relative balance between the federal government and the states has not significantly shifted over the past one hundred seventy-five years. The two levels of government have played the same respective roles in the system from the first, and these roles have not been significantly altered, despite the great changes that have taken place within the United States and in the world. Consequently, the pattern of American federalism in practice, in so far as it differs from the classic theory of American federalism, has certain fundamental implications in the context of American history and in the context of democratic theory.

PROGRAMS AND POLICIES: A REVIEW

From the first days of American independence, the controversy as to the scope of national vis-à-vis state powers has been part and parcel of the American political scene. While the controversy has continued to rage unabated, the American people have by and large endeavored to use both federal and state governments as means to achieve specific ends, rather than as ends in themselves. When problems arose, solutions were sought that would harmonize with the reality of the times, involving government whenever and wherever necessary, generally at every level. Out of these attempts to solve actual problems, there evolved a series of co-operative relationships between all levels of government.

As the new nation began to expand under the Constitution, expansion came to center primarily around movement westward, the conquest of the continent. Out of this expansion arose a number of major problems that required governmental consideration. Among them, three major categories stand out: internal improvements, education, and disposition of the public domain. A fourth major category centering around the slavery issue reached national prominence and forced the ultimate conflict as a result of problems arising from territorial expansion westward and the attempt to spread slavery to the land frontier. It should be noted that each of these major categories has its counterpart in the twentieth century, which has required governmental action just as its forerunner did.

The term "internal improvement" covered a multitude of specific problems, all basically concerned with facilitating the geographic and material expansion of the American people, while at the same time binding the various sections of the country more closely together as one political and economic system. Roads, canals, railroads, harbors, public buildings and institutions, river improvements, land reclamation, mineral production and extraction, agricultural development, and the creation of a banking system to finance all these projects, constituted the internal improvement programs of the day. All demanded a share of the interest, energy, and money, both public and private, of the expanding nation. Internal improvements provided a major portion of the intergovernmental programs that emerged during the century, simply because they provided a major portion of all governmental activity.

While much attention was directed toward material progress, no less was given to the development of a responsible and capable citizenry, particularly in the newly settled areas of the Midwest and Far West. The dominant educational problems were to provide a basic foundation for productive citizenship through the common schools and to advance intellectual, agricultural, and mechanical training of young men and women in colleges and universities. As the frontier advanced, so did the desire for education. Population groups demanded government programs to fill needs that the struggling pioneers could not meet alone. Once again, the use of co-operative government programs provided the vehicle whereby such aid could be rendered within the framework of the federal system.

Since our nation is dedicated to the task of providing opportunity for each individual to engage in the pursuit of happiness in a manner as nearly approaching his own definition of that goal as socially possible, the disposition of the major national resource, the public domain, in a manner consistent with that high purpose continued to be a leading problem. As the nation evolved a policy for the solution of the problem, the tension between public and private interests brought forth increasingly greater efforts on the part of all levels of government. From these efforts emerged the federal land grants to the various states for a multitude of purposes, ranging from veterans' benefits to railroad construction; the direct federal land grants for transportation and development companies; and finally, the land grants to individual settlers under the various homestead and pre-emption acts. Even before the adoption of the Constitution, it was determined that the disposition of the public domain would provide the means whereby the other problems were to be attacked, with land serving in place of cash as the substance of federal grants-in-aid.

Several basic patterns for the actual implementation of co-operative federalism developed in the nineteenth century. Informal relationships developed, primarily in the field, where officials of the federal government, the states, and the localities exchanged information or co-operated to solve specific problems. Examples of this informal co-operation cover the range of governmental activities. In relations with the Indians, the federal government theoretically held exclusive jurisdiction. Actually, federal authorities in any specific situation consulted with officials of the state and locality concerned and often relied upon their co-operation to implement a policy or subdue hostiles.[1] The co-operative relations between the second Bank of the United States and the various states in the development of a national monetary system were semiformal, based on national needs. Co-operation between the United States Army Corps of Engineers and state and local authorities in the construction and maintenance of river and harbor improvements made that program a shared

[1] For a few of the many examples of this, see records in the Thomas Gilcrease Institute of American History and Art, Tulsa, Oklahoma; the Indian Archives in the Oklahoma Historical Society Library, Oklahoma City, Oklahoma (these archives are themselves a grant from the federal government to the state of Oklahoma); the National Archives, Washington, D.C.; and "Miscellaneous Papers and Documents Relating to the Ute Uprising, 8/16/1887–5/28/1889" (microfilm) in the Colorado State Archives, Denver, Colorado.

one *de facto* long before such sharing was officially recognized in law. The localities contributed financial, material, and technical aid amounting to at least one-fifth of the cost of any Corps of Engineers project.[2] Problems of law enforcement also led to a number of informal co-operative relationships, both in routine law enforcement matters in which local police and United States marshals worked together and in more specialized fields such as control of smuggling and immigration.[3] Wherever the military was stationed, a series of informal co-operative relationships grew up, which covered a number of governmental functions; some were temporary reactions to emergency situations, and others ongoing relationships that continued for many years.

Other co-operative relationships that were never formalized grew up around federal programs designed to dispose of the public domain, which officially made no reference to the states and localities. These included the various homestead and reclamation programs, such as the homestead and pre-emption acts, the tree-culture acts, the town-site selection acts, and some parts of the desert lands and reclamation acts. As a general rule, whenever a federal program affected the citizens of a state, the state governments concerned became unofficial parties to, and even agents in, its administration.

For various reasons that were dealt with in previous chapters, a number of internal improvement programs were initiated through the federal government only. Certain western roads and railroads were constructed by the federal government or with direct federal aid generally because the regions they traversed were predominantly in the territorial stage of government. Little time elapsed before even these programs were incorporated into the co-operative system, originally with territorial and local authorities and ultimately with the state governments once they had been

[2] This figure is based on calculations made for specific projects selected at random from materials in the U.S. Army Corps of Engineers records, National Archives.

[3] William E. Burke, *Federal Finances* (Chicago: F. J. Schultze and Co., 1891). The enforcement of the federal fugitive slave laws provides an excellent example of both the operation and breakdown of intergovernmental co-operation in law enforcement. The laws not only took such co-operation between federal and state law enforcement officials for granted, but were based on such co-operation to attain any real effectiveness. When antislavery sentiment in the North forced the state and local lawmen to desist from aiding in the apprehension and return of fugitive slaves, the entire program broke down. For a view of the constitutional impact of this problem, see Carl Brent Swisher, *American Constitutional Development* (Boston: Houghton Mifflin, 1943), pp. 236-38.

formed.[4] Collaboration in these programs was almost always quasi-formal even from the outset, since any portion of the road or railroad that was to be built within an existing state forced the builders to obtain the approval of the state legislature, as required by the terms of the Congressional grant, and the legislature would often demand tailoring of the planned improvement to meet the needs of the state. In almost every case, co-operation had to evolve because every program involved some issues of interest to each level of government. The choices that confronted the political leaders were such that the alternatives to co-operation would have produced at best unmanageable chaos and at worst disunion.

Another by no means separate form of intergovernmental co-operation involved formally co-ordinated relationships. Programs in this category did not involve the exchange of money, land, or personnel, but instead action was co-ordinated pursuant to statutory provisions enacted by Congress and the participating state legislatures. Under such programs, the federal government and each participating state undertook to implement parts of a jointly produced nationwide or state-federal plan without sharing the costs for individual projects. This is the type of co-operation which the United States Constitution provides for the administration of national elections.

The master plan for an internal transportation and communications system designed by the United States Army Corps of Engineers in co-operation with the boards of public works in the various states in the early nineteenth century was of this nature. The public works that emerged from that joint endeavor still form part of the pattern of the twentieth-century American highway and railroad system. The sequence of national banking programs, which were designed to establish a national banking system with a stable nationwide currency, frequently provided other examples of this form of intergovernmental co-operation.

Many times, a co-operative program would be initiated as a co-ordinated activity only to be expanded as a formal federal-aid program at a later date. The inland waterways system designed by Albert Gallatin and others in Jefferson's administration fits into this category. The history of the Dismal Swamp Canal is illustrative of the tenuous line that often existed between co-ordinated and formal federal-aid programs. Intergov-

[4] See W. Turrentine Jackson, *Wagon Roads West* (Berkeley: University of California Press, 1956), for a discussion of the integration of wagon roads constructed by the federal government into the co-operative system.

ernmental co-operation in the field of education was exceptional in that it moved in the other direction, beginning as a federal-aid program in most states and later becoming almost entirely transformed into a co-ordinated activity until the mid-twentieth century.

Midway in scope between co-ordinated and formal grant-in-aid programs were some quasi-grant programs, which developed particularly in cases in which the federal government had to reimburse various states for money spent on its behalf for "national defense." While the reimbursement could not be earmarked for specific purposes under federal law, it was almost universally used by the state leadership as an opportune way to establish or supplement funds for the promotion of education. This general use of reimbursement funds for educational purposes was instrumental in obtaining Congressional and executive approval for many reimbursements that would otherwise not have been granted. The administration entailed in the transfer of funds for such reimbursements was of necessity co-operative. Other illustrative quasi-grant programs included the exchange of documents and scientific specimens, which were not grants so much as they were attempts to facilitate academic, legal, and cultural interchanges within the Union.

The most significant formal co-operative programs were generally those which involved federal grants of land, money, and services to the states. These programs can be divided into two categories: those that included both financial aid and the contacts with federal personnel necessary to implement the federal aspects of the program (grants-in-aid), and those that made only personnel available (services-in-aid). This study has concentrated on these programs as examples of the most rigorous and institutionalized form of federal-state co-operation.

Grants-in-aid in the nineteenth century took the form of land grants, grants of materials, cash grants based upon land sales, and direct cash grants, with land grants the most prevalent. Land grants were made to the states for education (common schools, colleges, and special educational institutions), internal improvements (roads, canals, river and harbor improvements, railroads), public purposes (public buildings, salt springs), reclamation (desert lands, swamp lands), veterans (bounty lands), and welfare (public institutions). Cash grants based on land sales were made for internal improvements and conservation. Direct cash grants were made for defense (the militia grants),[5] internal improve-

---

[5] Federal grants to arm and equip the state militias were initiated in 1808 as the first federal cash grants-in-aid to the states on record. An obvious example of co-opera-

ments (transportation and banking), veterans (soldiers' homes), education (land-grant-college supplementary aid), and agriculture (agricultural experiment stations). Materials grants included construction materials on public lands, plants, seeds, fish, publications, scientific specimens, and weights and measures. Services-in-aid included the sending of federal personnel to co-operate with state officials (road and canal construction, waterway improvements, agriculture); the sending of federal officials to prepare the groundwork for state programs (road, canal, and railroad surveying); and the lending of federal experts to the states for specific projects (road, railroad, and canal construction).

All these forms of intergovernmental co-operation involved considerable administrative interaction between federal, state, and local officials. This interaction was carried on through established departments and bureaus on the federal level and, usually, through boards and commissions generally comprised of ex officio elected officials on the state and local levels. The forms of this administrative interaction were quite fluid, since the entire system of co-operative relationships had to be developed through trial and error for each program.

While day-to-day operations rested largely with the various administrative bodies in the executive branches of several levels of government, the members of the legislative assemblies—and particularly the representatives of the states and localities in Congress—were alert and active in overseeing the numerous programs. The role of these politicians was an interstitial one. In a real sense, they provided the cement that held the bricks together and enabled the programs to function with a maximum of local control. Although this study could not deal with their activities in proper depth, in every program that involved federal action, they were continuously present and involved, always prepared to question an administrator's action, enlarge or decrease an appropriation, and contact the appropriate bureau on behalf of a public or private constituent. All this was in addition to the fundamental authority of Congress to establish the programs in the first place.

In addition to the formal administrative arrangements and the traditional role of the legislature, a spirit of professionalism arose among the officials implementing a particular program. Although it varied in inten-

---

tive federalism, the case of the militia has not been dealt with at any length in this volume dedicated to the "hard case." Information on intergovernmental co-operation in maintaining the militia in the nineteenth century is available in William H. Riker, *Soldiers of the States* (Washington, D.C.: Public Affairs Press, 1957).

sity from program to program, where the spirit of professionalism was strong, it was strong at all levels of government. This spirit led to the development of a professional interest in the implementation and expansion of each program, which meant that the professionals involved in it would strive to increase the amount of federal-state co-operation as an effective vehicle for the expansion of their own functions. Often, when political pressures formally lessened the amount of intergovernmental action in a given program, the professionals involved would find ways to continue the program in a manner closely approximating its previous level. There were times when existing programs were expanded and even new programs initiated by devoted professionals after Congress had hesitated to grant formal authorization. Often the federal professionals were abetted in this by the cabinet secretary under whom they served.

It might be said that the evolution of a co-operative system was the result of a considerable effort on the part of a number of men who, along with the founding fathers, may justly be termed the architects of the American federal system. These men could be found at all three levels of government (they usually served at more than one level during their public careers) and in all three branches of government. Some of them were prominent figures as well in their day, others were hardly known outside of their immediate circles. A few have been named in the preceding pages. All were indispensable in the evolution of the American partnership.

CO-OPERATIVE FEDERALISM: THE
ALTERNATE HYPOTHESIS

On the basis of the evidence presented in the previous chapters, and summarized in this one, it would seem necessary to develop a different theory to explain the nature of the American federal system and its character over time. Any new theory must take into account the continuous existence of an amount of intergovernmental collaboration equal to, and in fact greater than, the amount of separation (as traditionally defined) in the federal system. More precisely, the amount of intergovernmental collaboration in the nineteenth century in relation to the total amount of governmental activity in American life (what may be termed the velocity of government) was no less than, nor substantially different from, the amount of intergovernmental collaboration that exists in the mid-twentieth century in relation to the total velocity of government. Co-operative —not dual—federalism has been the mode since the establishment of the Republic, in the nineteenth century as well as in the twentieth.

Co-operative, or collaborative, federalism can be defined as the sharing of responsibilities for given functions by the federal and state governments. In this sense, it is conceived to be the opposite of dual federalism, which implies a division of functions between governments as well as a division of governmental structures. Although the theory of co-operative federalism assumes a division of structures, it accepts a system of sharing that ranges from formal federal-state agreements covering specific programs to informal contacts on a regular basis for the sake of sharing information and experience.

Even during the nineteenth century, when the ethos of the times called forth a theory of dualism that was based on a functional demarcation between governments, the actual exigencies of the operation of the federal system demanded co-operation. Consequently, federal-state co-operation was developed in a wide variety of cases. Though it was usually opposed on the theoretical level, it persevered in practice in many forms and under different guises. Its procedures were refined through trial and error and, often subtly, through the arrangements of dedicated public servants at a time when formally accepted doctrines were occasionally applied to prevent its open recognition. Officially recognized or not, a system of intergovernmental co-operation was evolved to serve the dual purpose of maintaining the federal balance while providing needed governmental services. Where co-operation did not develop but should have, both the system and the programs in question suffered.

In a sense, a substantial share of the history of American government has been the search for methods to provide for the necessary collaboration of the various units of the federal system while at the same time preserving and strengthening those units as separate bases for such collaboration. It has been shown that much of what historians have mistaken for the rejection of intergovernmental co-operation in the nineteenth century was, in reality, the rejection of certain methods of interaction as failing to meet one or both of the above criteria.[6]

[6] One final example, appropriate here since it is often cited to illustrate American rejection of federal participation in the construction of internal improvements, is Andrew Jackson's veto of the Maysville Road Bill on May 27, 1830. The Bill, in common with other measures passed during the period, authorized federal subscription of stock to the amount of $150,000 in the Maysville, Washington, Paris, and Lexington Turnpike Road Company, a joint-stock company for the construction of a road sixty

The federal government and the states together comprise the basic units of government in the United States. These units of government receive their power from the people primarily through the national Constitution, which defines and guarantees the existence of both the federal and state governments. The state governments are further defined by their own constitutions.

The federal Constitution grants certain specific powers exclusively to the people acting through the federal government and reserves other specific powers to the people acting through the states. However, the bulk of the powers of government are not allotted exclusively to either government. Constitutionally, then, the federal and state governments share authority and responsibility in a large area, an area of concurrent powers, while relatively small areas are exclusively allotted to each.

In handling specific programs, within this large area of concurrent powers, the federal and state governments can either divide the responsibility among their separate jurisdictions, with each responsible only for its own share of the divided responsibility ("dual federalism"), or divide the work of government co-operatively and share responsibility in each program, with all units directed toward common goals that extend along the entire chain of concurrent powers ("co-operative federalism") and generally overflow into the ostensibly "exclusive" preserves. Though precedent favors the latter approach, the decision must be made anew through the political process in each case.

The actual division of responsibility under the concurrent powers is

---

miles long entirely within the state of Kentucky. In his veto message, Jackson explicitly declared that since the road lay within the boundaries of a single state and had no connection with any established system of improvements of interstate importance, it was not eligible for federal aid. Jackson's view was that federal aid should be confined to projects of a general nature, unless the Constitution was otherwise amended. He approved a measure authorizing work on the National (Cumberland) Road four days later because it was a project of national interest and the keystone of a large system of interstate internal improvements. Although he continued to veto other such bills authorizing appropriations for local purposes, he did not significantly interfere with river and harbor improvements. He even developed a plan (never adopted) for federal aid for local improvements through the distribution of the federal surplus revenues to the states for use by them at their discretion. (Jackson's apparently negative stand on the internal improvement issue is closely connected with the struggle for power within his administration family between Van Buren and Calhoun.) See Charles W. Wiltse, *John C. Calhoun: Nullifier* (Indianapolis: Bobbs-Merrill Co., 1949), pp. 39–43. For a brief account of Jackson's position on internal improvements, see Richard B. Morris (ed.), *Encyclopedia of American History* (New York: Harper & Bros., 1953), p. 169.

primarily determined by the political process rather than through legal decisions. That is, the decisions as to the distribution of the areas of concurrent powers are made either on the political level or by constitutional interpretations based on political realities. Such decisions are recognized in constitutional law either after a political decision has been made or as a result of a constitutional interpretation that, sooner or later, must follow the polls.

In understanding our federal system, there is a basic conflict between simple rationalities and the logic of political experience. Simple rationalities demand that a federal system present a dual structure with a clear-cut division of powers that can easily be measured, whereas political experience, dealing with reality, demands a concurrent and co-operative approach to problem-solving. In the past, many Americans have been attracted to the simplistic approach in their verbal images, while, in actuality, they have not hesitated to ignore those same images when and where it seemed necessary to do so. That this has been true throughout American history is attested to by the development of co-operation as the dominant mode of the American partnership.

19

The Development of Co-operation

THE FOUNDING FATHERS AND THE CONSTITUTION

Just as the founding fathers did not perceive the future role of political parties in the United States, they also appear not to have planned for the development of co-operative federalism as we know it. The "intentions of the framers" of the Constitution are always difficult to uncover with any degree of certainty. The language of the Constitution is neither co-operative nor dualistic per se. The document does make explicit provision for some intergovernmental co-operation in several important fields as varied as national defense, conduct of elections, and standards of measurement. Other sections of the Constitution clearly provide for concurrent activities by the federal and state governments, which the framers may or may not have intended to become co-operative ones (see Table 21). Most sections, however, do not clearly indicate whether the powers of the two levels of government are to be exclusive or concurrent, leaving the matter open to interpretation. It is the extent and meaning of the concurrent powers that have been at the center of most controversies over the "intentions of the framers."[1] Despite this uncertainty, it seems clear that at least a majority of the founding fathers conceived of the system as dualistic in many ways, though the instrument they created made in-

---

[1] The dispute over the intentions of the framers has been revived in recent years with the publication of William W. Crosskey's remarkable work, *Politics and the Constitution in the History of the United States* (Chicago: University of Chicago Press, 1953). The evidence uncovered by Crosskey makes it necessary for historians to reassess the prevalent theories of the "intentions of the framers," even if Crosskey's conclusions are unacceptable. However, as William Anderson says in *The Nation and the States, Rivals or Partners?* (Minneapolis: University of Minnesota Press, 1955), Part II, pp. 53–139, this entire debate is generally couched in terms little relevant to understanding the development of American political institutions.

tergovernmental co-operation as necessary (and probably as inevitable) as the party system.

Within the framework of dualism, the founding fathers were generally identified with one of two schools of thought. The Jeffersonians viewed the system as dual and separate, with the states having the dominant role and the powers of the federal government being confined to the specifically enumerated objects. The Hamiltonians envisaged the federal union as one in which the national government would have the dominant role while the states would become relatively weak repositories of residual local powers.

TABLE 21

CONSTITUTIONAL PROVISIONS FOR SHARING

Constitutional Provision	Article	Section	Provision for Co-operative Relationship or Concurrent Power
Election of representatives..................	I	2	Co-operative
Apportionment of direct taxes..............			Co-operative
Filling Congressional vacancies.............			Co-operative
Election of senators.......................	I	3	Co-operative
Congressional election procedures..........	I	4	Co-operative
Taxing power.............................	I	8	Concurrent
Borrowing power.........................			Concurrent
Regulation of monetary standards...........			Co-operative
Standardization of weights and measures.....			Co-operative
Judicial powers..........................			Concurrent
Militia and national defense...............			Co-operative
Election of president......................	II	1	Co-operative
Judicial jurisdiction.......................	III	2	Concurrent
Full faith and credit of states' public acts, etc. .	IV	1	Co-operative
Privileges and immunities of citizens.........	IV	2	Co-operative
Republican form of government.............	IV	4	Co-operative
Amending the Constitution.................	V		Co-operative

In the pragmatic American way, neither of these theories was adopted in practice, though both were used as base points in the evolution of a functional federal system. The spokesmen of both schools were forced by the exigencies of public office to modify their views and, in doing so, to seek some middle ground. However, what emerged was not simply a compromise somewhere in between the two theoretical positions, but a new approach that embodied some of the principles of both schools amalgamated with new principles induced from the practical experience of the first years of the new government.

This new approach is what has since been labeled "co-operative federalism." It includes the basic idea of dualism in so far as the fundamen-

tal units of government ("sovereignties" is the traditional term) are maintained as separate entities with separate grants of authority from the sovereign people. In spirit, it embodies both the Hamiltonian idea of a
strong federal government and the Jeffersonian idea of strong states. It
is the tension between these two ideas, which unavoidably come into
conflict on some levels, that has created the great debate of American
federalism, which is so vital to the maintenance of the system. This debate is, in the last analysis, never resolved, since its resolution would of
necessity mean the end of the federal system as we know it. Translated
into practical terms, it has provided the major sources of tension within
the co-operative system as well as the means for compromise needed to
maintain both national authority and state power.

THE ARCHITECTS OF AMERICAN FEDERALISM

Despite their vital contributions to the development of American government in other ways, neither Hamilton nor Jefferson could become major architects of co-operative federalism because of their prior intellectual
commitments to their respective schools of thought. The architects of the
American federal system had to be of a different breed. They had to be
men who occupied key positions in the political process and consequently were in close contact with the practical problems of government, yet
who possessed sufficient breadth of vision to see the larger significance of
those problems without being bound by the theories of the dualistic
schools. The men who became the architects of American federalism did
not view the federal system as one in which there was to be either a perpetual struggle between the federal and state governments or an irrev-
ocable separation of their respective functions for the sake of amity between them. Avoiding the premises of legalistic thought, they did not
view the two governments as rivals, but as partners (to use William Anderson's terms), in government who were to share responsibility for a
wide range of activities for the mutual benefit of the nation as a whole
and for its constituent states.

These architects did not leave a formally organized and recognized
body of theory behind them because they wrote of their theories almost
exclusively in response to specific practical problems. Nevertheless, it is
possible to resurrect a body of theory developed by them. Examination of
their official reports and other documents that they produced during their

public careers reveals some very coherent patterns of thought on the proper nature and goals of American federalism.[2] Some of their theoretical formulations have been quoted or referred to in the preceding text.

Foremost among the men who led the movement toward intergovernmental co-operation to meet the problems of a dynamic society were Albert Gallatin and John C. Calhoun. Gallatin and Calhoun were not just responding to each external stimulus as it affected them at the moment. They did not reject the formulation of theories. What they avoided were many of the pitfalls of a priori theoretical formulations based on too rigid principles by establishing instead a series of guides based on some stated and unstated general premises that could and were to be applied and modified for each practical problem. This neglect of highly formal theorizing on the part of the "architects," while vital to the growth of the federal-state partnership in practice, left the field open to the more formal legalistic theorists, who pre-empted it to promote the doctrine of states' rights versus federal power. Unlike the architects of American federalism, who assumed that the federal and state governments had more shared than opposing interests, the legalists based their theories on the assumption that the two levels of government were natural (or potential) rivals, each of which would destroy the other if given the chance.[3]

Aside from these two principle architects of American federalism, many people made major contributions to the development of the federal system as we know it. Other top ranking officials in the federal executive branch, particularly in the Treasury, War, and Interior departments, led the federal government into the field of specific co-operative activities when co-operation, as such, was not popular as a doctrine. The professionals in the federal and state governments, such as the engineers and the educators, who were interested in promoting specific programs for

---

[2] In this respect, the architects' theories of federalism were developed in the same pattern as were the *Federalist* papers. Unfortunately, they have remained undiscovered, perhaps because they did not appear simultaneously but at sporadic intervals and, as a consequence, were allowed to remain buried in the mass of official documents that have accumulated over time.

[3] Calhoun in particular has provided the most comprehensive statement of the co-operative position, because he was the most theoretically oriented of any of the American statesmen of his age. In time, other circumstances came to cloud his role as an architect in favor of his role as a precursor of disunion (which he dreaded more than any of his erstwhile disciples could know). It was on the slavery issue that Calhoun was forced into the rigid position that he strove to avoid on other issues of federal-state relations. Even then, however, he did not alter his basic views as to the value and place of co-operation in the federal system.

the benefit of the whole nation and its constituent parts provided cadres for the initiation and implementation of co-operative programs in undramatic ways, while the rest of the country virtually ignored them and the governments they served. The advocates of specific programs, who were not in or of government at any level but who wanted to see the development of certain public activities at all levels (or regardless of level), provided a basis for the mobilization of popular support in those cases in which government took a hand. Finally, much of the development of the system was stimulated by the members of the Congress of the United States and the several state legislatures who, because of their interest in the general welfare or as an outgrowth of their localistic concerns, supported intergovernmental co-operation in those fields of endeavor that seemed most necessary to them despite an over-all theoretical disposition to limit government in general and to separate by level those few activities that were considered of legitimate governmental concern.

THE THREE PERIODS OF FEDERALISM

American federalism has evolved over three historical periods, all bound together by the thread of intergovernmental collaboration. A strong case can be made to demonstrate that the three periods of federalism correspond in general to the three major periods in postcolonial American history. The particular characteristics of federalism in these three periods can be identified by the forms of intergovernmental collaboration that predominated in each, though in every period the other forms of co-operation existed alongside the predominant ones. Thus, the difference between the three periods is not a difference in the nature of intergovernmental co-operation but in the predominant forms by which such co-operation was effected.

The first period encompassed the formative years of the American nation and its federal system. It can be said to have begun with the founding of the American confederacy in 1775, when the second Continental Congress was convened. Between 1775 and 1787, the basic procedures for co-operation within the new confederacy were initiated. They were formulated as part of the frame of government known as the Articles of Confederation.[4] The Constitution of 1787 provided a frame of government that

[4] Submitted to the Congress on July 12, 1776, and to the states for ratification in November, 1777, the Articles of Confederation were declared in operation on March 1, 1781.

refined some of these bases for co-operation, but otherwise only continued the co-operative procedures initiated under the confederacy on a different level.

The first period encompassed the Revolutionary and Federalist eras, the Jeffersonian "Revolution of 1800," the flourishing and subsequent decline of the Jeffersonians, and the rise of "Jacksonian Democracy." When the period came to a close in the mid-1840's, the United States had fought its second war of independence, turned its back on Europe to concentrate on westward expansion, and was just completing the continental expansion of the nation's boundaries.[5]

This period was also the period in which the mercantilist orientation of the American economy persisted and finally declined, to be replaced by the laissez faire persuasion. In fact, the last decade of this period was marked by the fluidity and confusion characteristic of a change in eras, both in the economic and governmental realms, since the changes in the forms of federalism coincided with the changes in economic organization.

In the realm of ideas, this first period contributed refined versions of the vital ideas of "natural law" and "constitutionalism" to the American mystique, as expressed in the basic documents that emerged from the revolutionary era. As part of this set of ideas, the basic idea of federalism was defined and its corollary concepts of structural dualism and functional co-operation were refined as well. Dominant in this formative period were the activities of the major architects of pre-twentieth-century co-operative federalism, Gallatin near the beginning and Calhoun near the end. The major vehicles of intergovernmental co-operation were the joint-stock company for long-term co-operative projects and the co-operative survey carried out with the widespread use of federal technicians by the states as a means of providing federal services-in-aid to the latter. During this period the majority of the states did not have extensive federal lands within their boundaries, so the tone of co-operation was set by programs designed for the states without public lands. Co-operation in the field of banking was the most uniformly structured throughout the Union. Internal improvement programs usually involved formal arrangements, but were almost always tailored to specific situations. Federal aid to education was vital but generally consisted of "back-door financing."

The landmark that comes closest to marking the end of the formative

[5] Texas was annexed in 1845, followed by the settlement of the Oregon question. In 1846, the Mexican War broke out, which culminated in 1848 in the Mexican cession of the bulk of what is today the American southwest.

period and the beginning of the second era in American federalism was
the Mexican War. After the war, the questions of manifest destiny, commercial expansion, and political democracy that had provided the impetus for government activities during the first period gave way to concern over a solution to the slavery question, industrialization, and the settlement of the newly acquired Far West, thus opening up a new set of
problems for government.

While the great land-grant programs were created during the formative period, and even antedated the other forms of co-operation, they
were almost entirely confined to the public-land states, which did not become major factors on the American political scene until the age of Jackson and did not begin to set the nation's pace and provide its tone until
the middle of the nineteenth century. The second period, that of the great
land grants, can be considered to begin when land-grant programs became the predominant form of intergovernmental co-operation, that is,
when their impact on government became greater than any other form of
co-operative federalism, and other forms of co-operation began to be
measured in relation to the level of collaboration in the public-land
states. The transition from the formative period began during Jackson's
administration with the demise of the United States Bank, the greatest of
all the joint-stock companies, and the distribution of the surplus revenue
in 1837, which was, at least in part, designed to balance the land grants
to the western states. By mid-century, the states admitted to the Union
after ratification of the Constitution outnumbered the original thirteen.
Though not all the former were public-land states, all except Maine and
Vermont shared in the problems of the West. They provided the support
necessary for the establishment of the land grant as a major means of
implementing national policy. The Land Grant College Act of 1862 marks
the triumph of this policy by its application to all the states, east and
west.

The second period lasted for the remainder of the nineteenth century.
During this period, the patterns of American democracy evolved after
1775 were subjected to their greatest domestic tests. In the political realm,
there was the challenge of classical states' rights, secession, and disunion.
In the economic realm, the complex of radical individualist and antigov-
ernment doctrines known as laissez faire was the order of the day. The
slavery issue and its outgrowth, segregation of the Negroes, tore at the
fabric of American democratic ideals. The era was dominated by the
Civil War, first by the threat of disunion, then by the war itself, and fi-

nally, by the process of reunion and reconstruction. Politically, this was the Republican era. The Democratic party, in power as the nation's majority party at mid-century, was dominated by a hesitant and overcautious leadership and was already declining. During the first decade of the second period, the Republican party wooed and won a working majority of the voters, who turned to it as the best vehicle available to respond to the era's major issues. Though challenged by Populists from its own ranks and by a Democracy led by the resurgent South, the Republican party managed to maintain its position throughout the period.

Between 1848 and 1913, the hope of the American people lay in the West as never before or since. The West, whatever it may have been in reality, became the shining haven of the American dream. It was this period that added the refined idea of the "frontier" to the American mystique, much as the earlier period had contributed the ideas of natural law and constitutionalism. And, in reality, it was in the West that co-operative federalism flourished and matured during those years. The great land-grant programs set the tone for intergovernmental co-operation in the older states because of their expansion in the new ones. Uniformly structured land grants for internal improvements and education dominated the stage, supplemented by various types of federal subsidies, new co-operative developments in the regulatory field, and an increasing amount of informal co-operation among professionals on all levels of government. Through the land grant, the impact of the federal government was felt in almost every field of activity throughout the West and in most of the East.

The last major land-grant program was inaugurated in 1894. Although selection of lands under the land-grant acts has persisted through the mid-twentieth century and the admission of Alaska to the Union in 1958 has once again placed the land-grant programs in the public eye, since 1913 the cash grant (usually called the grant-in-aid), coupled with the rising impact of professionalized co-operation within all levels of government, has represented the dominant form of intergovernmental co-operation. The modern cash grants had their origins in the later years of the land-grant period. Inaugurated in their modern form in 1886, they rose to predominance with the adoption of the specific programs embodied in Woodrow Wilson's "New Freedom" and were notably extended with the rise of the New Deal.

The third period does not fall under the purview of this book. Beginning in 1913 after a transitional decade not unlike that which closed the

first period, it is generally considered to be the era of co-operative federalism. American domestic political problems in this era have centered
around the rapid expansion of the velocity of government and the rise of
the so-called welfare state. Even greater than these domestic challenges
have been the pressures on the nation from abroad and the basic change
in American policy arising from an inescapable involvement in world affairs. By 1913, the end of the second period, the Democrats had already
seized the initiative in tackling the problems of the new century; and,
though the Republicans had yet to lose their majority, Woodrow Wilson's
election was a hint of things to come. After a postwar resurgence of Republicanism based primarily on an attempt to return to the "normalcy"
of the nineteenth century, the Democratic party became the majority party
because it had captured the position of pacesetter in this new era, much
as the Republican party had two generations earlier.

Economically, the successful completion of the first stage of industrialization led to an abandonment of the laissez faire dogmas and the evolution of a publicly regulated, corporation-dominated, welfare-oriented
capitalism with a "mixed economy" whose political doctrines were more
like those of the first period. In the social realm, there was a resurgence
of community co-operation as part of an over-all attempt to cope with the
social challenges to the American ideal.

Even during the second period, the old agricultural-land frontier had
been giving way to an urban-industrial one. In the third period, a new
frontier based on metropolitanism and technological advance captured
the imagination of restless Americans, gave them cause for concern, and
defined the bulk of the problems they had to face.

Perhaps the major contribution of the third period to the store of ideas
that comprise the American mystique has been the refined idea of "co-
operation." Just as the ideas of natural law and constitutionalism had existed prior to their refinement in the first period and the idea of the frontier prior to its refinement in the second, so was co-operation a part of
American life prior to the third. Because co-operation as such was refined
only in the third period, it is often conceived to be an invention of that
era. Nowhere is this better illustrated than in the case of federalism.

Needless to say, all the aforementioned changes had profound effects
on the expansion of government. Formally structured grant-in-aid programs of internal improvement had to share the center of the stage with
the "new federalism" of welfare. The less visible areas of intergovernmental collaboration expanded apace. As government became more per-

vasive, so did intergovernmental co-operation. The twentieth century was soon labeled the century of co-operative federalism, while the co-operative federalism of an earlier century was forgotten.

THE PLACE OF THE PUBLIC DOMAIN

The outstanding single feature of pre-twentieth-century America was the extensive unoccupied public domain. In the nineteenth century, before human settlement reduced its size, the public domain served as a source of government revenue much as the entire national product serves government in the twentieth. Whatever its successes and failures as a revenue source, it was the basis from which governments could draw the resources necessary to undertake those public programs acceptable at the time. As long as the land frontier lasted, it served as the greatest single source of national wealth, the foundation of the American economy. Even the development of the major industries of the nineteenth century—agricultural implements, railroads and telegraphs, machines for processing the products of the land, and the like—was directly tied to the development of the public domain. It is not surprising, then, that the land, since most of it was owned by the federal government, should have served as the foundation for intergovernmental co-operation in the expanding nation.

In so far as the existence of the public domain provided an integrating factor from which to view the grant-in-aid programs, the public-land states differed from their non-public-land counterparts in the nature of their co-operative relationships with the federal government. While this was a real difference in one sense, in the larger sense it was one of degree rather than kind. The existence of extensive federal lands within the boundaries of the public-land states only made it less difficult to justify major co-operative programs under the strict-constructionist ideology then dominant in Constitutional interpretation.

Considering only formal grants-in-aid, it is likely (though not certain) that the public-land states received more benefits than the others, and so it was argued on the floors of Congress when the states possessing no public lands wanted to gain additional benefits for themselves from the federal government. Yet, when all the other forms of intergovernmental co-operation and the direct federal aid to localities are totaled, the balance seems to have been rather adequately redressed and the amount of co-operation generally equalized. One brief example: the protective tariff was unquestionably a great aid to eastern manufacturing interests, often to the detriment of the West and the South. It was as much a federally originated benefit as any defense contract in the twentieth century, and had a similar impact on the nation's economic development. The tariff was considered by both its proponents and opponents to be a form of federal subsidization of industry and the industrial states. The eastern railroad companies coupled benefits gained from the protective tariff (or exemptions from the tariff, as was sometimes the case) with federal mail subsidies (the co-operative impacts of which were noted in chapter xiii) and additional direct state and local subsidies to construct the network of railroads east of the Great Lakes. They began to take advantage of these benefits even before the major railroad land grants were made and continued to do so subsequently as well.

The public domain was most significant as a vehicle for the introduction of co-operative programs as they became necessary, despite strong sentiments opposed to co-operation as such. Although the federal government contributed significantly to the growth of the eastern states, through the aforementioned subsidy system and in other ways, the lack of a convenient medium for intergovernmental co-operation that would satisfy the strict-constructionists hindered the development of large-scale formal co-operative programs in the East. What did develop was important but somewhat uneven in character. In the West, however, the availability of federal lands and the development of the "gift" theory of federal land grants, which was acceptable to all but die-hard strict-constructionists, made possible the creation and development of long-term, ongoing co-operative programs.

Frederick Jackson Turner, in stating his frontier hypothesis, emphasized the influence of the West—i.e., the states carved out of the public domain—in the development of American nationalism and governmental centralization. He maintained that the growth of the federal government was greatly fostered by the demands of the western settlers and their early experiences with federal officials, who preceded state governments in almost every new territory.[6] Turner's point is generally well taken. However, it is considerably more accurate to say that not only did the westward expansion increase central government activity at the federal level, but it did so primarily by increasing intergovernmental co-operation, formal and informal, thus also increasing the central governmental

[6] Frederick Jackson Turner, *The Frontier in American History* (New York: Henry Holt and Co., 1920).

activities of the states. The public domain served as a vehicle for the development of the role of the federal government in promoting national expansion while at the same time providing a means for the states and localities to share in this task.

The pattern of relationships that emerged from the manipulation of the public domain was carried over into the twentieth-century co-operative programs. It was the prior existence of this pattern that made the increase in velocity of government possible without major alterations in the operations of the federal system.

STATE LOYALTIES AND CO-OPERATIVE FEDERALISM: OLD STATES AND NEW

While the public-land states were more evenly integrated into the co-operative pattern than were their sisters lacking federal lands, this division seems to have produced no difference in their respective patterns of state loyalties. What few generalizations about state loyalties can be made without "hard" data must be based on the evidence provided by the recorded comments and actions of people living in the nineteenth century. Even the rich literature of the Civil War period avoids dealing with the question of state loyalties, though much of the literature contains implicit assumptions concerning the locus of southern loyalties.[7]

One might reasonably assume that the original thirteen states, which antedated the Union, would have provided stronger reasons for state attachments on the part of their citizens than the states admitted subsequently, which might be considered (practically, though not Constitutionally) to be the creatures of the Union. Even the brief references to the subject in this book indicate that although in Virginia this assumption may very well be valid, in the New Hampshire situation it does not appear to be. It is common knowledge that the southern states, whether of the original thirteen or of later origin (and whether carved from the federal public domain or not), have developed patterns of state loyalty that some of the original states in the northeast have not.

[7] There is as much reason to assume that southern loyalties were local or sectional (or rooted in economic interest), as there is to assume the pre-eminence of state ties. Robert E. Lee and other Virginians with backgrounds similar to his whose loyalties were to their state are outstanding and well-known exceptions to this. The Lees were counterbalanced, however, by the many soldiers of the South who enlisted in the Confederate States Army because all their friends were doing so or because they had heard that their *homes and families* (not states or even states' rights) were in danger.

One need only contrast the attitudes of citizens of Mississippi with those of New Jersey's citizenry to note that this difference is based on section rather than antiquity.

Yet sectional differences between North and South do not explain differences in state loyalties either. Some of the western states (among them, California and Colorado), among the newest in the nation, have a sense of state identity much more like that of the South than of the East, though they have been far more dependent on the federal government for fiscal and other forms of aid over the years. The western states, with sparse populations usually concentrated in central locations within each state, have developed relatively few permanent interstate contacts that transcend their boundaries, none of which compare to the commuting relationships that have developed along the east coast. At the same time, the level of contacts with the federal government has historically been much higher for them than for either the eastern or southern states. Consequently, strong traditions of state loyalty have developed alongside strong traditions of intergovernmental co-operation. Evidence of this type tends to indicate that the level of state attachments is much more a product of geography than of chronology.[8]

What the newer states had was a tradition of intergovernmental co-operation that antedated their admission to the Union. If the federal government did not always precede the first settlers into new territory, it almost invariably preceded the state government. From this arrangement emerged an implicit conception of the rightness of the role of the federal government as a major participant in the development of new territories and new frontiers. This conception then carried over after statehood was achieved.

[8] It is clear to even the most casual observer that citizens of some states seem to have much more of a sense of attachment to their states than do the citizens of others, and the reasons for this have yet to be investigated properly. Evidently, certain factors in the history of individual states, perhaps including early patterns of settlement, unique contributions or experiences, and place in the total scheme of American history, combine with certain geographic factors, perhaps including degree of isolation and uniqueness of topography, to cause the development of state loyalties of different strengths. Evidence in the author's files indicates that the level of peoples' attachment to their states today is often underestimated. This is at least partly because there is a tendency to evaluate loyalties on the basis of dualism, whereby the two loyalties are measured as to their mutual exclusiveness. In fact, the "man in the street" tends to consider these loyalties as concurrent. He does not choose between state and national loyalties but embraces them both. Indeed, one is usually considered to be a function of the other. One is a Minnesotan because one is an American and vice versa. This common sense approach has definite connections to the common sense attitude that has contributed so much to the evolution of co-operative federalism.

The movements to attain statehood reflected this tradition of intergovernmental co-operation. On one hand, they were certainly attempts to gain more power for local self-government. Even more important, the desire for statehood was linked to the perceived ability of states to gain more benefits from Washington than could territories. In almost all cases, land grants were not available until statehood was achieved. Lack of voting power in the national elections and full representation in Congress meant that a territory was dependent on favors from Washington over which its citizens had only a minimum of control. Statehood meant the right to participate in national politics as much as the right to manage one's local affairs. Elimination of control from Washington made it possible for the citizens of a new state to gain representation in Congress, which gave them the key to the benefits of the federal system. Through their senators and representatives, they were in a position to obtain their share of the federal largess, such as it was at any given time, and to decide the manner of its distribution. This was a most important achievement.[9]

CONTROL OVER THE GRANT PROGRAMS

The organization of control over the grant programs was another matter that tended to obscure the nature of the co-operative relationships in the nineteenth century. The evolution of formal federal controls did not signify changes in the fundamental policy of Congressional supervision of the programs, but did indicate that Congress, and the states represented in it, had learned from experience. The principle of federal control existed from the days of the earliest grants. At first, it was assumed that mere incorporation of certain principles into the state constitutions would be sufficient to ensure compliance with the spirit of the programs in question. To some extent, this method was successful and has continued to be so. If for no other reason than the general increase in the velocity of government, this method came to be too cumbersome. As it was seen that more specific controls were necessary, they were added by the representatives of the very states that would receive the grants. In addition, as

[9] The reasons why territories have desired admission to the Union as states have not significantly changed since the admission of Kentucky. A study of the campaigns waged by Alaska and Hawaii in the past few years indicates the same reasons and outlook, combining local patriotism with a desire for equal access to, and participation in, the federal government.

administrative complexities increased and new methods of enforcement besides the courts had to be found, they too were added, not as changes in policy but as improvements in method.

The question still arises as to the degree of enforcement of these provisions. There is no doubt that grants were not often revoked or lands often withheld, though enough cases of revocation and withholding of lands can be found to indicate that federal control could be carried to its ultimate implications in this manner. The absence of large-scale revocation of programs is due less to the failure of the federal government to enforce the terms administratively than to the political power of the states in the halls of Congress. This is no less true in 1962 than in 1862. Students of government have noted that since the rise of the great cash-grant programs following the New Deal, little money has been withheld from any of the states for maladministration or violation of the terms of the program in question. Attempts have been initiated by the federal executive to withhold funds from individual states for a number of reasons. In almost every case, these attempts have been overruled in Congress, or suitable compromises have been negotiated with Congressional help. When state violations of federal regulations occur, they are dealt with in less drastic ways, because Congress will not often allow the drastic solution and the federal administrators know this.

The revocation of one major railroad grant has already been described in the case of Minnesota. Between 1870 and 1900, the question of revoking some of the unfulfilled transportation land grants became a matter of some political importance. Congressional investigations into the uses of land grants by railroad companies were widespread during this period. Ultimately, federal-state land grants to eight railroad companies were revoked in whole or in part and steps were taken to withhold lands from the great transcontinental railroads as well.[10]

Although other federal grants to the states were not revoked, specific lands were frequently withheld by the federal government. It has been shown that, not infrequently, the states were even forced to re-cede lands already patented to them. As the available public domain diminished and the number of land-grant programs increased, the amount of control and intensity of supervision grew also, leading to greater exercise of federal authority, subject always to the formal and informal limitations imposed by Congress.

[10] Federal Co-ordinator of Transportation, *Public Aids to Transportation* (Washington: U.S. Government Printing Office, 1938), Vol. II, Part I, Sec. A.

20

The Roots of Co-operation

SERVING A FRONTIER SOCIETY

The roots of co-operative federalism can be traced to three fundamental aspects of American civilization: the dynamic American society typified by the frontier, the American constitutional structure, and the forms of political organization that have developed in the United States to maintain the Constitution while meeting the challenges of the frontier. American federalism in its present form is conceivable only as the product of a dynamic society. In a federal system serving a relatively static society, it is conceivable that a separation of functions between the central government and the constituent governments could be maintained, because the pressures for crossing the lines of demarcation would be considerably fewer. Indeed, in such a society, crossing the lines of demarcation would probably spell the end of federalism as a viable force, since one level or the other would soon gain the bulk of the power entrusted to government. In a dynamic society, however, attempts at separation are constantly challenged by the rise of new problems or the expanding scope of older ones, while the expansion of the society simultaneously provides room for both levels of government to act. Furthermore, the demands created by the new problems must be met by government on all levels if the society itself is not to be radically altered. It is this paradox that has helped to keep the functioning and consequences of the sharing principle obscured from general view.[1]

[1] As yet, little has been developed in the way of political theory to account for the political differences between static and dynamic societies. In this respect, practice (and the implicit theory that has grown out of it) has outstripped formal theory, which is still pre-eminently concerned with the old (static) pattern of society. It is the addition of a new dynamic dimension to American society that has made intergovernmental co-operation imperative. That same new dimension has also made the maintenance of federalism possible.

The dynamic civilization of the United States prior to the twentieth century was intimately connected with the land frontier. That is why so many of the innovations in American federalism stem from the conquest of the West or such related activities as transportation and internal communications. The needs which arose as a result of the westward expansion created problems for government unforseen by the founding fathers. The system that they had created, however, proved to be flexible enough to incorporate these new needs and problems into the governmental framework without significantly changing the basic principles of American government. The impact of the frontier was direct, through the settlement of new territories, and indirect, through the creation of needs for a new technology (and new industry to produce it) in order to develop the new lands. In both cases it was necessary to develop mechanisms of intergovernmental co-operation that might not have become necessary otherwise.

In the American experience, wherever strict adherence to the separatist theory of federalism was maintained in a major area of governmental concern, there followed a centralization of power in the hands of the federal government because no smaller unit of government could properly deal with the problems that arose. In most cases, however, the desire for local control over the effects of government locally, coupled with a realization of the need for some type of participation on the part of the federal government (usually fiscal or standard-setting), led to the emergence of a federalism based on the sharing principle. Perhaps, paradoxically, the development of intergovernmental co-operation has come to be a way to "have one's cake and eat it too" by enabling the society to change materially while maintaining its basic political institutions and values.

The constitutional structure of the United States was fitted to this dynamic civilization. While the Constitution itself does not explicitly provide for much intergovernmental co-operation, it does make such co-operation possible in most areas. Because of its provisions for joint responsibilities in the political arena, the Constitution actually provided a framework that encouraged co-operative federalism by making it possible for the states and localities to make demands on the general government without abdicating their own roles.

The political organization of the United States, which stems from this constitutional structure, provides the means for sharing functions. The non-centralized American party system, rooted in the states and localities but also responsible for the government of the nation, has encouraged the use of the federal government as the arm of a majority of the states by implicitly relying on Calhoun's doctrine that federal participation is proper when a project "is immediately beneficial to more than half of the states of the Union, and, without the aid of the Federal Government, would require their cooperation." At the same time, the state- and locally-oriented party organizations have been vitally interested in preserving state and local control over as many activities of government as possible. The only possible resolution of these somewhat contradictory tendencies has been through the sharing principle.[2]

THE CRITERIA FOR SHARING

Nevertheless, not all governmental activities were directly co-operative (though they all might ultimately interconnect), and some were more formally co-operative than others. What criteria were used to determine how each activity would be structured? Examination of the variety of programs does lead to the extraction of a set of criteria, which were generally implicit in each program rather than explicitly formulated. In most cases, decisions were not made on constitutional or ideological grounds, but on a case by case basis. Constitutional interpretation and ideology were more in the character of later justifications of basically pragmatic decisions. At most, they led to the creation of some political euphemisms,

[2] For a detailed exposition of the contemporary role of the party system in making intergovernmental collaboration possible, see Morton Grodzins, "American Political Parties and the American System," in *Western Political Quarterly*, XIII (December, 1960). (A summary of this hypothesis can be found in *Goals for Americans*, the report of the President's Commission on National Goals [New York: Prentice-Hall, 1960], chap. xii.) Grodzins' description of the role of the political parties in maintaining the American federal system in the mid-twentieth century is equally applicable in the nineteenth century. The undisciplined American political parties function as decentralizers (1) "by determining in legislation the basic sharing of functions between the federal government on the one hand, and state and local governments on the other"; (2) through "constant, effective, and institutionalized" Congressional "interference" in the national administrative process on behalf of state and local (and other) interests and interest groups; (3) by impelling "administrators to seek political support for their programs" and, consequently, to "play a political role" that redounds to the advantage of the non-central governments; and (4) by allowing and encouraging the operation of the "multiple crack" system in American politics, whereby a multiplicity of interests have multiple means of access and ways to take a crack at influencing government policy. The parties function in this manner because they are basically undisciplined on the national level, or quite often on any other, and are principally organized through the states (or on the local level, in some cases).

such as the "gift" theory, which were quickly abandoned when brought to a test. Legislators and officers of the federal and state governments were concerned with getting people on the land, with building railroads, and with providing educational and certain minimum welfare facilities, more than they were concerned with theory-building.

Though they are often used as a basis for analyzing American political behavior, Supreme Court decisions were not the significant factors in determining co-operation, separation, or variations of either. They were reflections, ratifications, and occasionally rejections of the pragmatic arrangements that were raised to the level of constitutional law by the holders of power of the time. When the court tried to alter the course of collaboration in the federal system through its decisions, as in the latter part of the nineteenth and early twentieth centuries, its specific successes were brief, soon circumvented, and subsequently reversed.

The decisions, then, seem to have been made by a broad group of policy-makers on the basis of four major criteria. The first was the issue itself. What was the proposed program and what was its nature? Thus, at one time, a relief program involving direct federal cash grants was not considered acceptable, whereas aid for internal expansion through railroad construction land grants was. Implicit here was the idea that each issue had to be judged on its own relative merits in the context of the times and that no blanket rule would suffice. In effect, it was recognized that different programs should be shared in different ways or, occasionally, not shared at all. It was considered possible for co-operation to take different forms, depending on the program in question, for the same program to pass through different stages of sharing, and for a program to be shared in different ways at different times. Furthermore, it was always possible to reconsider a decision, to alter the forms of co-operation applied in a given program, to include a program previously excluded, or occasionally, to exclude a program previously included.

Issue-by-issue decisions imply a tacit recognition of the principle that there may be and occasionally are qualitative differences between issues, which would indicate that different approaches to intergovernmental collaboration are not only politically necessary but normatively desirable.[3]

---

[3] This is apparent in a contemporary example. Intergovernmental co-operation in the field of education seems to be acceptable so long as it is piecemeal in nature and developed program by program. However, attempts to establish blanket programs of federal aid to education have been successfully resisted to date (1962), often by the same people who support the piecemeal programs. It would seem to this writer that here is a case in which a qualitative difference between education and, say, high-

The second criterion was the desire to preserve and develop the entire nation. As analyzed above, the desire for national development meant, in the main, the conquest of the land frontier in its broadest sense. Consequently, areas of technological development, the effects of which on the nation were related or very similar to those resulting from the development of the West, also figured prominently in co-operative activities. "Preservation" has been particularly important during wartime. The outstanding example of expanded intergovernmental co-operation for this purpose in the nineteenth century was the Civil War, which featured a great amount of federally dominated intergovernmental co-operation in the loyal states, which was temporarily instituted by the federal government and accepted by the states and localities in order to preserve the Union.[4]

Implicit in the desire to preserve and develop the entire nation has been a long-established feeling of national identity on the part of the American people. National and state loyalties were considered of a piece. Although many cases of state and sectional particularism could be found, this particularism was generally based on a concern that one's state or section was sharing fairly in the national expansion, rather than a parochial desire to exclude other states or sections from sharing as well. Rarely articulated and often obscure, there has generally been some sense of the national interest coursing through the near chaos of non-centralized interest competition that characterizes American democracy. This na-

---

way construction is implicitly accepted, and certain practical conclusions are drawn from the distinction that is made. This is evident in the debate that has surrounded various federal aid-to-education bills, in which opponents of federal aid dwell upon the nature of the educational process to caution the people against injecting the federal government into the education field in a manner that might lead to centralized control of the schools. Regardless of the validity of this argument, it implies the qualitative difference between education and other government functions.

The education issue also illustrates how the issue-by-issue approach provides for changing decisions over time. In the nineteenth century, blanket federal aid to education, with a minimum of conditions, through land grants and federal cash distributions was considered to be the best way to aid in the establishment of school systems, while specific programs were resisted. Now that the problem is no longer the establishment of school systems but their enrichment, blanket aid has been rejected while specific programs have grown considerably. Of course, by the same token, the decision may again be changed.

[4] For an excellent account of federal-state relations during the Civil War that documents this assertion, see William B. Hesseltine, *Lincoln and the War Governors* (New York: Alfred A. Knopf, 1955). The Minnesota State Archives has many documents that support this thesis also, in both the Governors' Archives and the Executive Records.

tional interest has generally been expressed governmentally through the device of co-operative federalism.

The third criterion was the desire to preserve and develop the states. Though co-operative programs reflected national interests, they also reflected a desire to act within the federal framework to preserve the power and autonomy of the states—to make government as comprehensive and efficient as necessary, yet as non-centralized and "close to home" as possible. Thus, the co-operative program, as well as any limits placed on it, was as much a vehicle by which the enlightened champion of states' rights might strengthen the states by giving them more to do and more power with which to do it, as it was a vehicle by which the nationalist might secure programs that covered the entire Union.

From the beginning, the feeling that the states should be preserved and developed has stood alongside the desire for preservation and development of the nation. In some respects, those who have conceived of the two ideas as mutually exclusive ones have learned to live with each other out of necessity, since neither group has won sufficient support to dominate the other. However, the two ideas have survived standing side by side, not as the end products of a compromise, but as the two legitimate faces of American federalism. It seems clear that a majority of those who have been actively involved in the political process have themselves desired the preservation and development of both the nation and the states, accepting the view that the two were not only compatible, but that their preservation was vital to the nation in its attempt to maintain the American way of life. Woodrow Wilson, who as president is considered to have been one of the major centralizers in American political history, provided what is perhaps the best statement of this view. Charles E. Merriam paraphrases it in *American Political Ideas* as follows:

Possibly the best presentation of the importance of the state in our system of government was made by Wilson. "Every commonwealth," he declared, "has been a nursery of new strength; and out of these nurseries have come men and communities which no other process could have produced. Self-government has here had its richest harvest." If our system of states had not come to us "by historical necessity, I think it would have been worth while to invent it." Local affairs are not uniform, and cannot be made so by compulsion of law. What we seek is co-operation, but not the strait jacket. Variety will not impair energy, if there is genuine co-operation.

Our states have not been created: they have sprung up of themselves, irrepressible, "self-originated, self-constituted, self-confident, self-sustaining, veritable communities demanding only recognition." The remedy [for the states' weaknesses] lies, not merely in changing the division of powers between state and nation, along lines of actual alteration of interest, but in reorganization of the state from within. Instead of upsetting an ancient system, we should "revitalize it by reorganization." "Centralization is not vitalization," said he, and the atrophy of the parts will result in the atrophy of the whole.[5]

In this sense, although the actual patterns of intergovernmental co-operation have been developed piecemeal, co-operative federalism as such has been a product of almost conscious design.

The fourth criterion was that of efficiency. When a specific program was being considered, the system or combination of systems that seemed likely to get the job done best, taking into consideration the first three criteria, would be the one chosen. "Efficiency" is used here in the political as well as the classic sense. Since the concept of efficiency in American political practice has out of sheer political necessity implicitly included the individualistic, pluralistic, and free-enterprise values of American democracy, not just a simplistic "economic" view of accomplishment, it has normally led to federal-state collaboration and the use of concurrent powers in order to include these individualistic, pluralistic, and free enterprise elements affected by government.[6]

[5] Merriam, *American Political Ideas* (New York, 1921), pp. 239–40 (quoted by permission of the Macmillan Co.).

[6] It can be said that contemplation of the individual decisions made by American governments and examination of the ways in which they are made is not often conducive to this view of efficiency as one of the criteria in the decision-making process. So-called rational decision-making procedures are not often visible in this process, primarily because the other criteria generally take precedence over considerations of classic efficiency. Nevertheless, these other criteria are intimately tied to the concept of political efficiency. During the period of the New Deal, the struggle between proponents of classic efficiency and political efficiency within the federal government reached a high point. However, even in the throes of a major depression, the proponents of political efficiency were more successful than their opposite numbers in securing Congressional consent for New Deal measures. This explains why the major new federal programs instituted in that period were designed as co-operative programs, despite strong pressures for centralization of power in the federal government within and outside of the Roosevelt administration. In essence, those officials who designed new programs on the basis of classic efficiency were generally disappointed. However, this did not mean that efficiency itself was no criterion. Other officials, with goals quite similar, designed new programs with an eye toward political efficiency and were generally able to see their most important measures adopted. The creation of the social security system is a case in point. For a brief history and analysis of this case, see R. G. Tugwell and E. C. Banfield, "Grass Roots Democracy—Myth or Reality," *Public Administration Review,* X (Winter, 1950), 48, 50; Frances Perkins, *The Roosevelt I Knew* (New York: Viking, 1946), p. 291; and Grodzins, *op. cit.,* pp. 978–79.

Under a co-operative arrangement, neither side of the partnership could work its will unopposed to cripple or destroy the other or the interests represented by the other. The temperament of the public would not allow that to happen, and their *political* sense of efficiency managed to keep things on a generally even keel. It is this temperament and political sense which have kept federalism in America alive and vibrant, just as they have served our political system as a whole.[7]

These four criteria were applied through the political process. Political leaders, legislators, administrators, and judges all shared in their application and in the decision-making process that determined how and where the criteria would be applied. The major medium for this decision-making was the party system, the central agency of American politics. The pragmatic arrangements referred to above were made through the give and take of politics and were absorbed and put into effect by the parties or the elected representatives of the people, who were products of the party system. The broad range of interpretation allowed by the Constitution itself makes room for this type of decision-making, which is reflected in the actions of Congress as well as in the decisions of the courts. The land-grant system was created pragmatically through political give and take. The Supreme Court never ruled directly on the constitutionality of the land-grant programs, but grants initiated by Congress were later recognized as enforceable by the Court in decisions related to specific problems created by their administration. This type of oblique consent is typical of the Court's ratification of many legislative innovations in the area of federalism.

SEPARATIST TENDENCIES

The importance of this system of co-operation between the units of government is best demonstrated when it is contrasted with separatist tendencies that were very strong during the first six decades of the nineteenth century and with the results of those separatist tendencies when they were translated into action.

The Civil War has often been used as the decisive example in presenting the case for nineteenth-century dual federalism. However, even the existence of extreme separatist tendencies on certain issues does not in it-

---

[7] For an excellent presentation of this view in a larger framework, see Herbert Agar, *The Price of Union* (Boston: Houghton Mifflin Co., 1950).

self tell the whole story about the state of intergovernmental relations on other issues. On the contrary, given the American penchant for approaching issues individually from a pragmatic viewpoint, it is entirely possible and even likely that separatist tendencies on one issue will exist side by side with continued and cordial co-operation on others. Mid-twentieth-century America is afflicted with a major disagreement quite similar to that which divided this country one hundred years ago. Yet, despite southern white reaction to attempts at integrating the Negroes, and their occasionally violent resistance to such attempts, co-operative programs in other areas of government have, without exception, been maintained and even expanded.[8] Though a few suggestions have been made to reduce or eliminate federal school aid to segregated schools, these proposals have not yet been seriously considered in Congress.

This is just as true of the nineteenth century as of the twentieth. When the states feel that the purposes of a federal aid program are in line with their own goals and that the program can be controlled by them to a reasonable degree, they will become fully involved in the co-operative arrangements, conditions and all, without feeling that their "rights" are being infringed upon. However, when there is a disagreement as to goals or policy, resistance may occur in several different ways. Only then is the cry of "states' rights" raised; and even then it is generally confined to the specific issue at hand.

It is significant that the co-operative programs that existed in the nation up to the outbreak of the Civil War were disrupted only by secession itself, not during the period prior to it when separatist tendencies were growing. Secession, then, was not of itself a demonstration that co-operative federalism did not exist within the federal system prior to its attempted dissolution. New co-operative programs were actually initiated throughout the 1850's by southern legislators in Congress and the state legislatures. In many cases, these were the same legislators who were

[8] The writer has data to this effect gathered in the summer of 1958 in thorough studies of two smaller southern cities, Benton, Arkansas, and Lafayette, Georgia, in "the year of Little Rock." In these communities, there was virtually unanimous opposition to desegregation in principle and substantial support for "states' rights" as exhibited in Little Rock. Nevertheless, not a single co-operative program was in the least bit altered as a result of the separatist tendencies manifested in the Little Rock situation. Benton, located twenty-four miles southwest of Little Rock, was benefiting from federal aid for schools as a federal impacted area. Not only was this aid continued there without interruption throughout the crisis, but Little Rock itself continued to receive federal aid for school construction while its Central High School was "occupied" by the United States Army.

otherwise occupied trying to lead the southern states out of the Union after 1851.

If further demonstrations of the possibility for co-operative and separatist tendencies to exist side by side are needed, the almost immediate re-establishment of co-operative relations between the federal government and the states of the former Confederacy after the end of the Civil War should serve the purpose. Despite the rigors of Reconstruction and the ill will generated by the clash of radicals on both sides, the previously existing grant-in-land programs were quickly resumed, and new ones, such as the agricultural college grant, were extended to those states that had been in rebellion in 1862. Indeed, Abraham Lincoln himself developed a theory of federalism designed to maintain these co-operative programs (as well as the Union in general) by ruling that the states had not themselves seceded but that their governments had been captured by rebels and insurrectionists.

The greatest example of an attempt to implement classic dual federalism was that made by Confederate officials on the national and state levels during the brief existence of the Confederate States of America. Admittedly, there are certain limitations to generalizing from this example, since a wartime situation, particularly one as difficult as that in which the Confederates soon found themselves, would impose great strains on any federal system. Nevertheless, many historians have provided evidence to the effect that Confederate officials on the state level asserted the most extreme doctrines of state sovereignty in their administrative actions, that they were abetted in their actions by officials of their federal government who went out of their way to avoid charges of interference with states' rights, and that this contributed significantly to the defeat of the Confederacy.

If the Confederate government could have mobilized the men and material that were available in the individual states of the South during the early days of the war when the Confederate armies were winning battles with considerable consistency, the course of the war might have been altered. Instead, each state stood on its constitutional rights (as the South had been habituated to do in the larger sectional struggles of the old Union) and refused to do more for the common cause than the individual governors thought was necessary. No real system of co-operation was developed during the entire course of the war because of this doctrinaire attitude on the part of the southern leadership. Case after case of state intransigence in the face of demands, requests, levies, and even cajolery on the part of the Richmond government can be found in the records of Confederate history. Governors withheld vitally needed supplies for use within their own states. State militia were held for "local self-defense" when they were needed in Confederate service at the front. State-controlled railroads refused to respond to Confederate requests to participate in a co-operative transportation effort. The record of dual federalism as practiced in the southern Confederacy is a long and sad one.

In the old United States, on the other hand, the co-operative experiences of the previous decades provided a basis upon which to build the expanded system of federal-state co-operation that finally enabled the North to preserve the Union. Lincoln, a man intimately familiar with such important co-operative enterprises in Illinois as the Illinois and Michigan Canal and the Illinois Central Railroad, was the architect of this policy of co-operation with the states. This is not to imply that the great increase in the amount of co-operation (which was simply part of the great, though temporary, increase in the velocity of government that took place during the war) was not subject to criticism and even some resistance on the part of state authorities. But verbal denunciations aside, the system of co-operation was expanded as the amount of government activity expanded. In the last analysis, wartime co-operation worked, and it was generally accepted by the nation.[9] The separatist tendencies of the Civil War are not an indication that American federalism demonstrated classic dualism during the ante bellum period. On the contrary, that war itself provides an example of the consequences of the classic theory when an attempt was made to translate it into action.

A demonstration of the need for superimposing a co-operative method of operation over a formally dual system of government in times of peace can be found in the prolonged struggle to develop a nationwide banking system. The nation has always been in need of a banking system that could mobilize the financial resources necessary for national development while providing a proper combination of stability and fluidity to foster their proper use. Hamilton and his Federalist colleagues recognized this in the earliest days of the Republic. Against the wishes of the Jeffersonian Republicans, they secured the establishment of the first Bank of the United States to co-operate with state and local banks in order to achieve

[9] For a discussion of this question, see William B. Hesseltine, *op. cit.* While Hesseltine takes the position that it was the Civil War itself that created a new national supremacy, a view not shared by this writer, he does document the development of wartime co-operation between the federal and state governments in the North and refers to the lack of such a relationship in the South.

that end. As a result of the Republicans' opposition, the charter of the first bank was allowed to lapse. It has been shown how the resultant problem was sufficiently grave to force the Republicans to change their position within five years and support the establishment of a second bank with a view to reintroducing and even strengthening a co-operative national banking system. Regardless of the wisdom of the action from other than a fiscal point of view, the destruction of this second bank and of the co-operative system it had fostered meant the beginning of a period of serious fiscal problems for the nation. A series of piecemeal attempts to restore the federal role was initiated almost immediately, albeit unsuccessfully until the passage of the National Banking Act of 1862 alleviated the problem somewhat. Only some fifty years later, with the creation of the Federal Reserve System, which essentially restored to the federal government the role that it held until the 1830's, was the problem met. During the interim, the money problem continued to plague the American people. The men who governed the nation and the states were taught relatively early in history that the natural expansion of a dynamic society necessitated either co-operation or federal control. Although the latter solution does not necessarily preclude the emergence of a great deal of local influence, it does tend to lessen the power of the states and their local subdivisions.

THE RISE OF THE DUALISTIC DOCTRINE

Despite the underlying facts of federalism in the nineteenth century, the outward appearances of the period were the ones that most influenced observers of the American political scene. Those outward appearances were dignified and consequently magnified by the utterances of the more articulate of the founding fathers, who were able to impute a separatist orientation to the Constitution itself. By what may have been just a quirk of fate, the most publicly articulate of the founding fathers, those who were active in politics for two generations after the Revolution, were also the major proponents of the theory of dual federalism as a means of safeguarding the states. The advocates of collaboration, such as Gallatin, Calhoun, and even John Marshall, were no match for Presidents Jefferson, Madison, and Monroe when it came to capturing the public eye. Furthermore, though the administrations of the aforementioned presidents were honeycombed with co-operative programs, the terminology employed by even the most realistic observers of the time tended to color the facts with a patina of dual federalism.

The public statements of these separationists were soon accepted as part of the American political tradition and were followed by an unceasing stream of comments from public officials of all governments that were based on, and in support of, the traditional doctrine of dual federalism. That these comments often went hand in hand with the enthusiastic participation of the same officials in specific co-operative activities did not alter their impact on American political theory, particularly since the theory of separatism was soon buttressed by the rise of the states'-rights movement. The major role played by southerners in the formulation of American political theory in the nineteenth century provided such additional impetus as was necessary. The entire theory of dual federalism was sharpened when the slavery issue came to dominate American politics (often at the expense of less glamorous but equally significant issues), since it united the diverse currents of separationist thought and focused them on the question of disunion.

In the formative period of the early Republic, intergovernmental co-operation seems to have been more or less taken for granted by the majority of politically aware Americans. It is significant that so many of the architects of co-operative federalism in this period were southerners. Calhoun, William Crawford, James Barbour, and others who were in the vanguard of the movement toward co-operation on the national level were prominent leaders of that section of the country. The South continued to supply leadership oriented toward collaboration until the nullification controversy at the beginning of the fourth decade of the nineteenth century, when the southerners began to realize that the North was surpassing their section in growth and would soon replace it in the national councils as the leading section. It was only then that the doctrine of states' rights and dual federalism emerged as an ideology, and the southern states began to assert their exclusive authority in order to preserve the exclusive identity of an embattled section.

So great was the influence of the southern conservative leadership that in this area as in so many others, they won acceptance for their doctrines from the inhabitants of all sections, even those who opposed them on specific issues, such as the slavery question. By appealing to a rising entrepreneurial group in the North that wanted to be free of all government regulation, the southerners were able to score some imposing practical victories for their doctrine of dualism. The destruction of the national banking system in the 1830's may have been one such victory. This coalition of southern agrarians and northern capitalists could win a few apparent victories, but they were unable to eliminate co-operative federalism simply because it remained necessary. What did happen was that federal-state collaboration took on new guises, and the myth of dualism was used to camouflage it on the surface.

The Civil War did not settle this conflict between theory and practice, but actually aggravated it. Once the southern leadership learned that it could not separate the South from the Union to preserve its way of life, it became all the more necessary for them to find ways to preserve that way of life within the framework of the Constitution. To this end, they again turned to the doctrine of separation of functions, to dual federalism. Once again, the best spokesmen for dual federalism in the post bellum period were southerners. Alexander Stephens of Georgia, through his books and articles, and Edward D. White of Louisiana, from his position on the Supreme Court, made the theory of dualism accepted doctrine in all sections of the nation. Since the doctrine was still very useful to northern business interests in their efforts to resist increasing pressures for government regulation of the newly developing corporations, they continued to accept and make use of it for their own purposes. Despite the official adoption of this theory by the Supreme Court during this period, co-operative programs continued to grow, suffering only occasional and temporary setbacks for doctrinal reasons.

CO-OPERATIVE FEDERALISM: CONTINUITY
OF DEVELOPMENT

The traditional theory of dual federalism erred in its "factual" description of government operations in nineteenth-century America and in its evaluation of the formula needed for the maintenance of the federal system as a bulwark of American liberties. The theory that the federal and state governments each had their own spheres of activity in which each operated independently of the other must be altered to show that at any given time in American political history the great majority of governmental activities were shared by all levels of government. Since intergovernmental collaboration was actually the norm, the maintenance of functional separation between the federal and state governments cannot be considered the key to the successful maintenance of the federal system.

This study should suggest that the success of American federalism in the nineteenth century was due to the ability of the several levels of government to adjust to new problems together, so that in each case all governments shared responsibility, each in its own way, and each gained new responsibilities as the need arose, thus preserving the system's balance through this sharing process rather than through separation into "independent spheres."

If co-operative federalism was the rule in the nineteenth century as well as in the twentieth, it is not the change from dualism to co-operation or from local control to centralization that is significant, but the progressive routinization of intergovernmental co-operation within the various governments of the United States. The actual sharing of functions can not only be traced back to the beginnings of the nation, but does not seem to have appreciably changed in relation to the total velocity of government at any given time. What has changed is the routinization of sharing procedures. In the beginning, the administration of co-operative activities was often an *ad hoc* process carried out through procedures developed in response to specific situations. In the passing of time, some precedents were set and some mistakes were rectified, so that as American governmental and political institutions developed patterns of routine, so did the institutions of intergovernmental collaboration.

The administrative history of American federalism is, on one hand, a history of this progressive routinization. It is also the history of the adaptation of new governmental activities into the pattern of the system. As new problems arose and required governmental attention, they were made to fit into the American federal model, rather than the model being changed to fit them. If this required apparent changes in the methods of dealing with the problems, these apparent changes were made in a manner calculated to interfere least with the sharing processes. When cash grants had to replace land grants, the change was not used as an excuse to transfer programs to the federal government; it simply provided a means for continued sharing by utilizing cash for grants-in-aid instead of land. The apparent changes in the forms of grant administration developed because the cash grants provided an excuse for increased routinization of procedures.

Although the grant-in-aid system has been the cornerstone of co-operative federalism, much governmental activity lies outside of the formal sphere of the grants. The crucial test of the similarities within the federal system over the past two centuries lies in assessing the amount of co-operation in all forms relative to the total velocity of government during that time span. Though no complete statistical accounting is available to indicate that, statistically, the major share of governmental activities in the nineteenth century was co-operative, the available evidence (statistical and non-statistical) does lead to that conclusion. Upon careful investigation, virtually every domestic governmental program has been revealed to have involved intergovernmental co-operation in some form. Not only that, but the range of forms—from grants-in-aid to exchanges of documents—was quite similar to that of the twentieth century. The criteria for allocating functions and the means of their subsequent control have also been developed in a continuing pattern. At least in the public-land states, it appears that even the percentage of federal funds in the states' budgets has not appreciably changed; in fact, the federal government may be contributing proportionately less to the budgets of many states in the mid-twentieth century than it did during the nineteenth.

This study has attempted to present examples of significant programs, and some examples of very ordinary ones, in certain representative states to illustrate the pervasiveness and depth of intergovernmental co-operation before 1913 and to probe the origins of and reasons behind the course of development of American federalism. If each state has shown certain differences in its handling of co-operative programs, this is merely an indication of the variety that can exist within the co-operative framework. The very existence of this variety is an indication of the health of the system in light of its chosen goal to balance unity and diversity. Certain basic patterns quickly emerge in this study and carry over from program to program and generation to generation. Among these are the sharing principle itself, the criteria for developing new governmental activities, the nature of federal administrative supervision that insists on details within the framework of the program but is governed by considerations of the political system around it, the development of co-operative routines, the variety of means of access to government that results from spreading responsibility, and, ultimately, the pattern by which new programs are assimilated into the system.

If there are truly unique aspects in the American political system, it may well be said that they lie imbedded in the ways and means of American federalism. Indeed, the creation of a viable and lasting federal system of government is probably the most unique American contribution to the political art. Throughout the history of human society, the problem of reconciling the virtues of local control with the need for centralized powers has troubled politicians and philosophers. Practical attempts to solve this problem have succumbed either to fragmentation of government and the destruction of the state or to centralization of power and the destruction of individual freedom. The United States can boast the first truly modern federal system to have been successfully established and maintained for any length of time. Through the development of collaborative techniques, this system has taken root and has been made to survive some of the most radical social changes ever faced by any government.

The federal principle has been adapted to a dynamic society which has developed in mankind's most dynamic period. It may some day be said that, indeed, it was the federal principle that provided the basis for the survival of the American government as a free government during these difficult times. American federalism has been able to combine strength at the center with local control and reasonably uniform national progress with opportunities for local diversity. Herein lies the system's greatness. Unfortunately the values of federalism, like all values, are difficult to measure. The federal system cannot be replicated in a laboratory, nor can an alternate system be tested alongside the present one. To a great extent, the American people have to take the American partnership on faith. Yet it is possible to examine the operations of American federalism and, through understanding them, to develop insights into the value of the system. As the knowledge gained serves to strip away the mysteries of the past and the myths of the present, it becomes less difficult to see the vital importance of federalism in the preservation and the extension of those political values most Americans hold dear.

Bibliography

GENERAL

BOOKS

AGAR, HERBERT. *The Price of Union.* Boston: Houghton Mifflin Co., 1950.

ANDERSON, WILLIAM. *The Nation and the States, Rivals or Partners?* Minneapolis: University of Minnesota Press, 1955.

BENTON, THOMAS HART. *Thirty Years' View.* New York: D. Appleton & Co., 1854–56.

BRYCE, JAMES. *The American Commonwealth.* 2 vols. New York: Macmillan Co., 1893.

CALHOUN, JOHN C. *Works.* 6 vols. New York: D. Appleton & Co., 1888.

CURTI, MERLE, *et al. The Making of an American Community.* Stanford, Calif.: Stanford University Press, 1959.

DUPREE, A. HUNTER. *Science in the Federal Government.* Cambridge: Harvard University Press, 1957.

EDDY, EDWARD D., JR. *Colleges for Our Land and Time.* New York: Harper & Bros., 1956.

HACKER, LOUIS M. *The Triumph of American Capitalism.* New York: Simon and Schuster, 1940.

HAINES, CHARLES G. *The Role of the Supreme Court in American Government and Politics, 1789–1835.* Berkeley: University of California Press, 1944.

HAINES, CHARLES G., and SHERWOOD, FOSTER. *The Role of the Supreme Court in American Government and Politics, 1835–1864.* Berkeley: University of California Press, 1954.

HESSELTINE, WILLIAM B. *Lincoln and the War Governors.* New York: Alfred A. Knopf, 1955.

MILLER, MARION MILLS (ed.). *Great Debates in American History.* Vol. X. New York: Current Literature Publishing Co., 1913.

MORRIS, RICHARD B. (ed.). *Encyclopedia of American History.* New York: Harper & Bros., 1953.

341

ORFIELD, MATHIAS N. *Federal Land Grants to the States with Special Reference to Minnesota.* Minneapolis: University of Minnesota Press, 1915.

RICHARDSON, JAMES D. (ed.). *Messages and Papers of the Presidents.* 9 vols. Washington: Bureau of National Literature and Art, 1908.

SLOSSON, EDWIN E. *The American Spirit in Education.* New York: Harper & Bros., 1956. (Esp. chap. xv, "The Morrill Act.")

SOUTHERN HISTORY PUBLICATION SOCIETY (ed.). *The South in the Building of the Nation.* ("Economic History.") 2 vols. Richmond: The Society, 1909.

SWISHER, CARL BRENT. *American Constitutional Development.* Boston: Houghton Mifflin Co., 1943.

TOCQUEVILLE, ALEXIS DE. *Democracy in America.* 2 vols. New York: Vintage Books, 1954.

WHITE, LEONARD D. *The Federalists.* New York: Macmillan Co., 1948.

———. *The Jacksonians.* New York: Macmillan Co., 1954.

———. *The Jeffersonians.* New York: Macmillan Co., 1951.

WILLIAMS, WILLIAM A. (ed.). *The Shaping of American Diplomacy.* Chicago: Rand McNally & Co., 1955.

WILTSE, CHARLES M. *John C. Calhoun.* 3 vols. Indianapolis: Bobbs-Merrill Co., Inc., 1944, 1949, 1951.

ARTICLES

CORWIN, EDWARD B. "National-State Cooperation—Its Present Possibilities," *Yale Law Journal,* XLVI (1937), 599–633.

DODD, GORDON B. "Arizona, Oregon, and the Nation," *Western Political Quarterly,* X (June, 1957), 398–404.

GRODZINS, MORTON. "American Political Parties and the American System," *Western Political Quarterly,* XIII (December, 1960), 974–98.

———. "The Federal System," in *Goals for Americans.* New York: Prentice-Hall, Inc., 1960. Pp. 265–84.

NETTELS, CURTIS P. "British Mercantilism and the Economic Development of the Thirteen Colonies," *Journal of Economic History,* XII (Spring, 1952), 105–14.

PUBLIC DOCUMENTS

U.S. Constitution.

U.S. HOUSE OF REPRESENTATIVES. *Laws of the United States of a Local or Temporary Character.* Misc. Doc. 45, Part 2. 47th Cong., 2d Sess., 1880.

U.S. HOUSE OF REPRESENTATIVES, COMMITTEE ON CLAIMS. "Report on the Interest Claim of Virginia," *House Reports of Committees.* No. 11. 18th Cong., 2d Sess., Vol. I, January 3, 1825.

U.S. SENATE. "Federal-State Relations by the Council of State Governments," *Report of the Commission on Organization of the Executive Branch of the Government.* Doc. 81. 81st Cong., 1st Sess., 1949.

U.S. SENATE. *Message of President Monroe.* Doc. 64. 18th Cong., 1st Sess., Vol. III, April 13, 1824.

U.S. SENATE. *Report on the President's Message as Respects the Distribution of the United States Surplus.* Doc. 139. 21st Cong., 1st Sess., 1830.

U.S. State Papers. Doc. 97. 13th Cong., 2d Sess., 1814.

U.S. Statutes at Large. Vols. XI, XIV, XVII.

U.S. SUPREME COURT.

Martin v. *Hunter's Lessee* (1 Wheaton 304 [1816]).

McCulloch v. *Maryland* (4 Wheaton 316 [1819]).

Cohens v. *Virginia* (6 Wheaton 413 [1821]).

Gibbons v. *Ogden* (9 Wheaton 1 [1824]).

Prigg v. *Pennsylvania* (16 Peters 539 [1842]).

Ableman v. *Booth* (21 Howard 506 [1859]).

Collector v. *Day* (11 Wallace 113 [1871]).

Munn v. *Illinois* (94 U.S. 113 [1877]).

Hammer v. *Dagenhart* (247 U.S. 251 [1918]).

Ponzi v. *Fessenden et al.* (258 U.S. 254 [1922]).

United States v. *Constantine* (296 U.S. 287 [1935]).

United States v. *Butler* (297 U.S. 1 [1936]).

Carter v. *Carter Coal Company* (298 U.S. 238 [1936]).

Ashton v. *Cameron County Water Improvement District No. One* (298 U.S. 513 [1936]).

ARCHIVAL MATERIALS

Oklahoma Historical Society Library, Oklahoma City. Indian Archives.

Thomas Gilcrease Institute of American History and Art, Tulsa, Oklahoma. Archives, particularly records of Indian affairs.

OTHER UNPUBLISHED MATERIAL

ELAZAR, DANIEL. "Federal-State Cooperation as Reflected in Supreme Court Decisions, 1851–58." Unpublished MS, Department of Political Science, University of Chicago, 1957.

GRODZINS, MORTON. "The American System." MS in preparation.

THEORY OF AMERICAN FEDERALISM

BOOKS

ANDERSON, JOHN M. (ed.). *Calhoun: Basic Documents.* State College, Pa.: Bald Eagle Press, 1952.

BECKER, CARL. *The Declaration of Independence.* New York: Alfred A. Knopf, 1941.

BENSON, GEORGE C. S. *The New Centralization.* New York: Farrar and Rinehart, 1941.

CLARK, JANE PERRY. *The Rise of a New Federalism*. New York: Columbia University Press, 1938.

COOPER, JAMES FENIMORE. *The American Democrat*. New York: Vintage Books, 1956.

CORWIN, EDWARD S. *The Commerce Power versus States'-Rights*. Princeton, N.J.: Princeton University Press, 1936.

——. *Total War and the Constitution*. New York: Alfred A. Knopf, 1947.

——. *The Twilight of the Supreme Court*. New Haven, Conn.: Yale University Press, 1934.

CROSSKEY, WILLIAM W. *Politics and the Constitution in the History of the United States*. Chicago: University of Chicago Press, 1953.

DEWEY, JOHN. *The Living Thoughts of Thomas Jefferson*. New York: David McKay Co., Inc., 1940.

HAMILTON, ALEXANDER; JAY, JOHN; and MADISON, JAMES. *The Federalist*. London: Everyman's Library.

HOLCOMBE, ARTHUR N. *Our More Perfect Union*. Cambridge, Mass.: Harvard University Press, 1950.

HUNT, GAILLARD (ed.). *The Writings of James Madison*. 9 vols. New York, 1900–1910.

JONES, W. MELVILLE (ed.). *Chief Justice John Marshall: A Reappraisal*. Ithaca, N.Y.: Cornell University Press, 1956.

KILPATRICK, JAMES. *Our Sovereign States*. Chicago: Henry Regnery Co., 1956.

KING, JOHN W. *Federalism: Or the Question of Exclusive Power*. N.p., 1899.

MORRIS, RICHARD B. (ed.). *The Basic Ideas of Alexander Hamilton*. New York: Pocket Library, 1956.

PADOVER, SAUL K. (ed.). *The Complete Madison*. New York: Harper & Bros., 1953.

——. *Thomas Jefferson on Democracy*. New York: Penguin Books, 1939.

SMITH, HERBERT A. *Federalism in North America*. N.p., 1899.

STEPHENS, ALEXANDER. *A Constitutional View of the War between the States*. 2 vols. Philadelphia: National Publishing Co., 1868.

TURNER, FREDERICK JACKSON. *The Frontier in American History*. New York: Henry Holt & Co., 1920.

FISCAL AFFAIRS AND BANKING

BOOKS

BROWN, WILLIAM H. *The Story of a Bank*. Boston: Gorham Press, 1952.

BURKE, WILLIAM E. *Federal Finances*. Chicago: F. J. Schulte & Co., 1891.

CATTERALL, RALPH C. H. *The Second Bank of the United States*. Chicago: University of Chicago Press, 1903.

CLARKE, M. ST. CLAIR, and HALL, D. A. *Legislative and Documentary History of the Bank of the United States*. Washington, 1832.

HAMMOND, BRAY. *Banks and Politics in America: From the Revolution to the Civil War*. Princeton, N.J.: Princeton University Press, 1957.

SHULTZ, WILLIAM J., and CAINE, M. R. *The Financial Development of the United States*. New York: Prentice-Hall, Inc., 1937.

PUBLIC DOCUMENTS

American State Papers, Finance. Washington, D.C., 1832.

U.S. COMPTROLLER OF THE CURRENCY. *Annual Report, 1955*.

ARCHIVAL MATERIALS

National Archives. Letters from Banks to U.S. Treasury Department. 1835–37; 1837–40.

National Archives. Letters sent by U.S. Treasurer. Book I (July 3, 1828–July 19, 1831).

National Archives. Letters to the Collector, Norfolk, Va., from U.S. Treasury Department. 1800–1833.

PUBLIC LANDS AND INTERNAL IMPROVEMENTS

BOOKS

ASHENHURST, JOHN and RUTH L. *All About Chicago*. Boston: Houghton Mifflin Co., 1933.

FEDERAL COORDINATOR OF TRANSPORTATION. *Public Aids to Transportation*. Vol. II (*Aids to Railroads and Related Subjects*). Washington, D.C.: U.S. Government Printing Office, 1938.

GREELEY, A. W. *Reminiscences of Adventure and Service*. New York: Charles Scribner's Sons, 1927.

HILL, FOREST G. *Roads, Rails, and Waterways*. Norman, Okla.: University of Oklahoma Press, 1957.

A History and Description of the Baltimore and Ohio Rail Road by a Citizen of Baltimore. Baltimore: John Murphy & Co., 1853.

HUNGERFORD, EDWARD. *The Story of the Baltimore and Ohio Railroad, 1827–1927*. New York: G. P. Putnam's Sons, 1928.

JACKSON, W. TURRENTINE. *Wagon Roads West*. Berkeley: University of California Press, 1956.

PUTNAM, JAMES W. *The Illinois and Michigan Canal*. Chicago: University of Chicago Press, 1918.

SANBORN, JOHN B. *Congressional Grants of Land in Aid of Railways*. Madison: University of Wisconsin, 1899.

SANDERLIN, WALTER S. *The Great National Project*. Baltimore: Johns Hopkins Press, 1946.

SMALLEY, EUGENE V. *History of the Northern Pacific Railroad.* New York: G. P. Putnam's Sons, 1883.

WAGGONER, MADELINE S. *The Long Haul West.* New York: G. P. Putnam's Sons, 1958.

YOUNG, JEREMIAH S. *Political and Constitutional Study of the Cumberland Road.* Chicago: University of Chicago Press, 1902.

ARTICLES

BROWN, ALEXANDER C. "The Dismal Swamp Canal," *American Neptune,* July, 1945.

HILL, FOREST G. "Government Engineering Aid before the Civil War," *Journal of Economic History,* Vol. XI (Winter, 1951).

PUBLIC DOCUMENTS

Acts of the States of Virginia, Maryland, and Pennsylvania, and of the Congress of the United States in Relation to the Chesapeake and Ohio Canal Company, etc. Washington, 1828.

Annals of Congress. 14th Cong., 2d Sess. (1816).

DISMAL SWAMP CANAL COMPANY. *Annual Reports.* 1837, 1839, 1843.

U.S. DEPARTMENT OF THE INTERIOR. *Annual Report of the Commissioner of the General Land Office, 1911.*

U.S. HOUSE OF REPRESENTATIVES. *Index to the Reports of the Chief of Engineers, U.S. Army, 1866–1912.* Vol. I (*Rivers and Harbors*). Doc. 740. 63d Cong., 2d Sess., 1914.

U.S. SENATE, SPECIAL COMMITTEE ON PUBLIC LANDS. *Report.* 18th Cong., 2d Sess., 1825.

U.S. WAR DEPARTMENT. *Annual Reports of the Chief Engineer.* 1852, 1853, 1854, 1856.

ARCHIVAL MATERIALS

National Archives. U.S. Army Corps of Engineers, Bulky File, Record Group 77.

National Archives. U.S. Army Corps of Engineers, De Grange Index, Record Group 77.

National Archives. U.S. Army Corps of Engineers, Files, Record Group 77.

National Archives. U.S. Corps of Topographical Engineers, Letterbook Number 5, Record Group 77.

National Archives. U.S. Treasury Department Records: Canals, 1833–1849. 1 vol.

National Archives. U.S. War Department, "Report of Lieutenant Colonel S. H. Long, William Howard, and Captain William McNeill on the Preliminary Survey of the Route of the Baltimore and Ohio Railroad, 1827," Baltimore and Ohio Railroad File.

COLORADO

BOOKS

COLORADO WRITERS' PROJECT. *Colorado.* New York: Hastings House, 1941.
STONE, WILBUR FISK (ed.). *A History of Colorado.* Chicago: S. J. Clarke, 1918.

PUBLIC DOCUMENTS

COLORADO. *Governor's Messages.* 1876–1902.
Colorado Constitution.
COLORADO SCHOOL OF MINES. *Annual Report, 1876.*
COLORADO STATE BOARD OF LAND COMMISSIONERS. *Annual and Biennial Reports.* 1879–1956.
COLORADO STATE PLANNING COMMISSION. *Yearbook of the State of Colorado, 1956–1958.* Denver, 1958.
Colorado Statutes. 1876–1904.

ARCHIVAL MATERIALS

Colorado State Archives. Colorado State Board of Land Commissioners' Records.
National Archives. "Miscellaneous Papers and Documents Relating to the Ute Uprising, 8/16/1887–5/28/1889." Microfilm in Colorado State Archives, Denver.

MINNESOTA

BOOKS

ANDERSON, WILLIAM. *Intergovernmental Relations in Public Finance.* Minneapolis: University of Minnesota Press, 1956.
CHRISTIANSON, THEODORE. *History of Minnesota.* New York: American Historical Society, 1935.
FEDERAL WRITERS PROJECT. *Minnesota: A State Guide.* New York: Viking Press, 1938.
FOLWELL, WILLIAM WATTS. *A History of Minnesota.* 4 vols. St. Paul: Minnesota Historical Society, 1921.
ORFIELD, MATHIAS. *Federal Land Grants to the States with Special Reference to Minnesota.* Minneapolis: University of Minnesota Press, 1915.
SANBORN, JOHN BELL. *Congressional Grants of Land in Aid of Railways.* Madison: University of Wisconsin, 1899.
SMALLEY, EUGENE V. *History of the Northern Pacific Railroad.* New York: G. P. Putnam's Sons, 1883.

PUBLIC DOCUMENTS

MINNESOTA. *Executive Documents.* 1860–1900.
MINNESOTA. *Report of the Warden of the State Prison, 1860–1900.*

MINNESOTA ADJUTANT GENERAL. "Report." *Executive Documents,* 1860–1900.

MINNESOTA BOARD OF REGENTS OF THE STATE UNIVERSITY. "Report of the Board of Regents of the University." *Annual Report of the Superintendent of Public Instruction, 1860–1900.*

MINNESOTA COMMISSIONER OF STATISTICS. *Annual Reports.* 1860, 1887–92.

Minnesota Constitution.

MINNESOTA RAILROAD AND WAREHOUSE COMMISSION. *Index of Railroads in the State of Minnesota, 1862–1936.* 1936.

MINNESOTA RAILROAD COMMISSIONER. *Reports.* 1871, 1872, 1873, 1882, 1883.

MINNESOTA STATE AUDITOR. *Annual and Biennial Reports.* 1863–1936.

MINNESOTA STATE FORESTRY ASSOCIATION. *Forest Culture.* 1874, 1876.

MINNESOTA STATE FORESTRY ASSOCIATION. *The Forest Tree Planter's Manual.* St. Paul, 1879–96.

MINNESOTA STATE FORESTRY ASSOCIATION. *Practical Suggestions on Forest Tree Planting in Minnesota.* St. Paul, 1874.

MINNESOTA STATE GEOLOGICAL SURVEY. "Report of the Chief of the State Geological Survey." *Executive Documents,* 1876.

MINNESOTA STATE LIBRARY. "Report of the State Library." *Executive Documents,* 1860, 1876.

MINNESOTA SUPERINTENDENT OF PUBLIC INSTRUCTION. *Annual Report, 1860–1900.*

Session Laws of the Territory of Minnesota. Extra Session, 1857.

Special Laws. 1861, 1878.

U.S. Statutes at Large. Vols. XI, XIV, XVII.

ARCHIVAL MATERIAL

Minnesota Historical Society. James C. Taylor Papers. 1842–94.

Minnesota Historical Society. Northern Pacific Railroad Company Letterbook. 1895–97.

Minnesota Historical Society. Southern Minnesota Railroad Company Papers.

Minnesota Historical Society. Stanford Papers.

Minnesota State Archives. Auditor's Records. 1858–1900.

Minnesota State Archives. Executive Department Records. 1860–85.

Minnesota State Archives. Governors' Archives. 1858–1900.

Minnesota State Archives. Minnesota Railroad and Warehouse Commission, Railroad History Files.

Minnesota State Archives. Minnesota State Forestry Association Records.

Minnesota State Archives. United States Land Office Archives. Vol. X, pp. 294–309.

UNPUBLISHED MATERIAL

ELAZAR, DANIEL J. "Federal-State Relations in Minnesota: A Study of Railroad Construction and Development." Unpublished Master's thesis, Department of Political Science, University of Chicago, June, 1957.

NEW HAMPSHIRE

BOOKS

FEDERAL WRITER'S PROJECT. *New Hampshire: A Guide to the Granite State.* Boston: Houghton Mifflin Co., 1938.

PUBLIC DOCUMENTS

NEW HAMPSHIRE. *Governors' Messages to the Legislature.* 1835–1900.

NEW HAMPSHIRE. *Reports of the Board of Managers of the New Hampshire Soldiers' Home.* 1889–1900.

NEW HAMPSHIRE. *Reports of the Commissioner of Common Schools.* 1847–59.

NEW HAMPSHIRE. *Reports of the State Board of Education.* 1861–75.

NEW HAMPSHIRE BANK COMMISSIONERS. *Annual Reports.* 1865–1900.

NEW HAMPSHIRE HOUSE. *Journal.* 1835–50.

New Hampshire Laws. 1835–1900.

NEW HAMPSHIRE STATE TREASURER. *Annual Reports.* 1835–1900.

TRUSTEES AND SUPERINTENDENT OF THE NEW HAMPSHIRE ASYLUM FOR THE INSANE. *Reports.* 1846–1900.

VIRGINIA

BOOKS

BUCK, J. L. BLAIR. *The Development of Public Schools in Virginia.* Richmond, Va.: State Board of Education, 1952.

FEDERAL WRITERS' PROJECT. *Virginia: A Guide to the Old Dominion.* New York: Oxford University Press, 1940.

MORRISON, A. J. *The Beginnings of Public Education in Virginia, 1776–1860.* Richmond, Va.: State Board of Education, 1917.

PUBLIC DOCUMENTS

Calendar of Virginia State Papers. 12 vols. Richmond, 1875–93.

VIRGINIA BOARD OF PUBLIC WORKS. *Annual Reports.* 1816–60.

VIRGINIA GENERAL ASSEMBLY, COMMITTEE OF ROADS AND NAVIGATIONS. *Report* (December, 1814) in *A Collection of All Laws and Resolutions of the General Assembly of Virginia Relating to the Board of Public Works, etc.* Richmond: 1819.

VIRGINIA HOUSE OF DELEGATES. *Journal.* 1814–60.

———. *Report of the Hartford Deaf and Dumb Asylum.* Doc. No. 7, 1833–34.

ARCHIVAL MATERIALS

Virginia State Archives. Board of Public Works' Files.

Virginia State Archives. Board of Public Works' Letter Book "B." April 5, 1837–May 15, 1840.

Virginia State Archives. Records on Banks and Banking.

Index

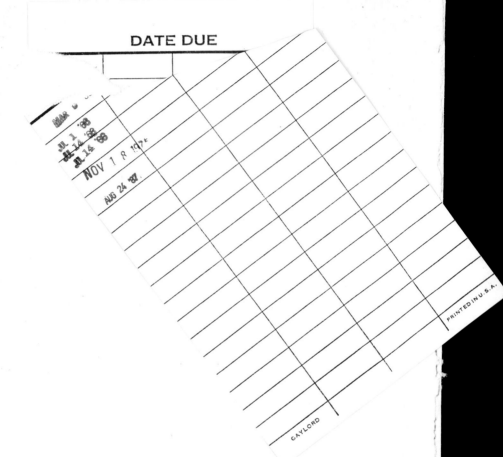